Contextualizing Inclusive Education

Inclusive education is one of the most dominant and controversial issues confronting educational policy-makers and professionals around the world today. What does inclusive education really mean? Is it a Western idea which cannot work in developing countries? Is it even working in Western countries?

Inclusive education is a complex and problematic concept that raises many questions. A team of prominent academics present fresh and critical perspectives on these issues, drawing upon their global resources and knowledge.

The over-arching theme of this book is that social, political, economic and cultural contexts play a central role in determining whether or not inclusive education is implemented in a range of regions and countries around the world. The book presents a series of original and provocative conclusions such as

- Inclusive education means creating a single system of education, which serves all children.
- Inclusive education is a site of conflicting paradigms of children with special needs, centred on a psycho-medical model and a socio-political model.
- While many countries seem committed to inclusive education in their rhetoric, legislation and policies, their practices often fall short.

This book is a major landmark resource for educational policy-makers, researchers, teacher educators, students and international agencies with interests in the education of children with special needs.

David Mitchell is an honorary professor of education at the University of Waikato and a research consultant to Waikato Institute of Technology in Hamilton, New Zealand. He is also Honorary Research Fellow at the University of Manchester. He has held visiting appointments in universities in several countries, including Japan and Singapore, and has worked as a UNESCO consultant in inclusive education in the Asia-Pacific region, particularly in Central Asia, where he has also worked with the Soros Foundation's Step by Step programme. He has published extensively in the fields of special and inclusive education, most recently editing the four-volume set, *Special Educational Needs and Inclusive Education: Major Themes in Education*, published by Routledge in 2004. E-mail: dmitch@waikato.ac.nz

Contextualizing Inclusive Education

Evaluating Old and New International Perspectives

Edited by David Mitchell

Routledge
Taylor & Francis Group

LONDON AND NEW YORK

First published 2005
by Routledge
2 Park Square, Milton Park, Abingdon, Oxfordshire, OX14 4RN

Simultaneously published in the USA and Canada
by Routledge
270 Madison Ave, New York, NY 10016

Routledge is an imprint of the Taylor & Francis Group

©2005 David Mitchell for selection and editorial matter; individual
chapters, the contributors

Typeset in Times and Gill Sans by Taylor & Francis Books
Printed and bound in Great Britain by MPG Books Ltd, Bodmin

British Library Cataloguing in Publication Data
A catalogue record for this book is available from the British
Library

Library of Congress Cataloging in Publication Data
A catalog record for this title has been requested

ISBN 0–415–31880–7

For Jill, and our grandchildren, Ayaka, Kiki, Tane,
Conrad and Zenji

Contents

Tables

Contributors

Alfredo Artiles's scholarship focuses on the intersections of culture, learning, and disability. He has worked and made presentations in the USA, Europe, Latin America, and Africa. Recent publications include (2003) 'Special education's changing identity: Paradoxes and dilemmas in views of culture and space', *Harvard Educational Review*, 73, 164–202 (2004); and 'Culturally diverse students in special education', in J. Banks and C. Banks (eds) *Handbook of Research on Multicultural Education*, 2nd edn (Jossey Bass) (with S. Trent and J. Palmer). He received the 2001 Early Career Award from AERA's Committee on Scholars of Color in Education. He is a principal investigator with the National Center for Culturally Responsive Educational Systems. E-mail: alfredo.artiles@asu.edu

Ronald C. Brown is the founding Executive Director of the Fawzia Sultan International School and Learning Institute in Kuwait. As a frequent guest lecturer and consultant, he has travelled in many Middle East countries, most recently in Iraq. He completed his Ph.D. in special education and psychology at the University of Pittsburgh; an M.A. in special education at New York University; and postdoctoral work in cultural anthropology at Columbia University and in educational leadership at the University of Pennsylvania. In the USA, he was Coordinator for the National Learning Resource Center and, later, Philadelphia's Director of Special Education. E-mail: RONCB123@aol.com

Ishwar Desai is a senior lecturer in education and a consultant on international projects and training in the Faculty of Education at the University of Melbourne, Australia. He has extensive experience in research, teaching, consultancy and capacity building in special education and inclusion. Recent projects have included training seminars in India funded by AUS-Aid and the World Bank. He has acted as a research consultant to the Department of Human Services, Disability Division, in Victoria, Australia, for a number of projects. In addition to a number of publications, commissioned reports and projects, he has presented over 100 papers, seminars and workshops in various parts of the world, including the USA, England, South Africa, Thailand, Singapore, Hong Kong, India and Australia. E-mail: i.desai@unimelb.edu.au

Alan Dyson is a professor of education at the University of Manchester, where his research focuses on the relationship between social and educational inclusion. He has been a member of the Westminster government's ministerial working group on Special Educational Needs, is a member of the National Education Research Forum and has worked with a range of government agencies both in England and abroad. He recently led the production of the Open File on Inclusive Education for UNESCO. He has worked in universities since 1988, having spent thirteen years prior to that as a teacher, mainly in urban comprehensive schools. E-mail: D.A.Dyson@man.ac.uk

Ingemar Emanuelsson is Professor Emeritus of Special Education at Göteborg University, Sweden. He has held appointments as Professor of Education and/or Special Education at Stockholm School of Education and the University of Trondheim, Norway. A main focus of interest is integration, as well as segregation processes, on different levels of the school system and special educational challenges related to school support as a precondition for giving individual support within integrated and inclusive education settings. He has published extensively on these issues in international journals and Scandinavian books. E-mail: Ingemar.emanuelsson@ped.gu.se

Todd Fletcher is an associate professor in the Department of Special Education, Rehabilitation and School Psychology in the College of Education at the University of Arizona in Tucson. He is a graduate of the University of the Americas in Puebla, Mexico and has worked throughout Latin America in the field of special education. He is co-editor of the book *Helping Individuals with Disabilities and Their Families: U.S. and Mexican Perspectives*, and has written numerous articles on special education reform and practice in Mexico. His research interests include educational policies and the implications for English language learners; assessment and instruction of English language learners with disabilities; and special education reform in Mexico and Latin America. E-mail: toddf@email.arizona.edu

Peder Haug is a professor of education at Faculty of Education, Volda University College, Norway and at the Norwegian Centre for Child Research, the University in Trondheim, Norway. He has had several appointments in The Norwegian Council of Research, leading research programmes. He has published in the fields of early child care, special education and inclusive education. E-mail: peder.haug@hivolda.no

Anne Jordan is Professor and Associate Chair of the Department of Curriculum, Teaching and Learning at the Ontario Institute for Studies in Education of the University of Toronto. She conducts research in the characteristics of effective teachers in inclusive classrooms and their impact on students, which has been published in international and North American journals. She has published three books, including a 1994 RoutledgeFalmer book *Skills in Collaborative Classroom Consultation*. E-mail: ajordan@oise.utoronto.ca

Margaret J. McLaughlin is Professor, Special Education and Associate Director, Institute for the Study of Exceptional Children and Youth, University of Maryland, College Park MD. She has been involved in special education all of her professional career. She earned a Bachelor of Arts from the University of Denver, a Master of Arts in Special Education from the University of Northern Colorado and her Ph.D. from the University of Virginia. She currently directs several national projects investigating educational reform and students with disabilities. These include studying the impact of high stakes accountability on students with disabilities. Dr McLaughlin also has worked internationally in developing inclusive education. E-mail: mm48@umail.umd.edu

Peter Mittler was the first director of the Hester Adrian Research Centre at Manchester University and later became Dean of the Faculty of Education. Following his retirement, he organized ISEC 2000, spent a year at Hong Kong University and has undertaken a range of consultancies for the United Nations, UNESCO, UNICEF and other international organizations. He has also been an adviser on disability and education to former UK ministers. He is a past president of Inclusion International and has published widely on intellectual disability and human rights. His most recent book is *Working Towards Inclusive Education* (Fulton, 2000). He now lives in Florence and Manchester. E-mail:Peter.Mittler@man.ac.uk

Sigamoney Manicka Naicker is currently National Director of Inclusive Education in South Africa's Department of Education. He taught at the University of the Western Cape and later moved onto the Western Cape Education Department, where he was responsible for learning support. Whilst in this position he was seconded to the curriculum unit of the province. He has written several publications both nationally and internationally, and is the author of *Curriculum 2005: A Space for All* (Renaissance, Tafelberg. 1999), an introduction to inclusive education, and co-editor of *Inclusion in Action in South Africa* (Renaissance, Tafelberg, 1999). E-mail: Naicker.S@doe.gov.za

Bengt Persson is a senior lecturer at Göteborg University in Sweden. He is also a visiting professor at Stavanger University College in Norway and has had different expert commissions in Scandinavia and England. He has published articles and books in Sweden as well as internationally. His research interests concern inclusive education in schools and how inclusive policies are being formulated and negotiated in the political arena. E-mail: bengt.persson@ped.gu.se

Roger Slee is Dean of the Faculty of Education at McGill University. Prior to this he was Deputy Director General of the Department of Education in Queensland. He has held chairs at the University of London and the University of Western Australia, and adjunct chairs at the University of Queensland and Griffith University. Roger is the founding editor of the *International Journal of Inclusive Education*. E-mail: roger.slee@mcgill.ca

Preface

Underpinned by the philosophy that all students belong and can learn in regular schools and classrooms, inclusive education is one of the most dominant and controversial issues confronting educational policy-makers and professionals around the world today.

Although the common denominator of approaches to inclusive education is the recognition and valuing of diversity in educational institutions, its scope in the literature varies. Some writers limit it to the education of students with disabilities and thus focus on the intersection between special and regular education. Others take a broader, education for all, perspective, arguing that all disadvantaged students – such as those from poverty backgrounds, ethnic minorities, isolated rural communities and, in some cultures, girls – should fall within its purview. For this book, authors were asked to focus on students whose special educational needs arise from disabilities, in particular those with behavioural and/or learning difficulties. While it is beyond the scope of the book to deal systematically with inclusion in its broadest manifestation, the authors were also asked to take cognizance of other sources of disadvantage, particularly where these intersect with disabilities.

In the literature, some writers portray inclusive education as a variant of education in general; others argue that it should be the main, or even the only, form of education. Whichever view is accepted, it is clear that all of the issues that confront education in general must also be addressed in inclusive education: curriculum, assessment, school management, teacher quality, pedagogy, and so on. As well, there are issues that are specific to the particular population(s) of students who form the focus of attention. In the case of those with disabilities, these include such matters as notions of special needs, curricular adaptations, individualization of programmes, and support services.

The over-arching brief for authors was to write chapters that examine the relationships that exist between the social, political and cultural contexts of inclusive education as it is being implemented in the period of compulsory schooling – or not implemented – in their regions of interest. The approach was to be explanatory and critical and not merely descriptive. To enable the writers to do justice to the contexts of their particular regions and countries, a rigid analytic structure was not imposed on them.

The motivation for *Contextualizing Inclusive Education* arose from my extensive international work on inclusive education, particularly my consultancies with UNESCO in the Asia Pacific region. In these, and other contacts with policy-makers, researchers, and teacher educators in a range of developed and developing countries, I have often been confronted with questions such as 'what does inclusive education really mean?'; 'who are the "targets" of inclusive education?'; 'is it a Western idea that would not work in developing countries?'; 'what factors make inclusive education seem to be accepted in some countries, but not others?'; 'how can general educators and parents be persuaded to accept inclusive education?'; and 'what models are there for introducing inclusive education?'. I hope that *Contextualizing Inclusive Education* will provide a major resource for educationists around the world as they confront the challenges of introducing or consolidating inclusive education and addressing such questions.

The book comprises twelve chapters, four of which explore broad issues to do with inclusive education, the remaining eight presenting analyses specific to various regions and selected countries within them. In Chapter 1, David Mitchell introduces the volume by presenting a series of sixteen propositions that address the main issues raised in the book, focusing on old and new paradigms in inclusive education and the range of contextual features that influence the purposes and forms it takes in different cultures. Chapter 2 contains Peter Mittler's analysis of the role of the United Nations in promoting inclusive education. In Chapter 3, Alfredo Artiles and Alan Dyson explore inclusive education in the globalization age and describe an approach to a comparative-historical analysis of the topic. Chapter 4 presents Alan Dyson's examination of the impact of various philosophies, political forces and economic considerations on inclusive education in England. In Chapter 5, Margaret McLaughlin and Anne Jordan examine the push and pull forces that shape inclusive education in USA and Canada. In Chapter 6, Ingemar Emanuelsson, Peder Haug and Bengt Persson outline the discrepancies between inclusive education rhetoric and policies in Western Europe, with particular reference to Norway, Sweden, the Netherlands and Greece. Roger Slee, in Chapter 7, presents a 'snapshot' of inclusive education in Australia. This is followed by Chapter 8, which presents David Mitchell and Ishwar Desai's analysis of the status and cultural underpinnings of inclusive education in Asia, with particular reference to China, India, Japan and Singapore. In Chapter 9, Todd Fletcher and Alfredo Artiles examine equity issues and inclusive education in Latin America, with a particular focus on Mexico. Sigamoney Naicker, in Chapter 10, discusses inclusive education in post-apartheid South Africa, while Chapter 11 presents Ron Brown's analysis of the intersection of inclusive education and traditional belief systems in the Middle East, with particular reference to Qatar, Bahrain and Kuwait. In the final chapter, Todd

Fletcher reflects on the issues raised in the book and presents his personal interpretation of future directions for inclusive education.

I believe that *Contextualizing Inclusive Education* is particularly timely as countries seek to honour the principles of the Salamanca Framework (UNESCO, 1994), with its focus on inclusive education, and the Dakar Framework for Action (2000), with its commitment to Education for All. It should appeal to the following readership: educational policy-makers, special education administrators, special education researchers, teacher educators (in general, as well as in special education), students of comparative education, international agencies with interests in education, disability advocacy organizations, school psychologists, and educational sociologists. As well, the book should be of interest to postgraduate students in inclusive education, special education, comparative education and educational policy.

David Mitchell

References

Dakar Framework for Action (2000) *Education for All: Meeting our collective commitments*. Paris: UNESCO.

UNESCO (1994) *World Conference on Special Needs Education: Access and Quality. Salamanca Declaration and Framework for Action*. Paris: UNESCO.

Chapter 1

Introduction

Sixteen propositions on the contexts of inclusive education

David Mitchell

> Educational inclusion requires careful consideration of every aspect of schooling and the social context in which it finds itself. Innovative approaches to educational inclusion will need to address issues at the macro, micro, personal and interpersonal levels and to recognise and engage with the political implications of working at these levels. Connections between school and community cultures have to be drawn, as well as between educational and community programmes of inclusion.
>
> (Sayed *et al.*, 2003, p. 245)

The theme of this book is that the characterization, purpose and form of inclusive education reflect the relationships among the social, political, economic, cultural and historical contexts that are present at any one time in a particular country and/or local authority. As Sayed *et al.* (2003) suggest in the above quotation, inclusive education is embedded in a range of contexts and consideration should be given to the relationships among them. The authors in this book present varying views on these relationships as they pertain to students with special educational needs, especially, but not exclusively, those with disabilities. They explore a range of issues, including: definitions of inclusive education; types of provisions for students with special educational needs; various forms of segregation or exclusion; paradigms of special needs; historical developments; the impact of contexts, including the role of economic considerations; the need to look beyond schooling; the justification for inclusive education; the ways in which indigenous and foreign values are blended; the relationship between inclusive education and education reforms; the gaps between rhetoric, policy and practices; and future trends. This chapter will provide a brief synthesis of these issues under a series of sixteen propositions. In developing these propositions, literature in addition to the chapters will be drawn upon.

Proposition 1

Inclusive education extends beyond special needs arising from disabilities, and includes consideration of other sources of disadvantage and marginalization,

*such as gender, poverty, language, ethnicity, and geographic isolation. The
complex inter-relationships that exist among these factors and their interactions with disability must also be a focus of attention.*

Many commentators on inclusive education argue that inclusion should be
concerned with making schools responsive to *all* students, not just those
with special educational needs arising from disabilities. As Booth (1996)
asserts, 'It makes little sense to foster the inclusion of some students
because they carry one label, whilst ignoring the lack of participation of
others' (p. 89). In a similar vein, Sayed *et al.* (2003) lament the fact that
'the complex inter-relationship of race, class, gender and other pivots of
injustice means that programmes promoting equality often tend to focus
on one of these at the expense of the others and so, loses the thread
connecting the others' (p. 240).

Three chapters in the present volume relate to these points. First, in
Chapter 9, Fletcher and Artiles point out that social inequalities in Latin
America mirror educational exclusion worldwide and place those at a social
disadvantage based on gender, disability, poverty, language, and ethnicity
on the margins of society. They note that in accordance with this view,
many countries in Latin America have extended the concept of 'special
education' beyond traditional disability categories, adopting instead the
much broader definition of a student with special educational needs as one
who, in comparison to his or her peer group, has difficulties learning the
established curriculum content, and as a result requires additional or
different resources. In Mexico, for example, in the 2001–2002 school year,
special education personnel provided some type of educational service for
525,232 pre-school, elementary, and secondary students, of whom only
112,000 were identified with a disability. Second, in Chapter 7, Slee argues
that inclusive education can best be understood by examining the experiences, conceptualization and struggles of other marginal identities that
arise from factors such as socio-economic disadvantage, gender, racism,
sexuality, mono-lingualism, and geographic isolation. In a similar vein, in
Chapter 10, Naicker points out that in post-apartheid South Africa, the
focus is 'not merely on disability but rather on all vulnerable children,
including over-age learners, children in prison, learners who experience
language barriers, or barriers such as the attitudes of others, lack of
parental recognition and poverty'.

While I agree with the argument that inclusive education should concern
all students, I decided that the main focus of this book should be on
students with disabilities (sometimes referred to as 'students with special
educational needs' in the text). Even so, as noted above, several chapters do
extend their coverage to include other groups and/or consider the interactions between disabilities and other factors. Also, I believe that many of the

principles discussed with reference to students with disabilities apply to other disadvantaged and marginalized groups.

Proposition 2

Inclusive education is a complex and problematic concept.

Almost every chapter in this volume refers to inclusive education as being a complex, if not a problematic, notion. For example, McLaughlin and Jordan, in their chapter on the USA and Canada (Chapter 5), note the lack of a commonly accepted definition of what constitutes 'inclusion'. The USA does not have an official definition of the term, although it has become synonymous with the placement of students with disabilities in the general education classroom. In contrast, Canada's federal charter has an understanding of inclusive education that is more aligned with the principles set forth in the Salamanca Statement (UNESCO, 1994). Dyson, in Chapter 4, notes that inclusion in England emerges as a complex and highly problematic phenomenon characterized by considerable ambiguities. These inevitably arise, he feels, from 'deep-seated dilemmas' that are, in turn, underpinned by fundamental social and economic processes. Similarly, in Chapter 11, Brown points out that 'confusion and controversy over the semantics of "inclusion" abound in many countries with long experience with its implementation', so that 'When the term crosses over into use in other cultures, it is no surprise that it is interpreted and applied in even more different and, sometimes, contradictory ways'. Chapter 9 makes similar points, with Fletcher and Artiles noting that one of the challenges to the consolidation of inclusive education models in Latin America is the lack of conceptual clarity, particularly with regard to disability definitions and the very notion of inclusion.

Given the above, it is not surprising to find that, as Artiles and Dyson point out in Chapter 3, the forms of educational practice that are labelled as 'inclusive education' have a strongly local flavour and that it would be chimerical to take a uni-dimensional perspective on the phenomenon. Rather, they argue, 'inclusive education is a multi-dimensional phenomenon, with different countries (and, we might add, different schools and classrooms) developing not simply at different rates but in quite different directions'. Another reason for such divergence can be found in economics, Artiles and Dyson further noting that

> the inclusion efforts of the affluent western democracies, where well resourced segregated forms of special education are being merged with equally well resourced regular education, seem to be quite different from those of many economically poorer countries where special education

has never been fully developed and where regular education is desperately lacking in resources.

Proposition 3

Although there is no universally accepted definition of inclusive education, there is a growing international consensus as to the principal features of this multi-dimensional concept. With regard to students with disabilities, these include the following: entitlement to full membership in regular, age-appropriate classes in their neighbourhood school; access to appropriate aids and support services, individualized programmes, with appropriately differentiated curriculum and assessment practices.

In seeking an understanding of what is meant by inclusive education, perhaps the first distinction to be made is between integration and inclusion. In addressing this issue, Ainscow (1995, p.1) states that the former refers to 'additional arrangements ... within a system of schooling that remains largely unchanged', while the latter aims 'to restructure schools in order to respond to the needs of all students'. Similarly, Antia *et al.* (2002), argue that inclusion denotes a student with a disability unconditionally belonging to and having full membership of a regular classroom in a regular school and its community. This is contrasted with integration, which implies that the student with a disability has the status of a visitor, with only conditional access to a regular classroom, and primary membership of a special class or resource room.

A second, and related, distinction is that inclusive education goes far beyond mere physical placement (sometimes referred to as 'locational' or 'proximity integration'), but instead involves attention being paid to all aspects of schooling – curriculum, assessment, pedagogy, supports, and so on. For example, Skrtic *et al.* (1996) argue that inclusive education involves schools meeting the needs of all their students within common, but fluid, environments and activities.

Given its international significance, it is worth describing at some length the concept of inclusive education as outlined in the Salamanca Statement (UNESCO, 1994), and as described by Mittler in Chapter 2. Included in the Statement were the following proclamations:

- every child has a fundamental right to education, and must be given the opportunity to achieve and maintain an acceptable level of learning,
- every child has unique characteristics, interests, abilities and learning needs,
- education systems should be designed and educational programmes implemented to take into account the wide diversity of these characteristics and needs,

- those with special educational needs must have access to regular schools which should accommodate them within a child-centred pedagogy capable of meeting these needs.

Proposition 4

From the perspective of placement criteria alone, there are three main types of provision for students with special educational needs: one-track (serving all students in one system), dual-track (serving students with special educational needs in one system and all others in another, main, system), and multi-track (serving various groups in different, parallel systems). Inclusive education for students with disabilities usually refers to a one-track system.

This distinction between the three different tracks is based on an analysis of different educational systems in Europe presented by Meijer *et al.* (2003). The one-track approach refers to countries that have developed policies geared towards the inclusion of almost all students in regular education, with support services. These include countries such as Italy, Portugal, Sweden, Greece and Norway (for a discussion of the last three countries, see also Chapter 6). To these countries could be added USA and Canada (Chapter 5), Australia (Chapter 7), China (Chapter 8), South Africa (Chapter 10), and some of the Latin American countries (Chapter 9), among the countries covered in the volume. South Africa, for example, is aiming at all students having equal access to a single, inclusive education system.

In two-track countries, there are two distinct education systems, with separate placements in special schools or special classes for students with special educational needs who follow a different curriculum to their non-disabled peers and sometimes come under separate ministries and administrative bodies. Meijer *et al.* (2003) cite Belgium and Switzerland as examples of this approach, while examples included in this volume would be Japan, Singapore, and the countries included in the chapter on the Middle East (Chapter 11). For example, in Singapore voluntary welfare organizations administer a special education system for students with moderate, severe or profound disabilities, while the Ministry of Education provides a regular education system for those without disabilities or those with milder learning, emotional, behavioural, sensory and physical disorders.

Also, as noted in Chapter 6, although the Netherlands has had a two-track policy for several decades, a growing group of policy-makers, educators and parents prefer inclusive education. Thus, in the Netherlands (and in other countries), the classification into one of these three categories is in a state of flux.

The countries coming under the multi-track approach have a multiplicity of approaches to inclusive education and offer a variety of services between the other two systems. In Europe, these would include such countries as

Denmark, France, Finland, the Czech Republic and Poland, and the United Kingdom (see Chapter 4 for the last-named, with reference to England). In the present volume, India and the Netherlands would probably fall into this category.

Proposition 5

The inclusive education/segregation divide is not limited to the regular class versus the special class/special school, but also covers a range of other educational provisions that separate students.

This proposition is based on Dyson's analysis in Chapter 4, in which he points out that many students with special educational needs, who are ostensibly integrated, are placed in segregated and semi-segregated provision within mainstream schools, largely in isolation from their peers. In some cases, the provisions for them effectively form mini-special schools attached to the mainstream. This point resonates with Sayed *et al.*'s (2003) argument that institutional access alone does not equate with educational inclusion: 'Besides issues of affordability, cultural and political environments and practices, both within and outside of educational institutions, may perpetuate exclusion even after students have technically been "placed" '(p. 242).

As well, Dyson points out that selection by ability and aptitude has been revived under New Labour governments since 1997 and the independent (private) sector educates well over half a million students, who are often selected on the basis of academic ability. He concludes that the impact of these various forms of selection, quasi-selection and grouping is that an unknown but significant number of students spend much of their school time in groups of 'like-ability' peers. There is no dispute, he claims, that English schools tend to be characterized by greater or lesser degrees of social segregation and that they tend not to educate children from clearly identifiable and homogeneous 'communities'.

Proposition 6

With regard to students with disabilities, inclusive education is a site of conflicting paradigms, centred on two different conceptualizations of special needs: (a) a psycho-medical model, and (b) a socio-political model.

Elsewhere, I have noted that the field of special education constitutes a site of conflicting paradigms that centre on the conceptualization of special needs (Mitchell, 2001). Several such paradigms may be identified, according to writers such as Clark *et al.* (1995). Two in particular stand out.

The first of these is referred to as the 'within-child model' (Lindsay, 2003), the 'medical model', the 'psycho-medical model' (Brown, Chapter

11; Clark *et al.*, 1995), the 'discourse of deviance' (Skidmore, 2002), the 'defect model' (Mittler, Chapter 2), the 'pathological model' (Naicker, Chapter 10), or the 'categorical model' (Emanuelsson *et al.*, Chapter 6). In this paradigm, school failure is ascribed to some defect, pathology, or inadequacy located within the student. As McLaughlin and Jordan (Chapter 5) note, this paradigm assumes that a disability is a stable, pathological trait within the individual that can be reliably diagnosed and categorically grouped. Resources are therefore tied to a diagnosis of a student's disabilities into one of the official categories and are usually delivered via some form of special schooling. Slee (Chapter 7) criticizes this model on the grounds that it reduces people to an essentialized set of characteristics that then forge teachers' expectations.

The second paradigm is variously referred to as the 'social model' (Mittler, Chapter 2; Lindsay, 2003), the 'socio-political paradigm' (Clark *et al.*, 1995), the 'deficient system' model (Naicker in Chapter 10), or a 'relational perspective' (Emanuelsson *et al.*, Chapter 6). In this perspective, special needs are portrayed as social constructs and special education as a system in which structural inequalities at the macro-social level are reproduced in institutional form. Under this paradigm, according to McLaughlin and Jordan (Chapter 5), it is assumed that society creates barriers which limit access for people with disabilities and which are constructed to serve the interests of the social majority. This point is further developed by Naicker (Chapter 10), who notes that theories underpinning much of the understanding around learning breakdown shapes the belief that problems are located within learners, with very little being said about system deficiencies.

In general, the within-child paradigm predominates. This would certainly be the case in most countries discussed in this volume, especially those in Asia (Chapter 8), Latin America (Chapter 9), and the Middle East (Chapter 11). There is, however, a growing awareness of the importance of the environmental paradigm, certainly in England (Chapter 4), the USA and Canada (Chapter 5), Western Europe (Chapter 6), and South Africa (Chapter 10). Even when the latter paradigm is gaining traction, vestiges of the former remain. This is no great pity, according to Lindsay (2003), who argues that it is not a matter of one or the other model but of finding the right balance between the two and of understanding how each interacts with the other.

Proposition 7

Inclusion goes beyond education and should involve consideration of employment, recreation, health and living conditions. It should therefore involve transformations across all government and other agencies at all levels of society.

This proposition has its basis in Sayed *et al.*'s (2003) thesis that:

> Educational inclusion ... presumes a broad-based collective will to effect transformation at every level of society. It requires grand schemes within an architecture that frames and facilitates transformation as well as political will at a sectoral, institutional and classroom level to create truly inclusive spaces.
>
> (pp. 244–245)

They go on to describe educational exclusion as operating 'in a sea of social exclusionary processes which affect access to basic rights in a number of domains: "adequate" or "quality" food, shelter, social security, employment, education, etc.' (p. 245).

Acceptance of the proposition requires, as Slee (Chapter 7) and Emanuelsson *et al.* (Chapter 6) indicate, not only a concern for education policy at large but also for the whole school community and other government departments to be inclusive.

Proposition 8

Inclusive education is not always made available to all students with special educational needs arising from disabilities, particularly those with severe or multiple disabilities.

It is probably safe to say that there is no country in the world where are *all* students with disabilities are enrolled in inclusive education settings. Even in those countries with the strongest commitment to inclusive education, it is seen as a conditional entitlement. In some cases, the grounds for excluding students are based on particular categories or on perceived severity of disability; in others it is a judgement exercised on a case-by-case basis. In still other cases, it reflects parents' choices.

In the US, as McLaughlin and Jordan point out in Chapter 5, the courts have held that violent or dangerous students who disrupt the education of others are never properly placed in a regular classroom setting. Further, the legal interpretations of the 'least restrictive environment' legislation support the preference that for inclusion to be justified, students should be expected to be able to achieve or acquire specific skills or certain levels of knowledge. In brief, in the US, inclusive education is not a right, but is dependent on an individual student's IEP goals. There are also differences in the use of inclusive placements when the data are examined by category of disability. For example, students with learning disabilities and speech and language impairments are most likely to be educated in general education classrooms, whereas a third of all students with emotional disturbance and over half of all students with mental retardation spend most of their school day outside general education classrooms. Similarly, in Chapter 7 Slee mentions that in Australia caveats are placed around the level of inclusion, so that the most difficult and different students don't disrupt the physical and educational capacity of current forms of schooling. Also, as noted by Mitchell and Desai in Chapter 8, the Learning in Regular Classrooms programme in China is usually made available only to students with sensory impairments and mild mental retardation; those with severe and multiple disabilities, and some with moderate disabilities, are still excluded and do not attend school. So, too, in Mexico, where those few students with severe disabilities who receive any education at all are placed in Multiple Attention Centers, rather than in regular classes.

Brown, in Chapter 11, raises yet another factor that works against inclusive education. With reference to Middle East countries, he notes that the 'invisibility' of the disability experienced by children with mild degrees of cognitive impairment, ADHD, ADD, speech and language impairment and specific learning disabilities, has created confusion and contradictory responses among parents and educators. He points out that at the same time that students in these categories may be more easily accommodated by inclusive educational practices, their identification in the schools is more likely to result in their exclusion as a condition for receiving special education and related services. A not too dissimilar point is made by McLaughlin and Jordan in Chapter 5, who note that different advocacy organizations in Canada and the US take contrasting stances towards inclusive education. Those representing students with complex disabilities argue for inclusion on the grounds of social equity and rights, whereas those representing learning disabled students seek to have them diagnosed and identified so that they can access specialized services.

Proposition 9

Inclusive education policies and practices must take account of reforms in general education, especially those that are derived from such neo-liberal philosophies as marketization, devolution, public choice, competition, and the setting of accountability criteria such as standards, outcomes and high-stakes testing. Since contemporary educational reforms often provide disincentives for schools to adopt inclusive education, the state has an obligation to intervene to ensure that such (usually unintended) consequences are prevented or ameliorated.

The context provided by neo-liberal market philosophies, which have characterized education reforms in many countries in the past couple of decades, contains many elements that tend to work against equity, the valuing of diversity and inclusive education (Blackmore, 2000; Mitchell, 1996). Several chapters in this volume discuss these reforms and their impact on inclusive education. Two inter-related themes in particular are addressed: standards and marketization. Each will be briefly examined, their impact on inclusive education discussed, and their implications for the state's responsibilities towards students with special educational needs suggested.

First, the economics-driven quest for 'excellence' or 'high standards' is referred to in several chapters. In his discussion of inclusive education in England, Dyson (Chapter 4) outlines the current standards-driven, highly accountable post-welfare society with its aim of developing individuals as a means of developing the economy. In this context, the emphasis is on excellence in education. Although the aim is to achieve excellence for the many, not the few, Dyson feels that the shift of focus to outputs in the education system is making 'unproductive' students less welcome in schools. Canada and the US are also undertaking what McLaughlin and Jordan (Chapter 5) refer to as 'standards-driven reform', which focuses on increasing the educational performance of all students, assessing these performances through 'high-stakes testing' and holding schools to more stringent levels of accountability. In this context, the focus of inclusive education shifts from access to outcomes and it thus becomes a means to an end and not the goal. Parents seeking inclusive education will increasingly be faced with regular classrooms that have an even more demanding curriculum and a pace of instruction that may not support inclusion. Other writers to touch on these issues include Brown (Chapter 11), who notes that in Middle Eastern countries the concept of excellence is perceived as being incongruous with the accommodation of learning diversity, and Slee (Chapter 7), who considers that narrowly defined notions of academic outcomes enforced through high-stakes testing 'is not the friend of educational inclusion'.

Second, it is frequently assumed that the adoption of marketization approaches to education will lead to excellence. Several chapters explore this theme and its impact on inclusive education. Most writers would agree with Blackmore's (2000) perception that marketization and the associated competitive relationships between schools and students has a negative impact on students with special educational needs. Such students, she argues, are seen as 'non-marketable commodities' (p. 381). This point is taken up by Dyson in Chapter 4, who notes that as low-attaining students are likely to depress the performance of schools, they are understandably wary about accepting such students or will place them in one of the multiple forms of segregated grouping, or seek to have them assessed as having special educational needs. Similarly, in Chapter 7, Slee writes that the intensification of competition between schools, resulting from parents choosing schools based on student results, amplifies and reinforces social division. This is compounded when schools are given permission through a quasi-market to become selective of their student cohort. He feels that the implications of this for students who are likely to jeopardize school results on academic performance league tables, and therefore for notions of inclusive education, are stark. In Singapore, too, where there is increasing stress on competition, with schools being ranked annually, the capacity of some schools to be selective provides them with an incentive for attracting students who are likely to be assets and, conversely, deters them from accepting students who might depress their scores (Mitchell and Desai, Chapter 8).

If the above risks to the education of students with special educational needs are to be avoided or ameliorated, there is an obligation on the state to intervene. As Blackmore (2000) argues, 'The first condition for quality education for all students is a reassertion of the value of a strong state supporting public education systems' (p. 383). Dyson, in Chapter 4, takes a similar tack, recommending that the operation of the market be supplemented with vigorous state intervention to ensure that its more perverse consequences are avoided. In particular, there is a need to ensure that those who are vulnerable in the market place are not so much protected as 'empowered to succeed', not least by gaining 'new knowledge and skill'.

Proposition 10

While many countries seem committed to inclusive education in their rhetoric, and even in their legislation and policies, practices often fall short. Reasons for the policy/practice gap in inclusive education are manifold and include barriers arising from societal values and beliefs (see Propositions 12 and 13); economic factors (see Proposition 14); a lack of measures to ensure compliance with policies; the dispersion of responsibility for education; conservative traditions among teachers, teacher educators and educational researchers; parental resistance; lack of skills among teachers; rigid curricula and examination systems; fragile democratic institutions; inadequate educational infrastructures, particularly in rural and remote areas; large class sizes; resistance from the special education sector (especially special schools); and a top-down introduction of inclusive education without adequate preparation of schools and communities.

Every chapter in this volume makes reference to a policy/practice gap in inclusive education, with a variety of explanations and possible solutions being advanced.

Even though the UN and its various agencies have been prime movers in persuading member countries to adopt inclusive education policies and to enact relevant legislation, turning these initiatives into reality is ultimately the responsibility of national governments. As Mittler points out in Chapter 2, each government will inevitably interpret such international guidance in the light of its own history, traditions, values and structures, to the point where the original policy may become unrecognizable. Fletcher, in Chapter 12, takes this point further, arguing for leadership to be exerted to bring about a world order in which diversity is honoured and equality of opportunity is provided for all citizens. The fact that we seem to be far away from such an ideal with respect to inclusive education often reflects the low priority accorded by most governments to children with disabilities. This is certainly the case in Singapore, for example, where, notwithstanding it being a signatory to important UN documents relating to the education of students with disabilities, it retains a largely segregated approach (see Mitchell and Desai, Chapter 8).

'Entre dicho y hecho hay mucho trecho' ('Between what is officially endorsed and what actually occurs, there is a gap'). According to Fletcher and Artiles (Chapter 9), this Mexican saying characterizes the chasm separating discourse and reality in ensuring inclusive education in Mexico, a chasm that could well be present in almost all of the countries discussed in this volume. So, too, the reasons. Among those identified by Fletcher and Artiles are the following: the structural adjustment policies required as part of the neo-liberal economic policies imposed by international donor agencies; the lack of accountability of schools to the parents and communities they serve; the lack of funds; the failure to infuse a social justice agenda in schools' work; exponential population growth; massive external debts and rampant poverty; fragile democratic traditions and institutions; the unavailability of social and educational infrastructure in rural and remote areas; the top-down manner in which the new system of 'educational integration' was imposed; the general lack of preparation prior to the implementation of integration, and the resulting confusion regarding the roles and responsibilities of practising regular and special education teachers; the absence of communication and dialogue among teachers working in integrated schools; the lack of administrative support to promote and support inclusive education practices; and little parent involvement.

Brown, in Chapter 11, points out that in the Middle East the effort to translate inclusive education rhetoric into action involves confrontation with the bedrock values and beliefs of the region. He states that while many of the basic cultural values and sentiments towards disabled persons provide a wellspring of potential support for inclusive thinking, deeply rooted cultural beliefs and traditions pose obstacles that are difficult to overcome. As can be seen in Chapter 8, the same could be said of the Asia region.

In South Africa, according to Naicker (Chapter 9), most South African educationists within mainstream education are perplexed by the notion of inclusive education simply because of a lack of exposure in the past and the current dominance of special education theory and practices. Specific barriers to implementing inclusive education policies include the following: socio-economic factors, attitudes, inflexible curriculum language and curriculum, inaccessible and unsafe environments, inadequate support services, lack of enabling and protective legislation and policy, lack of parental recognition and involvement, and lack of human resource development strategies.

According to Dyson (Chapter 4), despite the policy rhetoric of increasing inclusion in England, progress towards this goal is extremely slow. He attributes this, in part, to the way in which education is administered. In

England, local education authorities have responsibility for identifying and making provision for students with special educational needs, thus determining how far and how quickly an inclusion agenda is pursued, irrespective of central government policies. It is not surprising, therefore, that in some parts of the country, children are ten times more likely to be found in special schools than in others.

In Chapter 6, Emanuelsson *et al.* suggest that it is much easier to formulate than to practise inclusive education policies, and that there usually is a time lag between intentions being formulated and when they are put into practice, if ever. They note that in all four of the European countries they discuss, policies and regulations take a relational perspective, whereas the traditions within the school systems are based on a categorical perspective with a 'two-track' organization. With reference to Norway and Sweden, they suggest that one reason for this situation is the fact that most special education research is still mainly anchored in the traditional categorical perspective and does not subject the school environment to criticism. Another reason is related to the decentralization and deregulation that began in the early 1990s, which led to more conservative philosophies in education.

With the Australian state of Queensland as his reference, Slee (Chapter 7) points to the powerful special school sector as having a significant – and negative – impact on the spread of inclusive education. He argues that many students with disabilities would experience marginal engagement, neglect with respect to their diverse needs and even hostility in regular schools.

Artiles and Dyson (Chapter 3) outline yet another discrepancy – the potential contradiction between the outcomes that are intended by practitioners and policy-makers, on the one hand, and those that are actually generated for students, on the other. They argue that the efforts of policy-makers, practitioners, advocates and researchers have been weighted heavily towards what professionals intend to happen for learners, rather than towards robust evaluations of what outcomes actually materialize. Further, with reference to the USA and Canada, McLaughlin and Jordan (Chapter 5) highlight the research/practice gap, ascribing it to such factors as inadequately prepared personnel, large class sizes, lack of sufficient time, and lack of differentiation in the curriculum.

Proposition 11

Inclusive education exists in historical contexts in which vestiges of older beliefs co-exist with newer beliefs.

Every country has its own unique history of conceptualizing and responding to students with special educational needs. In order to understand current and planned approaches to inclusive education, it is necessary to consider past attitudes, policies and practices. In doing so, one should avoid taking either an unduly optimistic or an unduly pessimistic view of history. The optimistic perspective is premised on a notion of practice and policy in special education making uninterrupted progress over time (Dyson, 2001) or of it following 'a developmental pathway, away from superstition, prejudice and cruelty, and in the direction of greater enlightenment and humanity' (Armstrong, 2002, p. 437). The pessimistic perspective 'stems from powerful critical traditions ... which have uncovered ways in which vested interests in the education system and beyond have conspired to subvert any "progress" towards more liberal practices and forms of provision' (Dyson, 2001, pp. 24–25).

More appropriate ways of looking at the history of special education are advanced by Dyson (2001) and by Armstrong (2002). The former explores the potential of the concept of dilemmas as a means of understanding the field. Here, he argues that the history of special education 'can be seen as the product of the contradictory tendencies within the education system's responses to diversity and the resolutions of the "dilemmas of difference" to which those tendencies give rise' (p. 25). The latter cites with approval Safford and Safford's (1996) notion that human societies don't pass through discrete periods or stages, 'abandoning practices of one era as the next is born'. Instead, 'Vestiges of older beliefs remain, even today' (Armstrong, 2002, p. 437).

The importance of taking an historical perspective is highlighted in several chapters in this volume, many of which note the tensions between past and new paradigms. Even where the new paradigm of inclusion appears to be holding sway, it is clear that vestiges of old paradigms still exist. For example, Naicker (Chapter 10) describes the difficulties in moving teachers and teacher educators away from apartheid-era thinking to post-apartheid policies of inclusive education. He points out that South Africans, historically, had been exposed to very conservative theories and practices and that a narrow understanding of learning and teaching had bracketed out sociological considerations. Even in Sweden and Norway (Emanuelsson et al., Chapter 6), which are often held up as the pioneers of inclusive education, while policies are based upon thinking with roots in the relational perspective, the traditions within the school systems are essentially categorical and assume a two-track organization, with special education as one and regular education as the other track. With reference to Australia (Queensland in particular), Slee (Chapter 7), too, notes the tension between new inclusive education policies and the adherence to old special education perspectives. The latter is particularly evident among advocates for the large and resilient special school sector.

Proposition 12

Inclusive education is embedded in a series of contexts, extending from the broad society, through the local community, the family, the school and to the classroom.

A student with special educational needs simultaneously occupies a space within a regular classroom in direct interactions with his or her age-mate peers and with the teacher(s). In turn, the student is a member of a school with students of a particular range of ages, governance and management structure, and philosophy. The school is located in a community comprising the student's family, other families, various services, agencies, workplaces and recreational facilities, and so on. Communities exist within a broader society with a range of values, legislation, and resources. Each one of these features of a student's context has the potential to facilitate or hinder his or her inclusion into the school and the community. The necessity to take a systems perspective of inclusive education thus lies at the heart of this volume. In such a contextualist approach, according to Harry (2002), 'the individual is seen as embedded in a context, which is in turn embedded in a culture' (p. 132). Not only does such an approach draw our attention to issues such as those raised in the previous two propositions, but also, as Harry argues, it highlights the big cross-cultural differences in definitions of disabilities, the attributions of their aetiology and the stigma or value attached to various conditions. In a similar vein, Harvey (cited by Slee in Chapter 7) asserts that 'meaningful political action (and, for that matter, even meaningful analysis) cannot proceed without some embedded notions of value, if only a determination as to what is or is not important to analyze intellectually let alone to struggle for politically' (Harvey, 1996, p. 10).

In Chapter 3, Artiles and Dyson outline a comparative cultural historical framework that enables the multiple aspects of inclusive education to be organized systematically in such a way that is sensitive to local conditions, yet facilitates comparisons across cultural contexts. The framework encompasses several dimensions, including: participants, culture, and temporal. The participants dimension is concerned with the participants in the inclusive education system. The cultural dimension envisions culture as a cohesive system of rules and prescribed roles that mediate the actions and emotions of a cultural community. It comprises a regulative aspect, which helps us define the model of inclusion that is being implemented in a given locale; and an interpretive aspect, referring to the values, beliefs, knowledge, and emotions people use to interpret events; an instrumental aspect that considers the practices in which people participate. The temporal dimension focuses on the distribution of culture across time scales.

Proposition 13

Because cultural values and beliefs, levels of economic wealth, and histories mediate the concept of inclusive education, it takes on different meanings in different countries, and even within countries. The form taken by inclusive

*education in any particular country is influenced by the nature of the settle-
ments reached at any one time between (a) traditional values such as social
cohesion and group identity, collectivism, images of wholeness, fatalism, hierarchical ordering of society, and (b) modernization values such as universal
welfare, equity and equality, democracy, human rights, social justice, individualism, and parent choice.*

Artiles and Dyson (Chapter 3) observe that although inclusive education can
be seen as constituting a global agenda, in practice it takes on strongly local
flavours. This distinction between the global and the local is paralleled by an
equally powerful tension between modernization and traditionalism, a point
that is emphasized in several of the chapters in this volume (particularly
Chapters 8, 9, 10 and 11). As Brown points out in Chapter 11, for example,
while many of the basic cultural values and sentiments towards the disabled
provide a wellspring of potential support for inclusive thinking, deeply rooted
cultural beliefs and traditions pose obstacles that are difficult to overcome.

In some cases – for example, China, South Africa, the Middle East and
Latin America – these tensions are exacerbated by the rapidity of modernization processes that are taking place or are being advocated. Thus, with
reference to Latin America, Fletcher and Artiles (Chapter 9) refer to the
socio-historical contexts of inclusive education as being embodied in
tensions stemming from the dialectics of the global and the local and the
pressures to achieve economic development while strengthening democratic
traditions and institutions. In some cases (for example, Japan) traditional
value systems seem to be relatively impervious to Western models of inclusive education; in others, there appears to be a wish to modernize as quickly
as possible (South Africa, with its rapid shift to a post-apartheid era, is a
case in point). Whatever settlements are reached between the global/modern
and the local/traditional, three features stand out. First, the settlements are
complex; second, they are unique to each country; and third, they are in a
state of flux.

From a modernist (some would say Western) perspective, inclusive education is founded on many interlocking beliefs and values, three being given
prominence in this volume: First, several chapters (6, 7, and 10) emphasize
the relationship between inclusive education and democracy. For example,
Naicker in Chapter 10 describes deeper democracy in education structures
and processes as being one of the key transformation goals that underpinned post-apartheid policies in South Africa. Second, the related concepts
of equality, equity, social responsibility and freedom from discrimination
figure prominently as justifications for inclusive education in Chapters 5, 6,
7 and 10. Again, Naicker in Chapter 10 notes that a key aim of the new
South African policy was to address the inequalities of the apartheid past,
particularly those that were race-based. In Chapter 6, Emanuelsson *et al.*
describe the strong emphasis on equality and equity as being an important

basis of the 'Scandinavian welfare system', in which the state took care of the population by providing material security and satisfying psychological and cultural needs through social security, health and education. Third, inclusive education as an expression of individual human rights and social justice comes through in much of the literature in this field. In the present volume, this notion is emphasized in several chapters, particularly Chapters 5 and 10. For example, one of the first achievements in post-apartheid South Africa, according to Naicker, was the writing of a new constitution that attempted to entrench a human rights culture.

Traditional beliefs and values are outlined in some detail in two chapters: Mitchell and Desai's discussion of selected Asian countries (Chapter 8) and Brown's analysis of Middle Eastern cultures (Chapter 11). In India, according to Mitchell and Desai, the doctrine of karma has often militated against the disabled because it is believed that their disabilities represent retribution for sins committed in a previous incarnation and, therefore, any efforts to improve their lot would interfere with the workings of divine justice. This fatalistic attitude is often accompanied by feelings of guilt, stigma and fear. In seeking an explanation of China's evolving policies and practices in the education of students with special educational needs, Mitchell and Desai argue that consideration must be given to a complex amalgam of influences. These include traditional Confucian values, socialist ideologies, and, more recently, foreign (especially Western) influences, all overlaid by pragmatic economic considerations. For example, in Confucianism collective societal interests are emphasized and individualism is abjured. The Western concept of 'innate ability' is virtually non-existent; instead, teachers tend to believe that, with due effort, a child should be able to achieve the expected standard. Several interlocking core values also impinge on attitudes towards inclusive education in Japan, some also derived from Confucianism, others being indigenous to Japanese society. For example, Japanese schools are not much concerned with individual differences and provide education according to collectively established frames of reference. Individual differences are created through cumulative effort, not innate ability, and since all students are equal, any special attention is seen as discriminatory.

As noted by Brown in Chapter 11, since the concept of individualization is not generally understood in the Middle East, the organization of instruction represents a significant obstacle to the development of effective inclusive education practices. Where individualization is recognized, it becomes synonymous with exclusion, rather than a precondition for promoting inclusive practices. Thus, in the dominant collective paradigm, children are often seen as errant if they demonstrate individual needs separate from the communal group. Because the concept of disability contradicts the powerful cultural image of wholeness in the Middle East, the impetus for rejecting information that confirms the existence of any imperfection is strong. As in

India, disability is associated with some misdeed or condition created by a family member and thus results in shame and a loss of family honour.

Finally, it should be noted that this book's scope does not allow for consideration of within-country cultural variations. These, too, are very important if a full understanding of the context of inclusive education is to be achieved (see, for example, the contrasting viewpoints of Artiles [2003], and Macmillan and Rechsly [1998]).

Proposition 14

Economic considerations play a significant role in determining approaches to inclusive education. These include (a) a recognition that it would not be financially realistic to provide special schools throughout a country; (b) the adoption of a human capital policy of developing all individuals primarily as a means of enhancing the economy; and (c) an attitude that persons with disabilities are economic liabilities and are therefore of low priority.

There are two points here. The first is that some countries, particularly developing countries (such as China and India; see Mitchell and Desai, Chapter 8), are inclined to take a pragmatic, economically driven approach to inclusive education, recognizing that it would not be feasible to establish special schools throughout the country and that residential schools located in national or regional centres would be too expensive to operate. This point is also stressed by Artiles and Dyson (Chapter 3), who note that regular schools with an inclusive orientation represented the only realistic prospect in many countries of giving marginalized learners access to educational provision of any kind. The argument that inclusive education is both cost-efficient and cost-effective is also driving moves to rationalize the administration of special and general education (Peters, 2003, cited by Artiles and Dyson in Chapter 3).

Also pertinent is research reported by Meijer *et al.* (2003). In their study of fifteen European countries, they found a correlation of 0.60 between degree of segregation and population density. They explained this finding in both social and economic terms. It can be assumed, they argued, that in countries with low population density (e.g. Norway, Sweden, Greece), segregation in separate special schools has some clear disadvantages. First, great travel distances are time-consuming since children have to be transported to other towns or cities. Second, there are negative social consequences: children are taken out of their social environments and have less time for their friends in their own neighbourhood. Furthermore, special settings in low populated areas are not very cost effective. In countries with high population densities (e.g. the Netherlands, Belgium, Germany), special placements have less negative social and economic consequences.

The second point concerns the economic purposes of education for students who may never become highly productive in economic terms, an issue raised by Artiles and Dyson in Chapter 3. In some countries this matter is resolved simply by placing low priority on the education of such children. As noted by Mitchell and Desai in Chapter 8, Singapore is a case in point, with evidence that such persons are considered to be economic liabilities. In Latin American countries, too, as Fletcher and Artiles (Chapter 9) point out, an often-stated argument is: 'How can we afford to invest in social services for the small population of people with disabilities when size-able segments of our non-disabled populations still have such deep basic needs?' A contrary attitude is held in Canada and USA where, as McLaughlin and Jordan (Chapter 5) note, while the educational policies concerning students with disabilities represent strong statements of social equity and individual rights, there are also deep cultural values that support individual productivity, competition, and social competence. In post-welfare England, too, as Dyson (Chapter 4) explains, inclusion is seen not just as a matter of civil rights, but as part of an agenda that is driven by educational outcomes and, ultimately, by economic imperatives. With reference to Australia, Slee (Chapter 7) also notes the way in which government discourse talks of the depletion of social capital through exclusion and the requirement, therefore, for inclusive schooling.

Conclusion

Inclusive education reflects the relationships that exist at any one time among a country's social, political, economic, cultural and historical contexts. Given the issues raised in this volume regarding the relationships between inclusive education and its multi-dimensional contexts – some from within and others from without a country – the penultimate proposition must be:

Proposition 15

Since there is no one model of inclusive education that suits every country's circumstances, caution must be exercised in exporting and importing a particular model. While countries can learn from others' experiences, it is important that they give due consideration to their own social-economic-political-cultural-historical singularities. The challenge to 'importers' of inclusive philosophies and practices is to determine how far their country's indigenous philosophies, ideologies and practices should be encouraged, respected, challenged, over-thrown or blended with those from 'outside'. 'Exporters' of inclusive philosophies and practices have similar obligations to respect local values.

Inclusive education reflects the various settlements that are made between competing paradigms, and how various moral and professional dilemmas are resolved. This process is not without tensions, nor is it without frustrations as advocates of inclusive education confront obstacles and resistance. The chapters in this volume paint a somewhat bleak picture of the status of inclusive education around the world – at least in the regions and countries that are described. As will be seen in this volume, while there is ample evidence of good intentions, and occasional examples of inclusive education being implemented, practices do not always match the promises. There are even some signs in some countries that commitments to the philosophy of inclusive education may be stalling, if not in retreat.

In my work as a UNESCO consultant I sometimes liken students with special educational needs arising from disabilities to canaries in the coal mine: they tell us something about the quality of education systems in general. If schools will not or cannot adapt to such students, what does this tell us about their capacity to cater for diversity in general? Indeed, what does it tell us about their capacity to provide a quality education for any student? In Chapter 7, Slee raises this issue, commenting that 'Many of our neighbourhood schools are not good places even for those children whose right to a desk therein is never questioned'. Even so, he believes that there are sufficient examples of schools where inclusive education is being practised to justify rejecting the conclusion that inclusive education is a failed project.

Perhaps we should not be all that surprised to see resistance to implementing inclusive education. After all, it makes considerable demands on education systems and the participants within them. This is not limited simply to shifting attitudes towards students with disabilities and providing them with a desk in a regular classroom. To mix my analogies, I have also likened inclusive education to a Trojan Horse, in that it challenges education systems and schools to transform, re-align, and re-engineer their missions, structures, curricula and pedagogies (Mitchell, 2004). Not only does inclusive education reflect the ethos of the education system and the culture in which it is embedded, but it also contributes to its shaping. This is a process that some find compelling and others find unconvincing; and that some find liberating, while others find threatening. In brief:

Proposition 16

Inclusive education requires major shifts from old to new educational paradigms.

References

Ainscow, M. (1995) *Education for all: Making it happen.* Keynote address, International Special Education Congress, Birmingham, UK.

Antia, S.D., Stinson, M.S. and Gaustad, M.G. (2002) 'Developing membership in the education of deaf and hard-of-hearing students in inclusive settings' *Journal of Deaf Studies and Deaf Education*, 7, 214–229.

Armstrong, F. (2002) 'The historical development of special education: humanitarian rationality or "wild profusion of entangled events"?' *History of Education*, 31(5), 437–456

Artiles, A.J. (2003) 'Special education's changing identity: Paradoxes and dilemmas in views of culture and space'. *Harvard Education Review*, 73(2), 164–202.

Blackmore, J. (2000) 'Big change questions: Can we create a form of public education that delivers high standards for all students in the emerging knowledge economy?' *Journal of Educational Change*, 1, 381–387.

Booth, T. (1996) 'A perspective on inclusion from England'. *Cambridge Journal of Education*, 26(1), 87–99.

Clark, C., Dyson, A., Millward, A. and Skidmore, D. (1995) 'Dialectical analysis, special needs and schools as organisations'. In C. Clark, A. Dyson and A. Millward (eds) *Towards inclusive schools?* (pp. 78–95) London: David Fulton.

Dyson, A. (2001). 'Special needs in the twenty-first century: where we've been and where we're going'. *British Journal of Special Education*, 28(1), 24-29.

Harry, B. (2002) 'Trends and issues in serving culturally diverse families of children with disabilities'. *The Journal of Special Education*, 36(3), 131–138.

Harvey, D. (1996) *Justice, nature and the geography of difference*. Oxford: Blackwell.

Lindsay, G. (2003) 'Inclusive education: a critical perspective'. *British Journal of Special Education*, 30 (1), 3–12.

Macmillan, D.L. and Rechsly, D.J. (1998) 'Overrepresentation of minority students: The case for greater specificity or reconsideration of the variables examined'. *The Journal of Special Education*, 32(1), 15–24.

Meijer, C., Soriano, V. and Watkins, A. (eds) (2003) *Special needs education in Europe: Thematic publication* (pp. 7–18). Middelfart, Denmark: European Agency For Development in Special Needs Education.

Mitchell, D. (1996) 'The rules keep changing: Reforming special education in a reforming special education system'. *International Journal of Disability, Development and Education*, 43(1), 55–74.

——(2001) 'Paradigm shifts in and around special education in New Zealand'. *Cambridge Journal of Education*, 31(3), 319–335.

——(2004) 'Introduction'. In D. Mitchell (ed.) *Special educational needs and inclusive education. Major themes in education, Vol. II: Inclusive education* (pp. 1–10). London and New York: RoutledgeFalmer.

Peters, S.J. (2003) *Inclusive education: Achieving Education for All by including those with disabilities and special educational needs*. Washington: Disability Group, The World Bank.

Safford, E.J. and Safford, P.J. (1996). *A history of children and disability*. New York: Teachers College Press.

Sayed, Y., Soudien, C. and Carrim, N. (2003) 'Discourses of exclusion and inclusion in the South: Limits and possibilities'. *Journal of Educational Change*, 4, 231–248.

Skidmore, D. (2002) A theoretical model of pedagogical discourse. *Disability, Culture and Education*, 1(2), 119–131.

Skrtic, T.M., Sailor, W. and Gee, K. (1996) 'Voice, collaboration, and inclusion. Democratic themes in educational and social reform initiatives'. *Remedial and Special Education*, 17(3), 142–157.

UNESCO (1994) *World Conference on Special Needs Education: Access and quality. Salamanca Declaration and Framework for Action*. Paris: UNESCO.

Chapter 2

The global context of inclusive education

The role of the United Nations

Peter Mittler

> Each girl and boy is born free and equal in dignity and rights; therefore all forms of discrimination affecting children must end. We will take measures to ensure the full and equal enjoyment of human rights and fundamental freedoms, including equal access to health, education and recreational services, by children with disabilities and children with special needs to ensure the recognition of their dignity; to promote their self reliance and to facilitate their active participation in the community.
>
> (Statement by Heads of State, United Nations, 2002)

The commitment of the United Nations to human rights underpins the whole of its work in the social and humanitarian field, as first expressed in its Charter and in the Universal Declaration of Human Rights (1948), and most recently in the above commitment made by heads of state at the World Summit on Children in 2002. But since the UN can do nothing without the agreement and financial backing of its member states, it has to use its influence to ensure that the rhetoric of UN principles is translated to reality at national and local level by persuading governments to make a clear commitment to humanitarian and social development in general and to the human rights of disabled children and adults in particular.

The scope of United Nations initiatives

Up to this point, the UN has operated at a number of levels. First, it has created a number of legally binding international conventions, or treaties, together with mechanisms for public monitoring and accountability. The UN High Commission on Human Rights (UNHCHR) has now ruled that all UN conventions apply fully to disabled persons. These include conventions on Racial Discrimination (1965), Civil and Political Rights (1966), Economic, Social and Cultural Rights (1966), Women (1979) and Torture and Other Cruel, Inhuman or Degrading Treatment or Punishment (1984). In this chapter, I will focus on the impact of the Convention on the Rights of the Child (1989), as it illustrates the strengths and weaknesses inherent in the use of international treaties.

Quinn and Degener (2002) and Herr *et al.* (2003) have published detailed critiques of all UN conventions in relation to the rights of disabled people, while Lachwitz and Breitenbach (2002) have prepared a briefer analysis for the use of non-governmental organizations. These analyses are proving useful in work on a proposed new UN Convention on the Fundamental Rights and Dignity of Persons with Disabilities. The first steps have been taken but the process of drafting and securing agreement to such a convention will take many years and is not guaranteed a successful outcome, as several countries and groups have expressed strong reservations. Much will depend on the strength of the lobbies and their ability to maintain a united front.

In addition to the legally binding conventions, the UN has also issued a range of universal and specific Declarations on Human Rights which are not legally binding, but which have proved useful as a catalyst for the development of national policies and have provided a global framework for local advocacy and lobbying. The Universal Declaration on the Rights of Persons with Mental Retardation (1971) and the Declaration on the Rights of Disabled Persons (1975) were followed by a series of global programmes such as the International Year of Disabled Persons (1981) and the Decade of Disabled Persons (1983–1992). These were underpinned by the World Programme of Action (UN, 1982), which is still regarded as a beacon document. UN regional offices have launched two Asian Decades of Disabled Persons (1993–2002; 2003–2012) and the African Decade of Disabled Persons (2001–2010). The most influential initiative to date has been the UN Standard Rules on the Equalisation of Opportunities for Persons with Disabilities (UN, 1993) (to be discussed below). Although these initiatives have for the most part been beneficial and productive, the fact that they are not legally binding and that governments are not therefore held internationally accountable, has weakened their impact and strengthened the demand for a new convention to promote the rights of persons with disabilities.

In addition, many UN agencies have initiated their own programmes. I will consider the contribution of UNESCO in the field of inclusive education, with particular reference to the impetus created by the Salamanca Declaration and Framework for Action. Other relevant agencies include the World Health Organisation (WHO), the International Labour Organisation (ILO) and the UN Children's Fund (UNICEF). Many others with a more general remit are also now considering the needs of disabled children; these include UNHCHR and the High Commission on Refugees.

Human rights: inclusive or specific?

Some critics have argued that because disabled people are automatically included in universal human rights instruments, there is no need for separate initiatives specifically for them and that such campaigns can be counterproductive and increase rather than decrease discrimination (Helander, 1993).

Organizations of disabled people, as well as non-governmental organizations (NGOs) working in the field, have lobbied hard to ensure that their interests are included in these generic initiatives, but have met with only limited success. They complain that disability issues are either ignored completely, or subliminally subsumed under terms such as 'children in difficult circumstances', and that even when there is a specific reference to disability, this is lost in a long list of other marginalized groups and subsequently ignored.

This tension is fundamental to the struggle for inclusion. Disabled people want to be included as equals in society and its institutions, but experience of discrimination and exclusion at every level, including the UN itself, forces them to campaign for legislation which guarantees their specific rights and entitlements. They argue that once generic instruments effectively protect and promote the interests of disabled people, there will be no need for specific instruments. In the meantime, disabled people will fight for legislation that safeguards their rights.

Currently, the emphasis is on a twin, or multi-track, approach in which disability advocates campaign simultaneously for their full inclusion in both generic and disability-focused instruments and initiatives. There are indications that this is meeting with some success. An ongoing study by Inclusion International of a sample of the largest international aid agencies suggests that a disability dimension is now an integral element of policy in the majority of these agencies, even if the implementation of these policies is still at an early stage (www.inclusion-international.org). For example, the president of the World Bank has made a strong commitment to ensure that the needs of disabled people are specifically included in all development aid programmes supported by the Bank, and has appointed an experienced disability adviser to ensure the implementation of this policy (Wolfenson, 2002).

UN Convention on the Rights of the Child (1989)

The Convention on the Rights of the Child (CRC) addresses the rights of all children but also makes specific reference to children with disabilities. Every country in the world, with the exception of the United States and Somalia, has ratified it. Ratifying countries are required under international law to submit regular reports to the Committee on Children's Rights of the UNHCHR and to attend its hearings in Geneva. The Commission's reports on each country are published by the UN and on the internet. NGOs in the field of children's and disability rights have a key role in the monitoring process. Moreover, they have set up a strong communication and collaboration network and are well supported by the High Commission itself.

The International Save the Children Alliance published *Children's Rights: Equal Rights?* (2000), documenting examples of abuse of children's rights from twenty-six countries, including reports from governments and NGOs, as well as the Commission's own recommendations. The Alliance has also disseminated a CD-ROM that provides detailed information on the human rights of disabled children in most countries of the world (Jones, 2001) – an invaluable but alarming source of information.

Articles of the CRC

The four fundamental principles underlying the CRC apply to all children, without exception. These are non-discrimination (on any grounds, including disability); the best interests of the child; the right to life, survival and development; and the right to be heard and to participate. These are crosscutting principles and inform the interpretation and application of each article of the Convention for all children. Article 23 is specifically concerned with disabled children, but some of its language and concepts seem out of date by today's standards (see italics, added):

(i)   States Parties recognise that a mentally or physically disabled child *should* enjoy a full and decent life, in conditions which ensure dignity, promote self-reliance and facilitate the child's active participation in the community.
(ii) States Parties recognise the rights of disabled children to *special care ... subject to available resources ...*
(iii) Recognising the special needs of a disabled child, assistance extended ... *shall be provided free of charge, whenever possible, taking account of the financial resources of the parents* and others caring for the child, and shall be designed to ensure that the child has effective access to and receives education, training, health care services, rehabilitation services, preparation for employment, including his or her cultural and spiritual development.
(iv) States Parties shall promote, in the spirit of international cooperation, the exchange of appropriate information *in the field of preventive health care and of medical, psychological and functional treatment of disabled children*, including dissemination of and access to information concerning methods of rehabilitation, education and vocational services ...

In their detailed critique of the CRC, Quinn and Degener (2002) point out that access to appropriate services is not set out as a matter of right or as a general entitlement based on need. By failing to specify how states should secure these rights, the Convention treats disabled children less favourably than children who are refugees or those who are in need of protection from abuse. Furthermore, the wording throughout reflects a medical rather than a social model. This is also reflected in the reporting and monitoring arrangements that categorize disability as a health issue. Particular exception has been taken to references to the caveat, 'subject to available resources', because, even in 1989, it would not have been acceptable to discuss the education of girls or children from ethnic minorities in these terms.

Other articles of particular relevance to disabled children refer to the following rights: to remain with the family (9); views of the child to be taken into account (12); services to support parents (18); protection of children without families (20); refugee children (22); highest attainable standard of health and to facilities for treatment of illness and rehabilitation (24); periodic review of treatment (25); primary education free and compulsory to all, prevention of drop-out (28); education directed to the development of personality, talents and mental and physical abilities to their fullest potential (29); children of minorities or indigenous people (30); protection from work which interferes with education (32); protection from drug abuse (33); protection from sexual exploitation (34); protection from torture and deprivation of liberty (37); and rehabilitative care for victims of neglect, exploitation, abuse or degrading treatment (39).

Meeting the challenge of exclusion

The rights of children listed in the Convention stand in stark contrast to the statistics of exclusion which have been known for many years but which are only now beginning to impinge on the media and on the general public (e.g. UNICEF's [2003] annual reports on the *State of the World's Children*, Watkins, 2000). For example, 113 million children never attend school, two thirds of whom are girls. Another 150 million children drop out of school before they can read or write. One in four adults – 872 million people – cannot read or write; two thirds of these are women. For every child killed in armed conflict, three more are injured or permanently disabled. Ten million children are psychologically traumatized by armed conflicts. Less than 2 per cent of children with disabilities attend any form of school in income-poor countries.

Education For All: some landmarks

World Declaration on Education for All, Jomtien, 1990

As an immediate follow-up to the CRC, 155 governments and numerous NGOs concerned with children sent delegates to a major UN conference held in Jomtien, Thailand, in 1990, and agreed to aim for certain targets by 2000. Later in the same year, the world's leaders committed themselves to these targets at a one-day Summit on Children at the United Nations in New York. More targets were added in 1995 at the World Summits on Social Development in Copenhagen and on Women in Beijing. A ten-year review in Dakar, Senegal, in 2000, resulted in further revisions and new initiatives designed to speed up progress.

These targets include: the completion of the full period of primary education for all children by 2000 (now 2015); the reduction of adult illiteracy by half; the elimination of gender disparities (getting all girls into school would save two million lives a year); the reduction of infant and under-five mortality by one third by 2000 and two thirds by 2015; the reduction by half of severe and moderate malnutrition for children under five; and the reduction of the incidence of poverty by a half by 2015.

EFA was initially concerned with enrolment and completion rates and with gender disparities because these indicators are readily understood and publicized. But the emphasis has now shifted from access to schools to access to a reformed curriculum, full participation, and better methods of teaching and reform of teacher training.

Low enrolment rates, high drop-out rates and huge gender disparities cannot be blamed on family poverty and ignorance alone. The school system is itself at fault in most countries, partly because governments fail to invest in the education of their children or the training of their teachers, but also because the curriculum and the way it is taught fails to capture the interest of children or motivate them to learn and to participate. Reform of the school curriculum therefore lies at the heart of the inclusion movement, not only for disabled children, but also for all children.

There is a parallel here with the 'defect' and 'social' models of disability, the first seeing the problems as located largely within the child or family, the second emphasizing how different aspects of the environment have to change to meet the needs of all citizens. As an example of such a 'paradigm shift', the government of Brazil is paying the poorest families to send their child to school, in order to compensate them for the loss of income if their child was working.

World Education Forum: The Dakar Framework for Action (UNESCO 2000)

Ten years after Jomtien, the UN convened a follow-up meeting in Dakar to draw up a balance sheet of what had and had not been achieved. Although progress overall has been deeply disappointing, some positive outcomes can be celebrated. For example, the decline in school enrolments has been reversed (except in sub-Saharan Africa), there has been a slight reduction in the gender gap in primary education, and 300 million fewer adults are unable to read or write.

Overall, however, the failure of so many governments to meet or even approach the Jomtien targets makes it difficult to avoid the conclusion that children and education are a low priority and that a lack of political will, rather than lack of resources, lies at the root of the problem.

For example, some very poor countries have made a deliberate decision to invest in education; these include China, Cuba, Indonesia, Laos, Lesotho,

South Africa, Sri Lanka, Uganda, Vietnam, Yemen and Zimbabwe, all of whom perform at a much higher level than would be expected on the basis of their income levels (Watkins, 2000). Most of these countries are prioritizing inclusive education (UNESCO, 1999a; 1999b; 1999c; 2001a).

Early UN estimates indicated that it would cost 8 billion dollars to achieve universal primary education, and that donor countries would need to increase the proportion of their grants that go to education from two to eight per cent. This is the equivalent of 4 dollars per annum for each taxpayer in the donor countries. Paradoxically, proportions of aid earmarked for education have actually fallen by 16 per cent during the 1990s, the USA cutting its education aid by 58 per cent, the UK by 39 per cent and France by 22 per cent (Watkins, 2000). Donors have expressed doubts about the commitment of governments to reform education systems or have complained that the infrastructure was too weak to ensure that money reached those for whom it was intended. Be that as it may, school enrolments have actually fallen in sixteen countries in sub-Saharan Africa.

Oxfam has provided some figures to put the 8 billion dollars in perspective (Watkins, 2000). This amount represents four days of military spending; it is half of what is spent on toys in the USA, and it is less than Europeans spend on computer games or mineral water in a single year (these figures predate recent wars in Afghanistan and Iraq). Speaking at the Jomtien conference, the president of Ecuador stated that the cost of a single nuclear submarine would finance the annual educational budget of twenty-three developing countries and meet the needs of 160 million school age children. Some countries (e.g. Pakistan and India) choose to spend up to six times more on armaments than on the education of their children. Other countries are crippled by the burden of debt repayments to international agencies such as the World Bank and the International Monetary Fund. Furthermore, these agencies demand 'structural readjustment programmes' which require governments to reduce expenditure on public services such as health and education and to privatize others.

On the positive side, we are seeing a serious attempt on the part of a number of donor countries and agencies to reduce or even eliminate debt repayment, on condition that at least 80 per cent of the money thus saved is invested in the country's infrastructure, especially health and education. This programme and its variants (known as the Heavily Indebted Poor Countries, or Fast-Track, initiative) is welcome but has been heavily criticized for its slow speed of implementation.

Uganda was one of the first countries to benefit from debt relief, and provides a powerful example of what can be done when a country impoverished first by civil war and then by HIV/AIDS decides to prioritize education as the way to the social and economic regeneration and health of the whole country (UNESCO, 2001b). Free primary education is guaranteed to four children in every family, with first priority going to disabled children and to girls. As a direct outcome of this policy, 2 million additional children enrolled in school in the first two years, the net enrolment rate rising from 54 to 80 per cent. Public spending on education increased from 1.6 per cent of GDP in the early 1990s to almost 4 per cent in 2000 (Watkins, 2000). Targets for 2003 include 25,000 classrooms, water and sanitation for all schools, free textbooks for all primary age children, and an extensive teacher education programme. The Uganda government freely admits the immense obstacles facing the implementation of these policies (Arbeiter and Hartley, 2002), but a combination of political will and well targeted donor support has already achieved a great deal. Over and above enrolment rates, a higher quality of education is planned.

Although the example of Uganda is the most radical, it is clear that many other countries are moving towards inclusive practice in a variety of ways. In addition to the numerous reports published by UNESCO, mainly from income-poor countries, detailed reports have also been published by Save the Children (Miles, 2002a; Holdsworth, 2002 (on Lao PDR); and the Atlas Alliance (Stubbs, 2002) (see also Ainscow and Mittler, 2000; Armstrong and Barton, 1999; Daniels and Garner, 1999; and www.eenet.org.uk for many other country reports and summaries).

The Salamanca Declaration and Framework for Action (UNESCO, 1994)

As UNESCO and UNICEF began to monitor the impact of Jomtien, it became clear that although some governments were planning to reach targets for literacy and gender equality, very few were including disabled children within EFA. The Salamanca Conference was designed to redress the balance. It was hosted by UNESCO and the Spanish government and attended by representatives of ninety-four governments, UN agencies and many NGOs.

Salamanca significantly advanced the cause of inclusive education at several levels. It reminded governments that disabled children must be included within EFA and provided examples from a range of countries on ways in which disabled children could be more fully included in ordinary schools. The conference explored the implications of inclusive education for the training of teachers and for working with parents, NGOs and community agencies. Above all, Salamanca recommended that governments should adopt the principle of inclusive education as a matter of policy or law, 'enrolling all children in regular schools, unless there were compelling reasons for doing otherwise'.

The Salamanca conference seems to have had a positive impact on developments in a number of countries and at a variety of levels (UNESCO, 1999a). Some governments (including the United Kingdom) have explicitly committed themselves to implementing its recommendations. UNESCO's Inclusive Education Division has launched a series of new programmes and initiatives, and disseminated a great deal of information about the experiences of countries at all stages of development in moving towards more inclusive systems. It has also strengthened its teacher education programmes to focus more sharply on the education of children with disabilities in ordinary classrooms (UNESCO, 2001c). Two of its most recent programmes (Welcoming Schools and Inclusive Schools and Community Support) have reported pilot demonstration projects with inbuilt dissemination for sustainability; incorporation of innovations into national planning; changes in attitudes among policy-makers, administrators and the local community; knowledge, skills and human resource development at national and provincial levels, and enhanced managerial and leadership skills (UNESCO, 1999b; 1999c; 2001a).

Despite such positive examples, UNESCO's own conclusion five years after Salamanca effectively punctures complacency:

> The current Education for All strategies and programmes are largely insufficient or inappropriate with regard to the needs of children and youth with special needs. Where programmes targeting various marginalized/excluded groups do exist, they have functioned outside the mainstream – special programmes, specialised institutions, specialist educators. Notwithstanding the best intentions, it is conceded that too often the results have been exclusion – differentiation becoming a form of discrimination, leaving children with special needs outside the mainstream of school life and later, as adults, outside community, social, and cultural life in general.
>
> (UNESCO, 1999a, p. 10)

Although a ten-year review will certainly provide many more examples of positive national developments, some of the underlying tensions and contradictions of the Salamanca documents are now coming under critical scrutiny. For example, Lindsay (2003) argues that

> the Salamanca statement is based on a combination of a view of children's rights; of moral imperatives for action which do not directly relate to the right that is being proclaimed; and of an assertion of evidence. Also implicit is a tension between application of the proposed system for all children and a view that it may not be effective for all.
>
> (p. 4)

Lindsay's critique provides examples from the United Kingdom of fundamental tensions and contradictions between the government's simultaneous commitments both to inclusion and to policies and practices that create segregation and division within and between schools. These include competition between schools, a preoccupation with the raising of standards as reflected in the publication of test and examination results, and a paradoxical commitment to the continuation of special schools as 'part of the spectrum of provision in an inclusive system' (Mittler, in press; Rustemier, 2003).

Despite, or perhaps because of, these tensions and internal inconsistencies, UNESCO itself has done a great deal to provide helpful implementation guidelines which reflect the experience of many countries with very different education systems and attitudes to diversity and difference. For example, the *Open file on inclusive education* (UNESCO, 2001d) provides detailed guidelines for planners and policy-makers on moving towards more inclusive practice. Eight topics are discussed in some detail as being particularly relevant in planning for a more inclusive educational system. These include managing the transition, professional development, assessment, organizing support, families and communities, developing an inclusive curriculum, resourcing and funding, managing transitions throughout education, and working with schools. Most recently, UNESCO (2004) has published a *Toolkit for creating inclusive, learning-friendly environments* in the form of five booklets that reflect experience in a number of countries in the Asia and Pacific region (www.unescobkk.org). Since Dakar, UNESCO as a whole has been given a major monitoring mandate for EFA and has adopted inclusive education as a 'flagship programme' in order to ensure that the needs of disabled children are not once again overlooked or given a low priority.

UN Standard Rules on the Equalisation of Opportunities for Persons with Disabilities

The Standard Rules (United Nations, 1993) represent one of the influential initiatives taken by the United Nations. The twenty two Rules are firmly based on the social model of disability and have a twin agenda of empowering disabled people and creating an accessible society by removing obstacles to their participation. The Rules are basically a set of standards or quality indicators for a wide range of rights, needs and services relevant to disabled people of all ages, in all countries. They cover education, employment, family life, personal integrity, culture, recreation, sports, religion, income maintenance and social security.

Rule six is concerned with education, and is followed by nine further specific points of guidance:

> States should recognise the principle of equal primary, secondary and tertiary education for children, youth and adults with disabilities, in integrated settings. They should ensure that the education of persons with disabilities is an integral part of the education system.
>
> (UN, 1993, p. 23)

An important feature of the Rules is that they include an element of continuous monitoring carried out by the Special Rapporteur on Disability to the

UN Secretary General. Until December 2002, this was Mr Bengt Lindqvist, a former minister for social welfare in Sweden, and himself blind. He has been supported from the outset by a small expert committee consisting of two representatives of each of the main international disability NGOs: Disabled Persons International, Inclusion International, Rehabilitation International, World Blind Union, World Federation of the Deaf, and the World Federation of Psychiatric Users. Lindqvist's position enabled him to write to all heads of state, asking specific questions concerning their legislation and provisions for disabled people. He has made regular reports to the General Assembly of the UN and written personally to the heads of state of the many countries that he has visited officially. The Rules are currently being revised and a new rapporteur is being appointed.

The Standard Rules have had a major impact at a number of levels. First, they have influenced the UN and its agencies in seeing disability as a human rights issue and in using the Rules to ensure that disabled persons are included in all aspects of the work of the agency. For example, the World Health Organisation has developed a human rights based disability policy across all aspects of its work, not just in the section concerned with rehabilitation and development (www.who.int).

Second, follow-up surveys by the rapporteur suggest that the Rules have influenced many national governments in drawing up new legislation and by setting up or strengthening national coordinating councils responsible to the head of state. In their review of the impact of UN human rights initiatives on disabled people, Quinn and Degener (2002) reported that thirty-nine states in all regions of the world have adopted anti-discrimination legislation in the context of disability, and that national governments are increasingly including information on disability in their reports to the UN bodies monitoring the implementation of UN conventions. Third, organizations of disabled people are much more centrally and powerfully involved in the process of policy development at both national and international levels, especially when they speak to governments and the UN with a single voice.

Nevertheless, in his final report to the UN, Bengt Lindqvist expressed his disappointment that the Rules have had relatively little impact in developing countries, and in particular that there has not been more progress for children. In an earlier reference to the Convention on the Rights of the Child, he stated that 'when we relate the meaning of these principles to the actual situation of disabled children, we see, with shocking clarity, how far we are from complying with them' (Lindqvist, 1997).

Conclusions: from rights to reality

Turning rights into reality is a challenge for the UN, but above all a responsibility for national governments. As we have seen, children are not a high priority for most governments, and children with disabilities are particularly vulnerable to being overlooked and forgotten. Recent assessments raise fundamental questions about the impact of the whole range of UN initiatives on the day-to-day lives of disabled children and their families, especially in developing countries (Price, 2003).

In 1998, Mary Robinson, then High Commissioner of the UNHCR, gave expression to the challenge:

> Disabled people frequently live in deplorable conditions owing to the presence of social and physical barriers which prevent their integration and full participation in the community. Millions of children and adults worldwide are segregated and deprived of their rights and are, in effect, living on the margins. This is unacceptable.
>
> (Robinson, 1998, p. 1)

The disappointment expressed by world leaders illustrates the difficulties which arise when an international organization tries to provide leadership and guidance in encouraging national governments to change their policies and practice, however desirable or justified such a change may be. Inevitably, each government will interpret such international guidance in the light of its own history, traditions, values and structures, to the point where the original policy may become unrecognizable.

The story of UNESCO's leadership in the field of inclusive education can be compared with the work of the World Health Organisation in the parallel field of community-based rehabilitation (CBR). In the 1980s, WHO developed an impressive series of training manuals to support the inclusion of disabled people and their families in primary health care and community development, and used its influence and prestige to ensure that CBR was delivered according to what was initially presented as a standard WHO model. After twenty-five years, it is now accepted that each country will introduce CBR in its own way, even if this is far removed from the original blueprint developed in Geneva (see Thomas and Thomas (2002) for an authoritative history of CBR).

Despite disappointingly slow progress towards inclusive education, conditions seem favourable for a more positive and determined effort to achieve universally agreed goals. The quotation at the head of this chapter from the heads of state taking part in the 2002 World Summit on Children represents an accountable commitment to include disabled children in developing provision in their countries. These commitments are being followed up and monitored (e.g. Global Movement for Children, 2003). Furthermore, disability rights will become more prominent within the UN as a whole as a result of discussions designed to lead to a convention on the Rights and Dignity of Disabled Persons.

Governments are now more accountable for their policy and practice, and information about provision is increasingly in the public domain and subject to open monitoring at many levels. This includes the UN itself, through its mechanisms for monitoring and publicizing the implementation of the international conventions. Similarly, NGOs have published information about the record of all governments in implementing the Convention on the Rights of the Child in favour of disabled children (Jones, 2001). Because all governments are currently reviewing their EFA targets, there are opportunities for advocacy organizations to remind them that disabled children must be included in all EFA initiatives.

Finally, parents of disabled children all over the world are demanding inclusive education for their children and are putting pressure on governments to bring about the necessary reforms (Miles, 2002b). Experience in many countries has shown that organized and informed pressure from parents is irresistible and that change invariably follows.

References

Ainscow, M. and Mittler, P. (eds) (2000). *Including the excluded: 5th International Special Education Congress, University of Manchester*. CD-ROM. URLs: www.inclusivetechnology.co.uk and www.isec2000.org.uk

Arbeiter, S. and Hartley, S. (2002). 'Teachers' and pupils' experiences of integrated education in Uganda'. *International Journal of Disability, Development and Education*, 49(1), 61–78.

Armstrong, F. and Barton, L. (eds) (1999). *Disability, human rights and education: Cross-cultural perspectives*. Buckingham: Open University Press.

Dakar Framework for Action (2000). *Education for All: Meeting our collective commitments*. Paris: UNESCO.

Daniels, H. and Garner, P. (eds) (1999). *World yearbook of education: Inclusive education*. London: Kogan Page.

Global Movement for Children (2003). *The UN Special Session on Children: A first anniversary follow-up*. Woking, England: Global Movement for Children. URL: www.gmfc.org

Helander, E. (1993). *Prejudice and dignity: Community based rehabilitation*. Geneva: United Nations Development Programme.

Herr, S.S., Gostin, L.O. and Koh, H.H. (1993). *The human rights of persons with intellectual disabilities*. Oxford: Oxford University Press.

Holdsworth, J. (2002). *Seeking a fine balance: Lessons from inclusive education in Lao PDR*. London: Save the Children.

International Save the Children Alliance (2000). *Children's rights: Equal rights?* London: International Save the Children Alliance.

Jones, H. (2001). *Disabled children's rights: A practical guide*. Stockholm: Save the Children Sweden. (accompanying CD-ROM: *Examples of good practice and violations from around the world*). URL: www.rb.se

Lachwitz, K. and Breitenbach, N. (2002). *Human rights and intellectual disability: A guide to international human rights instruments for persons with intellectual disability*. London: Inclusion International. URL: www.inclusion-international.org

Lindqvist, B. (1997). *Statement to the Committee on the Rights of the Child*. Geneva: UN High Commission on Human Rights.

Lindsay, G. (2003). 'Inclusive education: A critical perspective'. *British Journal of Special Education*, 30(1), 3–12.

Miles, S. (2002a). *Schools for all: Including disabled children in education*. London: Save the Children UK. URL: www.savethechildren.org.uk/development

——(2002b). *Family action for inclusion in education*. University of Manchester: Enabling Education Network. URL: www.eenet.org.uk

Mittler, P. (2000). *Working towards inclusive education: Social contexts*. London: David Fulton Publishers.

——(in press). 'Why are special schools returning so few children to mainstream education?' *Special!*.

Price, P. (2003). 'Education for All: An elusive goal for children with disabilities in developing countries in the Asian and Pacific Region'. *Asia Pacific Rehabilitation Journal*, 14(1), 3–9.

Quinn, G. and Degener, T. (2002). *Human rights are for all: A study of the current and future potential of the United Nations human rights instruments in the context of disability*. Geneva: United Nations High Commission on Human Rights.

Robinson, M. (1998). Foreword to *Are disabled people included?* New York: United Nations. (fiftieth anniversary of 1948 Universal Declaration of Human Rights).

Rustemier, S. (2003). *The case against segregation into special schools*. Bristol: Centre for Studies in Inclusive Education.

Stubbs, S. (2002). *Inclusive education: Where there are few resources*. Oslo: Atlas Alliance. URL: www.atlas-alliansen.no

Thomas, M. and Thomas, M.J. (2002). 'Some controversies in community based rehabilitation'. In S. Hartley (ed.) *CBR: A participatory strategy in Africa*. London: Centre for International Child Health, University College.

UNESCO (1994). *World Conference on Special Needs Education: Access and quality. Salamanca Declaration and Framework for Action*. Paris: UNESCO.

——(1999a). *Salamanca five years on: A review of UNESCO activities in the light of the Salamanca Statement and Framework for Action on Special Needs Education*. Paris: UNESCO.

——(1999b). *Welcoming schools: Students with disabilities in regular schools*. Paris: UNESCO.

——(1999c). *Inclusive schools and community support programmes: Report on phase 1 (1996–1997)*. Paris: UNESCO.

——(2000). Dakar Framework for Action. *Education for All: Meeting our collective commitments*. Paris: UNESCO.

——(2001a). *Inclusive schools and community support programmes. Report on Phase 2 (1998–2001)*. Paris: UNESCO.

——(2001b). *Including the excluded: Uganda*. Paris: UNESCO.

——(2001c). *Understanding and responding to children's needs in the inclusive classroom: A guide for teachers*. Paris: UNESCO.

——(2001d). *Open file on inclusive education: Support materials for managers and administrators*. Paris: UNESCO.

UNICEF (2003a). *State of the world's children 2003*. New York: UNICEF.

——(2003b). *Including disabled children*. Florence: UNICEF, Innocenti Research Centre Digest.

United Nations (1982). *World Programme of Action Concerning Disabled Persons*. Adopted by the United Nations General Assembly at its 37th regular session. New York: United Nations.

——(1993). *UN standard rules on the equalisation of opportunities for persons with disabilities*. New York: United Nations. URL: www.un.org/esa/socdev/enable

——(2002). *A world fit for children*. New York: United Nations and UNICEF.

Watkins, K. (2000). *The Oxfam education report*. Oxford: Oxfam International.

Wolfenson, J.D. (2002). 'Poor, disabled and shut out'. *Washington Post*, 3 December.

Chapter 3

Inclusive education in the globalization age

The promise of comparative cultural-historical analysis

Alfredo Artiles[1] and Alan Dyson

In this chapter, we wish to explore a tension that is at the heart of all attempts to trace international 'movements' in education. On the one hand, such movements are recognizable as international precisely because different national systems begin to show similar features at the same time. On the other hand, whenever these apparent similarities are examined in detail, they tend to dissolve into the local forms and practices that characterize different national contexts. Inclusive education clearly is one such international movement, contributing, as it does, a significant dimension to the education policies of countries across the world and supported, as it is, by international declarations and international organizations (UNESCO, 1994; 1999; 2001). There is, therefore, a very real sense in which inclusive education constitutes what one group of commentators has called 'a global agenda' (Pijl *et al.*, 1997). At the same time, however, it is equally clear that the forms of educational practice that are labelled as 'inclusive education' have a strongly local flavour. The inclusion efforts of the affluent Western democracies, where well resourced segregated forms of special education are being merged with equally well resourced regular education, seem to be quite different from those of many economically poorer countries where special education has never been fully developed and where regular education is desperately lacking in resources. This is, of course, quite apart from the differences in the scope and definition of special education in different countries, or the exclusion and marginalization of different groups of learners in different countries and regions.

The question of whether inclusive education is best understood as a global or a local phenomenon cannot, we suggest, be separated from the location of that phenomenon at a particular historical moment. If inclusive education is global, that is because it has emerged in a period that is characterized by globalization in many aspects of human activity. And if the global nature of inclusive education cannot quite obscure its local flavours, that is because of the ambiguous nature of globalization itself.

Globalization refers to the tendency for human activities which occur at places geographically remote from each other nonetheless to interact with each other so that local practices – in terms, say, of culture, politics or economics – become overlain, or are entirely swept aside, by global patterns. Globalization in this sense is multifaceted, though there are three aspects that might demand particular attention (Suárez-Orozco, 2001): the development of communication technologies that have changed modern understandings of time and space as people increasingly have instantaneous access to events that are unfolding on the other side of the globe; the consolidation of regional and global markets and the emergence of information-knowledge economies; and an unparalleled mass migration, mostly from developing to developed countries.

The implication of globalization from a policy perspective is that countries are likely to be well informed about how policy questions are handled elsewhere and at the same time cannot develop their own policies without reference to how global developments impact on their own situation. The effects of this global interactivity are not necessarily benevolent. For instance, it is creating paradoxical conditions for the consolidation of democratic systems, particularly in developing nations. In the Latin American region there is evidence about both the strengthening of economies and a decline in investment in social programmes – the emerging outcome is that poverty levels during the 1990s remained virtually unchanged while equity indicators in the education sector reflect troubling trends (e.g. differential access to school, school completion and grade repetition, particularly for marginalized groups) (Arnove and Torres, 1999; Reimers, 1991). More generally, global economic conditions are widely seen as inhibiting the implementation of the Education for All agenda in economically poorer countries (World Education Forum, 2000). Indeed, education systems are notably vulnerable to these globalizing trends. As national markets become consolidated into regional and global ones, the level of investment in education is determined by global trends as much as by local decisions. At the same time, pressure builds on education systems across the world to deliver a workforce that is appropriately equipped to service these markets, and educational provision becomes shaped by these ends.

Within this situation, inclusive education can be seen as both a response and a contribution to global economic and other trends. This is true in two senses: first, it is supported by a globalized discourse of rights and entitlements; second, it is linked to global economic developments.

The discourse of inclusion

Daniels and Garner (1999), reviewing the international development of inclusive education, make the point that inclusive education is essentially based on a rights discourse:

The concept of 'inclusion' is by no means new ... its roots have been sown by a succession of educationalists and philosophers throughout the twentieth century – but it is the recent widespread and increasingly vociferous demand to establish individual rights as a central component in policy-making that has provided the impetus to place inclusion firmly on the agenda of social change.

(Daniels and Garner, 1999, p. 3)

Such a discourse lends itself easily to international declarations. In 1994, delegates from ninety-two governments and twenty-five international organizations, meeting under the aegis of UNESCO, adopted the Salamanca Statement on Special Needs Education (UNESCO, 1994) – a document which has gone on to exert a powerful influence on education policies across the world. The Statement sets out a commitment to inclusive education in ringing tones:

We believe and proclaim that:

- every child has a fundamental right to education, and must be given the opportunity to achieve and maintain an acceptable level of learning,
- every child has unique characteristics, interests, abilities and learning needs,
- education systems should be designed and educational programmes implemented to take into account the wide diversity of these characteristics and needs,
- those with special educational needs must have access to regular schools which should accommodate them within a child centred pedagogy capable of meeting these needs,
- regular schools with this inclusive orientation are the most effective means of combating discriminatory attitudes, creating welcoming communities, building an inclusive society and achieving education for all; moreover, they provide an effective education to the majority of children and improve the efficiency and ultimately the cost-effectiveness of the entire education system.

(UNESCO, 1994, pp. viii-ix)

This formulation bears some analysis. Its extraordinary power – and its worldwide influence – comes to a significant extent from its ability to deal in absolutes. In part, this comes from its reliance on a notion of children's rights which is, not surprisingly, grounded in other United Nations declarations – the 1948 Universal Declaration of Human Rights, the 1990 commitment to the right of education for all, and the 1993 Standard Rules on the Equalization of Opportunities for Persons with Disabilities (UNESCO, 1994, p. vii). In part, however, it comes from an extension of this absolute approach from questions of rights into questions of how those rights might be delivered. The right to education slips easily into an assertion of individual learner uniqueness and thence into assertions that education systems should be designed around uniqueness, that children with special educational needs 'must' attend regular schools and that inclusively oriented schools produce a range of educational and social benefits. In other words, the universalizing discourse is based not simply on its assertion of universal human rights, but on the universalization of theories of human difference, policy prescriptions and largely unsubstantiated empirical claims. It is but a short step from here to asserting that the forms of inclusive education that are desirable and effective in one national context must be equally desirable and effective in all such contexts.

Inclusive education and global economics

Despite the salience of rights within its discourse, inclusive education is also inextricably bound up with the need of countries to compete (or at least survive) in a global economic market place. As the Salamanca Statement makes clear, inclusive education is seen by UNESCO and the governments that follow the UNESCO lead as a means of 'achieving Education For All' (EFA). In turn, the World Education Forum, sponsored by a range of international bodies, including UNESCO and the World Bank, argues that EFA is strongly linked to national economic development and hence to the world economic and political order:

> it is unacceptable that more than 113 million children have no access to primary education, 880 million adults are illiterate, gender discrimination continues to permeate education systems, and the quality of learning and the acquisition of human values and skills fall far short of the aspirations and needs of individuals and societies. Youth and adults are denied access to the skills and knowledge necessary for gainful employment and full participation in their societies. Without accelerated progress towards education for all, national and internationally agreed targets for poverty reduction will be missed, and inequalities between countries and within societies will widen.

> … Education is a fundamental human right. It is the key to sustainable development and peace and stability within and among countries, and thus an indispensable means for effective participation in the societies and economies of the twenty-first century, which are affected by rapid globalization. Achieving EFA goals should be postponed no longer. The basic learning needs of all can and must be met as a matter of urgency.

> (World Education Forum, 2000, p. 8)

In this situation, inclusive approaches to education are essential, not simply on the basis of a notional right to participation in common social institutions, but because 'regular schools with this inclusive orientation' represent the only realistic prospect in many countries of giving marginalized learners access to educational provision of *any* kind:

> There is an urgent need to adopt effective strategies to identify and include the socially, culturally and economically excluded. This requires participatory analysis of exclusion at household, community and school levels, and the development of diverse, flexible, and innovative approaches to learning and an environment that fosters mutual respect and trust.
>
> (World Education Forum, 2000, p. 20)

As one might expect in the context of globalization, such arguments are not restricted to UNESCO, nor to economically poorer countries. As the chapter on England in this collection shows, policy-makers there make similar links between inclusive education and economic development. Similarly, in the USA, policy-makers routinely present their reform initiatives (in particular, the No Child Left Behind Act) as an attempt to include historically marginalized groups in an overall raising of standards – an attempt, moreover, which is driven by the need to make those groups economically competitive and which is explicitly linked to the global EFA initiative (see, for instance, Paige, 2004a; 2004b).

The economic analyses that underpin these arguments are highly influential in policy terms. In a paper commissioned (significantly) by the World Bank, the disability researcher Susan Peters sets out the complex interconnections between domestic economics, global economics, EFA and inclusive education which drive development in this field:

> Financing and support of educational services for students with special needs is a primary concern for all countries, regardless of available resources. Countries of the North are experiencing constraints as well as countries of the South, albeit with vast disparities. ... Regardless of relative wealth, education in all countries has had to compete with other economic priorities such as health care, social welfare, and defence budgets. However, education is widely seen as a means to develop human capital, to improve economic performance, and to enhance individual capabilities and choices in order to enjoy freedoms of citizenship. The strategy of Education for All is driven by a human-rights discourse and clear economic purpose linked to development.
>
> Within this global context, the Salamanca Statement of 1994 and a growing body of research assert that Inclusive Education is not only cost-efficient, but also cost-effective. ... Within education, countries are

increasingly realizing the inefficiency of multiple systems of administration, organizational structures and services, and the financially unrealistic options of special schools.

(Peters, 2003, pp. 4–5)

The globalizing aspect of these drivers is clear. The global economic position creates resource pressures in all countries while at the same time requiring them to develop as highly educated a workforce as possible to enhance their national economic competitiveness. In this situation, separate educational sub-systems for different groups of learners come to seem inefficient (or, in the case of poorer countries, non-viable), while approaches which focus on educating all learners in regular schools and enhancing the quality of those schools hold out the promise of both greater efficiency and greater effectiveness.

The 'global agenda': enlightenment or conspiracy?

Looked at in this way, inclusive education is both an outcome of global economic trends and itself an instrument of the globalization of educational policy and ideology. This dual nature can easily lead to the cynical conclusion that the high ideals of inclusion are simply a smokescreen for baser economic motives, and to a deep suspicion of the international traffic in inclusion consultants spreading the word of inclusion chiefly from the economically richer Western democracies to the economically poorer countries of the South. Indeed, some commentators believe they can smell the unpleasant odour of Western cultural imperialism in this movement (Haskell, 1998).

However, globalization is not necessarily or homogeneously negative in its consequences. The effort to define rights and entitlements in ways which rally action across the world, or to learn in one country from practices and forms of provision developed elsewhere may be enormously positive in a world situation where millions of learners are unable to participate fully in current educational arrangements. The potential for negative consequences arises not from such efforts *per se*, but if and when the globalizing tendencies of inclusion lead us – as commentators or advocates, practitioners or policy-makers – to overlook legitimate local differences. These may be in the way rights are understood in different cultural contexts, differences in the role ascribed to education, differences in forms and processes of exclusion, or simply differences in what is practicable. Under these circumstances, universal principles and prescriptions may simply lead to a false belief that the transfer of policy and practice between contexts is anything other than hugely problematic.

Equally, the universalizing discourse of inclusive education may draw attention away from its relationship to global economic imperatives and the way these imperatives play out in different contexts. It is not self-evident that the 'human-rights discourse and clear economic purpose' to which Peters refers are everywhere and always compatible. Certainly, the economics of the relationship between education and economic development are hugely contested (Robinson, 1997; Wolf, 2002), as is the question of whether the aims of education can be reduced to economics in the first place. In inclusive education, there is the further complexity of the economic purposes of education for learners who may never become highly productive in economic terms.

None of this is intended as a straightforward critique of inclusive education in the style of some of its self-professed opponents and sceptics (see, for instance, Garner and Gains, 2000; Kauffman and Hallahan, 1995). To ask whether inclusive education is 'right' or 'wrong', whether it 'works' or 'does not work' is, we suggest, to miss the point. Inclusion is, as Booth (1995) points out, a slippery concept that means different things in different systemic, socio-economic and cultural contexts. If the common language of inclusion is not simply to over-ride local concerns and conditions, the global inclusion 'movement' must engage in dialogue with – and be engaged in dialogue by – the local and the context-specific. For this reason, we suggest that those who wish to understand the global phenomenon of inclusive education need to do so from a perspective which takes due account of context. In the remainder of this chapter we will describe and argue for just such a perspective.

Comparative inclusive education: towards a cultural historical map of the dialectics of the local and the global

Arnove (1999) argues for a comparative perspective on education, and identifies three dimensions that characterize such an approach, namely the scientific, the pragmatic, and the global. A comparative education model is concerned with the generation of knowledge and theory-building characteristic of all scientific fields; the premise is that all sciences are comparative in nature. From this perspective, comparative analyses enable researchers to understand variations and to identify patterns in the ways in which educational systems around the globe are shaped by societal, political, economic, and cultural forces (Bray and Thomas, 1995). The pragmatic dimension aims to 'discover what can be learned that will contribute to improved policy and practice at home' (Arnove, 1999, p. 6). This means comparative analyses enable nations to engage in processes of knowledge transfer (what some called 'lending and borrowing') to improve their educational systems. The global perspective, in turn, contributes to an understanding of local educational processes as shaped by proximal and distal forces. As explained above, globalization reminds us of the international interdependencies that affect local events.

The contemporary proliferation of inclusive education suggests that researchers and policy-makers can benefit from comparative analyses for scientific, pragmatic, and global purposes. Comparative analyses enable us to examine fundamental aspects such as the definition of inclusive education that is used in a given context, the purposes and functions that inclusion serves in the target context, and the historical (global and local) precursors that shaped the development of an inclusive education system. In addition, a comparative analytic framework needs to acknowledge the interlocking of general and special education and it must examine such fusion as embedded in political and cultural arenas. In this vein, aspects of analytic interest include the power and status of groups being served in and excluded from education, the social locations of advocates and detractors of inclusive education, and the consequences of inclusion for all individuals involved (Artiles, 2003; Artiles and Larsen, 1998).

The comparative cultural historical framework we outline in this chapter enables us to organize systematically the multiple aspects of interest in such a way that is sensitive to local conditions yet grounded in broad parameters that facilitate comparisons across cultural contexts. The framework encompasses four dimensions as follows: participants, culture, history, and outcomes.

The participants dimension

This dimension is concerned with the participants in the inclusive education system. Comparative analyses of inclusion must begin with a description of the grouping dimensions of importance to local actors and the inclusion movement. This description should include first the target group(s) purportedly benefiting from the inclusive education system or model. Are these participants individuals with disabilities? Are these groups defined by categorical classifications or are groups defined by the more fluid notion of special needs education? If a categorical system of disabilities is used, which disabilities are being targeted for inclusion? How are these categories defined and operationalized? What are the other groups of participants expected to support the inclusion of the target groups?

Second, it is equally important to describe these populations in terms of key additional demographic information, such as socio-economic background, race and/or ethnicity, language, gender, and religion. These demographic descriptions need to include the families of participants as well. Last, the same descriptors should be used to characterize the professionals and staff working in the inclusive education model or system. It is desirable to describe the professional participants in terms of their qualifications (e.g. highest degree attained, certification, participation in mentoring and professional development programmes) and other indicators of quality.

The cultural dimension

The second dimension focuses on culture. This is indeed a challenging domain to address in comparative analyses, as culture is considered one of the most complex constructs in the English language (Williams, 1983). The view of culture that informs our framework aims to address the limits of traditional definitions and, thus, we endorse a multidimensional framework. For this purpose, we draw from cultural historical theory (Cole, 1996; Rogoff, 2003). Culture is defined as 'an historically unique configuration of the residue of the collective problem solving activities of a social group in its efforts to survive and prosper within its environment(s)' (Gallego *et al.*, 2001, p. 12).

From a cultural historical perspective, culture embodies three constitutive aspects, namely *regulative, interpretive, and instrumental* (Erickson, 2001; Gallego *et al.*, 2001). We typically envision culture as a cohesive system of rules and prescribed roles that mediate the actions and emotions of a cultural community. From a *regulative* perspective, the patterning that characterizes a group's identity is foregrounded. That is, a key assumption of the regulative aspect is that cultures are cohesive. For a system of regulations to work, a group must agree on the need for and content of the rules. Moreover, the group is required to pass on information about this regulative dimension to newcomers so that cultural continuity is ensured. The byproduct of this logic is that it is in a group's best interest to reproduce its culture and the implicit regulative model; indeed, a central premise of this dimension is that culture must reproduce its legacies in order to survive (Erickson, 2001).

The regulative dimension of culture helps us define the model of inclusion that is being implemented in a given locale. This is no easy task as there is a variety of inclusive models being implemented, even within the same nation (Dyson, 2001). Models, therefore, vary in core aspects such as the official definition of inclusion, the stated goals of the general education system, the stated vision of an inclusive society that supports the model, and the regulations and norms that govern the organization and administration of inclusive schools. To take one small but telling example, the French government has recently published a bill proposing the banning of outward symbols of religious faith – including the Muslim headscarf – in public schools. Such a move is, one press report states, seen by the government as raising no issues of inclusion or exclusion because, 'The principle of secularism, which expresses values of respect, dialogue and tolerance, is at the heart of France's republican identity' (an A.P. reporter and Dakroub, 2004).

However, in England, where there is no equivalent principle of secularism and where inclusion is taken (not least by government) to imply particular sensitivity to ethnic, cultural and religious differences, this move has been met with widespread incomprehension amongst educational liberals. In this respect, the models of inclusion in two otherwise similar countries derive from quite different cultural norms.

Culture also embodies an *interpretive* aspect. Some scholars argue culture is located in people's subjective understandings of the world, that is, in the values, beliefs, knowledge, and emotions used to interpret events (Eagleton, 2000). As Erickson (2001) explains, we 'live in webs of meaning, caring, and desire that we create and that create us' (Erickson, 2001, p. 38). Individuals are apprenticed to ways of interpreting the world in their cultural communities. Note that the weight of cohesion (i.e. group patterning) and reproduction is still emphasized in this aspect of culture, as it is implicitly suggested that people use their group's ways of interpreting the world to mediate their actions and ultimately ensure the survival of their culture. An important insight from this aspect of culture is that people navigate the regulative streams of culture by using cultural filters (values, beliefs) to decode and interpret the world.

This dimension compels us to understand how actors involved in the implementation of inclusive education systems make sense of their labour. The interpretive dimension focuses on the meaning-making processes that mediate local actors' efforts to forge an inclusive education culture. Note that actors interpret and make sense of the regulative aspects of the local inclusion education model through the beliefs, values, and expectations that each brings to the work; after all, participants are engaged in biographical projects that are shaped by race, gender, class, and language background, among others. This means that analyses should document participants' beliefs to gain deeper understandings of their interpretive processes. This information will enable researchers to explain how, despite the existence of official definitions of inclusion, there still are multiple and often partial understandings of the programme.

Culture also embodies an *instrumental* aspect that infuses a dynamic spin to the understanding of culture described thus far. In fact, this notion enables us to gain a deeper understanding of the indivisibility of the regulative, interpretive and instrumental aspects of culture. Culture is indexed in the practices in which people participate. The notion of practice has gained considerable currency in the last two decades in the social sciences, as a means to transcend the longstanding dualisms of structure v. agency, nature v. nurture, or individual v. social. Indeed, the work of scholars such as Bourdieu, Foucault, Giddens, Scribner, and Lave has enabled us to tackle these dichotomies through the adoption of practice as the unit of analysis. Giddens explains that

> the use of *practice* as the unit of analysis assists us to substitute the central notion of *duality of structure*. By the duality of structure, I mean the essential recursiveness of social life, as constituted in social practices: structure is both medium and outcome of the reproduction of practices, and 'exists' in the generating moments of this constitution.
>
> (as cited in Cole, 1996, pp. 138–139, emphases in original)

An implication of the central role of practice is that the nature of ethnic groups, for example, as culture-bearing communities should be regarded as an *outcome* of people's engagement with practices, as opposed to a definitional feature of such groups (Barth, 1969).

The instrumental aspect of culture helps us envision the tension that inhabits the stability of culture; that is, the dialectic of production and reproduction. The pressure to reproduce culture in any situation stems from the presence of established regulative systems, and from the fact that individuals enter social encounters with a toolkit or repertoire of practice appropriated through participation in their cultural groups (Gutiérrez and Rogoff, 2003). Hence, analyses of inclusion cannot focus solely on the regulative aspects of inclusion programmes, participants' assumptions or beliefs about inclusion, or even on how individuals' beliefs affect the ways in which they engage with inclusive programmes. This linear thinking artificially separates individuals' cognitions from context characteristics; sometimes it even implies that group membership determines people's ways of thinking and acting (e.g. learning styles linked to ethnic heritage) and, thus, it implicitly suggests that culture is stagnant. Although the instrumental aspect of culture does not deny people's proclivities to use certain repertoires of cultural practices, it also requires researchers to focus on individuals' histories of participation in cultural practices; that is, the focus is on processes of change.

This means that cultural historical analyses of inclusion need to document how people participate in inclusive practices as they use their cultural toolkits in their attempts to enact the vision of inclusion that structures the programme, and as they cope with the immediate demands of the tasks they are trying to accomplish. When individuals are committed to the vision of inclusion that informs their programme, and if they have adequate resources to achieve the programme goals, it is likely their efforts will contribute to reproducing the envisioned culture of inclusive education.

Let us assume, for example, a school community commits itself to creating an inclusive education programme that stresses placement of students with special needs in general education classrooms; features of the programme include some supports (teacher aids) and adaptations (basic curriculum and instructional modifications). A cultural historical analysis would require the observation of people's participation in key activities (defined theoretically or through consensus building procedures) of the inclusion programme. In addition, the analysis would be informed by an understanding of how participants' beliefs in key domains (e.g. inclusive education, teaching, learning, special needs) mediate their participation in the programme's practices. In other words, the analytic focus is on people's engagement with the activities of the inclusion programme (i.e. cultural practices) because culture 'is experienced in local, face-to-face interactions that are locally constrained and heterogeneous with respect to both "culture as a whole" and the parts of the entire toolkit experienced by an given individual' (Cole and Engestrom, 1993, p. 15). Over time, a culture is crafted to instantiate the inclusion programme – i.e. participants develop shared understandings of what it means to engage in inclusive practices, traditions emerge, the coordinated use of rules and roles is agreed upon, and regularities crystallize over time to constitute the cultural identity of this inclusive education programme (Rogoff, 2003). People's participation in these practices contributes to the reproduction of such culture.

However, there is always considerable unpredictability in the social ecology of life and, thus, culture is not fate (Erickson, 2001). Again, the notion of practice as the unit of analysis allows us to understand that social encounters always afford people the possibility to counter cultural reproduction or to innovate traditions. Specifically, as people navigate the regularities of a cultural community, tensions arise between the traditional cultural practices and the emergent goals that are shaped by the specific circumstances surrounding local events. Individuals negotiate these tensions by using their agency (use cultural resources) to adapt to ecological factors, resist local demands, or renew cultural legacies. It is important, therefore, to understand people's use of cultural rules and meaning-making processes as always mediated, not only by their individual toolkits and the cultural norms of their community, but also by the immediate contexts and ecological circumstances in which events take place. This is how the dialectic of cultural stability is crafted, how cultural production and reproduction co-exist.

Following with the aforementioned example of 'inclusion as placement' (Dyson, 2001), it is possible that a practitioner realizes, while reviewing with a colleague a reading lesson plan for special needs students, that their inclusion model did not examine critically curriculum and instructional barriers that could stifle their efforts. She also becomes aware that the current inclusion programme does not include accountability provisions to ensure special needs students attain at comparable levels to their non-disabled peers. These insights obtained as she plans a reading lesson prompt her to question some of the basic postulates of the school's inclusion programme. As a result, the school community embarks on a process of redefining its vision of inclusive education. This hypothetical example illustrates the value of using practice as the unit of analysis, because it helps us understand how people's participation in cultural practices can contribute to both cultural reproduction and change.

Note also that the dialectic of the stability of culture shapes the construction of a culture's cohesion; that is, cultural patterning and within-group diversity. Just as distinctive boundaries can be drawn between cultural groups, there are important variations in the ways in which people participate in their community's practices (Rogoff, 2003). The cohesion of culture, then, refers to the fact that people within a cultural group learn differing sets and subsets of culture (Barth, 1969; Erickson, 2001). Indeed, one of the most fascinating features of culture is the construction of its cohesion – i.e. how a culture gets distributed, similarly and differently within and across groups and within and between generations (Erickson, 2001). Like culture's stability, the cohesion of culture is crafted in the moment-to-moment history of events. As Varenne and McDermott (1999) explain, 'the coherence of a culture is crafted from the partial and mutually dependent knowledge of each person caught in the process. It is constituted, in the long run, by the work they do together' (p. 137). Through such processes, within-group diversity emerges in every culture as individuals negotiate emergent goals and cope with local demands to reproduce and innovate cultural legacies. This shift from individuals as mere carriers and reproducers of cultural codes to active creative agents and producers of culture is a welcome emphasis in contemporary culture theory, particularly in complex, stratified, multicultural societies where resistance might play a key role (Holland *et al.*, 1998; Holland and Lave, 2001; Varenne and McDermott, 1999).

This facet of culture is an important source of insight, since it affords researchers an analytic tool to explain that although the model of 'inclusion as placement' can be described as a cohesive whole, there are also participants (certain parents or teachers) who have different understandings of inclusive education or perhaps even oppose the inclusion programme. As explained above, the variability within the cultural community of this inclusion model can be crafted during the negotiated interactions between people who bring different commitments or understandings of the community's vision.

Furthermore, the role of *power* is crucial to an understanding of culture. As Erickson (2001) suggests, culture's webs of meaning and practices 'also hang in social gravity. Within the webs all our activity is vested in the weight of history; that is, in a social world of inequality all movement is up or down' (p. 38). The role of power reminds us that the analysis of culture should always be grounded in a relational and comparative framework (Holland and Lave, 2001; Rosaldo, 1993). This is an important insight for at least two reasons. First, it emphasizes the need to identify actors' perspectives to make visible what otherwise would be regarded as 'natural.' The assumption is that an actor's perspective is always invisible since it is the cultural medium through which events are experienced. Critics of traditional social science practices, for example, have identified how, although implicit Eurocentric assumptions permeate understandings of human development and culture, such suppositions are never made visible (Rosaldo, 1993). For example, the expectations, biases, evaluative criteria, or beliefs of European fieldworkers or observers are never acknowledged in descriptions or studies of Asian, African, or Pacific Islander cultural communities (Said, 1979; Tuhiwai Smith, 1999). The result is that such non-European groups are depicted as exotic or 'different'; hence, the Eurocentric gaze is deemed 'natural'.

The second reason is that the power dimension of culture enables us to understand how a cultural boundary – i.e. the objective presence of cultural difference – can be transformed into a cultural border, which is defined as a social construct that is political in origin. Through such process power is exercised because actors with differential access to power or who possess high-prestige cultural knowledge engage in the politics of difference as they turn boundaries into borders. From this perspective, the notion of difference is the product of political processes. As Minow (1990) explains, difference,

> after all, is a comparative term. It implies a reference: different from whom? ... But the point of comparison is often unstated. ... If we identify the unstated points of comparison necessary to the idea of difference, we will then examine the relationships between people who have and people who lack the power to assign the label of difference. If we explore the environmental context that makes some trait stand out and some people seem not to fit in, we will have the opportunity to reconsider how and for what ends we construct and manage the environment. The difference will no longer seem empirically discoverable, consisting of traits inherent in the 'different person.' Instead, perceptions of difference can become clues to broader problems of social policy and human responsibility.
>
> (pp. 22–23)

The dimension of power, therefore, reinforces the adoption of a unit of analysis that bridges agency and structure; it compels us to use a micro-macro gaze so that we envision events 'as a hybrid of the local and the socio-historical levels of analysis' (Gallego *et al.*, 2001, p. 957). Attention to power can afford important insights that are not typically addressed in the conventional scholarship in education. The role of certain markers of difference in the history of a given society or community, such as race, class, gender or language background, can help researchers contextualize further how power issues may mediate the implementation of inclusive education models. Questions such as the following can enable researchers to begin to explore power issues: Is there silence about certain issues, groups, or practices? What are the ideological underpinnings of inclusion goals and means? What does it mean to be included for various groups in the target community? When do certain types of difference count, under what conditions and in what ways and for what reasons? (Varenne and McDermott, 1999).

The temporal dimension

Level of analysis is a key aspect of this framework and a temporal dimension allows us to address it. Work on the temporal distribution of culture across time scales can assist us in this regard (Cole, 1996; Dien, 2000; Lemke, 2000). It is argued, for example, that the role of culture in human development can be studied at the cultural historical level that gives us access to the history of a given group or community. The focus is on the distinctive patterns that characterize a community's identity. However, cultural processes can also be examined at the individual level in terms of the life history trajectories of members of a given group. Interestingly, culture mediates processes at yet another temporal scale, the so-called moment-to-moment history of events, or the microgenetic scale. A key assumption is that these temporal scales are embedded and mutually influence one another. From this perspective, we can characterize this multilevel temporal model as a *temporal heterarchy* – i.e. the 'interdependence of processes at very different timescales ... of an organizational hierarchy in a complex self-organizing system' (Lemke, 2000, p. 280). It is important to note that the temporal levels unfold simultaneously (Scribner, 1985).

This dimension enables researchers to select the temporal scale at which an analysis is conducted. This is an important advantage of the model as it allows access to multiple levels of analysis of inclusive education, from the scrutiny of moment-to-moment interactions between teachers and students to the evolution of the cultural history of entire programmes. Moreover, analyses can be conducted diachronically or synchronically, depending on the needs and goals of the researchers.

The outcomes dimension

The outcomes of the inclusive education movement need also to be described. To some extent, this can be done within standard taxonomies of educational outcomes. However, there are two additional levels of complexity in the case of inclusive education. First, there is the potential contradiction between the outcomes that are intended by practitioners and policy-makers on the one hand, and those that are actually generated for learners on the other. The intended outcomes emerge out of processes of cultural reproduction – the existing understandings of inclusion and the purposes of education. The actual outcomes, however, have the potential to feed back into processes of production as they confront practitioners with realities that create new demands. It is probably true to say, however, that the efforts of policy-makers, practitioners, advocates and researchers have been weighted heavily towards what professionals intend to happen for learners rather than towards robust evaluations of what outcomes actually materialize (see, for instance, Dyson *et al.*, 2002).

Second, both the intended and actual outcomes of inclusive education are complex and multidimensional. For instance, the *Index for Inclusion* (Booth and Ainscow, 2002), which is used as an indicator system in a range of countries, views these outcomes in terms of the enhanced participation of all learners in the cultures, curricula and communities of their schools. This goes well beyond the simple 'integration' of learners with disabilities into regular schools and begs the question of whether these forms of participation are outcomes in their own right or are simply mediating processes leading to more standard academic and social learner outcomes. However, the Salamanca Statement that we examined earlier goes further still, talking in terms of a wide range of outcomes for communities and for society as a whole. Indeed, the economic imperatives that, we have argued, underpin to some extent the inclusive education movement, would seem to require that the economic impacts of inclusion be considered alongside those that are more personal or social.

Using the framework

It is not our intention to suggest that the framework we have proposed should be applied mechanistically to the analysis of inclusive education in particular contexts. It guides, but does not replace, contextual sensitivity and interpretive skill. Nonetheless, it does, we believe, have considerable heuristic power, and an example of how this works might be helpful. Since this collection is primarily concerned with country studies, our example is drawn from a lower system level – that of the school.

One of us (Dyson) has recently completed a study with colleagues of the development of inclusive practices in twenty-five schools in three English local education authorities (LEAs).[2] The study involved a collaborative action research process between university researchers and teams of leaders and teachers in each of the schools, lasting for some three years. Each of the school teams identified some aspect of practice in the school that was less inclusive than it would have liked, took action to develop practice in a more inclusive direction and monitored the impact of that action. The findings of the full study are being reported elsewhere (e.g. see Ainscow and Dyson, in press; Ainscow et al., 2001; 2004; Dyson, 2004; Dyson et al., 2003; Gallannaugh and Dyson, 2003). However, for our purposes, it is sufficient to focus on a single school – Broadmeadow primary school.

Broadmeadow educated children aged 5–11 who were predominantly from low-income, white families living on a large social housing estate. In common with all the other schools in the study, the Broadmeadow team were invited to identify for themselves the aspects of the school's practice that were less inclusive than they wished. By implication, of course, they had to define what they meant by 'inclusion'. In doing this, they were offered some guidance by the relatively recent national commitment to the development of an inclusive education system (DfEE, 1997). This guidance, however, was deceptive. Although the government drew upon the discourse of rights and even aligned itself with the principles of the Salamanca Statement, it adopted what it described as a 'pragmatic, not dogmatic' approach which accepted that some children could not be educated in mainstream schools, foresaw a continuing role for special schools, and laid down few if any prescriptions about what inclusive education would look like in terms of school and classroom practices.

Government ministers at the time also tended to elide the issue of including children with disabilities and special needs with the issue of 'social inclusion', by which they meant the wider problems of low attainment, unemployment and disaffection which were reckoned to afflict a sizeable minority of the population (Blunkett, 1999). Moreover, at the same time the government was pursuing a so-called 'standards agenda' which focused heavily on driving up levels of measured attainment and institutional performance through a process of national target-setting and high levels of school accountability. This placed considerable premium on the attainments of children who were just below the borderline level set by national targets. Since the target was for 80 per cent of children in primary schools to reach the specified level, the borderline group was effectively those whose attainments were somewhat below the national mean, but not those with the very lowest levels of attainment.

In this context, the Broadmeadow team decided that their focus should not be on children formally identified as having special educational needs (SEN). In the view of the head teacher, the school had already made a major commitment to these students and they were, therefore, well provided for and as fully 'included' as was possible. Instead, the team focused on children in the 'borderline' group:

> They [the target group]'re underachievers. They're actually children of the broadly average ability but who are underachieving. Whereas our SEN children on the whole they haven't got the average learning potential – they're below average, and some are significantly below average.

The explicit aim was to enable these children to reach the national standard. As the head teacher commented: 'It's all about level 4s [the national standard] really, isn't it?'. The 'borderline' children, the head felt, presented particular problems:

> We're always playing catch up with some children, but it's too late. The catch-up's coming too late. And the sort of catch-up we're doing, it goes some way, but it's building bricks – it's like building a wall isn't it? And the top row's going to be very wobbly if you haven't got the bottom right. And some of those early layers of bricks are either missing completely, or they're very insecure. And this is obviously impacting. And it's the barrier – it's what's stopping these children attaining what they should attain for children of their age.

The origins of these difficulties were understood as lying in the home, with parents who failed to provide books and reading opportunities for their children. There was, teachers told us, 'a loss of family life and the talking that goes on in it'.

Specifically, children suffered from a language deficit acquired in the home:

> the children we take in particularly have problems with language. Because I think their first-hand experience is quite little … I think their lack of experience with language, perhaps at home, already has created a problem when they come into school.

In addition, this lack of preparedness for schooling was said to be exacerbated in the case of boys by the existence of what was variously described as a local 'yob' or 'northern lad' culture, within which boys were expected to behave in stereotypical ways and influenced each other adversely as they grew older. As one teacher told us:

> I think so far as language skills are concerned, there's a difference between boys and girls – no matter what we all might say. … Female language centres are more highly developed, aren't they? … I think girls' language development is much quicker than boys' … I think schools are set up to be the sort of places girls would like, more than boys. Boys want to rush around and do exciting things and not sit there reading and writing – we make them do it. I mean it isn't a natural boy thing to do, is it, at that age?

In response to this situation, the team decided to shift the emphasis of teaching in the school from a largely instructional mode to one that made good some of the children's supposed deficits and allowed them to capitalize on their existing skills. Instead, therefore, of placing more emphasis on the technical skills of writing, they offered their students a range of practical experiences as a precursor to writing, encouraged them to talk about these experiences in collaborative groups and engaged them in what they called 'thinking skills' activities. The intention was that they would build up a sound experiential and cognitive base – the foundations of the 'wall' – out of which writing would flow more naturally. As the school's deputy head teacher explained:

> if you think of like a triangle or pinnacle thing – at the end of it we would like to see, from the school's point of view, a specific improvement in attainment in some areas [such as] writing. But we felt that the opportunity with this project would be to influence kind of a cultural change, in staff as well. And we could use it to look at teaching styles, learning styles, expectations, but with the focus that all these strategies and ideas towards thinking, a whole host of things, will benefit writing.

Applying the framework

This mention of cultural change brings us back to our proposed cultural-historical framework. Although it is not possible here to develop a full analysis of what was happening in this school, some of the dimensions of such an analysis are already clear. For instance, the chosen temporal scale for the analysis is the cultural historical level, as the focus is on the transformation of school culture(s). However, it would be possible to analyse, in addition to the school culture(s), processes of change at the individual level by crafting a case study on the learning trajectories of a particular 'type' of student and/or teacher(s).

As it happens, we know relatively little about the teachers themselves as individuals (since this was not a focus of the study). However, we do know that, as a profession, teachers in England are graduates (and therefore academically successful learners themselves), that they are relatively highly trained, that they earn well above the national average wage and that they are regarded as being members of the middle class. This information may be important if the target temporal scale of the analysis was concerned with the individual level, in this case focusing on teachers to understand how the teachers in this school interpret and respond to the challenges presented by the academically less successful children they teach and the predominantly working-class community served by the school.

Attention to the participants dimension of our framework suggests that the target group supposedly benefiting from the school's attempt to become more inclusive is not the children with disabilities and/or special educational needs who frequently form the focus of such efforts, but children on the borderline of the national standard in measured attainment. We also know that this identification derives from the *de facto* requirement on schools to categorize their students in terms of where they stand in relation to national assessments – those who will easily achieve the national standard, those who cannot achieve the national standard and those who are on the borderline. However, this categorization is crosscut by other, perhaps more deeply rooted systems. Hence, we see teachers making a series of distinctions: between underachievers with 'learning potential' and children with special educational needs who do not have 'learning potential'; between girls with highly developed 'language centres' and boys with poorly developed 'language centres'; and between the 'children we take in' who have language problems because of their home background and some implicit ideal group of children whose language develops rapidly in 'supportive' homes.

We know that the 'culture' of the school is something of which the teachers were struggling to become aware in order that they might change it. We see the dialectic between cultural production and reproduction that arises as old practices prove inadequate to meeting new demands and as the teachers who participate in the school culture(s) seek to develop new practices. However, we also see the mediating force of power at work within and upon the culture(s) of the school. There is the most obvious form of power exerted by national government through the demands and accountabilities it imposes on the school. Significantly, however, this is not the simple power of command. The demands of national government are internalized by teachers so that the national system of attainment targets transforms itself into a quasi-categorization system that becomes a way of 'seeing' the schools' students.

Moreover, the accounts which teachers give us of their students, the difficulties they experience, the origin of those difficulties in family and area and the likely impacts of different approaches to teaching are not accounts of some objective reality. These accounts themselves are cultural products that, amongst other things, demonstrate the power of the school to represent its students in particular ways and to use these representations as a means of rationalizing actions in respect of those students. In this sense, the framework's multilevel nature allows us to understand the interplay between structural forces (as represented in the school narratives of students located at the cultural historical level) and individual trajectories at the ontogenetic level (as indexed by teachers' uses of such narratives to interpret student performance in daily interactions).

Although this study was not truly longitudinal, we could nonetheless see how these accounts and the cultures from which they emerged might change over time. The new demands that the teachers were facing arose at particular points in time; these demands embodied complex tensions in the stability (reproduction v. production) and cohesion (group patterns v. within-group diversity) dimensions of culture. The new demands arose as the result of multiple events: the intensification of the standards agenda by the incoming 'New' Labour government in 1997; its introduction at the same time of a rather prescriptive national literacy strategy; a mini-crisis in 2000 about the apparent failure of the literacy strategy to improve attainments in writing, just as the schools in the project were choosing a focus for their work. These policy developments created pressure at the local level to *reproduce* traditional practices that would ultimately stratify student performance (i.e. by privileging particular measures of student competence without reconfiguring the very structures that produced the achievement differentials) while the policies purportedly aimed to *produce* a new culture of school practices (i.e. evidence-based accountability).

These historical events were compounded by other, more local events – notably, the coming together shortly before the project started of a relatively youthful head and deputy head teacher determined to make their mark on the school and committed (albeit in different ways) to the principles of inclusive education as they understood them. Analysis at the cultural historical level would enable us to document the school's *cultural patterning* as it strived to become inclusive, while the study of ontogenetic trajectories (e.g. certain teachers and students) would enable us to document variability in the school's characteristic patterns (i.e. within-group diversity).

We can also characterize at least some of the outcomes from the model of inclusive education pursued by this school. In terms of raising the measured attainments of the target group of 'borderline' students, the school did rather well. It was also able to document changes in classroom practice, some changes in the discourses of teaching and learning that were used by the staff, and changes in the level of engagement by students with learning activities. At the same time, some outcomes seemed likely to reinforce the status quo, which had generated the very problems that the school's actions sought to address. Nothing the school did challenged the hierarchies established by the national testing regime, or the social conditions out of which children's difficulties (if such they were) emerged, or the relationship between the process of schooling and the 'habitus' of working-class children. Arguably, indeed, the school's willingness to take up the challenge issued by the government in precisely the terms in which that challenge was issued did little but legitimate the essentially exclusive tendencies of the existing system. Again, our multilevel framework enables us to document the complex tensions between macro and micro issues in order to understand the cultural historical nature of local practices.

Analysis, ambiguity and inter-national learning

It is common for educationalists to talk about the development of inclusive education as if it were a race towards a single, clearly defined and consensually understood finishing post. We find ourselves talking about schools, or administrations or national systems that are 'ahead' in terms of inclusion, or that 'got into inclusive education early' or that are 'lagging behind' the others. What this analysis demonstrates, we suggest, is that such unidimensional perspectives are simplistic. From a cultural-historical perspective, the development of inclusive education is a multidimensional phenomenon, with different countries (and, we might add, different schools and classrooms) developing not simply at different rates but in quite different directions. It follows that comparisons of countries (as of schools and classrooms) are not possible in any simple and straightforward way. One of the manifestations of the globalization of education is, of course, the extent to which systems for making international comparisons of educational performance – such as the PISA study (OECD, 2001) – have flourished and become increasingly influential in shaping national policies. The implication of our analysis, however, is that there can be no equivalent in inclusive education, and that even the relatively sophisticated indicator systems that are currently gaining international adherence (e.g. see Booth and Ainscow, 2002) have to be treated with considerable caution.

This in turn has implications for the transferability of educational practices between countries (or between schools or classrooms). Because such practices are embedded in local cultures, histories and conceptualizations, they are unlikely to survive in their original form unless the complex contexts out of which they grow are transplanted at the same time. Not only is such transplantation hugely problematic, but also it may mean no more than riding roughshod over local contexts. In this situation, Haskell's (1998) characterization of the inclusive education movement as a form of cultural imperialism will be amply justified.

There is one further cautionary note to be sounded as a result of our analysis. The contextualized nature of inclusive education means that in any given form, it always reflects the outcome of historical and cultural choices. The corollary of this, of course, is that other choices were always theoretically possible and inclusion could have taken some other form. In the case of Broadmeadow primary school, for instance, some group other than the 'borderline' students could *theoretically* have been the focus of the school's efforts, some other analysis of children's difficulties could have been made and some other actions could have been taken. Under these circumstances, any form of inclusion is always ambiguous because behind it lie the choices that were not made, the other forms of inclusion that were rejected. This inevitably compounds the problem of international transfer. It is not simply that inclusion is multidimensional, or that it is embedded in complex historical and cultural contexts. The ambiguity of any one form of inclusion means that there is no 'perfect' model of inclusion that can be exported around the world.

Do these difficulties with the notion of international transfer mean, then, that there is nothing that national systems can learn from each other and that the contributions to a collection such as the present one have little more than curiosity value to readers in other countries? Our answer to this question is to assert that this need not be the case, provided that the emphasis is indeed on learning rather than on transfer. As we argued above, culture is not fate. Cultural reproduction can always potentially be countered; the 'choices' made can always theoretically be otherwise. Given the dynamic tension between reproduction and production, the presence of alternative cultural practices is a powerful means of problematizing the choices that have always been made and opening up new possibilities for seeing and doing. This is as much true at institutional as at national level. One of the factors in Broadmeadow school's development of its new approach to literacy, for instance, was when the staff had access to a skilled teacher from outside the school who worked with students in ways quite different from those to which they were accustomed. Indeed, across the project as a whole, the impact of accessing alternatives – seeing teachers teach differently, spending time in schools that organized themselves differently, or visiting cities which had very different policies on inclusion – was the most powerful factor we could find in catalysing inclusive developments. It is not that teachers 'borrowed' educational practices from these alternatives, but that they used alternatives to enable them to reflect on their own practices. In this sense, such alternatives acted as what we have called 'interruptions' (Ainscow and Dyson, in press), 'contradictions' or 'disruptions' (Artiles *et al.*, 2000; Engestrom, 1993) to the taken-for-granted reproduction of established practice.

In much the same way, encounters between national systems, whether actual – through visits and exchanges – or virtual – through accounts such as those in this collection – have the potential of 'making the familiar strange'. This is a much less certain process than that of technology transfer in which techniques, procedures and structures from one system are imported into another. It depends on the willingness of national systems to open themselves up to international scrutiny and, even more so, on their capacity to use what they learn about other systems to reflect on why things are the way they are in their own system. It also then depends on their capacity to take action to make things in some culturally specific way 'better'.

Such a process is genuinely international without at the same time being in a negative sense globalizing. Because it uses experience from elsewhere as a catalyst rather than a template, it respects local cultures and promotes local solutions without at the same time implying that the local should be accepted uncritically simply because it *is* local. Moreover, it delineates an important role for international scholarship of a particular kind – scholarship which focuses on penetrating the complexities of local practices while it strives to discern regularities in the midst of diversity, uncovering their roots in local cultures and histories and making them available for scrutiny from outside. It is the attempt to represent the local in a form with which those from elsewhere can engage, which represents the core purpose of this collection.

Notes

1 Dr Artiles acknowledges the support of the National Center for Culturally Responsive Educational Systems (NCCRES) under grant no. H326E020003 awarded by the US Department of Education, Office of Special Education Programs.
2 *Understanding and Developing Inclusive Practices in Schools*, funded by ESRC (L139251005) as part of the Teaching and Learning Research Programme and undertaken by teams from Christchurch University College Canterbury, the University of Manchester and the University of Newcastle.

References

Ainscow, M., Booth, T. and Dyson, A. (2004). 'Understanding and developing inclusive practices in schools: A collaborative action research network'. *International Journal of Inclusive Education*, 8(2), 125–139.

Ainscow, M., Booth, T., Dyson, A., Gallannaugh, F., Howes, A., Millward, A. and Smith, R. (2001). Understanding barriers to participation in education. Paper presented to American Educational Research Association Annual Meeting, 1–5 April 2001, New Orleans, Louisiana.

Ainscow, M. and Dyson, A. (in press). 'Standards and inclusive education: Schools squaring the circle'. *British Educational Research Journal*.

An AP reporter and Dakroub, H. (2004) 'Muslim girls may quit classes'. *TES* (London), 16 January 2004. URL: http://www.tes.co.uk/search/ search_display.asp?section=Archive&sub_section=News+percent26+opinion&id 389357&Type=0 (accessed 1 April 2004).

Arnove, R.F. (1999). 'Reframing comparative education: The dialectic of the global and the local'. In R.F. Arnove and C.A. Torres (eds) *Comparative education: The dialectic of the global and the local* (pp. 1–23). Lanham MD: Rowman and Littlefield.

Arnove, R.F. and Torres, C.A. (eds) (1999). *Comparative education: The dialectic of the global and the local*. Lanham MD: Rowman and Littlefield.

Artiles, A.J. (2003). 'Special education's changing identity: Paradoxes and dilemmas in views of culture and space'. *Harvard Educational Review*, 73, 164–202.

Artiles, A.J. and Larsen, L. (eds) (1998). 'Special issue: International perspectives on special education reform'. *European Journal of Special Needs Education*, 13, 5–13.

Artiles, A.J., Trent, S.C., Hoffman-Kipp, P. and Lopez-Torres, L. (2000). 'From individual acquisition to cultural-historical practices in multicultural teacher education'. *Remedial and Special Education*, 21, 79–89.

Barth, F. (1969). 'Introduction'. In F. Barth (ed.) *Ethnic groups and boundaries: The social organization of cultural difference* (pp. 9–38). Bergen/Oslo: Universitets Forlaget.

Blunkett, D. (1999). *Social exclusion and the politics of opportunity: A mid-term progress check. A speech by the Rt Hon. David Blunkett MP*. London: DfEE.

Booth, T. (1995). 'Mapping inclusion and exclusion: Concepts for all?' In: C. Clark, A. Dyson and A. Millward (eds) *Towards Inclusive Schools?* (pp. 96–108). London: David Fulton.

Booth, T. and Ainscow, M. (2002). *Index for inclusion: Developing learning and participation in schools*. Bristol: Centre for Studies on Inclusive Education.

Bray, M. and Thomas, R.M. (1995). 'Levels of comparison in educational studies: Different insights from different literatures and the value of multilevel analysis'. *Harvard Educational Review*, 65, 472–490.

Cole, M. (1996). *Cultural psychology: A once and future discipline*. Cambridge MA: Harvard University Press.

Cole, M. and Engestrom, Y. (1993). 'A cultural-historical approach to distributed cognition'. In G. Salomon (ed.) *Distributed cognitions: Psychological and educational considerations* (pp. 1–46). New York: Cambridge University Press.

Daniels, H. and Garner, P. (1999). 'Introduction'. In H. Daniels and P. Garner (eds) *World Yearbook of Education 1999: Inclusive education* (pp. 1–10). London: Kogan Page.

DfEE (1997). *Excellence for all children: Meeting special educational needs*. London: The Stationery Office.

Dien, D.S. (2000). 'The evolving nature of self-identity across four levels of history'. *Human Development*, 43, 1–18.

Dyson, A. (2001). *Varieties of inclusion*. Paper presented to the IV Jornadas Científicas de Investigación sobre Personas con Discapacidad, 17 March 2001. Salamanca, Spain.

——(2004). 'Inclusive education: a global agenda?' *Japanese Journal of Special Education*, 41(6), 613–625.

Dyson, A., Gallannaugh, F. and Millward, A. (2003). 'Making space in the standards agenda: developing inclusive practices in schools'. *European Educational Research Journal*, 2(2), 228–244.

Dyson, A., Howes, A. and Roberts, B. (2002). 'A systematic review of the effectiveness of school-level actions for promoting participation by all students' (EPPI-Centre Review, version 1.1). In *Research Evidence in Education Library*. London: EPPI-Centre, Social Science Research Unit, Institute of Education. URL:http://eppi.ioe.ac.uk/EPPIWeb/home.aspx?page=/reel/review_groups/inclusion/review_one.htm (accessed 1 April 2004).

Eagleton, T. (2000). *The idea of culture*. Oxford: Blackwell.

Engestrom, Y. (1993). 'Developmental studies of work as a testbench of activity theory: The case of primary care medical practice'. In S. Chaiklin and J. Lave (eds) *Understanding practice: Perspectives of activity and context* (pp. 64–103). New York: Cambridge University Press.

Erickson, F. (2001). 'Culture in society and in educational practices'. In J. Banks and C.M. Banks (eds) *Multicultural education: Issues and perspectives* (pp. 31–58). New York: Wiley.

Gallannaugh, F. and Dyson, A. (2003). *Schools understanding inclusion: issues in inclusion and social class*. Paper presented to the BERA Annual Conference, 11–13 September 2003, Heriot-Watt University, Edinburgh.

Gallego, M.A., Cole, M. and Laboratory of Comparative Human Cognition (LCHC) (2001). 'Classroom cultures and cultures in the classroom'. In V. Richardson (ed.) *Handbook of research on teaching* (4th edn) (pp. 951–997). Washington DC: American Educational Research Association.

Garner, P. and Gains, C. (2000). 'The debate that never happened'. *Special!*, autumn, 8–11.

Gutiérrez, K.D. and Rogoff, B. (2003). 'Cultural ways of learning: Individual traits or repertoires of practice'. *Educational Researcher*, 32(5), 19–25.

Haskell, S.H. (1998). *Inclusive schooling: The contemporary cultural imperialism of western ideologies*. Paper presented to the Second International Exhibition and Congress on Rehabilitation, 29–31 March 1998, Dubai, United Arab Emirates.

Holland, D., Lachicotte, W., Skinner, D. and Cain, C. (1998). *Identity and agency in cultural worlds*. Cambridge MA: Harvard University Press.

Holland, D. and Lave, J. (eds) (2001). *History in person: Enduring struggles, contentious practice, intimate identities*. Santa Fe NM: School of American Research Press.

Kauffman, J.K. and Hallahan, D.P. (eds) (1995). *The illusion of full inclusion*. Austin TX: PRO-ED.

Lemke, J.L. (2000). 'Across the scales of time: Artifacts, activities, and meanings in ecosocial systems'. *Mind, Culture, and Activity*, 7, 273–290.

Minow, M. (1990). *Making all the difference: Inclusion, exclusion, and American law*. Ithaca NY: Cornell University Press.

OECD (2001). *Knowledge and skills for life: First results from the OECD Programme for International Student Assessment (PISA) 2000*. Paris: OECD.

Paige, R. (2004a). 'A better education for all children in the United States'. *Education Today – Newsletter*, January-March 2004, UNESCO: Paris. URL: http://portal.unesco.org/education/ev.php?URL_ID=27743_DO=DO_TOPIC_SECTION=201 (accessed 1 April 2004).

——(2004b). Remarks of Secretary Paige before the Florida Atlantic University School of Education Conference on Reading Literacy, Boca Raton FL. Washington: US Department of Education. URL:

http://www.ed.gov/news/speeches/2004/01/01302004.html (accessed 1 April 2004).

Peters, S.J. (2003). *Inclusive education: Achieving Education for All by including those with disabilities and special educational needs.* Washington DC: Disability Group, The World Bank. URL:
http://wbln0018.worldbank.org/HDNet/hddocs.nsf/65538a343139acab85256cb70
055e6ed/8a1681957d70149f85256d7c004d9a61/$FILE/InclusiveEdEnglish.pdf
(accessed 1 April 2004).

Pijl, S.J., Meijer, C.J.W. and Hegarty, S. (eds) (1997). *Inclusive education: A global agenda.* London: Routledge.

Reimers, F. (1991). 'The impact of economic stabilization and adjustment on education in Latin America'. *Comparative Education Review*, 35, 319–353.

Robinson, P. (1997). *Literacy, numeracy and economic performance.* London: Centre for Economic Performance, London School of Economics.

Rogoff, B. (2003). *The cultural nature of human development.* New York: Oxford University Press.

Rosaldo, R. (1993). *Culture and truth: The remaking of social analysis.* Boston MA: Beacon Press.

Said, E.W. (1979). *Orientalism.* New York: Random House, Vintage Books.

Scribner, S. (1985). 'Vygotsky's uses of history'. In J.V. Wertsch (ed.) *Culture, communication, and cognition* (pp. 119–145). New York: Cambridge University Press.

Suárez-Orozco, M.M. (2001). 'Globalization, immigration, and education: The research agenda'. *Harvard Educational Review*, 71, 345–364.

Tuhiwai Smith, L. (1999). *Decolonizing methodologies: Research and indigenous peoples.* New York: Zed Books.

UNESCO (1994). *Final Report: World conference on special needs education: Access and quality.* Paris: UNESCO.

——(1999). *Salamanca five years on. A Review of UNESCO activities in the light of the Salamanca Statement and Framework for Action. Adopted at the World Conference on Special Needs Education: Access and Quality.* Paris: UNESCO.

——(2001). *Open file on inclusive education. Support materials for managers and administrators.* Paris: UNESCO.

Varenne, H. and McDermott, R. (eds) (1999). *Successful failure: The school America builds.* Boulder CO: Westview Press.

Williams, R. (1983). *Culture and society.* New York: Columbia University Press.

Wolf, A. (2002). *Does education matter? Myths about education and economic growth.* London: Penguin Books.

World Education Forum (2000). *The Dakar Framework for Action. Education for All: Meeting our Collective Commitments.* Text adopted by the World Education Forum, Dakar, Senegal, 26–28 April 2000. Paris: UNESCO.

Chapter 4

Philosophy, politics and economics?

The story of inclusive education in England

Alan Dyson

> We want to see more pupils with SEN included within mainstream primary and secondary schools. We support the United Nations Educational, Scientific and Cultural Organisation (UNESCO) Salamanca World Statement on Special Needs Education 1994. This calls on governments to adopt the principle of inclusive education, enrolling all children in regular schools, unless there are compelling reasons for doing otherwise. This implies a progressive extension of the capacity of mainstream schools to provide for children with a wide range of needs.
>
> (DfEE, 1997a, p. 44)

With these words in October 1997, the recently elected 'New' Labour government aligned the English education system for the first time with the international movement towards inclusive education. This was, in many ways, a remarkable move. Not only was the language of 'inclusion' a relatively new phenomenon in England, but also it is rare for English governments to align themselves with principled international declarations – particularly in the field of education, or even to look abroad for models on which to develop policy. The government therefore positioned itself at – or at least close to – the forefront of thinking in the field and all seemed set fair for the rapid development of an education system that would be a world leader in terms of inclusion.

Much that followed seemed to confirm this expectation. In 1998, the government produced a Programme of Action that sought, amongst other things, to find practical ways of acting upon the commitment to inclusive education (DfEE, 1998). In the following year, the agency responsible for overseeing the National Curriculum issued statutory guidance on inclusion as part of a wide-ranging revision of the curriculum (DfEE and QCA, 1999). In 2001, a Special Educational Needs and Disability Act extended protections against discrimination on the grounds of disability to children in school and strengthened the rights of parents of children with special educational needs to choose a regular ('mainstream') placement for their child. At about the same time, the national schools inspectorate, Ofsted, issued guidance on how to inspect the inclusiveness of schools (Ofsted, 2000), while the government issued guidance to local education authorities (LEAs) on how best to fund inclusive provision in their areas (DfES, 2001a) and to schools on how to interpret the new legislation (DfES, 2001b). Recently, a second Programme of Action has been produced (DfES, 2004), which promises to give new impetus to the inclusion agenda.

On the face of things, therefore, England would appear to be a country that is moving rapidly along the path to full inclusion. However, all is not quite as it seems. Despite the steps that have been taken, a minority of students continue to be educated in special schools. Currently, the national figure stands at something over 1.1 per cent (National Statistics, 2003d). In the English system, however, local education authorities (LEAs) have a major role in determining provision at the local level, and here there is considerable variation. In some parts of the country, children are ten times more likely to be found in special schools than in others (Audit Commission, 2002b) and this seems difficult to explain simply in terms of the differing demographics of these areas. Moreover, despite the policy rhetoric of increasing inclusion, progress towards this goal is extremely slow. Overall, the special school population fell slightly from 97,700 in 1999 to 93,900 in 2003 (National Statistics, 2003d). Again, though, there are significant local variations. At current rates of change, for instance, many less inclusive LEAs will take decades to reach the levels already achieved by more inclusive LEAs (Norwich, 2002).

Moreover, the figures relating to special school placement do not tell the whole story. Many students are placed in segregated and semi-segregated provisions within mainstream schools. These 'units' or 'resource bases' may in practice be highly integrated with the rest of the school; some, however, educate children largely in isolation from their peers and effectively form mini-special schools attached to the mainstream. In addition, students may be placed in off-site 'Pupil Referral Units' (PRUs), often because they have been excluded for disciplinary reasons. Government figures (National Statistics, 2003c; 2003d) show some 32,000 students (0.34 per cent) educated in this way, though this may well be an underestimate.

Perhaps most significantly, mainstream schools have, in recent years, been encouraged to develop a range of grouping systems that place children in different settings and on different curriculum pathways on the basis of their perceived ability and aptitude (DfEE, 1997b; DfES, 2001c; 2002; 2003a). In addition, selection by 'ability' and 'aptitude', long a minor but significant feature of the English education system, has received a new lease of life under 'New' Labour governments since 1997. This, of course, is to say nothing of the 'independent' sector which educates well over half a million students (National Statistics, 2003c), often selected on the basis of academic 'ability' and very largely selected on the basis of their parents' ability and willingness to pay. The impact of these various forms of selection, quasi-selection and grouping is difficult to assess, but two consequences seem to be fairly certain. The first is that an unknown but significant number of students spend much of their school time in groups of 'like-ability' peers. In some (though not all) cases, the provision that is made is not unlike that of the special classes (Tansley and Gulliford, 1960) and behaviour units (Galloway and Goodwin, 1979) of bygone days that sought to replicate aspects of special school provision in mainstream settings.

The second consequence is that few if any mainstream schools in England educate all of the children who live in their localities. The combined effects of special schools, resource bases in mainstream schools, PRUs and various forms of selection are enough to ensure that school populations are skewed and truncated in various ways. These patterns are compounded by the effects of parental 'choice'. The education reforms of the 1980s and 1990s, centred on the 1988 Education Reform Act, removed the power of LEAs to place children in local schools and gave parents the right (with certain restrictions) to choose a school for their child. The net effects of this change are hotly disputed (Ball, 1993; Ball *et al.*, 1996; Gewirtz *et al.*, 1995; Gorard, 2000), but there is no dispute that English schools tend to be characterized by greater or lesser degrees of social segregation, and that they tend not to educate children from clearly identifiable and homogeneous 'communities' (Crowther *et al.*, 2003). Whether such schools can in any meaningful sense be described as 'inclusive' is highly doubtful.

There are, moreover, further complicating factors. Children are identified in England as having 'special educational needs' (SEN) on the basis of the difficulties they experience in school, rather than simply on the basis of any impairments or medical conditions that they experience (DfES, 2001d). Whatever the virtues of this system, it means that a large minority of children – around 18 per cent in primary schools and 15 per cent in secondary schools (National Statistics, 2003d) – is identified as having SEN and that 'objective' measures of impairment play only a minor role in the identification process. It is perhaps not surprising, then, that this population is skewed in various ways and particularly by poverty, ethnicity, gender and age. For instance: students eligible for free school meals (a widely used indicator of poverty) are at least twice as likely to be identified as having SEN as their peers; 'Black Caribbean' heritage children in mainstream schools are about one and a half times more likely to be identified than 'White British' children (National Statistics, 2003d); boys are about twice as likely to be identified as girls; and students at the end of the primary or beginning of the secondary phase are something like twice as likely to be identified than students at the start of the primary phase.

These distortions reflect more fundamental inequalities in the English education system, where outcomes for students within that system are heavily differentiated by class, gender and ethnicity (Bradshaw, 2001; Ennals, 2003; Gillborn and Mirza, 2000). Moreover, a particularly worrying phenomenon is that educational risk factors tend to become concentrated in particular areas and in particular schools, which then have to fight against the odds to offer their students a good education. As the Chief Inspector of Schools has recently pointed out, there is increasing evidence that, despite multiple initiatives in recent years, an irreducible tail of low-performing schools remains (Bell, 2003). This parallels a similar tail of low achievement across the student population as a whole. Although England's overall performance in international comparisons has improved remarkably in recent years, the gap between higher and lower achievers has not reduced (OECD, 2001). The implication is that those students who are most disadvantaged socially and economically – that is, those who live in (relative) poverty, come from the most disadvantaged ethnic groups and attend the most 'difficult' schools – continue to suffer the greatest educational disadvantages. Moreover, it is precisely these students who are disproportionately represented in the various forms of special provision.

Within this context, the extent to which the government's commitment to developing inclusive education has been realized seems doubtful, to say the least. Inclusion in England emerges as a complex and highly problematic phenomenon characterized by considerable ambiguity. In the remainder of this chapter, therefore, I wish to explore and, if possible, explain some of these complexities. I shall begin by examining briefly some of the social, cultural and political factors that underpin the current situation. I shall then look at some of the ways in which England has traditionally addressed issues we now label as 'inclusion'. I shall then attempt to explain the way in which recent education policy has led to the current situation. Finally, I shall propose a 'local theory' to help us to understand the English situation.

The social, cultural and political context

Politics and governance

England is a post-imperial and (increasingly) post-industrial Western European liberal democracy. All of these labels, though necessarily crude, are important for understanding the current situation in respect of inclusive education. The English democratic system, based on 'first past the post' elections of popular representatives and effectively dominated by two major parties – the Conservatives and 'New' Labour – guarantees regular turn-over of power, but within a context that is remarkably stable. Given that most voters are rather set in their voting habits, a good deal of effort on the part of all major parties goes into wooing 'middle England', a relatively small group of voters who can swing elections one way or the other. The consequence is that there is an inbuilt bias within the system against radical changes that might alienate this electorally powerful group. A genuine commitment to inclusive education, of course, might be seen as just such a radical change.

It may also be relevant that England has no written constitution and, unlike some other countries, has not historically underpinned its legislation with an explicit statement of civil rights. Even with the advent of the European Convention on Human Rights, such rights as exist are not derived from universal first principles, but have had to be defined in specific areas (as they have been in the area of disability, for instance) and argued for in particular cases. Significantly, the English, as they are occasionally reminded, are not 'citizens' but 'subjects', and whatever rights they have operate within a network of duties, obligations and expectations. It is indicative that, although all children between the ages of 5 and 16 are entitled to an education, this is not because of any statement of *rights*, but because *duties* are placed on LEAs to provide school places for them and on their parents to present them for schooling. Indeed, parents can be (and are) fined or imprisoned if they fall down on this duty.

This mention of LEAs points to another feature of how England is governed. The country is justly proud of the major public services – health, policing, transport and, of course, education – which grew up during the nineteenth century and took on a major new significance with the founding of the welfare state after the Second World War. However, the governance of these services has a strong local dimension, not least because the role of central government tends to have been to rationalize and extend what had already been developed through local initiative, rather than to initiate provision. This is certainly true of the education system, where LEAs, faith groups and the private sector continue to play a significant (though changing) role in determining the shape and direction of local provision, and where even state-maintained schools are answerable to a local governing body. As a result, there is something of a patchwork of provision, with different types of school overseen to different extents by central and local administrations, and with LEAs able to control significant aspects of local policy.

It is, for instance, the LEA that has the responsibility to identify and make provision for students with special educational needs. It is, therefore, the LEA that determines how many special school places to maintain and which students to place in them – and in doing so it will often make use of private providers for a small minority of children. Consequently, it is, in practice, the LEA that will determine how far and how quickly to pursue an inclusion agenda – with the consequent variations in pace of change that we noted earlier. If we add to this the effect of the differential policies of the faith sector, the private sector and school governing bodies, it is clear that there are formidable challenges to any government, even if it did wish to see a policy of inclusion implemented throughout the system.

Social and economic change

Although this traditional pattern of governance continues to hold good, there were social and economic changes in the last part of the twentieth century that brought about significant political changes. For generations after the Industrial Revolution, England relied for its wealth to a significant extent on a manufacturing industry that in turn sustained, and was sustained by, its overseas possessions. The country's prosperity and its need for cheap labour drew in successive waves of immigration, with the result that England is a multi-ethnic, multi-lingual and multi-faith country. For instance, in the 2001 census, 9 per cent of the population identified themselves as belonging to minority ethnic groups and over three per cent identified themselves as Muslims (National Statistics, 2003a). These overall figures, of course, disguise high concentrations of ethnic and faith minority groups in particular areas, towns and cities.

After the post-Second World War boom, however, English manufacturing industry, in common with that in many parts of the 'developed' world, went into a significant decline and the balance of industrial composition shifted markedly from manufacturing to service industries (Lindsay, 2003). This in turn had implications in terms of rising unemployment, increasing labour market 'flexibility' (such as part-time employment), declining male participation in the workforce and high levels of industrial unrest. The consequence of these phenomena, coupled with the policy response to them, was a polarization of society between those who were more and less well equipped to take advantage of the new situation. In broad terms, the gap between rich and poor increased, with poorly qualified men doing particularly badly and concentrations of disadvantage appearing in particular areas, towns and cities (Darton et al., 2003; Darton and Strelitz, 2003; Howarth et al., 1998). In many (though not all) cases, the places where disadvantage concentrated were also the places where ethnic minority groups concentrated, and some members of these groups continue to do particularly badly in terms of employment and income (National Statistics, 2003b).

Not surprisingly, these economic developments were reflected in significant political shifts from the 1970s onwards. Following the Second World War, England had adopted a welfarist position in which it was accepted that the duty of the state was to protect its citizens from the ravages of poverty and illness, to offer them something more than a basic education, and in other ways to protect and enhance their well-being. This would inevitably involve, amongst other things, redistributive taxation policies, the protection of workplace rights, and government intervention in the economy to protect jobs and promote growth. However, the industrial realignment of the last quarter of the century placed enormous strain on this position. It was unclear, to say the least, whether government intervention was simply shoring up the unsustainable and whether, in the new economic realities, the state could continue to finance large-scale public services and benefits payments out of taxation.

The Conservative governments from 1979 to 1997, led first by Margaret Thatcher and then by John Major, proposed an apparently radical alternative. Progressively, they withdrew state support from 'ailing' industries, tolerated increasing levels of unemployment and sought to reduce levels of personal taxation and, at the same time, of benefit dependency. This had implications for public services, which could no longer automatically be provided with increasing levels of funding from taxation. The emphasis shifted, therefore, to improving the quality and efficiency of those services by taking increasing levels of central control and by introducing 'internal markets' which required different delivery units within these services to compete against one another.

Educational change

In education, the pressure for change had been building long before the first Thatcher government took office. In 1976, the Labour prime minister, James Callaghan, delivered a landmark lecture at Ruskin College, Oxford, which is widely seen as a turning point in education policy. At the time, the economic changes outlined above were beginning to shake the old certainties as to how the liberal ideal of education as personal development and the more instrumental task of preparing young people for the labour market could be reconciled. In the face of growing unease (from the right at least) that quality and relevance had been sacrificed to 'liberal' and 'progressive' approaches, Callaghan explored the tricky balance that education policy had to achieve:

> The goals of our education, from nursery school through to adult education, are clear enough. They are to equip children to the best of their ability for a lively, constructive place in society, and also to fit them to do a job of work. Not one or the other but both. For many years the accent was simply on fitting a so-called inferior group of children with just enough learning to earn their living in the factory. Labour has attacked that attitude consistently. … There is now widespread recognition of the need to cater for a child's personality to let it flower in its fullest possible way. The balance was wrong in the past. We have a responsibility to see that we do not get it wrong again in the other direction. There is no virtue in producing socially well-adjusted members of society who are unemployed because they do not have the skills.
>
> (Callaghan, 1976)

Callaghan called for a 'great debate' that would explore a new balance. However, that debate was superseded by the advent of the Thatcher governments that showed little sympathy with notions of 'personality flowering'. Their agenda culminated in the Education Reform Act of 1988 and various other measures at around the same time that initiated a series of changes:

- the introduction of a National Curriculum with an associated testing regime;
- the creation of an education quasi-market in which schools competed with each other to attract families and in which school funding was closely tied to the numbers of students;
- the encouragement of multiple types of school so that there were more alternatives between which choices could be made;
- the publication of inspection reports and performance data so that parents and carers had information on the basis of which to 'choose' their children's schools;
- an increase in the autonomy of schools *vis-à-vis* their local education authorities by enabling them to manage, amongst other things, their own budgets and requiring LEAs to reduce their involvement with 'successful' schools;
- a strong emphasis on the role of the head teacher as 'chief executive' of the school's governing body.

In other words, schools were encouraged to operate like little businesses, seeking ways to maximize their income by increasing the numbers of children they taught, managing many aspects of their internal affairs, but operating within a strong regulatory framework which ensured minimum national standards (Bash and Coulby, 1989; Bowe *et al.*, 1992).

There is little doubt that these 'new right' policies had a significant impact (for better or worse) on the education services, as on other public services, on the labour market and on the economy. However, they also had some significant perverse consequences. Letting the market take its course led to high levels of unemployment that increased benefits claims whilst decreasing the tax base out of which those claims could be met. Old manufacturing skills were lost and, insofar as these were not replaced by new skills, inward investment depended on the country's being able to sell its low-skilled labour cheaply – a hopeless task in an increasingly globalized economy (Ball and Bradshaw, 1991). At the same time, the increasing polarization of society and the concentration of disadvantage in particular areas meant that significant minorities of the population were in danger of feeling that they were cut adrift – a feeling that was embodied particularly in growing outbreaks of urban unrest amongst young people. Moreover, these were the very people who relied on public services that were in considerable turmoil, whilst their more successful peers increasingly bought their way out of such dependency by turning to the private sector – thus further concentrating the most difficult problems in the public sector.

As this situation began to unfold in the 1990s, the challenge to main-stream politicians – and particularly to the Labour Party – was clear. The unravelling of its welfarist position and the advent of Thatcherism had thrown Labour into turmoil. Its salvation – if such it was – came through the invention of the Third Way. Tony Blair defines this in terms that are worth quoting at length:

> the third way represents a historic realignment of economic and social policy, at a time when the old boundaries between economy, state and society are breaking down. For years, the economic framework of the British left was dominated by questions of public ownership. Markets were poorly understood, their obvious limits leading the left to neglect their great potential for enhancing choice, quality and innovation. ... Effective markets are a pre-condition for a successful modern economy. The question is not whether to have them, but how to empower individuals to succeed within them. What used to be socially important is now an economic imperative. Individuals need opportunities as well as safeguards within the market – above all opportunities to gain new knowledge and skill to develop their potential. Without the assertion of equal worth, without the extension to all of basic entitlements at work, and without investment in their talents, both economy and society are impoverished. Social exclusion, poor education, high unemployment, racism and sexism, are not just socially wrong but economically inefficient.
>
> (Blair, 2001)

What we have here, then, is a wholehearted embrace for the principle of market economics, but sitting alongside an acknowledgement of the need to supplement the operation of the market with vigorous state intervention to ensure that its more perverse consequences are avoided. In particular, there is a need to ensure that those who are vulnerable in the market place are not so much protected as 'empowered to succeed', not least by gaining 'new knowledge and skill'.

This mixture of faith in market forces and intervention to enable the most disadvantaged to survive in the market place has been evident throughout 'New' Labour policies from 1997 onwards. So, there have been limits on personal taxation, incentives to move people off benefits, increases in the autonomy of public service delivery units and continuing tight controls on trade union activities, at the same time as there has been a strategy to combat childhood poverty, support to enable the long-term unemployed find work, targeted funding for disadvantaged areas, tax credits for low-income parents, and so on. Public services, of course, play a central role in this 'Third Way' strategy, since they are a principal means of identifying, supporting and 'empowering' disadvantaged groups and individuals. Although, therefore, the quasi-markets introduced by the Thatcher and Major governments have been maintained and even extended, public services have been driven by centrally determined targets and, increasingly, funded through centrally planned projects and initiatives.

It is no accident in this context that Tony Blair famously declared his three priorities to be 'education, education and education'. Before his election, he explained these priorities in the following way:

> Since I became leader of the Labour Party, I have emphasized that education will be a priority for me in government. I have done so because of the fact – increasingly recognized across our society – that our economic success and our social cohesion depend on it. An Age of Achievement is within our grasp – but it depends on an Ethic of Education. That is why in my party conference speech I said that my three priorities for government would be education, education and education.
>
> (Blair, 1996)

He then went on to set out an agenda which has turned out to be very much the one to which his governments have adhered:

> A new Labour government will focus on standards, especially in the basics of literacy and numeracy, in all our schools. We will expect education – and other public services – to be held accountable for their performance; we will urge teachers to work in partnership with parents, business and the community; and we will balance parents' rights with recognition of their responsibilities. These ideas have one aim – to improve the educational experience, and raise standards of achievement, for the majority of children.
>
> (Blair, 1996)

In practical terms, this agenda has retained virtually all the components of the Thatcher and Major governments' agendas, but has strengthened and extended them in various ways. At the school level, these have included:

- a greater emphasis on the 'basics' of literacy and numeracy, especially in primary schools;
- a tightening of the accountability framework by setting schools' and LEAs' performance targets (in terms of student outcomes) which they are required to meet;
- an increasing specification of teaching methods and intended outcomes, principally though detailed numeracy and literacy strategies in primary schools and a 'Key Stage 3 strategy' in secondary schools;
- an extension of the diversity of school type, so that at secondary level very few schools will be what one government spokesperson famously described as 'bog standard comprehensives';

- a further increase in central direction, particularly by directing funding centrally through multiple 'initiatives';
- a growing encouragement of multiple pathways through a loosening curriculum framework, especially for older students who are disaffected from the academic curriculum and are deemed to need more vocationally oriented experiences.

Running through all of these strands has been a concerted attempt to raise the standards of the lowest-attaining students and lowest-performing schools through a series of vigorous interventions. These have included multi-agency support for the families of young, disadvantaged children, customized strands in the national strategies, the development of data systems for tracking low-attaining students, direct intervention in low-performing schools and LEAs, pressure to reduce disciplinary exclusions from schools, and the targeting of substantial funding to schools serving disadvantaged areas. These interventions are frequently badged as attempts to prevent 'social exclusion' – a concept to which we shall return in the next section.

Significantly, Blair's outlining of the Third Way cited above comes from a lecture he gave at Ruskin College Oxford to commemorate Callaghan's lecture twenty years before.

Callaghan and Blair stand at different points in the process of transition through which England passed in the last quarter of the twentieth century. For both of them, as, in different ways, for Thatcher and Major between them, the erosion of the country's manufacturing base and the change in the industrial composition of the economy make the old certainties about education unsustainable. The country, they believe, cannot survive by preparing the majority of its young people for low-skilled jobs, and neither can it any longer afford education that focuses on personal development rather than on the demands of the labour market.

For all of them, the 'quality' of education, as measured by its outputs, is vital. The education system has to drive up the attainments of the majority of young people so that they become the highly skilled workers demanded by a modern, post-industrial economy. This means that the education system, as Blair argues, has to become standards-driven, highly accountable and outward looking. For Blair and the 'New' Labour governments in particular, an additional but related concern is the fate of those who have traditionally been educational 'failures'. If they do not begin to succeed, these 'failures' will find themselves unemployable, benefit-dependent and, ultimately, alienated from society. The emphasis, therefore, has to be on excellence in education, but on 'excellence for the many, not the few' (Blunkett, 1999a).

This transition, from the post-Second World War settlement to the 'Third Way', has been characterized also as a transition from a welfare to a post-welfare view of society, the state and public services (Tomlinson, 2001). In terms of education, this helps to highlight a shift from seeing education (and other public services) as something provided to support the welfare of individuals towards seeing it from a 'developmentalist' perspective (Paterson, 2003), that is, as developing individuals primarily as a means of developing the economy. It is, I wish to suggest, the incomplete nature of this shift and the inherent contradictions in the positions at either end of that shift that explain the complex and ambiguous nature of inclusive education in England. Although, therefore, economic restructuring and the reform of public services may seem a long way from inclusion, as we normally understand it, it is to the relationship between these disparate phenomena that I now wish to turn.

Welfarism, post-welfarism and inclusive education

I have argued elsewhere (Dyson and Millward, 2000) that inclusive education should be seen as an attempted resolution of a dilemma that is fundamental to mass education systems: the dilemma of commonality and difference. Put simply, such systems have to offer something recognizably common – an 'education' – to learners who are recognizably similar, while at the same time acknowledging that those same learners differ from each other in important ways and therefore have to be offered different 'educations'. Looked at in this way, inclusion, understood as a movement for educating learners with special educational needs in mainstream schools and classes, is a resolution that emphasizes the commonality pole of the dilemma. It focuses on learners who are 'different' in ways that have the most obvious educational significance, and argues for their right to be educated alongside their peers, within a common institution and, frequently, within a common curriculum. In England, as in many other parts of the world, this resolution is often proposed from a highly principled and rights-oriented perspective, as though policy and practice should – or, indeed, could – follow from the simple adherence to principle. The reality is, however, that the principle of inclusion enters policy and practice arenas that are characterized by the sorts of transitions we have explored in the previous section.

Inclusion and the Warnock settlement

The current framework for special needs education in England was effectively outlined by the Warnock Report (DES, 1978) in the late 1970s – at about the same time, in fact, as Callaghan's Ruskin College lecture. The Warnock settlement is, I suggest, strongly welfarist in tone. The Report sets out its rationale in the following terms:

> The purpose of education for all children is the same; the goals are the same. But the help that individual children need in progressing towards

them will be different. Whereas for some the road they have to travel towards the goals is smooth and easy, for others it is fraught with obstacles. For some the obstacles are so daunting that, even with the greatest possible help, they will not get very far. Nevertheless, for them too, progress will be possible, and their educational needs will be fulfilled, as they gradually overcome one obstacle after another on the way.

(DES, 1978, section 1.4)

There are two things to note about this passage. The first is that the language is very much one of help and support offered to individuals who are deemed to be 'in need'. The second is that the goals of education are conceptualized as overarching aims rather than specific items of knowledge or skill. In line with Callaghan's 'flowering of the personality', Warnock defines these goals in broad, humanistic terms as being 'to enlarge a child's knowledge, experience and imaginative understanding' and 'to enable him to enter the world after formal education is over as an active participant in society' (*ibid.*).

This broad definition of educational goals, together with the concept of individual needs that arise in relation to reaching those goals, led Warnock to formulate a framework for the SEN system, which was largely established in the 1981 Act and which continues to underpin special needs education in England. This framework had five elements that are significant from our perspective:

- children's 'special educational needs' were defined in very general terms as 'difficulty in learning' – effectively, difficulty in progressing towards the goals of education;
- a large minority of children (one in six at any one time) was deemed to have these needs and many of these would be maintained in mainstream schools;
- special educational needs were to be assessed on an individual basis by teachers, educational psychologists, doctors and other professionals;
- the assessment would lead to the LEAs making provision to meet the needs; and
- provision could equally well be made in mainstream as in special settings.

Again, the welfarist tendencies are clear. The Warnock system is about the state's responsibility (delegated to the LEA) to identify and meet the needs of its citizens in relation to some broad notion of well-being. The assumption is made that those needs will be self-evident (in the way, say, that hunger, poverty and ill-health are self-evident), that they can be assessed objectively by 'experts', that the state will provide whatever resources are necessary to meet these needs and that no outcome need be specified other than the well-being of the individual.

More than this, the framework is highly individualized. Despite the evidence, cited above, that special educational needs are related to the characteristics of socio-economic groups (as defined, for instance, by ethnicity, class and gender), the Warnock framework constructs such needs as the outcomes of the biological and psychological characteristics of individuals. This is partly a reaction against the previous, rather crude – and ultimately unworkable – categorization of learners on the basis of their 'handicaps'. This explains why Warnock offers no diagnostic criteria for, and nothing but the most general definitions of, special educational needs, preferring instead to rely on individual assessment. However, as Warnock has subsequently revealed (Warnock, 1999), this is also partly the result of a direction the Committee received from ministers not to explore the relationship between poverty and children's difficulties in schooling. As critics at the time observed, the Committee lacked a sociological input that might have addressed some of the underlying socio-economic causes of those difficulties (Lewis and Vulliamy, 1980).

What results from Warnock, therefore, is a welfarist approach to educational difference – and, specifically, to educational difficulty – but one which remains at the individual level. The consequences for special needs education and thence for inclusion in England have been significant. First, at a time when education has increasingly been driven by economic imperatives and, latterly, when educational 'failure' has become a salient policy issue, special needs education has had little contribution to make to the debate (Dyson, 1997; 2002). Indeed, its individualized approach has effectively disqualified it from contributing to whole-school reform efforts or to the development of new pedagogies (Dyson, 2003).

Second, the individualized and criterion-free framework has created extremely permeable boundaries around the special educational needs population, with groups of children being moved in or out almost at will. The Warnock Report itself extended the population significantly by embracing within it children who were placed in mainstream schools. In 1994, the then Conservative government extended formal identification, assessment and planning procedures to this new population, thus apparently cementing their position (DFE, 1994). A few years later, the 'New' Labour government tried to reverse this trend somewhat by removing children with lower levels of 'need' from the framework (DfES, 2001d). These changes, of course, are in addition to the impacts of the expansion of old conditions and impairments or the 'discovery' of new ones, such as dyspraxia, ADHD and autism.

This permeability might matter less if there were fewer vested and conflicting interests at work in determining the nature and size of the special needs population. Parents, lobby groups, schools, professionals, LEAs and central government all have interests in arguing that particular children or groups of children should or should not be regarded as having special educational needs. A major driving force of these interests, of course, is the welfarist principle that needs can be identified objectively (or at least consensually) and, once identified, that the state and its agents will meet them. This immediately creates a contest between those, like parents, who want to secure additional resources by having children's needs recognized and others, like LEAs, who have to manage the budgets out of which resources to meet those needs must be found. The sometimes bitter disputes that arise around the formal 'statements' of the needs of individual children remain, in particular, a blot on the English special education system (Audit Commission, 2002a).

These permeable and contested boundaries, of course, create an unpromising arena within which to develop national inclusion policies – a situation which is compounded by a third consequence of the Warnock framework. The pre-eminent position within that framework accorded to meeting individual needs makes the principle of inclusion, which is not immediately related to needs in this sense, of secondary importance. The post-Warnock position in England has therefore been that it may well be possible to meet many needs equally well in either a special or mainstream setting – or, indeed, that some children may 'need' a special school placement. Shortly after taking office, the first 'New' Labour government reiterated this position in the following terms:

> Promoting inclusion within mainstream schools, where parents want it and appropriate support can be provided, will remain a cornerstone of our strategy. ... For those with more complex needs, the starting point should always be the questions, 'Could this child benefit from education in a mainstream setting? If so, what action would be needed, by whom, to make this possible? What are the parent's and the child's views?' ... For some children, a mainstream placement may not be right, or not right just yet. We therefore confirm that specialist provision – often, but not always, in special schools – will continue to play a vital role.
>
> (DfEE, 1998, p. 13)

On the face of it, this is a strange position for a government purportedly committed to inclusive education to adopt. Indeed, the question arises as to why, given all its problematic features, the Warnock framework was not swept away long ago. It is not that these problems are unknown to policy-makers. Two reports from the Audit Commission (2002a; 2002b), for instance, were highly critical of the system and called for a high-level review of its operation. However, these simply repeated much of what was said by reports from the same body a decade earlier (Audit Commission and HMI, 1992a; 1992b) and what many others had long been saying.

The response of governments has not been to opt for fundamental reform; the recent call for review, for instance, has been ignored in favour of a new 'programme of action' (DfES, 2004) that seems to change little.

Instead, they have strengthened and formalized procedures, chiefly as a means of regulating the contests around identification and resource-allocation (DFE, 1994; DfES, 2001d). At the same time, in line with the principle of consumer choice in post-welfare public services, they have increased the power of parents, giving them an independent tribunal where they can appeal against LEA decisions (DFE, 1994) and making parental wishes the *de facto* determinant of placement (DfES, 2001b). Finally, in the case of 'New' Labour governments in particular, they have sought to align special needs education more closely with the mainstream 'standards' agenda. It is no coincidence, for instance, that the new programme of action (DfES, 2004) is called *Removing barriers to achievement*.

In terms of inclusion, these responses are ambiguous at best. The strengthened procedures arguably do no more than incorporate yet more children in decidedly non-mainstream forms of provision and practice. The enhanced rights of parents do nothing to guarantee that parents will opt for inclusive solutions. The 'SEN achievement' agenda, meanwhile, is premised on the notion that achievement can be high in any setting and not simply in inclusive settings. Moreover, through all this, the broad features of the Warnock framework remain firmly in place, despite the radical reshaping of other aspects of the education system that has taken place since Callaghan's Ruskin College speech. Why should this be so?

The reasons are doubtless complex, but two in particular spring to mind. First, in the context of consumer (or citizen) choice, governments are even less likely than previously to engage in principled reform unless they can be sure that the principles in question command widespread support from those consumers – and this is certainly not the case with inclusion. Rather than imposing inclusion on often sceptical parents and lobby groups, therefore, 'New' Labour governments in particular opt for what are effectively modified market solutions. Although schools and LEAs may be discouraged from expanding segregated provision, ultimately it is the demand from parents which will either cause such provision to wither on the vine or, more likely, create an equilibrium in which supply and demand are balanced.

Second, given the major economic and hence educational changes that I have outlined earlier in this chapter, the structures and systems of special needs education are essentially something of a sideshow. If they do not contribute to major government agendas, neither do they detract from them to any significant extent. This is not to say, of course, that there are not many children labelled as having special educational needs who could participate in these wider changes. Through its inclusion agenda, its focus on 'achievement' and its attempts to reduce the special needs population, 'New' Labour is clearly attempting to link as many of these children as possible into its broader educational agenda. It is no coincidence, for instance, that the various national strategies which now direct the work of teachers in schools set out approaches and programmes to raise the attainments of chil-

dren who previously would have had their 'needs met' through the procedures and practices of special needs education.

Insofar as this strategy is successful, the partial or total withering on the
vine of special schooling will be paralleled by an equivalent withering of
special needs provision in mainstream schools. As the new programme of
action declares,

> This strategy aims to personalise learning for all children, to make
> education more innovative and responsive to the diverse needs of indi-
> vidual children, so reducing our reliance on separate SEN structures
> and processes and raising the achievement of the many children – nearly
> one in six – who are considered to have SEN.
>
> (DfES, 2004, Introduction)

The implications for inclusion are clear. The archaic Warnock framework, which predates the dramatic changes of recent decades, is slowly
becoming an irrelevance. To that extent, the 'merger' of special and general
education, so long anticipated by inclusion advocates (Gartner and Lipsky,
1987), may at last be taking place. However, this is not inclusion as a matter
of civil rights into the pluralist micro-societies of regular schools where all
differences are recognized and validated. On the contrary, this is inclusion
into mainstream agendas that are driven by educational outcomes and, ultimately, by economic imperatives.

The ways in which these agendas have played out in England in recent
years are complex and, from the point of view of inclusion, highly problematic. It is to this story that I now wish to turn.

Social inclusion and post-welfarist approaches

The agendas that have preoccupied recent governments in fact have a long
history. The English inclusion scholar, Tony Booth, has long argued that
inclusive education in England has to be understood as part of a much wider
concern with issues of social justice in the education system (Booth, 1983;
1995). His point is that the inclusion of children 'with special educational
needs' in the mainstream school is a particular instance of the attempt in this
country to develop 'comprehensive community education' – that is, an education system in which common schools will educate all learners and, moreover,
will do so in close relation to the communities where those learners live.

Certainly, the big agenda from a welfarist perspective – as Callaghan's
Ruskin College lecture indicates – has been how an allegedly 'inferior' group
of children can be offered an education which will offer them more than a
minimal level of instruction and will, in the long run, contribute to a more
just and a more equal society. What happens to children with disabilities –
and, latterly, those with special educational needs – is only a small part of

that agenda. It is no coincidence, for instance, that the integration movement of the 1970s coincided in England, as in many other countries of Western Europe (Vislie, 1995), with attempts to develop Booth's 'comprehensive community education'.

Post-welfarist approaches to education, however, have introduced new imperatives that have had significant implications for this search for social justice. Those implications have, I suggest, been contradictory. On the one hand, they have shifted the focus of the education system to outputs and, in so doing, have made 'unproductive' students less welcome in schools. On the other hand, they have tried to make at least some of those students more productive than in the past, and in doing so have positioned them closer to the centre of schools' agendas.

As schools in England have first been required to compete against one another in a quasi-market and then have increasingly been held accountable for meeting demanding performance targets, their attitudes towards the lowest-attaining students, including those with special educational needs, has hardened (see, for instance, Booth *et al.*, 1998; Dyson and Millward, 2000; Gillborn and Youdell, 2000; Gold *et al.*, 1993; Rouse and Florian, 1997). A number of processes seem to have been at work. Low-attaining students depress the performance of schools as measured in the annual 'league tables' which report the average attainments of a school's students in national assessments. Moreover, since the targets set for schools are in terms of what *most* but not *all* of their students should achieve, the presence of these students does nothing to enable schools to meet these targets. This then makes schools vulnerable to receiving poor reports when they are inspected (until recently, every four years) and the league tables and inspection reports together may make schools less attractive to families in their areas. In the worst case scenario, schools can be placed in 'special measures', which means that they lose a good deal of their autonomy, may well mean that the head loses his/her job and could ultimately lead to closure. Almost as bad, however, a declining local reputation could lead to declining student numbers, shortfalls in the budget and the loss of students from the most aspirational families, leaving the school with an uphill struggle in its efforts to 'improve'.

Under these circumstances, many schools are understandably wary about accepting students who they feel might hamper their performance. Such students may find themselves discouraged from applying to the school in the first place, or encouraged to leave as problems begin to appear, or, eventually, may be excluded from the school. If they remain, the school will almost certainly place them in one of the multiple forms of segregated grouping we discussed earlier, and may well seek to have them assessed as having special educational needs. Students whose behaviour presents difficulties to teachers appear to be particularly vulnerable in these respects. Not only does their own low attainment drag down the school's overall performance, but also their presence is likely to interfere with the ability of other students to do well. The concern in schools about the 'problem of behaviour' is such that many secondary and some primary schools serving urban areas have now established, with government funding, 'learning support units' (LSUs) – often, ironically, known as 'inclusion units' – where difficult students can be educated separately from their peers and which are themselves separate from the schools' special educational needs systems. Likewise, the government has had to invest significant funding in a 'Behaviour Improvement Programme' (BIP) to help schools in the most disadvantaged areas to manage their students' behaviour.

The latter developments, however, are illustrative of the second implica-tion of the current government's overall approach to schooling. Central to that approach, as we have seen, is the notion of 'excellence for the many, not the few'. This is not simply a welfarist concern with the most disadvantaged. As Blair (2001) argues, 'Social exclusion, poor education, high unemploy-ment, racism and sexism, are not just socially wrong but economically inefficient' (Blair, 2001). The notion of 'social exclusion' is crucial here. For 'New' Labour, the socially excluded are those who get left behind in the effort to modernize the economy, who become unemployable, who live in poverty and who ultimately become alienated from mainstream society. As Blair puts it elsewhere:

> We came into office determined to tackle a deep social crisis. We had a poor record in this country in adapting to social and economic change. The result was sharp income inequality, a third of children growing up in poverty, a host of social problems such as homelessness and drug abuse, and divisions in society typified by deprived neighbourhoods that had become no go areas for some and no exit zones for others. All of us bore the cost of social breakdown – directly, or through the costs to society and the public finances. And we were never going to have a successful economy while we continued to waste the talents of so many.
>
> (SEU, 2001, Foreword)

The implication is that those who are at risk of social exclusion in this sense have to be offered whatever support, incentives and targeted interven-tions are necessary in order to enable them to 'catch up'. In educational terms, this means initiatives such as LSUs and BIP. It also means, quite liter-ally, catch-up programmes within the national strategies to ensure that low attainers do not get left too far behind, together with all the other programmes and initiatives which we referred to in the previous section. The implications from an inclusion perspective are threefold.

First, the pressures to marginalize low-attaining students are balanced, to some extent, by countervailing pressures to direct energy and resource to precisely these students. Consequently, while schools might, from a perspec-tive of self-interest, prefer not to have such students in their populations, where they do have them in significant numbers, they are almost certain to take advantage of any initiatives they can access to help them manage them better.

Second, the nature of schools' role *vis-à-vis* these students changes. Whereas inclusion as a principle may be based on notions of rights to equal access and participation, the new agenda is very much outcomes-driven. For the government and for many schools in England, therefore, 'inclusion' is simply a sub-set of 'social inclusion' (see, for instance, Blunkett, 1999a; 1999b; 2000); children with special educational needs are present in mainstream schools not as a right – or at least, not simply as a right – but because that is where they stand the best chance of attaining highly. As the government argues:

> There are strong educational, as well as social and moral, grounds for educating children with SEN, or with disabilities, with their peers. ... An increasing number of schools are showing that an inclusive approach can reinforce a commitment to higher standards of achievement for all children.
>
> (DfEE, 1998, p. 4)

Consequently, the 'inclusive' task of schools is not simply to make children with special educational needs feel welcome, but to find ways of driving up their attainments along with those of a wide range of other groups at risk of social exclusion. When, therefore, schools are inspected for their 'inclusiveness', it is on this ability to raise standards for all 'at risk' groups that they are judged (Ofsted, 2000).

The third implication follows from this. If inclusion, as usually understood, is simply a means to an end, then the key values of inclusion – presence and participation in 'common' settings – are ultimately subordinate to the imperative to raise standards. It is for this reason that schools sometimes describe their LSUs as 'inclusion units'. From their point of view, the students remain in the mainstream school, remain connected to the mainstream curriculum and have a far greater chance of achievement than if they were removed from the school entirely. Likewise, this is another reason why the government is happy to see special schools as part of an 'inclusive' system (DfES, 2003b) and why it has no compunctions about promoting grouping by 'ability' or alternative curriculum pathways for 'disaffected' older students. Although there is a presumption that most students will do best in mainstream settings, *where* children are educated is less important than *how* they are taught and, in particular, than the standards they achieve.

There is a final issue for inclusion which arises in 'New' Labour policy. It is no coincidence that, in explaining his commitment to education, Blair declared his aim to be 'to improve the educational experience, and raise standards of achievement, for the *majority* of children' (Blair, 1996, my emphasis). The difficulty with linking the purposes of education so strongly to a human capital notion of economic development is that it begs the question of why those who are likely to remain economically unproductive throughout their lives – that is, those experiencing the most significant educational difficulties – should be educated at all. 'New' Labour has largely sidestepped this issue by focusing on the 'majority' where economic productivity is a realistic aim and by relying heavily on a particularly heroic version of school effectiveness research which seems to have assumed that generating high levels of achievement from all students is simply a matter of finding the right techniques (see, for instance, Reynolds and Farrell, 1996).

However, as government policies increasingly come up against students and schools that are stubbornly resistant to 'improvement' (see, for instance, Bell, 2003), the question of how to include this recalcitrant minority in the form of education that has developed in English schools becomes an issue of growing significance. In terms of the 'dilemma of difference', to which I referred earlier, 'New' Labour has come up with an interesting resolution. It de-emphasizes the importance of commonality in terms of place and, increasingly, of curriculum. However, it emphasizes a form of commonality in terms of its commitment to basic levels of achievement for all and its faith in the ability of policy to generate these levels. My argument has always been that resolutions of dilemmas inevitably fall apart as a result of the tensions that arise from the poles they have neglected. In this case, it seems to me entirely likely that the 'New' Labour resolution will founder on its failure sufficiently to acknowledge the differences between students or to find ways of accommodating those differences within a more meaningful common framework. Significantly, we are already seeing a marginal turning away from the culture of target-setting and an even more modest acknowledgement that there might be more to education than attainment (DfES, 2003a), together with a new rhetoric of 'personalized learning' (Miliband, 2004), which seems to prefigure the proliferation of individual pathways through an increasingly diverse education system. Whether these cracks in the edifice widen and what the implications for inclusion will be of any reorientation of the government's approach, remains to be seen.

The ambiguities of inclusion: towards a local theory

Reviewing the history that is set out here, it seems to me that it is possible to some extent to understand it in terms of the changing resolutions of this dilemma of difference. However, focusing on this dilemma does not – and was never intended to – explain *why* and *how* different resolutions appear at any given time. The issues we have touched on here begin to indicate what may be a more powerful explanatory framework in terms of the English experience – and one, moreover, that may have resonance in other parts of the world.

Intersecting the 'dilemma of difference' is a second dilemma which we can see underpinning the shift in education policy in England between the mid-1970s and the present day. This is to do with the extent to which the purposes of education are seen as being located at the level of the individual or of the state. In particular, is education a benefit provided by the state to its citizens in order to promote their personal well-being and development? Or is education an instrument used by the state to equip its citizens with the means of serving its own social and economic ends? As with all dilemmas, the resolutions that have emerged are subtle and complex reconciliations of these two poles, but reconciliations that nonetheless emphasize one or other. In the post-Second World War settlement, the emphasis was, perhaps, marginally on the role of education in the process of individual development. In the 'post-Ruskin' era, the emphasis has shifted markedly towards an emphasis on the state and, more specifically, the economy and the labour market.

These shifts have then had implications for how commonality and difference have been understood – from the rigid categorization systems of the post-war years, to the more liberal attempts to emphasize common access and entitlement in the 1970s, to what sometimes seems a 'dragooning' of difference under 'New' Labour. In turn, the interaction between how difference was understood and how the state/individual balance was struck has had implications for notions of shared participation, 'integration' and, latterly, inclusion. Equally significantly, these shifts in understanding have been clearly tied to changes in the economic infrastructure of society.

Although these understandings are doubtless arrived at differently in the different national contexts, it does seem to me that similar issues are likely to arise. In the economically developed countries of the North and West particularly, it may be that similar adjustments to economic change will have to be made. This, I believe, is highly significant. Inclusion is, as I suggested earlier, often advocated and understood as a relatively simple phenomenon – a single principle which can be adhered to more or less resolutely and which can be realized in practice with a sufficient level of commitment and a few well chosen techniques. The analysis I am proposing here suggests that this is far from the case. Inclusion may be a principle for some, or simply a convenient and ambiguous language for others. Either way, it enters an arena that is characterized by the complexities and ambiguities that inevitably arise from deep-seated dilemmas. Moreover, the resolutions of those dilemmas, and hence the trajectory of inclusion, are not determined simply by high-minded debate, nor even by the practicalities of education policy-making. Underpinning them are more fundamental social processes and, in the case of England at least, fundamental economic processes. One does not have to be a fully fledged Marxist to agree with the dictum that 'it's the economy, stupid!'.

References

Audit Commission (2002a). *Policy focus paper: Statutory assessment and statements of SEN*. London: Audit Commission.

——(2002b). *Special educational needs: A mainstream issue*. London: Audit Commission.

Audit Commission and HMI (1992a). *Getting the Act together: Provision for pupils with special educational needs: A management handbook for schools and local education authorities*. London: HMSO.

——(1992b). *Getting in on the Act: Provision for pupils with special educational needs: The national picture*. London: HMSO.

Ball, C. and Bradshaw, D. (1991). *Learning pays: The role of post-compulsory education and training*. Address to the Association of Colleges for Further and Higher Education summer conference, 5 June 1991, the Central Hotel, Glasgow. London: Association of Colleges for Further and Higher Education.

Ball, S.J. (1993). 'The market as a class strategy in the UK and US', *British Journal of Sociology of Education*, 14(1), 3–19.

Ball, S.J., Bowe, R. and Gewirtz, S. (1996). 'Circuits of schooling: A sociological exploration of parental choice of school in social class contexts'. *Sociological Review*, 43, 52–78.

Bash, L. and Coulby, D. (1989). *The Education Reform Act: Competition and control*. London: Cassell.

Bell, D. (2003). *Access and achievement in urban education: Ten years on*. Speech to the Fabian Society by David Bell, Her Majesty's Chief Inspector of Schools. London: Ofsted. URL: http://www.ofsted.gov.uk/news/index.cfm?fuseaction=news.details&id=1506 (accessed 28 November 2003).

Blair, T. (1996). *The twentieth anniversary lecture given by the Rt Hon. Tony Blair, 16 December 1996*. Oxford: Ruskin College, URL: http://www.ruskin.ac.uk/original/archives/ (accessed 24 December 2003).

——(2001). 'The Third Way: Phase two'. *Prospect Magazine*, March 2001, London: Prospect Magazine. URL: http://www.prospect-magazine.co.uk (accessed 6 April 2004).

Blunkett, D. (1999a). *Excellence for the many, not just the few: Raising standards and extending opportunities in our schools. The CBI President's Reception Address by the Rt Hon. David Blunkett MP, 19 July 1999*. London: DfEE.

——(1999b). *Social exclusion and the politics of opportunity: A mid-term progress check. A speech by the Rt Hon. David Blunkett MP*. London: DfEE.

——(2000). *Raising aspirations for the 21st Century. Speech to the North of England Education Conference, Wigan, 6 January 2000*. London: DfEE.

Booth, T. (1983). 'Integration and participation in comprehensive schools'. *Forum*, 25(2), 40–42.

——(1995). 'Mapping inclusion and exclusion: Concepts for all?' In C. Clark, A. Dyson and A. Millward (eds) *Towards Inclusive Schools?* (pp. 96–108). London: David Fulton.

Booth, T., Ainscow, M. and Dyson, A. (1998). 'England: Inclusion and exclusion in a competitive system'. In T. Booth and M. Ainscow (eds) *From them to us: An international study of inclusion in education* (pp. 193–225). London: Routledge.

Bowe, R., Ball, S.J., with Gold, A. (1992). *Reforming education and changing schools.* London: Routledge.

Bradshaw, J. (2001). *Poverty: The outcomes for children.* London: Family Policy Studies Centre.

Callaghan, J. (1976). *Towards a national debate (the full text of the speech by Prime Minister James Callaghan, at a foundation stone-laying ceremony at Ruskin College, Oxford, 18 October 1976). Guardian,* London. URL: http://education.guardian.co.uk/print/0,3858,4277858–109002,00.html   (accessed 24 December 2003).

Crowther, D., Cummings, C., Dyson, A. and Millward, A. (2003). *Schools and area regeneration.* Bristol: The Policy Press.

Darton, D., Hirsch, D. and Strelitz, J. (2003). *Tackling disadvantage: A 20-year enterprise.* York: Joseph Rowntree Foundation.

Darton, D. and Strelitz, J. (eds) (2003). *Tackling UK poverty and disadvantage in the twenty-first century.* York: Joseph Rowntree Foundation.

Department for Education (DFE) (1994). *Code of practice on the identification and assessment of special educational needs.* London: DFE.

Department for Education and Employment (DfEE) (1997a). *Excellence for all children: Meeting special educational needs.* London: The Stationery Office.

——(1997b). *Excellence in schools.* London: The Stationery Office.

——(1998). *Meeting special educational needs: A programme of action.* London: DfEE. URL:
http://www.teachernet.gov.uk/_doc/5915/Action_Programme_Full.doc (accessed 6 April 2004).

Department for Education and Employment (DfEE) and Qualifications and Assessment Authority (QCA) (1999). *The National Curriculum: Handbook for primary/secondary teachers in England.* London: DfEE and QCA.

Department for Education and Skills (DfES) (2001a). *The distribution of resources to support inclusion.* London: DfES.

——(2001b). *Inclusive schooling: Children with special educational needs.* London: DfES.

——(2001c). *Schools achieving success.* London: DfES.

——(2001d). *Special educational needs code of practice.* London: DfES.

——(2002). *14–19: Extending opportunities, raising standards: Consultation document.* London: The Stationery Office.

——(2003a). *Excellence and enjoyment: A strategy for primary schools.* London: DfES.

——(2003b). *Report of the special schools working group.* London: DfES.

——(2004). *Removing barriers to achievement: The government's strategy for SEN.* London: DfES, URL: http://www.teachernet.gov.uk/wholeschool/sen/senstrategy/ (accessed 10 April 2004).

DES (Department of Education and Science) (1978). *Special educational needs: Report of the Committee of Enquiry into the Education of Handicapped Children and Young People (The Warnock Report).* London: HMSO.

Dyson, A. (1997). Social and educational disadvantage: Reconnecting special needs education. *British Journal of Special Education,* 24(4), 152–157.

——(2002). Special needs, disability and social inclusion: The end of a beautiful friendship? In B. Norwich (ed.) *Disability, disadvantage, inclusion and social inclu-*

sion: Special Educational Needs Policy Options Steering Group policy paper 3 (4th series). (pp. 9–18). Tamworth: NASEN.

——(2003). Decision-making in special needs education. Is a rational model really possible? In D. Galloway (ed.) *Children with special educational needs: A response to the new Code of Practice. ACPP Occasional Papers no. 20* (pp. 13–23). London: ACPP.

Dyson, A. and Millward, A. (2000). *Schools and special needs: Issues of innovation and inclusion.* London: Paul Chapman Publishers.

Ennals, P. (2003). *Child poverty and education: Briefing paper.* London: End Child Poverty with National Children's Bureau.

Galloway, D. and Goodwin, C. (1979). *Educating slow-learning and maladjusted children: Integration or segregation.* London: Longman.

Gartner, A. and Lipsky, D.K. (1987). 'Beyond special education: Toward a quality system for all students'. *Harvard Educational Review*, 57(4), 367–395.

Gewirtz, S., Ball, S.J. and Bowe, R. (1995). *Markets, choice and equity in education.* Buckingham: Open University Press.

Gillborn, D. and Mirza, H.S. (2000). *Educational inequality: Mapping race, class and gender. A synthesis of research evidence for the Office for Standards in Education.* London: Ofsted.

Gillborn, D. and Youdell, D. (2000). *Rationing education: Policy, practice, reform and equity.* Buckingham: Open University Press.

Gold, A., Bowe, R. and Ball, S. (1993). 'Special educational needs in a new context: Micropolitics, money and 'education for all''. In R. Slee (ed.) *Is there a desk with my name on it? The politics of integration* (pp. 51–64). London: Falmer Press.

Gorard, S. (2000). Questioning the crisis account: A review of the evidence for increasing polarisation in schools. *Educational Research*, 42(3), 309–321.

Howarth, C., Kenway, P., Palmer, G. and Street, C. (1998). *Monitoring poverty and social exclusion: Labour's inheritance.* York: Joseph Rowntree Foundation.

Lewis, I. and Vulliamy, G. (1980). 'Warnock or warlock? The sorcery of definitions: The limitations of the report on special education'. *Educational Review*, 32(1), 3–10.

Lindsay, C. (2003). 'A century of labour market change: 1900 to 2000'. *Labour Market Trends*, 111 (3), March 2003, pp. 133–144. URL: http://www.statistics.gov.uk/articles/labour_market_trends/century_labour_market_change_mar2003.pdf (accessed 10 April 2004).

Miliband, D. (2004). *Personalised learning: building a new relationship with schools.* Speech to the North of England Education Conference, Belfast, 8 January 2004. London: DfES.

National Statistics (2003a). *Census 2001: People and places: Census results on ethnicity, marriage and families.* London: National Statistics. URL: http://www.statistics.gov.uk/cci/nugget&_print.asp?ID=299 (accessed 26 December 2003).

——(2003b). *Ethnicity: Low income.* London: National Statistics. URL: http://www.statistics.gov.uk/cci/nugget_print.asp?ID=269 (accessed 12 December 2003).

——(2003c). *Statistics of education: Schools in England.* London: The Stationery Office. URL: http://www.dfes.gov.uk/rsgateway/DB/VOL/v000417/schools_volume_2003.pdf (accessed 19 April 2004).

——(2003d). *Statistics of education: Special educational needs in England: January 2003*. London: The Stationery Office. URL: http://www.dfes.gov.uk/rsgateway/DB/SBU/b000429/specialneeds.pdf (accessed 10 April 2004).

Norwich, B. (2002). *LEA inclusion trends in England 1997–2001: Statistics on special school placements and pupils with statements in special schools*. Bristol: CSIE.

OECD (2001). *Knowledge and skills for life: First results from the OECD Programme for International Student Assessment (PISA). 2000*. Paris: OECD.

Ofsted (2000). *Evaluating educational inclusion*. London: Ofsted.

Paterson, L. (2003). 'The three educational ideologies of the British Labour Party, 1997–2001'. *Oxford Review of Education*, 29(2), 165–186.

Reynolds, D. and Farrell, S. (1996). *Worlds apart? A review of international surveys of educational achievement involving England*. London: Ofsted.

Rouse, M. and Florian, L. (1997). 'Inclusive education in the market-place'. *International Journal of Inclusive Education*, 1(4), 323–336.

SEU (Social Exclusion Unit) (2001). *Preventing social exclusion*. London: Social Exclusion Unit. URL: http://www.socialexclusionunit.gov.uk/publications/reports/html/pse/pse_html/index.htm (accessed 6 April 2004).

Tansley, A.E. and Gulliford, R. (1960). *The education of slow learning children*. London: Routledge and Kegan Paul.

Tomlinson, S. (2001). *Education in a post-welfare society*. Buckingham: Open University Press.

Vislie, L. (1995). 'Integration policies, school reforms and the organisation of schooling for handicapped pupils in western societies'. In C. Clark, A. Dyson and A. Millward (eds) *Towards inclusive schools?* (pp. 42–53). London: David Fulton.

Warnock, M. (1999). 'If only we had known then …' *Times Educational Supplement*, London, 31 December, p. 33.

Chapter 5

Push and pull

Forces that are shaping inclusion in the United States and Canada

Margaret J. McLaughlin and Anne Jordan

This chapter discusses current interpretations of 'inclusive education' in Canada and the United States within the context of the rapidly evolving educational policies occurring in both countries. These policies are characterized by their focus on increasing the educational performance of students and closing the achievement gap between traditional 'high achievers' and those students who have traditionally not benefited from public education to the same extent. This demand for equality of educational achievement is redefining educational equity in both countries. The similarities and contrasts between Canada and the US in terms of how special education policy and practice are evolving within the changing concept of equity are made evident in this chapter, with particular attention to how the policies are exacerbating the ambiguities surrounding the concept of 'inclusive education'.

There are a number of difficulties inherent in constructing a cross-country analysis of inclusive education as it pertains to students with disabilities, one of which is the lack of a commonly accepted definition of what constitutes 'inclusion'. The US does not have an official definition of the term, although the word has become synonymous with placement in the general education classroom. In contrast, Canada's federal Charter has an understanding of inclusive education that is more aligned with the principles set forth in the Salamanca Statement (UNESCO, 1994). However, both countries' use of the term obscures the complexities of their respective special education policies and traditions. Both Canada and the US are caught between what Dyson (1997) has described as the two dominant discourses of inclusion: the 'rights and ethics' discourse and the 'efficacy' discourse. That is, while the educational policies concerning students with disabilities in both countries represent strong statements of social equity and individual rights, both countries also have deep cultural values that support individual productivity, competition, and social competence. Educational policies in both countries reflect a tendency toward minimal intrusion of government into individual lives, although the US has a much stronger tradition in this area. The assumptions are that individuals are best served if they are allowed to make most decisions regarding their lives as well as accept responsibility for those decisions. Thus, both countries have long traditions of highly decentralized educational policies, instead deferring to local and state or provincial preference.

Within the US, local control of education is based in the US Constitution under the 'General Provision' clause, which delegates to states all powers not specifically enumerated for the federal government. The notion of local control extends to some 15,000 independent school districts whose boards also serve to set and interpret state and federal policy requirements. In Canada, each of the ten provinces and three territories is responsible for administering its own School Act or Education Act. Thus, provincial and state governments retain enormous authority over educational policy, such that almost all federal or national policies enacted in either country have always permitted local interpretations.

To some degree, the traditions of decentralization in both the US and Canada are being reshaped by recent educational reforms that focus on setting ambitious standards, assessing student performance, and holding schools to more stringent levels of accountability. These standards-driven reforms are reinterpreting education in both countries. In the sections that follow we will discuss how special education policies surrounding inclusion are being considered in the US and Canada within these reforms. In addition, we will discuss how both countries will need to confront what it means to provide 'inclusive education' within the context of new demands that all students meet common and rigorous educational standards. Given this broad introduction to commonalities between Canada and the US, we now turn to a more in-depth analysis of each country's current special education context. In the sections that follow we also discuss the historical context of Canadian and US special education policies. We will then summarize our chapter with observations about the implications of the emerging policies for the principles and practices of inclusion.

Inclusion in Canada: new meanings and dilemmas

Canadian education legislation has evolved province-by-province in relation to the federal Charter of Rights and Freedoms, and in response to the persuasive legal influence of US policies and legislation. In Canada, since education comes under the purview of the ten provinces and three territories, special education is therefore delivered in somewhat different ways and under different regulations, funding formulae and guidelines from one jurisdiction to another.

Historically, parents of students with complex disabilities sought 'normalization' (Wolfensberger, 1975) for their children, defined as 'making available to all mentally retarded people patterns of life and conditions of everyday living which are as close as possible to the regular circumstances of society' (Nirje, 1979, p. 173). Parent organizations with political and legal representation pressed for the de-institutionalization of their children and for universal access to public education that is adapted to their needs (Nolet and McLaughlin, 2000). The first time that any province in Canada specified that students with disabilities could have access to schooling without payment of fees was in Ontario in 1980, although the legislation stopped short of mandating that such access should be inclusive.

In 1985, Canada repatriated its Constitution from Britain. This led to the creation of the Canadian Charter of Rights and Freedoms, which makes explicit in Section 15 that all individuals in Canada have equality rights and freedom from discrimination where such discrimination is based upon, among other conditions, their disability. However, since education is a provincial rather than a federal responsibility, provincial special education policies and practices have proceeded along their own course, shaped largely by the interests of the popular majority (Jordan, 2001). It is this disjunction between the federal and provincial political contexts that sets the stage for the push and pull for and against inclusive education.

In 1989, Canada was a signatory to the UN Convention of the Rights of the Child[1]. Article 23 in this Convention represented a major leap forward in international understanding of the rights of students with disabilities. But it did not shed light on the issues that dominate the inclusion discourse in Canada, the equity issues surrounding the identification and grouping of people with disabilities into legally defined categories, or the rights of people with disabilities to inclusive placements. All provinces and territories subscribe, in varying degrees, to five themes: freedom from discrimination, access to schooling at public expense, assessment of educational needs and appropriate placement, appropriate services, and provision for self advocacy (due process) by or on behalf of students with disabilities (Andrews and Lupart, 2000). Canadian interpretation of inclusion has been forged primarily in court challenges to one or more of these issues as represented in provincial education legislation. The challenges are litigated by advocacy groups who represent one or another category of disability. Such groups take opposing positions, however, and each hopes to push its arguments for or against inclusion through the various levels of provincial court hearings to the federal Supreme Court of Canada where the challenges to the province's education law can be examined within the terms of the Canadian Charter rights.

Provincial educational regulations and policies have been influenced by the evolution of legislation and policies in the US, often containing the principles of US policies but allowing for greater discretion in their compliance. Requirements that are typically prescriptive and fundamental to US law are made into permissive policies in Canada. The tendency of law-makers in Canada has been to follow the legislation put in place in the US by implementing similar requirements, but following a delay of several years, and without the conviction of the principles contained in the original. For example, the provision of Individual Educational Plans (IEPs) which is integral to the principles of appropriate education in the US (see below), are routinely prepared for Canadian students with disabilities, but they do not carry the force of law of their US counterparts.

Inclusion as a concept is interpreted, therefore, through the requirement first to identify students as having special education needs, i.e. as being 'exceptional.' Identification of students as exceptional is required in all provinces. Identification is generally the prerogative of each school board, and entails designating the student within a category of disability. In three provinces, Ontario, Quebec and Saskatchewan, the categories are governed by binding definitions.

The right to a placement of the parent's choosing is not provided in any province, although Quebec provides for a choice of public schools. Inclusion has been litigated in several provinces, and the right to an appropriate placement has been understood by some to mean inclusion in a regular classroom and by others as provision of specialized programs in small class settings.

In addition to differences in the judicial traditions of the US and Canada, a second factor has influenced the evolution of Canadian special education law. Advocacy groups for students with disabilities hold differing assumptions about the nature of disability, and this difference is reflected both in the nature of the cases that they bring to the courts, and in the influence that they exert in shaping the provisions mandated in provincial policies. One set of assumptions emphasizes the pathological nature of disability; it is assumed that a disability is a stable, pathological trait within the individual that can be reliably diagnosed and categorically grouped. Resources are therefore tied to a diagnosis of a student's disabilities into one of the official categories. In Ontario, for example, funding for students with low-incidence disabilities is dependent on such categorization. On the other hand, disability can be defined in terms of social responsibility. Here it is assumed that society creates barriers which limit access for people with disabilities and which are constructed to serve the interest of the social majority (Kalyanpur and Harry, 1999; Oliver, 1990; Rioux, 1997; 2001; Shakespeare and Watson, 1997; Slee, 1997). People who hold this perspective see disability as 'an artificial and exclusionary social construction that penalizes those people with impairments who do not conform to mainstream expectations of appearance, behavior, and/or economic performance' (Tregaskis, 2002, p. 457). As will be seen in the following section, in the US such an assumption is exemplified in a recent Presidential Commission recommendation that many students identified as having learning disabilities may have experienced inadequate early literacy instruction. In this view, it is the responsibility of the social agencies to reduce or remove barriers to access, especially by providing resources for intensive early interventions.

The third, and relatively recent, factor that has influenced the development of Canadian legislation is the political agenda of efficacy and productivity. At the provincial level, this has taken precedence over the rights and ethics agenda of the Charter. The efficacy and productivity agenda promotes the public belief that schools aspire to low standards, are wasteful of resources, and lack accountability (Jordan, 2001). The assessment of literacy for students aged sixteen, known as the Grade 10 literacy test, was introduced in 1998. All students, regardless of disability, language proficiency, or other circumstances, must pass the test if they are to receive a high school graduation diploma. While Ontario has just recently introduced a high school course designed to provide remedial intervention for those who fail the test, there is clearly an assumption in the requirement that literacy is a stable trait that is somehow linked to ability and not influenced by previous opportunity to learn. At the time of going to press, a parent advocacy group on behalf of students with disabilities is taking the provincial government to court to challenge the constitutionality of the literacy test.

The three factors – judicial traditions, contradictory assumptions about disability, and the agenda of efficiency and productivity – have influenced special education law and practices in Canada. To illustrate how these interplay, we examine the procedures in one province, Ontario, which has the largest school population of the thirteen territories and provinces. In 1974, when the US enacted *PL 94:142: The Education of All Handicapped Children Act*, Ontario drafted the first mandatory legislation for special education in Canada. *An Act to Amend the Education Act of Ontario, 1980* received a third reading in the Ontario legislature and was passed into law for enactment in 1985. This new legislation made no mention of inclusion, or of the clauses pertaining to Least Restrictive Environment that was central to the US legislation. Instead, the *Ontario Amendment Act* focused on the *identification* of a student as 'exceptional' in terms of a label or a category that identifies the disability, and the appropriate *placement* for that student, a location in which services would be delivered.

In Ontario, an Identification, Placement and Review Committee (IPRC) makes the identification and placement decisions on behalf of a School Board. Parents may appeal these recommendations, but the appeals are limited to the technical definition of 'exceptional,' i.e. that the child merits the *identification* as exceptional and the *placement* is determined in accordance with that identification. Technically, the recommendation for a placement need consist of no more than a statement such as 'placement will be in the classroom for children with this identification.' The child's programme and the services once in the placement do not need to be specified and are not open to parental appeal.

Other provinces have provided for the right to a regular class placement, but only subject to a standard of practicality. The provisions in the North West Territories Act, for example, entitle a student with a disability to education in the community school. They, however, list exceptions, one of which is '[if] the presence of the student in the regular instructional setting would unduly interfere with the delivery of educational programs to other students' (Education Act, s.7).

Since the Charter legislation was enacted in 1985, there have been various challenges to the constitutionality of Ontario's restriction on parental appeals, as well as challenges based on the Charter's guarantee of freedom from discrimination. As yet, however, the legal requirement to specify placement is not attached to any policy for inclusion beyond a 1998 Ontario regulation that forbids the IPRC from deciding the programs and services to be delivered in the placement[2] (although it may recommend doing so). The regulation further suggests that when recommending a placement for an exceptional student, the IPRC should first consider placement in a regular (general education) classroom, 'where the placement meets the needs of the exceptional pupil and the parent so agrees.' This is as close as the Canadian legislation gets to a policy of inclusion.

Issues surrounding the identification criterion

Influential advocacy organizations on behalf of disability groups have, unfortunately, taken opposite positions in the inclusion debate. There is much at stake for both advocacy positions in securing resources that are currently tied to the formal designation of a student as 'exceptional.' Defining which children can be designated as 'exceptional' is a major focus of certain parent and advocacy organizations. In particular, the limitations placed on the identification are of great concern to parents of students with school-task-related, high-incidence difficulties such as learning disabilities.

Parent organizations for these children with learning disabilities have created legal and political pressures to ensure official recognition for their children's identification as learning disabled. One such group is the Learning Disabilities Association (LDA), an organization with membership chapters throughout the US and Canada, and which is politically active in both countries. Half of the students designated as exceptional in each country fall within the definition of 'learning disabled.' Since funding for special programs is contingent upon valid identification, much effort has been vested in refining the categorical definition so as to eliminate children who do not meet its stringent discrepancy criteria. The LDA in Ontario has attempted to restrict the numbers of students whom it represents by narrowly defining the criteria by which they can be identified through promoting the 'discrepancy hypothesis' as a component of its definition. According to this hypothesis, learning disability can be determined only in children who have at least an average score on assessed intellectual potential, as measured by IQ tests, and levels of assessed achievement which are significantly discrepant from the norm, particularly in the areas of reading and literacy. Under this definition, students who show evidence of more pervasive developmental disabilities, or who have the complicating factors of attention difficulties, emotional problems or for whom English is a second language, are ineligible for the identification. The definition of learning disability is highly controversial and is not supported by Canadian research (Siegel, 1989a; 1989b; Stanovich, 1991; Stanovich and Stanovich, 1996). Unfortunately, the definition has guided the criteria used by government agencies to fund remedial programmes in several provinces.

The LDA definition of learning disabilities also claims that there is a neurological deficit associated with the syndrome, another controversial issue from a research standpoint (Davidson, 2002). One anomaly arising from this discrepancy definition is that students with *average* levels of achievement but very high levels of assessed IQ potentially qualify for the identification of 'Gifted Learning Disabled' and therefore for the same intensive financial resources as students with highly complex, severe disabilities. Inevitably, this gifted LD group raises questions about the equity of resource distribution.

The desire of the learning disabilities advocacy groups to define their children by these criteria is understandable in view of a history of experiencing inadequate support for their children (Winzer, 1996, p. 219). These parent organizations generally view the current movement to inclusion as an indication that their children will remain undiagnosed, and their needs will be unmet. Inclusion is therefore viewed as synonymous with failure to recognize and remedy individual needs specific to school tasks.

The advocacy groups' definition of learning disability is consistent with an efficacy perspective, focused on the medical-pathological characteristics of students as proof of their lack of individual productivity (Dyson, 1997). In addition, authorization by medical personnel is required to admit a child to this designation, emphasizing the pathology of the identification process. In order to access the funding for specialized programmes and services, responsibility falls on parents to collect and present the evidence to substantiate the claim that the child is eligible to be labeled 'learning disabled.'

Issues surrounding the placement criterion

In contrast, advocacy groups for children with complex and severe intellectual and developmental disabilities have focused their attention on the *placement* criterion in Ontario's identification requirements. The limitations present on the placement are of great concern to parents of students with complex disabilities. There is relatively little debate that these children merit the identification of 'exceptional.' Instead, parents' organizations have made a major push in legal disputes to define the placement criterion as inclusive placement, on the grounds that it benefits the social and linguistic integration and participation of their children. In contrast to the position that focuses on identification, parents and advocates who subscribe to inclusive placement hold the social responsibility and equity perspective. They claim that society-at-large and school systems in particular are responsible for removing barriers for their children to allow them to access and to benefit from inclusive classrooms and to participate fully with their non-disabled peers.

In summary, Canada's current provincial education legislation makes scant mention of inclusion and permits broad interpretation of 'inclusive' placements. Legally, a student with a disability is one who has been identified as being a member of a labeled or categorical group, and whose educational placement is defined in terms of a location. Needed programmes and services are prescribed in an IEP, at the discretion of the school board. The result is that two powerful advocacy lobby groups have emerged, each consisting of affiliated organizations. One has focused on the identification criterion. Its arguments are based on the efficacy and educational productivity initiatives current in general education: that children with learning disabilities should receive compensatory resources and supports if they are to compete on standards-based measures of achievement. The equally powerful group representing students with complex disabilities has little interest in academic productivity for its children, and prefers to take up the placement argument as a social equity and rights issue. Each seems to stand in opposition to the other.

Efficacy and educational productivity v. social equity rights

Within this ideological divide, there have been opportunities for provinces to promote their agendas of efficacy and productivity over the rights and ethics agenda of the Charter. The standards-driven system of monitoring student progress through provincially mandated high-stakes assessments, introduced in 1995, adds to Dyson's (1997) distinction between rights and ethics v. efficacy. Resources are centrally deployed to school systems, resulting in a competition between school systems (Mitchell, 1996). The funding formulae that support special education in Ontario exemplify this move to a market-driven system. One component, the Intensive Support Amounts (ISA), was and continues to be hotly contested. In keeping with an efficacy perspective, the ISA funds are allocated on a case-by-case basis. For students for whom it can be shown that specialized programmes are required for more than 50 per cent of the school day, ISA funding is provided for the equivalent of the salary of a half-time para-educator or Educational Assistant (EA). For students requiring 80 per cent or more, the ISA grant covers 100 per cent of the EA's salary (Ontario Ministry of Education, 2000). To apply for funding, school systems must supply the documented medical and psychological test evidence to demonstrate that each exceptional student meets every one of the stringently defined medical, behavioral and psychological criteria for one of the eight prescribed categories of exceptionality. It is notable that proof of a significant behavioral problem must be supplied in order for students to qualify in four of the eight categories. A team of centrally deployed Ministry auditors audits each application annually. Responsibility for collecting the evidence for eligibility for funding falls upon the school system, which then passes the responsibility to the child's family to secure medical and psychological test records to support the funding application. The parent organizations for high-incidence disabilities, with assistance from cash-strapped school boards, are thus motivated to maximize resources for their children in the form of EA salaries, despite the evidently negative assumptions that are implied about the students.

Parent organizations representing students with low-incidence disabilities have balked at the categorical definitions and at the demands for proof of eligibility through medical and psychological test data. The ISA funding policy represents the antithesis of their understandings about their children's needs. The family and advocacy organizations representing students with low-incidence disabilities argue against the placement provisions in legislation, by claiming that segregated placement is inherently discriminatory.

Their arguments for inclusive placements, however, have also been seriously challenged in the courts on the grounds that inclusion as a placement does not fit the Charter requirements for freedom from discrimination and equality rights. The 1997 landmark *Eaton* decision at the Supreme Court of Canada addressed the serious question of whether *identification*, i.e. whether designating a child with a disability as being identifiable as a member of a predefined category or group, results in attributing to the child a set of 'stereotypical characteristics' and whether such an attribution is discriminatory. The Supreme Court of Canada interpreted the meaning of the equality rights clause of the Canadian Charter of Rights and Freedoms in the case of Emily Eaton, a severely disabled child, who was placed in a segregated special education class in her local school system, against the wishes of her parents. Following a series of appeals and tribunal hearings, the Supreme Court upheld the school board's decision to place the child in a segregated class, which was viewed as a blow to those who support inclusion. However, the decision of the Court supported neither the identification nor the placement criteria used by the province, but proposed a third criterion for providing resources to students with disabilities. The Court determined that the Charter clearly provides for the equality rights of exceptional students by providing differences in treatment where necessary to ensure equality of outcomes. The ultimate test of inclusion must be 'a determination of the appropriate accommodation for an exceptional child ... from a subjective, child-centred perspective, one which attempts to make equality meaningful from the child's point of view' (*Eaton v. Brant County Board of Education* [1997] 1 S.C.R.241, [1977] 142 D.L.R. [4th] 385. *Education Act*, R.S.O., 1990, c.E.2 at pp. 272–273).

The court further stated 'It is the failure to make reasonable accommodations, to fine-tune society so that its structure and assumptions do not result in the relegation and banishment of disabled persons from participation, which results in discrimination against them.' The demand for inclusion as a *placement* can result in 'reverse discrimination or stereotyping which, by not allowing for the condition of disability in the individual forces him or her "to sink or swim in the mainstream environment"' (*ibid.* at pp. 272–273).

The court's use of the terms 'appropriateness' and 'accommodations' are to be applied to the individual child in the individual circumstances in which that child is located. The interpretations should not be viewed as endorsing any overall preconceptions or presumptions in favor of any particular placement or programme or service (MacKinnon, 2001). The onus is on society to seek accommodations that maximize the individual child's 'equality from the child's point of view.'

The distinctions made in the *Eaton* decision between the rights of individuals and their placement could, however, serve as a possible way out of the impasse that dominates the inclusion debate in Canada. The decision maintains that the rights of students with disabilities are not secured on the basis of their eligibility for designation as a member of one or another disability category. Membership in a category does not in itself guarantee the rights of its members. Neither are their rights preserved by being placed in an inclusive classroom setting without regard for what takes place in that setting. Both the focus on identification as a means to qualify for resources, and on inclusive placement as a formula to satisfy individual students' rights, are misleading, if not wrong. Instead, rights are preserved by supplying accommodations that are appropriate to the needs of each student on an individual basis. Such accommodations, including the location in which such accommodations are to be delivered, must be interpreted on a case-by-case basis.

One danger in the Court's decision is that it seems to render redundant the role of category-linked parent advocacy groups. In their place, school systems will be required to operate as advocates on behalf of each individual child. This is a tall order since the mainstream educational system is fixated on meeting the demands of high standards set by the reform policies of the provincial governments. Minority families, such as those with children with disabilities, tend to be ignored in the efficacy and productivity agenda that marks the political right. The court leaves open the question of who is responsible for ensuring social equity. If school personnel are to assume this moral undertaking, much needs to be done to infuse resources into teacher support and training. Our research with general education teachers in inclusive classrooms has shown that a policy of inclusion at the school and school system levels serves as a strong impetus for professional development. Teachers who hold assumptions about disability that are aligned with the social equity perspective have instructional practices that contain the elements of individualization, instructional intensity, and explicit instruction that are effective for students both with and without disabilities (Jordan and Stanovich, 2001; 2003; McDonnell *et al.*, 1997; Stanovich and Jordan, 1998; 2002). But few teachers are equipped and willing to provide the degree of individualization and intensive instruction that is needed in a modern diverse classroom. The resources that are available have been largely monopolized by the activities related to ISA funding, leaving largely under-served both classroom teachers and their students with learning difficulties.

As the Canadian understanding of inclusive education evolves, there are major challenges to creating a truly inclusive and seamless educational system that is designed for the needs of all students. Among the challenges is the need to create a continuum of curriculum and instructional supports within schools that can be provided without concern for labels or location of delivery, but which protects basic equity rights for students with disabilities on an individual needs basis.

Inclusion in the US: multiple meanings and multiple demands

As noted earlier in this chapter, the term 'inclusive education' is not defined in US law or policy. Within the US, the term 'inclusion' has been associated primarily with education in the general education classroom and is considered as only one option within a broader definition of policies surrounding educational placement. Among the two basic legal entitlements set forth in the Individuals with Disabilities Education Act (IDEA), which is the US special education legislation, are the entitlement to a free and appropriate public education (FAPE) in the least restrictive environment (LRE). The constructs of FAPE and of LRE have been the foundations of US special education policy since the passage in 1975 of PL 94–142. Federal regulations accompanying IDEA provide guidance with respect to what constitutes an 'appropriate' education and the 'least restrictive environment.' But both entitlements have been subjected to numerous legal interpretations and varied implementation across the fifty states of the US. Before discussing the current interpretations and evolving understandings, it is important to understand how policies surrounding FAPE and LRE are affected by the classification of a child as 'disabled.'

The US, similar to Canada, has witnessed substantial growth in the numbers of students being classified as having a disability. In particular, the growth in the numbers of students classified as having learning disabilities has created major tensions within the professional and advocacy communities within the US with respect to what constitutes FAPE and LRE. According to recent data reported by the US Department of Education (2002), 5.7 million students with disabilities were served in special education during the 1999/2000 school year. This number represents an increase of over 30 per cent within the past decade and is currently about 11.5 per cent of the estimated total student enrolment in grades pre-kindergarten through 12. The growth in special education enrolment is substantially above the 12 per cent growth in the population of 6–21 year-olds that occurred during the same decade (US Department of Education, 2002).

The federal government reports special education data according to thirteen disability categories, which define which students are eligible to receive special education under the IDEA. Of the thirteen disability categories covered under IDEA, four account for 87.7 per cent of students with disabilities aged 6 through 21. The specific learning disabilities category accounts for half of the students served, speech or language impairments for 18.9 per cent and mental retardation and emotional disturbance for 10.6 per cent and 8.2 per cent respectively. The one characteristic shared by these students is academic underachievement in one or more areas. For more than 50 per cent of the school-age students currently being served in special education, referrals from classroom teachers or parents are the primary mechanism for triggering eligibility. Research (Hosp and Reschly, 2004; Reschly, 2000) has confirmed extreme variability across states in both classification rates and factors that contribute to classification, such as definitions of disabilities and assessment procedures.

Moreover, there are longstanding issues surrounding the disproportionate representation of minority students, specifically black males, in special education (National Research Council, 2002; Hosp and Reschly, 2004). For example, black males are two and a half times more likely to be classified as having mental retardation than white males. Such disproportionate representation of minority students in special education has been evident since the early 1900s with the advent of special education classes.

While the federal government does not require that data be reported on the socio-economic status of students identified as eligible for special education, some research has demonstrated a strong relationship between poverty and the probability of being identified as having one of the previously noted four categories (Countinho et al., 2002; National Research Council, 2002; see also Macmillan and Reschly, 1997). A recent Presidential Commission that examined a number of issues relating to special education policy (President's Commission on Excellence in Special Education, 2002) concluded that many students who have been identified as having a learning disability are more likely to be students who have experienced inadequate early literacy instruction. The President's Commission and a recent National Academy of Science Committee that examined the issues related to disproportionate representation (National Research Council, 2002) recommends that changes be made to the special education identification procedures, specifically for the category of learning disabilities. Recommended changes include removing the requirement in federal law for measuring a student's IQ and instituting, instead, a 'response to intervention' approach to diagnosis. This approach would require that before a student is considered eligible for special education under the learning disability category, they have demonstrated a failure to respond to a systematically implemented, scientifically based intervention. Pending legislation that will reauthorize IDEA includes a new provision that will permit local school districts to use up to 15 per cent of the federal special education funds for preventative early intervention as a way to reduce special education identification rates.

The foregoing issues surrounding classification have influenced interpretations of inclusion, as well as perspectives on what constitutes an appropriate education. Parents and advocates of students with learning disabilities have long endorsed educational productivity as the chief purpose of special education. An 'appropriate' education tends to be measured in terms of scholastic outcomes, and equity is defined in terms of closing the achievement gap between students with and without disabilities. In comparison, many parents and advocates for children and adolescents with intellectual and developmental disabilities have traditionally had among their top goals the social integration and full inclusion of their children in general education classrooms and schools. Attainment of specific knowledge and skills has been secondary to the provision of equal access to the same environments as typical peers. Educational outcomes are defined in large part by the quality of interactions and in part by the individual's ability to access integrated environments through use of natural support systems and relationships.

What constitutes an 'appropriate education'?

The cornerstone of US federal special education law is the individual student's entitlement to a 'free appropriate public education' (20 USC. 1401(8)). As defined through regulation, this term means special education and related services that are provided at public expense, under public supervision, and according to an Individualized Educational Plan (IEP). By law, an IEP must include each child's present level of performance, a statement of annual goals and short-term objectives and benchmarks, a statement of all special education and related services that will be provided, the extent to which the student will participate in general education, and schedules for annual review.

At the time of the passage of PL 94–142, the US Congress clearly indicated that the requirement for individualized programs was essential to achieving the ambitious goals of the legislation (Ballard and Zettel, 1977; Levine and Wexler, 1981). However, neither the term 'appropriate' nor the IEP was an entirely new concept. A number of state statutes and judicial decrees had already required that the education of children with disabilities be 'appropriate' or 'suitable' and that it include 'specialized instruction' (Ballard *et al.*, 1982, p. 20). Yet, the definitions of these terms

have had certain circularity. The US Supreme Court has played a significant role in determining what constitutes an 'appropriate' education for
students with disabilities. In *Board of Education of Hendrick Hudson
Central School District v. Rowley (458 US 176, 1982)*, the Court held that:

> Insofar as a State is required to provide a handicapped child with a 'free
> appropriate public education,' we hold that it satisfies this requirement
> by providing personalized instruction with sufficient support services to
> permit the child to benefit educationally from that instruction. Such
> instruction and services must be provided at public expense, must meet
> the State's educational standards, must approximate the grade levels
> used in the State's regular education, and must comport with the child's
> IEP. In addition, the IEP ... should be formulated in accordance with
> the requirements of the Act and, if the child is being educated in the
> regular classrooms of the public education system, should be reasonably
> calculated to enable the child to achieve passing marks and advance
> from grade to grade.

Through this court interpretation, the IDEA and its regulations delegate
to states the more substantive decisions of what constitutes an 'appropriate
education' for any given student and only establishes a 'floor of educational
opportunity' (Center for Education and Employment Law, 2003). The
Rowley interpretation suggests that a child's education is considered appropriate if it is designed in conformity with the procedures specified in the
IDEA and if the child is making reasonable progress based on professional
judgment of their capabilities (McDonnell *et al.*, 1997; Smith and Brownell,
1995).

In the 1997 amendments to the IDEA, states were challenged to turn
their focus to what students with disabilities are learning. A number of new
provisions began to shift the emphasis in the law toward a focus on educational outcomes such as graduation and improving student achievement.
Language in the law exemplified the focus on student results:

> Disability is a natural part of the human experience and in no way
> diminishes the right of individuals to participate in or contribute to
> society. Improving *educational results* [italics added] for children with
> disabilities is an essential element of our national policy of ensuring
> equality of opportunity, full participation, independent living, and
> economic self-sufficiency for individuals with disabilities.
>
> (20 USC. Â§1401(a)(17)(1))

The 1997 IDEA amendments also introduced the concept of 'effective'
education. The legislation notes that an effective educational system now
and in the future must maintain high academic standards and clear perfor-

mance goals for children with disabilities, consistent with the standards and expectations for all students in the educational system (IDEA 97, 20 USC. Â§651(a)(6)(A)).

The new requirements in the 1997 IDEA amendments are aligned with the components of standards-driven reform. These include changes in IEPs that require specific attention to how an individual student will access the general education curriculum *regardless of the setting in which she/he will receive special education and related services* (Nolet and McLaughlin, 2000).

Specific requirements added to IDEA in 1997 include:

- A statement of the child's present levels of educational performance, *including how the child's disability affects their involvement and progress in the general curriculum*. For pre-school children, there must be a statement of how the disability affects the child's participation in appropriate activities.
- Measurable annual goals, including benchmarks or short-term objectives, related to meeting the child's needs that result from her or his disability. These goals and objectives must enable the child to be involved in and progress in the general curriculum while at the same time meeting each of the child's other unique educational needs.
- A statement of the special education and related services, supplementary aids and services, or programme modifications that are to be provided to the child. Also, there must be a description of any modifications or supports for school personnel that are necessary for the child to advance toward attaining the annual goals, be involved and progress in the general curriculum, participate in extracurricular or other non-academic activities, and to be educated and participate in activities with other children with and without disabilities.
- An explanation of the extent, if any, to which the child will *not* participate with the children without disabilities in general education classes and activities.
- A statement of any individual modifications in the administration of state or district assessments of student achievement that are needed for the child to participate in the assessment. If the IEP team determines that the child will not participate in the assessment, the IEP must include a statement that tells why that assessment is not appropriate, along with a description of how the child's achievement will be measured.
- A statement of how the child's progress toward the annual goals will be measured and how the child's parents will be regularly informed of that progress. This notification also must include an assessment of whether the student's progress is sufficient to enable him or her to achieve the goals by the end of the year.

What constitutes the 'least restrictive environment'?

The IDEA states that an appropriate education should occur in the least restrictive environment (LRE). The original regulations developed in accordance with PL 94–142 defined LRE in terms of a 'continuum of placements' that were to be available to a child with a disability. The law gave preference to educating children with disabilities in the same environment, as much as possible, as students who do not have disabilities, and recognized that supplementary aides, supports, and services may be needed to achieve this goal. The current LRE requirement in IDEA is essentially unchanged from its original statement in PL 94–142 and has resulted in different interpretation by different courts (Douvanis and Hulsey, 2002). However, 'the law continues to express a preference rather than a mandate for placement of students with disabilities in the regular classroom' (Bateman and Linden, 1998, p. 13).

The determination of what is the least restrictive environment for any given child with a disability is only to be made following the specification of what constitutes an 'appropriate' education for that child. The team that develops the IEP is to specify individual learning goals. Based on a judgment of what will be required in terms of special education and related services to achieve those goals, the IEP team then determines which setting or combination of settings will result in progress toward the goals. Some special education professionals (e.g. Bateman, 1992; Kauffman and Smucker, 1995) have argued that national or federal pressure to promote inclusion diminishes the importance of the individualized decision-making process required by IDEA. They argue that it is inherently unequal treatment to not educate a child with a disability in the setting that supports the attainment of IEP goals and objectives. At least one lower-level US federal court agreed with this view, stating:

> Under IDEA, mainstreaming is a policy to be pursued so long as it is consistent with the Act's primary goal of providing disabled students with an appropriate education. Where necessary for educational reasons, mainstreaming students assumes a subordinate role in formulating an educational program.
>
> (McLaughlin *et al.*, in press)

Yet, case law in the area of least restrictive environment is often contradictory. Because the US Supreme Court has refused to hear the appeals of cases that relate specifically to LRE, local and regional interpretations remain the rule of law.

The lower courts have established tests to address issues related to LRE. For example, in *Roncker v. Walter (700 F.2d 1058)* (6th Cir. 1983) the court developed the following two-part test to guide the appropriate placement for a student with a disability: (1) Can the educational services that make the segregated setting superior be feasibly provided in a non-segregated setting?

(If so, the segregated placement is inappropriate.) (2) Is the student being mainstreamed to the maximum extent appropriate? In *Greer v. Rome, 950 F.2d 688* (11th Cir. 1991), the court stated that schools must first consider the least restrictive setting prior to making a placement in a segregated program. In *Oberti v. Clementon, 995 F.2d 1204* (3rd Cir. 1993) the court held that inclusion was a 'right' not a privilege. This decision marks the first time that the word 'inclusion' rather than 'mainstreaming' was used in relation to IDEA. In *Sacramento v. Rachel H. 14 F.3d 1398* (9th Cir. 1994), the court ruled that in determining placement, the educational benefits of the general education classroom with supplemental aids and services must be compared to the educational benefits of the special classroom. The non-academic benefits of interaction with non-disabled students also must be considered. Further, the effect of the student's presence on the teacher and on other students must be evaluated.

Courts have also placed limitations on inclusive placements. They have held that violent or dangerous students who disrupt the education of others are 'never properly placed in a regular classroom setting' (*Light v. Parkway 41 F.3rd 1223* [8th Cir. 1994]). Some courts have determined that inclusion in the general education classroom should be based on the judgment of professionals and that it may not be appropriate for children who are not receiving an educational benefit but only a social benefit (*Hartmann v. Loudoun, 118 F. 3d 996* [1997]).

The legal interpretations of LRE seem to support the preference that students achieve or acquire specific skills or certain levels of knowledge. Social benefits of inclusion are not considered to be on a par with academic or functional skill acquisition. In addition, courts appear to interpret that a student with a disability must conform to a particular classroom setting, as opposed to having the classroom support the needs of the student, and that education in general education classrooms is not a right but dependent on an individual student's IEP goals.

Trends in placement in inclusive settings

Despite the mixed legal interpretations and the lack of an explicit federal directive, inclusive education in the US has steadily increased over time. The US Department of Education annually reports on the extent to which students who receive special education are being educated in the least restrictive environment. Each state (and US territory) reports on the daily per centage of time that students with disabilities are educated in general education classrooms, as well as on the per centage of students educated outside of general education buildings. The data are reported in terms of daily per centage of time that students are educated outside of general education classrooms. The most recent report (US Department of Education, 2002) indicates that the per centage of students with disabilities aged 6–21 who are being educated in regular schools and general education classrooms has increased significantly over a fifteen-year period. During the 1998/1999 school year, 96 per cent of all students in special education were educated in regular schools and 47 per cent of these students were educated in general education classrooms for 80 per cent or more of the school day. The latter statistic represents almost a 20 per cent increase since data were first collected on this placement option in 1984/1985 (US Department of Education, 2001).

However, there are some notable differences in the use of inclusive placements when the data are examined by category of disability. For example, students with learning disabilities and speech and language impairments are most likely to be educated in general education classrooms for 80 per cent or more of the school day. In contrast, a third of all students with emotional disturbance and over half of all students with mental retardation spend 60 per cent or more of their school day *outside* of general education classrooms.

Placement trends also differ by race and ethnicity. During the 1998–1999 school year, 70 per cent of the students with disabilities educated in the general education classroom for 80 per cent or more of the day were white, 14 per cent of the students were black, and 12 per cent were Hispanic. Compared to the composition of the total population of students with disabilities who receive special education (e.g. white = 63 per cent; black = 20 per cent; and Hispanic = 14 per cent), it is apparent that students of color are more likely to be educated outside of the general education classroom. In fact, black students were more likely to spend less time in the general education classrooms than any other racial or ethnic group (US Department of Education, 2001).

The federal government has increased its scrutiny and emphasis on inclusion through its recently developed strategy for monitoring state compliance with IDEA. Using the state-reported LRE data described above, the federal government is engaging in a process called 'targeted focused monitoring.' The process uses state-level data on a variety of indicators, including LRE, to identify individual states needing improvement. The federal government and the state administrators then negotiate improvement goals, set targets and develop improvement goals and timelines.

Current dilemmas in inclusive practice in the US: new accountability demands

The 1997 IDEA amendments clearly establish the importance of improving 'results' and 'outcomes' for students with disabilities and begin to link these to concepts of 'appropriate.' New provisions requiring that students with disabilities have access to and make progress in the general education curriculum and participate in state and local assessments, explicitly align US special education policy with standards-driven reform, the latter of which are grounded in challenging academic standards, assessments, and rigorous accountability. Education policy in the US is now being driven by the standards-driven requirements set forth in the *No Child Left Behind Act* (NCLBA), which is the renamed and amended Elementary Secondary Education Act (ESEA).

The ESEA is the largest k-12 education law in the US, providing $12.5 billion to US schools. The educational goals articulated in NCLBA reflect longstanding policy goals of closing the achievement gap between traditionally high and low performing groups of students. Specifically, the NCLBA requires that states establish challenging content standards in (at least) reading, math, and science, annually assess the performance of *all* students in grades 3–8, disaggregate assessment results by specific student subgroups (including students with disabilities), and create an accountability system of sanctions and rewards based on student results. Under the new NCLBA accountability requirements, states must set school and district level performance goals for each subgroup of students to ensure that each group makes 'adequate yearly progress' (AYP) toward specified levels of achievement on assessments. Calculations of AYP must include the assessment results of 95 per cent of the students in each subgroup. Regulations specify that for students with disabilities, the 95 per cent must include those students identified as having the most significant cognitive disabilities who may take an assessment based on alternate achievement standards. States and school districts can count the 'proficient and advanced' scores of these students against alternate achievement standards, as long as the number of such scores does not exceed one per cent of all students in the grades tested. The policies apply to all students with disabilities educated in public education settings, including charter schools, special centers, and alternative schools.

Ensuring that students with disabilities are included in the standards-driven reform has been a goal of special education policy-makers, professionals and advocates, under the assumption that holding schools accountable for student performance will ensure that students with disabilities receive the benefits of reform initiatives. However, there are a number of challenges facing educators in the US. As McLaughlin *et al.* (2001) note, there are ' "paradoxes and dilemmas" faced by special education researchers and practitioners who are seeking to create socially just education systems' (p. 164). They assert that the increasing concerns about over-identification and disproportionate representation of culturally diverse students in special education, coupled with the demands of school reform, are colliding with the discourse community of inclusion. Inclusion in the current policies of educational reform requires that student achievement of specific standards take primary position above all other educational goals.

Educational productivity, as measured by assessed student performance, is the driving force in US schools today. The requirement that schools should produce certain uniform levels of student performance is now trumping discussions of inclusion and is bringing to the fore a new perspective of social equity, one that focuses on equality of outcomes, not access. In this new notion of equity is a certain dissonance between the right to an 'individualized education' and the requirement to meet standards. Like the experience of Canada's policy-makers, some see a possible trade-off between effectively educating a student according to externally imposed standards and inclusive education. For other parents, NCLBA and its focus on accountability for results means that their children will have access to a more challenging curriculum and higher expectations. In the face of increased learning demands and accountability, the focus is on ensuring adequate resources to achieve standards. Still, parents are concerned that their children will not be able to meet the new rigorous demands and may be scapegoated by schools, suffer repeated failure or face serious consequences such as failure to receive a high school diploma.

While there was never unanimity surrounding the goal of universal inclusion, many parents of children with disabilities have opted for inclusive education as a means of providing greater opportunity to learn important content, as well as social and communication skills. Educators and advocates also believe that inclusive classrooms promote broader social goals by preparing all students for adult life in a diverse democracy. However, all US schools must now come to terms with the central educational goal of increasing performance and results for all students, even those few who may be held to alternate achievement standards. Presence and participation in school communities is no longer sufficient; all students must now contribute to the overall school productivity. Parents seeking inclusion as a goal will be faced with general education classrooms that have an even more demanding curriculum and pace of instruction (McLaughlin *et al.*, 1997) that may not support inclusion. Further, as new alternate achievement standards are developed by individual states, it is feasible that some may not be met in fully inclusive environments.

Still, the new reforms are changing the practice of special education in schools in some positive ways. Based on our own extensive field work in 'high reform' districts, we find that special and general educators are now more than ever being pushed to collaborate and communicate, and that standards provide a common language for that commitment (Caron and McLaughlin, 2003). Furthermore, the emphasis on improving achievement has resulted in a surge in intensive instruction in reading and math, with an emphasis on prevention of later school failure.

In summary, inclusion today within the US means an inclusive accountability system in which the performance of every student counts. Inclusion means having access to the same curriculum and to the same content standards and performance as all other students. The goal of reducing the physical segregation of students with disabilities remains, but the national energy and focus is on improving student achievement. From this perspective, inclusion in the US needs to be viewed as a means to an end and not the goal. That is, students should be educated in inclusive classrooms because that is the setting that will maximize each student's opportunity to gain the critical knowledge that will result in better achievement. The hope is that all students will also learn the dispositions that will result in them being better citizens in a democratic society.

Summary and conclusions

In this chapter, we have attempted to provide an overview of the complex tensions within US and Canadian policies resulting from two equally important goals: greater educational productivity and inclusive education. The dilemma is compounded by the struggles to develop an irrefutable and educationally defensible classification system for what constitutes a school-related disability.

Resolving the tension within special education policies is complicated by the research that has examined the impacts of inclusive classrooms with both groups of students. The efficacy of 'inclusion' for students with learning disabilities has been defined in terms of the acquisition of specific literacy or academic skills and has been found lacking (Fuchs and Fuchs, 1988; Vaughn et al., 1997). In contrast, the effects of inclusion on students with more significant intellectual and developmental disabilities have been measured in terms of language and social development.

Ideally, there should be no distinction between an inclusive education and one that results in the achievement of standards for students with high- and low-incidence disabilities. However, US research on strategies that are known to promote more inclusive education (e.g. cooperative learning, peer-assisted instruction) do not universally result in improved learning for students with learning disabilities (Zigmond et al., URL).

There is, however, substantial evidence that supports a set of basic instructional principles that work for all learners. Three research-based principles that have emerged from decades of research are individualization, instructional intensity, and explicit instruction (McDonnell et al., 1997; McLaughlin et al., 2000). These instructional principles are not placement-specific; they describe how effective instruction occurs, not where instruction takes place. Yet, the effectiveness of these principles in providing the level of achievement expected in today's assessment is unknown.

Further, application of such principles within fully inclusive and heterogeneous classes has been stymied by, among other things, inadequately prepared personnel, class sizes, lack of sufficient time, and lack of differentiation in the curriculum, all of which contribute to the research-practice gap (McLaughlin et al., 1998; Zigmond and Baker, 1995). Creating the conditions that support effective instruction within inclusive classrooms will require extensive political will as well as resources. Moreover, it will also require a new conceptualization of 'special education,' defined as a means of providing access to general education curricula offered in general education classrooms resulting in student attainment of higher levels of assessed performance.

Notes

1 Convention of the Rights of the Child. UN do.A/RES/4425, 20 November 1989; entry into force 2 September 1990; in force for Canada 13 December 1991, Can. T.S. 1992, Article 28.
2 O.Reg. 181/98 Identification and placement of exceptional pupils. S.15(2)(3).

References

Andrews, J. and Lupart, J. (2000). *The inclusive classroom: Educating exceptional children* (2nd edn). University of Calgary: Nelson Thomson Learning.

Ballard, J., Ramirez, B.A. and Weintraub, F.J. (eds) (1982). *Special education in America: Its legal and government foundations*. Reston VA: Council for Exceptional Children.

Ballard, J. and Zettel, J. (1977). 'Public Law 94–142 and Section 504: What they say about rights and protections'. *Exceptional Children*, 44(3), 177–184.

Barnes, C., Mercer, G. and Shakespeare, T. (1999). *Exploring disability: A sociological introduction*. Cambridge: Polity Press.

Bateman, B. (1992). 'Learning disabilities: The changing landscape'. *Journal of Learning Disabilities*, 25, 29–36.

Bateman, B.D. and Linden, M.A. (1998). *Better IEPs: How to develop legally correct and educationally useful programs* (3rd edn) Longmont CO: Sopris West.

Board of Education of Hendrick Hudson Central School District v. Rowley (458 US 176, 1982).

Caron, E.A. and McLaughlin, M.J. (2003). 'Indicators of "Beacons of Excellence" schools: Collaborative practices?' *Journal of Educational and Psychological Consultation*, 13(4), 285–313.

Center for Education and Employment Law (2003). *Students with disabilities and special education law* (20th edn) Malvern PA: Author.

Countinho, M.J., Oswald, D.P. and Best, A.M. (2002). 'The influence of sociodemographics and gender on the disproportionate identification of minority students as having learning disabilities'. *Remedial and Special Education*, 23(1), 49–59.

Davidson, R.J. (2002). *Emotion, plasticity and the human brain: An overview of modern brain research and its implications for education*. AERA Presidential Invited Address, the American Educational Research Association annual meeting, New Orleans, April 2002.

Douvanis, G. and Hulsey, D. (2002). *The Least Restrictive Environment mandate: How has it been defined by the courts?* ERIC Clearinghouse on Disabilities and Gifted Education. Arlington VA: Council on Exceptional Children.

Dyson, A. (1997). 'Social and educational disadvantage: Reconnecting special needs education'. *British Journal of Special Education*, 24(4), 151–156.

Fuchs, D. and Fuchs, L.S. (1988). 'Mainstream assistance teams to accommodate difficult to teach students in general education'. In J.L. Graden, J.E. Ains and

M.J. Curtis (eds) *Alternative educational delivery systems: Enhancing instructional options for all students* (pp. 49–70). Washington DC: National Association of School Psychologists.

Hosp, J.L. and Reschly, D.J. (2004). 'Disproportionate representation of minority students in special education: Academic, demographic, and economic predictors'. *Exceptional Children*, 70(2), 185–199.

The Individuals with Disabilities Education Act of 1997. US PL 105–17, 20 USC. 1401(8) et seq.

Jordan, A. (2001). 'Special education in Ontario: A case study of market-based reforms. Special issue: International perspectives on school reform and special education needs'. *Cambridge Journal of Education*, 31(3), 349–371.

Jordan, A. and Stanovich, P. (2001). 'Patterns of teacher-student interaction in inclusive elementary classrooms and correlates with student self-concept'. *International Journal of Disability, Development and Education*, 48(1), 43–62.

——(2003). 'Teachers' personal epistemological beliefs about students with disabilities as indicators of effective teaching practices'. *Journal of Research in Special Education Needs*. URL: http://www.nasen.uk.com/ejournal

Kalyanpur, M. and Harry, B. (1999). *Culture in special education.* Baltimore: Paul H. Brookes.

Kauffmann, J.M. and Smucker, K. (1995). 'The legacies of placement: A brief history of placement options and issues with commentary on their evolution'. In J.M. Kauffmann, J.W. Lloyd, D.P. Hallahan and T.A. Astuto (eds) *Issues in educational placement: Students with emotional and behavioral disorders* (pp. 21–46). Hillsdale NJ: Erlbaum.

Levine, E.L. and Wexler, E.M. (1981). *PL 94–142: An act of Congress.* New York: Macmillan.

MacKinnon, M. (2001). *Special education and human rights.* Unpublished manuscript. Toronto: Justice for Children and Youth, 15 November.

Macmillan, D.L. and Reschly, D.J. (1997). Issues of definition and classification. In W. MacLean (ed.) *Handbook of mental deficiency: Psychological theory and research* (3rd edn) (pp. 47–74). Hillsdale NJ: Lawrence Erlbaum.

McDonnell, L.M., McLaughlin, M.J. and Morison, P. (1997). *Educating one and all: Students with disabilities and standards-based reform.* Washington DC: National Academy Press.

McLaughlin, M.J., Artiles, A.J. and Pullin, D. (2001). 'Challenges for the transformation of special education in the 21st century: Rethinking culture in school reform'. *Journal of Special Education Leadership*, 12(2), 51–62.

McLaughlin, M.J., Blacher, J., Duffy, S., Hardman, M., McDonnell, J., Nisbet, J., Safer, N. and Snell, M. (2003). *Effective education in the least restrictive setting.* Unpublished paper prepared for National Goals Conference: State-of-Knowledge and National Research Agenda, Washington DC.

——(in press). In K.C. Lakin and A.Turnbull (eds) *National goals and research for persons with intellectual and developmental disabilities.* Washington DC: American Association on Mental Retardation.

McLaughlin, M.J., Fuchs, L. and Hardman, M. (2000). 'Individual rights and students with disabilities: Some lessons from US policy'. In P. Garner and H. Daniels (eds) *The 1999 World Yearbook of Special Education* (pp. 24–35). London: Kogan Page.

McLaughlin, M.J., Henderson, K. and Morando-Rhim, L. (1997). *Snapshots of reform: A report of reform in 5 local school districts*. Alexandria VA: Center for Policy Research on the Impact of General and Special Education Reform, National Association of State Boards of Education.

——(1998). *Snapshots of reform: How five local districts are interpreting standards-based reform for students with disabilities*. Alexandria VA: Center for Policy Research on the Impact of General and Special Education Reform, National Association of State Boards of Education.

Mitchell, D. (1996). 'The rules keep changing: Special education in a reforming educational system'. *International Journal of Disability, Development and Education*, 43(1), 55–74.

National Research Council (2002). *Minority students in special and gifted education*. Committee on Minority Representation in Special Education, M.S. Donovan and C. Cross (eds), Division of Behavioral and Social Sciences and Education. Washington DC: National Academy Press.

Nirje, B. (1979). 'Changing patterns in residential services for the mentally retarded'. In E.L. Meyen (ed.) *Basic readings in the study of exceptional children and youth* (pp. 172–187). Denver CO: Love Publishing.

Nolet, V. and McLaughlin, M.J. (2000). *Assessing the general curriculum: Including students with disabilities in standards-based reform*. Thousand Oaks CA: Corwin Press.

Oliver, M. (1990). *The politics of disablement*. Basingstoke: Macmillan.

The Ontario Education Amendment Act, Revised Statutes of Ontario, 1980, c. 129; R.S.O. 1990, c. E2.

Ontario Ministry of Education (2000). *2000–2001 Resource Manual for the Special Education Grant Intensive Support Amount (ISA). Guidelines for School Boards*. Queen's Printers for Ontario. URL: http://www.edu.gov.on.ca

President's Commission on Excellence in Special Education (2002). URL: http://www.ed.gov/inits/commissionsboards/whspecialeducation/

Reschly, D.J. (2000) 'The present and future status of school psychology in the United States'. *School Psychology Review*, 29(4), 507–22.

Rioux, M. (1997). 'Disability: The place of judgement in a world of fact'. *Journal of Intellectual Disability and Research*, 41(2), 102–111.

——(2001). 'Bending toward justice'. In L. Barton (ed.) *Disability, politics and the struggle for change* (pp. 34–47). London: Fulton.

Shakespeare, T. and Watson, N. (1997). 'Defending the social model'. *Disability and Society, 12(2), 293–300.*

Siegel, L. (1989a). 'Why we do not need intelligence test scores in the definition and analysis of learning disabilities'. *Journal of Learning Disabilities*, 22(8), 469–478.

——(1989b). 'IQ is irrelevant to the definition of learning disabilities'. *Journal of Learning Disabilities*, 22(8), 469–478, 486.

Slee, R. (1997). 'Imported or important theory? Sociological interrogations of disablement and special education'. *British Journal of Sociology of Education*, 18(3), 407–419.

Smith, S.W. and Brownell, M.T. (1995). 'Individualized education program: Considering the broad context of reform.' *Focus on Exceptional Children*, 28(1), 1–10.

Stanovich, K.E. (1991). 'Discrepancy definitions of learning disability: Has intelligence led us astray?' *Reading Research Quarterly*, 26(1), 7–29.

Stanovich, K.E. and Stanovich, P.J. (1996). 'Rethinking the concept of learning disabilities: The demise of aptitude/achievement discrepancy'. In D.R. Olson and N. Torrance (eds) *The handbook of education and human development* (pp. 117–147). Oxford: Blackwell.

Stanovich, P. and Jordan, A. (1998). 'Canadian teachers' and principals' beliefs about inclusive education as predictors of effective teaching in heterogeneous classroom's. *Elementary School Journal*, 98(3), 221–238.

——(2002). 'Preparing general educators to teach in inclusive classrooms: Some food for thought'. *The Teacher Educator*, 37(3), 173–185.

Tregaskis, C. (2002). 'Social model theory: The story so far…' *Disability and Society*, 17(4), 457–470.

UNESCO (1994). *The Salamanca Statement and Framework on Special Needs Education* (Paris: UNESCO). URL:
http://www.unesco.org/education/educprog/sne/salamanc/index.html

US Department of Education (2001). *Twenty-third annual report to Congress on the implementation of the Individuals with Disabilities Education Act*. Washington DC: US Government Printing Office. URL:
http://www.ed.gov/about/offices/list/osers/osep/research.html

——(2002). *Twenty-fourth annual report to Congress on the implementation of the Individuals with Disabilities Education Act*. Washington DC: US Government Printing Office. URL:
http://www.ed.gov/about/offices/list/osers/osep/research.html

Vaughn, S., Bos, C.S. and Schumm, J.S. (1997). *Teaching mainstreamed, diverse, and at-risk students in the general education classroom*. Boston MA: Allyn and Bacon.

Winzer, M. (1996). *Children with exceptionalities in Canadian classrooms*. Scarborough, Ont.: Allyn and Bacon.

Wolfensberger, W. (1975). *The origin and nature of institutional models*. Syracuse NY: Human Policy Press.

Zigmond, N. and Baker, J.M. (1995). 'An exploration of the meaning and practice of special education in the context of full inclusion of students with learning disabilities'. *Journal of Special Education*, 29(2), 1–25.

Zigmond, N., Jenkins, J., Fuchs, L., Deno, S., Fuchs, D., Baker, J.N., Jenkins, L. and Couthino, M. *Special education in restructured schools: Findings from three multi-year studies*. URL:
http://www.newhorizons.org/spneeds/inclusion/systems/jenkins.html

Chapter 6

Inclusive education in some Western European countries

Different policy rhetorics and school realities

Ingemar Emanuelsson, Peder Haug and Bengt Persson

This chapter discusses the present state of inclusive education in some Western European countries by approaching the relationship between intentions and realities in special education. We are well aware that inclusive education is not an equivalent to special education. The responsibility to create inclusive education must be much broader than special education alone; it is a concern for education policy at large and for the whole school community (Vislie, 2003).

At the same time, it is our conviction that what goes on in special education, both in policy and in the practice of schools, is a very good indication of the how inclusive education is understood, developed and practised. We will also concentrate our efforts on the primary schooling. As a rule, the struggle for inclusive education in most countries started in primary education. Even if the differences between some of the countries are noticeable in many respects, it is in primary education that inclusive education is most developed, and it is here that the challenges are most visible.

The main theoretical basis for the analysis in this chapter is the conflicting and competing perspectives labelled *categorical* and *relational* views on the challenges in special education. These views define two different paradigms, understood as ideal types, developed by Emanuelsson *et al.* (2001), derived from previous work by Persson (1998) and Dyson (1999) (cf. also Emanuelsson, 2001). The different perspectives can be applied to, among other things, the ontology of special needs, epistemology, approaches to difference, provisions of support, understanding of special education competence and reasons for special education needs. The model is illustrated in Table 6.1. In the categorical perspective, children's difficulties in school are explained by individual diagnoses describing pathological deviations, and with special provisions as the main educational strategy. The relational perspective refers to special needs as social constructs, with integrated and inclusive provisions as the main educational strategies.

In educational policy, as in policy in general, it is of utmost importance to distinguish between the formulation and the realization of political intentions. The former deals with what has been politically decided and formulated as objects and status. The latter tells what has really been done and how this functions. It is no exaggeration when we suggest that it is much easier to formulate than to practise. Yet we often can witness that formulations have been taken for realization. This also would mean that there usually is a time lag between the point of time when intentions have been decided, and when they have been put into practice, if ever.

The selected European countries for this presentation are Greece, the Netherlands, Norway and Sweden. This choice of countries was made to indicate variance and difference between European countries.

Norway

The presentation of the conditions in Norway mainly deals with two issues. The first one is the relationship between formulated political intentions and how these have been practised during the years from the 1950s and onwards.

Table 6.1 Consequences for special education activities depending upon perspective chosen

	Categorical perspective	Relational perspective
Ontology of special needs	Special needs refer to actual characteristics of individuals.	Special needs are social constructs.
Approach to difference	Differentiating and categorizing	Unifying
Major contribution	Mapping and systematizing the field	Problematizing and deconstructing the field
Disciplinary basis	Establishing special education as a 'scientific' discipline	Establishing special education as a social scientific discipline
Implication for provision	Special provision	Integrated /inclusive provision
Understanding of special educational competence	Superior support directly related to diagnosed difficulties among students	Superior support for incorporating differentiation into instruction and content
Reasons for special educational needs	Students with difficulties. Difficulties are either innate or otherwise bound to the individual.	Students in difficulties. Difficulties arise from different phenomena in educational settings and processes.

Source: This table was published in the International Journal of Inclusive Education, 2003, 7(3). 271–280. The permission of Taylor and Francis to re-publish the table is gratefully acknowledged.

The second is a presentation of the parallel developments in Norwegian special education research.

Inclusive school as a political intention

After passing through periods of segregation and integration, the present Norwegian compulsory school system became formally and legally characterized by inclusion. Children shall attend their home school and be taught together in classes with other children of the same age, as is the case for about 99 per cent of the children. The ideas of fellowship, participation, democratization and benefit in education are of paramount importance, as they are formulated as a basic principle for schools in the national curriculum for compulsory education (KUF, 1996). We also will find corresponding formulations in the National Education Act.

Intentions of inclusive education are very often taken to mean that there have been wide agreements about this education policy in Norway, that this policy in detail is implemented as decided and that results have been reached as intended. We will argue that neither is the case, as exemplified by the present state in special education. Special education was for a long time mainly organized as separate and segregated provisions in regular schools. The number of pupils in special education increased enormously from almost zero in 1955, when the municipalities were obliged to provide special support for pupils with special needs, to about 8 per cent of pupils in 1975. In 2002 the figure was 6–7 per cent.

The reason why Norwegian compulsory education has not been as segregated as in many other countries, seems to be that the special school system expanded very slowly and at a late point in time. Very few special schools had to be closed to make education more inclusive for all children. Because of a lack of official political interest in children with disabilities and special needs for more than two-thirds of the twentieth century, it was not so difficult as it could have been to construct what at that time was called 'integrated compulsory education'. It became easier than it might have been to go into the integrated, and later inclusive, alternatives acceptable from the late 1960s onwards (Haug, 1998).

Up till 1975, children with different kinds of learning difficulties and special needs had two main educational possibilities, both based on the categorical view of special education needs. They were either to attend a centralized special school system, which was insufficiently developed, with too few places for only some categories of disabilities. Or they had to be specially educated in segregated groups in the ordinary school system that was not prepared for them. Some children did not receive any education at all. When the debates about further developments of special education started in the 1960s, social and cultural values had changed, as a part of the general development in the strategies of the 'Scandinavian welfare state'.

All children should now receive education, and it was not possible to expand the relatively small and insufficient system of centralized special schools any further. Gradually, all children were supposed to attend their community school (Dahl *et al.*, 1982). This did not, however, initially imply a change of paradigm from a categorical to a relational view on special education (OECD, 1984).

The initiatives and the push both for education for all children and for an integrated school system, although diffusely understood and defined, came from outside the political and professional groups as a bottom-up process (Haug, 1998). In the late 1960s, a few active and interested researchers, special teachers, parents and citizens started it all. People in politics, bureaucracy and teaching unions did not receive demands for a radical change of special education policy with enthusiasm. The reactions against change actually were very strong. In particular, these groups mentioned above heavily defended the established special school system. In spite of this, and not least due to the general trend in state administration and policy towards decentralization and normalization, the unacceptable situation for children with special educational needs was gradually recognized and the documented needs for reforms gained political and professional support.

The process of formal and legal political change in these issues started in the late 1960s and ended in 1975, when the integrated compulsory school became the ideal and the result. Integration meant that all children should have educational opportunities, and at the neighbourhood school. This was, however, only a partial victory for those seeking reform, because of the differing interpretations of what had been decided. The decision in Parliament was followed by a long period of discussion. What was meant to be, and also appeared as, a straightforward implementation process from 1975, therefore turned into further policy-making and struggle between the same interest groups as before. The discussions primarily dealt with students with the most serious disabilities, and not the majority of students with special needs requiring support. They got access to 'the school for all', but the organizing of their education within this concept of the school differed greatly. The main matter of discussion can be attached to a categorical and a relational view on special education.

For reasons of simplicity, it is possible to divide the different actors into two groups, according to the type of support given to the idea of the integrated school or to 'the school for all', being the concept most frequently in use at the time. Both groups mainly wanted all children to get their education in their home school, in the framework of the ordinary class and most preferably together with all the other students in an ordinary classroom, but on different grounds. The two alternatives can be named 'inclusive integration' and 'segregated integration' (Fulcher, 1999; Haug, 1999). The concept of integration was understood differently. Inclusive integration meant that all children should have access to individually adapted teaching in the ordinary class in their home school – a relational view on education. Segregated integration meant a wider and more open definition of integration, where the criterion for inclusion was that the child should be able to have a certain reciprocal communication with other students and teachers. This implied that the student would become an active part of the social community, be able to take advantage of its offerings, and be able to take on responsibilities and duties. Each student should, in other words, have certain qualifications to be allowed into the ordinary school, a categorical view on education. If this was not the case, each individual student should have the education organized to best benefit that student elsewhere.

The political strategies for solving the problems of special education differed between the two groups. The supporters of inclusive integration wanted all students to be present at school, and then to use that as a lever for further developing the organization and working methods to make schools more inclusive. The supporters of segregated integration wanted everything to be prepared and planned before students with special needs were allowed into the school, to ensure that the teaching would be of sufficient quality.

The supporters of inclusive integration wanted the process of change to go very fast. This was partly because of the principles of social justice for all, and partly for economic reasons. The Norwegian special school system did not enrol many students, but was very expensive. To close down these schools and transfer both money and professional staff to the ordinary school system would be of great help to the local communities. The supporters of segregated integration wanted to reduce the speed of change, even to postpone the whole reform because of the lack of money and competence. They claimed that, for a long time, the local schools would not be able to give an inclusive education of sufficient quality. Therefore, they also wanted to retain the special school system.

Slowly during the 1980s, the ideals of inclusive integration began formally to be accepted as special education policy in Norway, not least due to what actually went on in the schools. The leading pedagogical and organizational principle for this new school was individual adaptation, meaning that every student had a right to an education adapted to his or her personal needs, interests and capabilities. The special schools were reorganized into resource centres to assist municipalities in their struggle with special education (1992). Over a period of thirty years, special education had formally moved from one paradigm to another. That could have been the end of the segregated organization of special education, but it was not.

Because of the political disagreements and the differing interests of the existing institutions and professions, this sector still has many structural indicators of a segregated system and a categorical view, contrary to intentions and ideals. There are still segregated special schools and classes. Special education is explicitly mentioned in the Education Act governing primary schools; special education is funded separately; Norway still has special teachers and a special institute for educating special teachers; the teaching unions have their own departments for special teachers; there have been special research programmes for this field; and the regulations allow deviation from the rule of inclusive integration.

The curriculum and educational methods for the different conceptions of the inclusive school had to be developed parallel to the political clarifications. They did not exist beforehand. Because of reforms in state administration, the responsibility for developing the school had been gradually decentralized since the 1970s. The central bodies for knowledge development were closed down or they mostly supported local development. In general, the decentralized development strategy did not function as intended. The organization and methods of the inclusive school were not developed as they should have been or could have been, due to lack of resources, competence, interest and consensus. To meet the new groups of students, the schools were forced into one of two existing solutions. They either had to import the educational tradition from the special schools to the compulsory school system, or they had to adapt the existing educational tradition from compulsory school to special education. When we analyse special education research in Norway, these two patterns dominate, and the individually adapted teaching in the classroom is often missing. Children are still either taken out of the class to receive special education alone or in small groups, as in special schools, and/or they stay in a class where the teaching is collective and not adequately individually oriented, as is the case in the traditional school. Deviations from this pattern can be found, but they do not dominate.

Special education research

The efforts and achievements in special education research have increased enormously in Norway during the period 1960–2000. What we find as most striking is not only the growth, but also the lack of change in research orientation. The degree of stability in the basic values and conception of this research is very characteristic (Haug, 2000). The most striking feature is that special education research to a large extent is still oriented around the categorical perspective and not the relational and inclusive, as should be expected. This is the situation, contrary to pressure from new regimes of research, contrary to changes of educational policy and even contrary to formulations made by the research community itself. During the short history of special education research in Norway, the ideals of the categorical perspective have dominated, and still dominate, even though there is a growing opposition to this. This general conservatism in research is well known; it is no surprise or novelty. Although there are exceptions, it seems clear that the research community does not share the views and ideals of the relational perspective.

The field of special education research has a short history, the competence is limited, and its prestige is low. This may well have been further strengthened by the early monopolization of special education research in the country. One single institute has in reality dominated both education and research in the entire field up until the 1990s. Most persons in special education and special education research have, in one way or another, been connected to this institute. This concentration of resources for teaching and research can be effective in many ways, but can also be an obstacle to processes of renewal. We have also seen very strong bonds between teaching and research institutions and the professional interests in the field. A surprisingly large number of special educators in the profession actually disagree with the political developments in the field, and support the basic system and categorical conception of special education as it was first established.

Sweden

The intention in this section is to describe and analyse how special education in Sweden was developed and established as an educational discourse, with reference to three different aspects. The first aspect is political, the second is focused on research, while the third aspect is related to practice. The survey starts in the 1940s but the emphasis will be on the period from the beginning of the 1990s up to the present time.

The politics of special/inclusive education

An important task for the post-war social democratic government was the question of differentiation. In 1948, the government published a report that proposed a nine-year comprehensive and compulsory school for all. One important purpose was to make use of what was called the 'reserve talents', in order to raise the general level of competence in the country. This group included people often from rural areas whose access to education was traditionally limited. This green paper was followed by the 1957 school committee report, which proposed a differential system of special education. The philosophy at this period was dominated by the belief that the pupil him/herself was the cause of his/her school problems and therefore should be taught in a way that matched up with the specific difficulties in evidence. In the first Swedish National Curriculum (Lgr 62), the contents and organization of special education were carefully specified and the accompanying proposal was for a system of coordinated special education as an alternative to remedial and special classes.

During the 1960s and 1970s, Swedish social democratic and liberal education policies were marked by a centralized approach, leaving little scope for local policy- and decision-making. During this period, the political influence upon educational policy-making decreased at the same time as civil service departments and public authorities increased their power. National curricula and syllabi manifested central planning and educational research was regarded as reliable and trustworthy (Lindensjö and Lundgren, 2000). Starting in the early 1960s, the parallel school system was replaced by a comprehensive school system. This proved to have unexpected consequences for special education in such a way that the number of pupils judged to have special educational needs grew at a record-breaking pace. The 1969 National Curriculum recommended increased integration of pupils with various forms of handicap into regular classes, and it was noted that the individual school's environment was possibly a cause of pupils' difficulties in fulfilling the school's demands.

The subsequent 1980 National Curriculum attempted to reduce the difference between special education and regular education. The most important goal in this plan was to prevent the child from having difficulties in school. In addition, the importance of the individual child who received help in a special education group returning to his/her regular group was emphasized.

Since the 1960s, the amount of special education has grown steadily in the Swedish elementary school. Critics have claimed that this is a result of schools' inability to cope with all children. Some children were filtered out and educated in special groups with special methods parallel to the regular education in the classroom. During this period, the number of special education teachers steadily increased and there appeared to be an unspoken agreement between the class teachers and the special education teachers, which allowed increased resources for special education.

Starting in the early 1990s, a period of decentralization and deregulation began to take shape. The former national management failed to implement what were regarded as important and necessary reforms, and incompatible interests made the reforms more ambiguous than previously. The present era may also be characterized by a declining confidence in educational research and continuous party-political conflicts.

During this recent period, the educational system has gone through a kind of legitimacy crisis that has led to diminishing confidence in education. The former consensual relationship between liberals and social democrats has turned into demands for a return to another type of schooling, characterized by law and order, discipline and an authoritarian leadership. Advocates of such views also assert ability grouping to be necessary if the quality of education is to be maintained.

This political disunity has come to produce somewhat contradictory messages, depending upon the arena where they were formulated. The School Act, the School Ordinances and the National Curricula all emphasize the importance of solidarity, the right to education of equal value and the right for pupils who experience difficulties for various reasons to receive the help and support they need. Local schools, however, often find this unrealistic, which indicates that the gap between political intentions and practical realities is considerable.

This gap is especially interesting with reference to inclusive education. Emanuelsson (1998) finds inconsistent and contradictory expressions, even in national curriculum texts, and writes: 'Use of inclusive language also means that you talk about students *in* difficulties rather than students *with* difficulties' (p. 170). This is a distinct example of how political language sometimes hides frozen ideologies behind opportunistic rhetoric. Ware (2000) also gives powerful examples of this from the US and defines inclusion very broadly: 'I view inclusion as a social justice project that begins with understanding how exclusionary we are in schools and in society, how we are sanctioned to maintain exclusion, and how we are rewarded to remain exclusionary' (p. 43). Inclusion thus has to be understood as part of social progress and must not become restricted to classrooms or schools.

The question, then, is whether inclusion may be understood as a distinctive trait of the Swedish school or not. Around 99 per cent of all children between 7 and 16 go to the comprehensive school. A little more than one per cent go to special schools due to moderate-to-severe learning difficulties or other disabilities. Sweden, however, has undergone dramatic budget cuts during the 1990s, with severe consequences for schools. Support for children who experience difficulties in school have been reduced and the former role of the 'special teacher', whose task was to teach pupils in smaller groups, is slowly but steadily becoming replaced by special educators whose field of activities is wider than that of the special teacher. It might be seen as contradictory, but recent research in Sweden and elsewhere has shown that a high level of special educational support in ordinary schools does not guarantee higher standards in achievement among these target pupils (Moen and øie, 1994; Persson, 1998).

The role of special educators is very different from the role of special teachers who were trained before 1990. In addition to carrying out teaching tasks, the special educator is trained to give guidance to his/her colleagues in the working team and to initiate and lead developmental work in the local schools. According to Solity (1992), it is important to confront ordinary teachers with the whole range of differences in the school and not hand over problematic children to experts such as special teachers. It is necessary also for all pupils to confront themselves with the whole range of diversity that exists among us. Solity writes:

> Children need to engage in a variety of activities to indicate that they have learned successfully. It is not sufficient for young children to demonstrate that tasks can be performed accurately, or are remembered over time. They need to learn to generalize their knowledge and apply it to real-life problems and situations. They also require opportunities to work independently and cooperatively with peers. When given a

balanced range of learning experiences, children who have difficulties neither require nor will benefit from high levels of direct pupil-teacher contact time.

(p. 48)

Here Solity captures some of the most important reasons for a changing special education professional role in Sweden. It is assumed that special educational knowledge is best put into practice by working together with colleagues in the working team.

Special education research in Sweden

During the last 20–30 years, the narrow aims and directions, as well as the limited paradigmatic perspectives in special education research, have become subject to criticism. Haug (1997) claims that researchers working in the field of special education have been extremely loyal and uncritical and trusting of official publications in their analyses. This in turn has implied that official objectives, intentions and visions are to be taken for granted. Even if some researchers and research groups have contextualized their research in a pioneering way, most research still focuses on disability/difficulty/dysfunction, thereby omitting to subject the environment to criticism. Rosenqvist (2000) writes that

> Only few studies are dealing with the education processes in schools for former so-called mentally retarded students at the expense of studies dealing with issues concerning the mental retardation per se. Even those studies dealing with the school and the educational process are, with some exceptions ... often avoiding the problematization of the categorization of the students.

(p. 2)

Even if an individualistic approach to students' difficulties still dominates, a development characterized by considerable orientation towards diversification of perspectives and paradigmatic understanding has appeared. This development should, however, not be described as a paradigm shift in the spirit of Thomas Kuhn. Instead it would be fair to say that different ways of understanding special education still work as parallel systems, not least in schools and other educational institutions. With reference to the model presented earlier in this chapter, the categorical perspective still dominates special education research in Sweden. Not very much seems to have happened during the last five years, compared to what, among others, Emanuelsson (1983) found in a survey from the early 1980s and Rosenqvist (1994) in the early 1990s. One of their conclusions is that the need for research within the categorical perspective has been sufficiently covered. This does not mean that knowledge developed from this research is not needed or useless, but that its aims are most often focused upon individual treatment and the effects of such treatment. The problem is that this research has little or no implications for pedagogical practice. Its knowledge is, to a high degree, based upon psychology or medicine and tells us little about how to find pedagogical strategies to deal with the problems. An interesting finding is that some of the research within the categorical perspective has elements from the relational perspective. Sometimes it seems as if this is a kind of 'add-on' to the individual-based research. However, research within the relational perspective also suffers from shortcomings. Teachers and other professionals tend to conceive it as ideological, utopian and not at all anchored in their practical realities.

An important question to raise is: whose special needs is special education expected to meet? The Swedish experience shows that it is not just a matter concerning individual students. Rather, special education should be understood as a responsibility of the whole school, thereby contributing to the development of deeper knowledge of how to deal with the whole range of difference between pupils.

The Netherlands

In comparative studies, as well as in statistical reports on special education issues from later decades, The Netherlands often stands out as reporting higher proportions of students registered in special schools and/or special classes than in most other European countries (Pijl, 2000).

For several decades, Dutch educational policy has been described as a 'two track' policy: one track being regular education and the other special education. It was widely accepted that handicapped pupils and those with learning and/or behaviour problems were referred to separate special schools. The special system was seen as reflecting concern for special needs pupils. However, more and more policy-makers, educators and parents have voiced their concern that the growing number of special education placements is socially unacceptable. An increasing number of parents want their special needs child to be in a regular school or in the same school as his or her siblings, and for him/her to be educated together with non-special needs children. They also consider segregation to be in conflict with widely accepted human rights (Pijl, 2000).

Until recently, financing of special needs education in mainstream schools has been restricted, which has hindered the development of further inclusiveness. Mainstream schools, for instance, find it difficult to cope with special needs pupils in the classroom. The available support is located outside the school building, in special schools and school counselling services. A way out for teachers is to refer such children to these special schools that have more time and expertise available. Special and mainstream education have long worked independently of each other. Special help was only available when pupils attended a special school. This always meant that pupils with special needs had to be taken to the facilities available, instead of vice-versa. Although the regulations for peripatetic teaching introduced in 1995 have resulted in a growing number of special needs pupils attending mainstream schools, these regulations are complex and funding has been available only under strict conditions.

The development of such a segregated educational system may also be seen as part of what is characteristic of the Dutch policy of school establishment. Parents' opportunities for choice of school for their children are greater in this country than in many others. This has also meant that it has been rather easy to start new schools, including special schools for different kinds of disabilities and impairments, and to have them funded by government. According to a recent national overview (Pijl, 2003), special education has ten different categories located in a system of separate schools. In these special schools there are also specialist departments for certain kinds of more severe disorder.

The participation rate varies according to handicap and age group, but the overall proportion of students of primary and secondary school age referred to separate special education is close to 4 per cent. There has been a rather broad acceptance of the need for this segregated approach to organizing special education, and it has not been seen as a problem until recently. For instance, there have not been any parent organizations challenging these issues and trying to change attitudes and opinions towards furthering less exclusion in favour of more inclusive mainstream education. One exception is the advocacy carried out by parents of children with Down's syndrome. During the last decade they have increasingly succeeded, at least in primary schools, in having their children placed in mainstream schools, where they get extra support.

However, there is today a growing concern over the extensive and increasing separation of so-called special needs students. Demands for mainstream education to be more inclusive are being advanced in several arenas in Dutch society, and for many different reasons. The earlier view, that the highly differentiated and extensive special system was a sign of positive concern for students with special needs, has been put under scrutiny instead of being taken for granted. Growing numbers of parents, as well as educators and policy-makers, are of the opinion that segregation has gone too far. In this debate, references to other countries and school systems are common. Questions like 'If it is possible for integration in those countries, why should it not be the case in our country?' are raised. Like parents of children with Down's syndrome, other groups of parents are increasingly demanding better opportunities for their children to be included in neighbourhood schools, together with their siblings and friends.

In the political arena, there have been increasing demands for integration of students with special needs. Their rights to participate in regular education is stressed in, for instance, the Primary Education Acts from 1985 and 1998, as well as in several policy papers. Most important is a 1990 government policy document with the heading 'Weer Samen Naar School' ('Together to school again'). This document is often referred to as a most comprehensive and serious statement in favour of integrating special needs pupils into mainstream schools. At the school system level, measures were taken to reduce the number of different kinds of special schools from ten to four: for those with visual handicaps, communication disorders, physical and mental handicaps, and behaviour problems. Even more important may be the measures taken to bring special and regular schools into closer collaboration by forming regional clusters with one or more special schools for pupils with learning difficulties and the mildly mentally disabled, together with a number of primary schools, twenty-seven on average (Pijl, 2003). These changes also mean that regular schools have to take part in decisions on how to collaborate on these matters, which implies that the earlier 'two track' approach is to be dismantled.

In 1995, the Dutch parliament also changed the rules for funding special education provisions. The main intention was to give schools opportunities to take services to the students instead of transferring students to the services. Successively, funding will be placed at the disposal of clusters instead of special schools. In this system, it is possible for clusters to maintain special schools or to use available resources for other kinds of support within more inclusive mainstream educational settings. Questions of how to allocate resources to special schools and resource centres or how to keep them integrated within mainstream regular schools are no longer to be exclusively dealt with by special education personnel, but become the responsibility for all cluster schools. The same is the case in questions as to which students are identified as in need of support. A key issue, for reorganization, often a stressful one, concerns questions of how to find the best ways to give support according to students' needs. What types of special schools are really needed, and if so, for what reasons? The overriding intention is to make mainstream schools more inclusive. Parliament's decision was made in 1998 and became fully operational from 2002.

Since 1998, special secondary education for learning-disabled and mildly mentally retarded students has also changed, consistent with the 'together to school again' policy. It is no longer part of separate special education, but a part of the 1998 Secondary Education Act. Secondary special education is reconstructed into pre-vocational secondary education, and special education support ensures that as many students as possible obtain secondary school qualifications. For those who, in spite of having considerable support, cannot reach a certificate level, there will be practical training courses to qualify them for low-skilled jobs.

A regional referral committee decides on eligibility for learning support or practical training. This committee also develops and applies criteria for placements, usually related to IQ range, level of learning backwardness and/or social-emotional problems. After a four-year phase-in period, this support structure was fully implemented from 2002.

Until recently, students with sensory, physical, and mental disabilities or behavioural problems could not receive services without being admitted to full-time special schools. A policy paper from 1996, the 'Back Pack', however, outlined plans to stop financing places in special schools and, instead, linked funding of special services to the students, regardless of the type of school. This is referred to as *demand-oriented* funding. As an important consequence, parents have more influence in making placement decisions for their children. Parents and students can choose a school and they can decide together with school personnel how to use student-bound resources. Even if a regular school cannot be forced to accept such a student, the changed policy requires the school to give good reasons for not doing so. This means a changed perspective, relational instead of categorical, in dealing with inclusion issues, with a requirement to express reasons and motives for exclusion instead of the earlier practice of trying to find motives for inclusion.

Both the new funding system and the re-organization of special education, including converting the many different special schools into four so-called expertise centres, were approved by Parliament in late 2002. More decisive legislation was accepted and the full implementation is now under way.

There are also fairly new plans for reconstructing parts of secondary special education into lower secondary mainstream education. Some pilot studies are in progress and experiences from those projects are supposed to steer further development and implementation. At present, however, there are few signs of success in this. The position of special schools is reported to be rather unclear, though. There is still much to be done before the innovative plans could be said to be working in practice.

In teacher training, there is an introductory component that includes education of students with special needs. Government policies also require a more extensive knowledge within the field as part of the programme, but this has been difficult to implement because of an overly full curriculum. Related to this is the fact that a growing number of teachers have qualified for the special education certificate, although this is not obligatory. There are also training programmes for so-called *begeleiders* (Special Education Needs Coordinators) in progress at some universities and colleges.

Special education research

The Dutch education system has a centralized evaluation policy that includes the qualities of special education. Important instruments are school inspections and national assessments. Another evaluative instrument is special education research, although the amount of research directly referred to or reported on current issues is very restricted.

In the national overview referred to earlier (Pijl, 2003), it is evident that the reforms have so far not been easy to implement, including the development of inclusive education. There are many obstacles to be overcome. At the same time, no more comprehensive evaluative research studies are planned (personal correspondence with Sip Jan Pijl, GION, University of Gröningen).

Karsten *et al.* (2001) found few differences when at-risk students in regular education settings were compared with their counterparts in special schools. This was in contrast to broadly accepted expectations that special school placement was a necessity for these students. They also reported great variation in most relevant aspects within both groups of students. Pijl and van den Bos (2001) report an extensive questionnaire study on working conditions for *begeleiders* and their role and success in assisting regular education to become more inclusive. As a rule, they met many difficulties and obstacles and on many occasions they felt more or less alone in their strivings. Most often they thought that they had too little time allocated for their manifold duties. They declared their main duty to be coordinating work with regular and special education teachers and to giving support needed to students as an integrated part of regular teaching. In that sense, they would take a proactive role in the further development of education to become more inclusive. However, this role was very often not welcomed by regular teachers, who were used to relying on special educators to take care of the problem in separate classes or schools. A consequence of this, and of the restricted time given to the *begeleiders*, tended to be that they took a more reactive role instead, giving most of their time and resources to individually focused special support in traditional special education ways. They often felt that they themselves had to take the whole burden for developing inclusiveness, which became too much and an impossible a task for them (see also Emanuelsson, 2001).

In many ways, the Netherlands can be said to be rather slow in striving for inclusion, compared with many other Western European countries. There are several reasons for this. First, for reasons dealt with above, the special school system was far more extensive than in most other countries. There were also many characteristics of the Dutch educational system that could be seen as favouring such an extension of special schools and separated special education. In that sense, traditions in the Netherlands and ways of thinking and understanding special needs education have been deeply rooted in a categorical perspective of understanding and reasoning until very recently. However, this has changed during the past decade, and such changes are working parallel to and are also supportive of the reforms introduced by government and authorities. Statistically based comparative studies from international organizations, etc., have also been of great importance for changing opinions, not least among politicians and policy-makers, as well as parents of students with special needs (Pijl, 2003). However, most policy and reform documents are still founded on a categorical perspective, especially so in the identification of special needs. As a rule, they are considered to be individual-bound characteristics and diagnoses. This may be problematic in relation to achieving the aims of inclusive education.

There seems to be a great need for comprehensive and critically evaluative research studies of the implementation of inclusive education in the Netherlands. Given that the country is rather slower in this development than other Western European countries, it is a challenging task for researchers to plan such studies on a comparative basis.

Highly related to the above comments about the still dominating categorical perspective in dealing with special education issues, is a comment given in a national report on the Netherlands (Pijl, 2000):

> In general, parents appear in favour of current integration policy. However, substantial numbers of both mainstream and special education teachers as well as some parents of pupils with special educational needs question integration. Whilst not reflecting the push for more integration in principle, they believe special needs pupils are better off in segregated settings, as they need the highly differentiated and therefore more effective teaching and counselling available in special education provision. In accordance with this view of the 'specialness' of special education, they consider pupils to have profound and special problems which make mainstream schooling inappropriate.
>
> (p. 6)

Moreover, these kinds of worries and opinions point in the direction of a great need for rather extensive research on necessary preconditions for, as well as obstacles to, developing a more inclusive education.

Greece

The development of special needs education in Greece is rather similar to that of other industrial countries in the West, even if its political influences to a high degree originate from Britain. Vlachou-Balafouti and Zoniou-Sideris (2000) claim that, although the political rhetoric asserts the right of vulnerable children to receive high-quality education, the Greek education system has not yet arrived at a stage of democratization where this can be implemented. The authors claim that there are several reasons behind this, such as:

> serious socio-political and economic problems associated predominantly with a number of successive, devastating wars. Given the above context,

a strong discourse on defectology in the child and psychopathology was developed which strengthened, and was strengthened by, the increased powers attributed to the medical profession. The strong influence of the defectology discourse on issues of deviance has been until now one of the main models of resistance towards the creation of more inclusive educational communities.

(p. 31)

The consequences of defectology as a basic idea of understanding students' difficulties, combined with the ambition to support disabled children, led to the establishment of different kinds of private special schools in the country. One important reason for this was the conviction that ordinary schools were incapable of dealing with these children. On the pattern of the British Warnock Report, 'special needs' was designed to conceptualize the needs of these children, even if ten categories of disability were used simultaneously as a basis for placement in different kinds of special schools. Nicodemos (1994) estimated the number of pupils with 'special needs' at about 200,000, among whom only about 14,000 had access to special educational support, almost without exception in special classes or groups. As the total number of students within the compulsory school system, according to Meijer (1999), was fully 1.6 million, this means that less than 1 per cent received special educational support.

The ideology of integration, according to Vlachou-Balafouti and Zoniou-Sideris (2000), has been difficult to implement, primarily because the vast majority of students with special needs were left to their fate in the ordinary classes. The authors write that

the fact that the vast majority of children with special educational needs are in ordinary schools does not justify political claims of supporting integration. It rather indicates that the official definition of integration remains at the level of locational integration. But locational integration alone, in practice, means total rejection.

(p. 36)

Also, research in special needs education has accordingly become focused on how to render special schools more effective by developing and adapting teaching methods to the needs of these students. Priority has been given to research within the so-called psycho-medical perspective in order to meet students' learning and behavioural difficulties. The need for the development of pedagogical strategies in order to meet the needs of students with special educational needs has led to national research projects, often conducted within the EU framework. However, Vlachou-Balafouti and Zoniou-Sideris (2000) claim that 'the area of special education has started to become a developing industry with the involvement of more professional groups which endeavour to establish and develop their interests' (p. 36).

EU membership has involved a dominant Western World orientation within the field of special needs education, followed by an official aim of complying with the recommendations of the Salamanca Declaration (UNESCO, 1994). Moreover, Greek universities have been particularly active within EU-supported research projects. The strongly centralized university system also facilitates orientation towards fields in need of empirical and theoretical development, as government has the power to direct research towards neglected areas. The field of special needs education belongs to these prioritized areas.

As indicated above, special needs education in Greece has its roots within a psycho-medical perspective. This orientation has involved scepticism regarding the question of whether the establishment of an inclusive system is possible or not. These doubts become recognized also in other national contexts, where attempts have been made to change direction in favour of a more inclusive educational system. The question, then, is if and how it may be possible to 'integrate' disabled children into mainstream classes, rather than how schools can adjust to the needs of all pupils. Advocates of different disability categories and parents' organizations often act as supporters of segregated educational settings and for the expansion of the special school sector.

During the 1980s and 1990s, post-secondary education in Greece extended considerably. This development has also involved special needs education and research at most universities in the country. Supported by government funding, the University of Thessaly in Volos has established Greece's first department for special education. This should be understood as a manifestation of a national interest in the development of research in special needs education. Influenced by British inclusive education movements, the visions of the department have been summarized as follows:

- To educate and train the specialized staff that our country requires in order to fulfill its duty towards children with special needs.
- To ascertain the possibility of equal educational opportunities for special children through complete scientific knowledge and instruction and through specialization of their educators according to the latest data of modern science.
- To cultivate and promote scientific knowledge in the field of special education with academic and applied teaching and research in our country.

(Department of Special Education, University of Thessaly, 2000)

However, the above visions indicate that the roots in defectology still dominate special needs education, even in one of the most prominent universities in Greece.

At Kapodistrian University in Athens, some researchers of special education take a critical standpoint towards the dominant research paradigms in
special needs education. Athina Zoniou-Sideris (2000) is one of the
researchers in Greece who strongly supports an inclusive perspective in
which 'the complicated procedure of disabled pupils' incorporation in public
schools' becomes focused (p. 36). In the critical analyses of the preparedness
and inclination of Greek education to work in the direction of inclusive
education, alternative strategies for the development of special needs education as a vital part of the entire educational system become essential. The
establishment of a 'meta-modern' school is therefore required, which
involves a pedagogy adapted to the needs of *all* students. In such schools,
the categorization of students' disabilities is toned down and innovative
solutions introduced within the existing educational framework.

This understanding of pupil's difficulties is also salient at Aristotle
University in Thessalonica, as well as at the University of Crete, both of
which challenge the traditional roles of special teachers. It is no longer practicable to call for experts as soon as problems occur. Instead, regular
teachers need to widen their range of pupil acceptance, thereby supporting
the variation of children's differences. However, if changes in the directions
mentioned above are realized, it will be necessary to adapt the School Act,
national curricula and teacher training in such a way that inclusion becomes
the hallmark of change. Even if this is also the official policy, the roots of
special needs education in defectological or psycho-medical thinking most
likely entail a protracted process of educational change.

Concluding comments

In the introduction to this chapter, we referred to two conflicting and
competing theoretical perspectives for understanding challenges and
dilemmas within the field of special education. The two perspectives,
labelled *categorical* and *relational*, are also of crucial relevance for understanding the contextualization of inclusive education. In all the Western
European countries referred to in this chapter, the political and policy
steering documents and regulations are based upon understanding and
thinking with roots in the relational perspective. Attempts to implement
inclusive education and processes of development towards more inclusiveness in national school systems demand that kind of theory-based
understanding. In that sense, the relational perspective may be seen as a
necessary precondition for inclusive education development. This is also
clearly reflected in political and policy documents from all the countries;
moreover, they clearly stress the need for education and teaching to be inclusive instead of segregative and exclusive. In all four countries, however, the
tradition within the school systems is a categorical perspective based on a
'two track' organization, with special education as one and regular educa-

tion as the other track. Historically, the two tracks have been more or less completely separated from each other. This tradition has lately been increasingly challenged in favour of the relational-based inclusive policies and regulations – 'one school for all' or 'together to school again'. The similarities are more striking than the differences between countries. What differs most clearly is the starting point, where the Scandinavian countries were earlier than Greece and the Netherlands. In all countries, but more clearly so in the latter two, international recommendations and agreements like the 1994 Salamanca Declaration and the 1991 Jomtien report are referred to as demanding and challenging for national politics and policy development.

With the exception of some rather rough descriptive statistical reports, there is very little special or other education research done on inclusive education matters. This is another thing that all countries have in common, a state of the art that must be judged as alarming and demanding. For instance, there are very few studies to be found on processes of development in schools or student groups when they try to move from being exclusive towards becoming more inclusive. As a rule, studies are restricted both in scope and even more so according to time perspectives. One reason for this situation must be a consequence of the fact that most special education research is still mainly anchored in the traditional categorical perspective. As long as this perspective is the dominant one, the most important critical and challenging research questions to be studied are at great risk of never being formulated and dealt with. Here we can see an essential part of an explanation of why results from special education research are, as a rule, very seldom referred to in connection with inclusive education policies and strivings. This pattern is more or less evident in all the countries considered in this chapter, and it is no less serious when similar things can be said about education research more broadly.

When inclusive education is dealt with as an issue within the categorical perspective, this leads to certain contradictory consequences for the development of inclusiveness. This is also a common problem that can be recognized in all four countries. One evident consequence is that the issue and problem of inclusion tends to be understood as belonging to special educators and as their special responsibility and task. They are supposed to make students who are diagnosed as special or deviant suitable for being included for their sake, but not in order that regular education might become more inclusive. Now and then, one hears talk about some students as being the ones 'included', and it is seen as a special education task to adapt students to this. The same pattern is often also seen in so-called evaluative studies, which, as a rule, are restricted to the same individual-bound perspective. These are merely examples of a complete misunderstanding of the real meaning and challenge of inclusive education as such. They might be understood as examples of what Haug (1998) refers to as 'segregating integration'. One further consequence from this categorical-dominated view and understanding is that evaluative studies of what is happening in so-called including classrooms will never be done. Nor will they be asked for in regular education, because of the problem as such being seen as a responsibility of special education. Such a category-based process and thinking is often still practised in all the countries, and it can be seen as an important explanation for why real inclusiveness, in terms of not excluding, is proceeding at such a slow rate. Sometimes, for the same reasons, one can see a kind of backlash pattern, with some schools developing an even more segregated 'two track' perspective again.

Inclusive education understood and dealt with in a relational perspective means challenges and tasks common for whole working teams, a shared responsibility for everyone. Studies reported from what is judged as successfully developing inclusive education very often talk about some kind of cooperative ways of working. For instance, Lundgren and Persson (2003) found such cooperation to be a crucial factor for developing education to be more inclusive in the schools studied. This is presented as a necessary precondition, both in personnel teams and in classroom teaching and work. The lack of research on these kinds of development processes in schools and classrooms may have contributed negatively to the contextualization of inclusive education. This can then be seen as one reason for the evident gap between education policies and school reality, which can be recognized in all the countries.

An interesting issue can be identified, perhaps most clearly in the context of the Netherlands. There, one can occasionally see that motives for striving for inclusion are understood to be so self-evident that the onus is put on schools and personnel to clearly express the reasons for exclusion, if judged to be necessary, instead. Such developments must be interpreted as indicating that the whole issue of inclusive education has moved into the appropriate perspective of understanding – the relational. This is, of course, an oversimplified way of dealing with the problem of discrepancies between politics and policies on the one hand, and school reality on the other. However, a necessary precondition for research to constructively contribute to school development are studies on challenging issues and questions based on and formulated from a more convinced choice of a relational perspective. This does not mean that special education research should be carried out only on premises dictated by politicians and authorities. On the contrary, the need for critical research, for instance on motives for inclusion and/or exclusion, is an essential element of what is highly necessary, again in all the countries. Similarities and differences identified between the countries are in themselves good incentives for making such studies comparative.

Opportunities for parents to choose schools for their children is another interesting issue in relation to inclusive education. Such parental choice puts individual schools into the market place, where they have to compete in attracting 'customers', i.e. students. We have not identified any case in any of the four countries, where a school has used its capability to be inclusive for all children as its 'trade mark'. In periods of increasing numbers of new special schools, as in Sweden today and the Netherlands in the 1980s, there is also a kind of differentiation of the market, which may be of certain interest for special educators. A research and evaluation issue of great interest for increasing knowledge and understanding of inclusive, as well as exclusive, processes in the school system, would be studies of what kind of schools special education teachers tend to work in and for what reasons. But, even if they tend to stay in the same school, it is an increasingly important and interesting question as to what roles they take or are given. Development of inclusive education demands proactive roles rooted in a relational perspective and supported by school principals. As referred to earlier, in all four countries, reactive roles are, instead, more common among special education teachers and special needs coordinators. The consequence is that schools remain locked into the categorical, traditional, segregative and exclusive way of teaching and working – the 'two track' model.

In all four countries, it is possible to identify a common pattern in development processes. When schools are put under stress, or if teachers and other personnel have such feelings, this tends to work against the development of inclusive education. Such stress factors are, for example, school budget cuts, new national assessment systems, changed systems for evaluating students' work, and increasing competition between schools. In many schools, such issues encourage them to remain exclusive and segregative and/or to return to a more traditional way of working, which feels safer. This tendency must not be taken to mean that if or when such stress factors are eliminated or reduced then inclusive education will dramatically flourish as a result. It has been documented that diminishing stress automatically leads to changes in opinions and ways of working. But to the contrary, studies in Sweden, for example, show that there are clear tendencies for schools to adjust their traditional ways of working to new preconditions rather than take opportunities from the altered conditions to change their organization and working models. As Sweden is not unique in these respects, this knowledge may also be seen as a challenging problem area for further research, as well as creating obstacles to the development of inclusive education.

Western European countries are often internationally referred to as good examples of well developed inclusion in their schools. There may be reasons to be found for this, but at the same time it is of utmost importance to recognize that this is far from the dominating pattern. There is much to be done, even if one can find good examples, and maybe also well developed school regulations and policies. A conclusion drawn from experiences in most of the countries is that it is more fruitful to talk about inclusion and inclusive education in terms of dilemmas and processes and not in terms of complete solutions. This is also in accordance with the relational-based theory. Inclusion and inclusive education are, as we have learned from experiences in four Western European countries, undergoing developmental processes in groups and schools. The far-reaching goal is better-functioning togetherness, where exclusion as such is rendered unnecessary and undesirable. The incentives for such school goals or aims are to be found in overruling political and policy discussions taken by majorities in parliaments and the like. As such, the goals can never be seen as guaranteed forever, nor can they automatically be expected to be fully accepted by every member of a working team in a school or among students and their parents. Developing inclusive education means taking these kinds of challenges as dilemmas and to see them as important issues in ongoing schoolwork and learning.

The above presentation of the intentions and practices of inclusive education in four different Western European countries produces a complex picture. The basic reasons for inclusive policies differ from country to country, the history of inclusive education is not the same, and, moreover, the practices differ.

For some time, the two Nordic countries have adopted integration, and later inclusion, as an ideal for education. At one time, they were probably among the world's leading countries in formulating these ideals, and, later, in trying to realize them in schools. The reasons for this seem to be a consequence of what has been called the 'Scandinavian welfare system', in which the state takes care of the population by providing material security and satisfying psychological and cultural needs through social security, health and education. An important basis for this policy has been a very strong emphasis on equality and equity. The process of developing these welfare systems began early in the twentieth century, and accelerated especially after 1945.

The two other countries considered, the Netherlands and Greece, have had quite different pathways because of other political regimes and ideals that have dominated their policies. They both have longer histories of categorically based, separated (two track) special education systems. Until very recently, this separation has also been clearly accepted by most parents, as well as by school personnel and authorities. In the case of Greece, traditional influences from defectology have been particularly strong and resistant to change.

Following different tracks, the four countries have come to formulate inclusive education as an ideal, albeit one that is coming under great strain. Inclusion as an ideal is based on values indicating that people should take care of each other. It means accepting that some of us are not able to contribute as much as others, but still have the right to a decent life and in fellowship with all others. From certain perspectives, it is quite surprising that inclusion has become an ideal, contrasting as strongly as it does with the increasing market orientation and globalization that is taking place. These latter trends represent other values: competition, economic profit, individualization, privatization, and, in some cases, even personal egoism. There is a shift of orientation from state responsibility for all, to the single individual's responsibility for oneself. Therefore, it could be said that welfare systems are unwinding, which may bode ill for inclusive education.

References

Dahl, M., Tangerud, H. and Vislie, L. (1982). *Integration of handicapped pupils in compulsory education in Norway*. Oslo: Universitetsforlaget.

Department of Special Education, University of Thessaly (2000). *Foundation and profile of the Department*. Promemoria.

Dyson, A. (1999). *International trends in special education research*. Keynote paper presented at the Research Council of Norway's Conference, Oslo, Norway, 4 May 1999.

Emanuelsson, I. (1983). *Verksamhet bland elever med svårigheter eller arbete med elevers svårigheter? En kunskapsöversikt* [Working among students with disabilities or working with students' disabilities? A review]. Stockholm; Skolöverstyrelsen.

——(1998). 'Closing reflections'. In P. Haug and J. Tøssebro (eds) *Theoretical perspectives on special education* (pp. 165–172). Kristiansand: Høyskoleforlaget.

——(2001). 'Reactive versus proactive support coordinator roles: an international comparison'. *European Journal of Special Needs Education*, 16(2), 133–142.

Emanuelsson, I., Persson, B. and Rosenqvist, J. (2001). *Specialpedagogisk forskning – en kunskapsöversikt*. Stockholm: Skolverket.

Fulcher, G. (1999). *Disabling policies? A comparative approach to education policy and disability*. Sheffield: Philip Armstrong Publications.

Haug, P. (1997). 'Status for spesialpedagogisk forsking i Noreg'. *Spesialpedagogikk*, 1, 31–40.

——(1998). 'Integration and special education research in Norway'. *International Journal of Educational Research*, 29(2), 119–130.

——(1999). *Spesialundervisning i grunnskolen. Grunnlag, utvikling og innhald*. Oslo: Abstrakt.

——(2000). *Regimes of special education research: Trends in special education research in Norway*. Paper presented at the European Educational Research Association, Edinburgh, 20–23 September.

Karsten, S., Peetsma, T., Roeleveld, J. and Vergeer, M. (2001). 'The Dutch policy of integration put to the test: Differences in academic and psychosocial development of pupils in special and mainstream education'. *European Journal of Special Needs Education*, 16(3), 193–203.

KUF (1996). *The Curriculum for the 10-year compulsory school*. Oslo: Ministry of Church, Education and Research.

Lindensjö, B. and Lundgren, U.P. (2000). *Utbildningspolitik och politisk styrning*. Stockholm: HLS.

Lundgren, M. and Persson, B. (2003). *Proactive and reactive work. Collaboration as idea and problem with children and youth at risk*. Paper presented at the International Week in Bremen, 23–27 June 2003. URL: http://brs.leeds.ac.uk/cgi-bin/grs_engine

Meijer, C. (1999). *Financing of special needs education*. Middelfart: European Agency for Development in Special Needs Education.

Moen, V. and øie, A. (1994). *Spesialundervisning. En kartlegging av undervisningen for barn og unge med sarskilte behov i grunnskolen og i den videregaende skolen*.

[*Special education. A mapping of training of children and youth with special needs in primary and secondary education*]. Report no. 9403. Volda: Moreforsking.

Nicodemos, A. (1994). *Special education in Greece today*. Information Bulletin of Special Education. Directorate of Special Education. Athens: OEDB.

OECD (1984). *The handicapped adolescent. Integration of handicapped pupils in compulsory education in Norway. An appraisal of current policies and practices*. Paris: OECD/CERI.

Persson, B. (1998). *Den motsägelsefula specialpedagogiken. [The contradictions of special education]*. Special Educational Reports no. 11. Göteborg University, Department of Education.

Pijl. S.J. (2000). Special education in the Netherlands. In C.R. Reynolds and E. Fletcher–Janzen (eds) *Encyclopedia of Special Education* (2nd edn) (pp. 1253–1256). New York. John Wiley.

——(2003). *National Overview. Netherlands*. URL: http://www.european-agency.org/national_pages/netherlands/national_overview/no01.html

Pijl, S.J. and van den Bos, K. (2001). Redesigning regular education support in the Netherlands. *European Journal of Special Needs Education*, 16(2), 111–119.

Rosenqvist, J. (1993). Special education in Sweden. *European Journal of Special Needs Education*, 8(1), 59–73.

——(1994). *Specialpedagogiska forskningsmiljöer – En analyserande översikt*. Göteborgs universitet, institutionen för pedagogik.

——(2000). Current trends in special education research in Sweden: Outline of research about the school for students with severe learning disabilities in Sweden. Paper presented to the European Conference on Educational Research, Edinburgh, Scotland, 20–23 September.

Solity, J. (1992). *Special education*. London: Cassell.

Stasinos, D.P. (1992). Special education in Greece: Historical, current, and future trends. *International Journal of Special Education*, 7(1), 42–48.

UNESCO (1994). *The Salamanca Statement and Framework on Special Needs Education*. Paris: UNESCO.

Vislie, L. (2003). 'From integration to inclusion: Focusing global trends and changes in the western European societies'. *European Journal of Special Needs Education*, 18(1), 17–35.

Vlachou-Balafouti, A. and Zoniou-Sideris, A. (2000). 'Greek policy practices in the area of special/inclusive education'. In F. Armstrong, D. Armstrong and L. Barton (eds) *Inclusive education: Policy, contexts and comparative perspectives* (pp. 27–41). London: David Fulton.

Ware, L. (2000). 'Sunflowers, enchantment and empires: Reflections on inclusive education in the United States'. In F. Armstrong, D. Armstrong and L. Barton (eds) *Inclusive education: Policy, contexts and comparative perspectives* (pp. 42–59). London: David Fulton.

Zoniou-Sideris, A. (2000). *The necessity of incorporation: Speculations and perspectives*. Promemoria. Volos: University of Thessaly.

Chapter 7

Education and the politics of recognition

Inclusive education – an Australian snapshot

Roger Slee

Writing about schooling and education in Australia for an international audience is not an easy task. Now resident in Canada, I appreciate it is no less difficult for colleagues in any jurisdiction. The view from the outside often misses complexities obscured by distance. Having previously met with senior officials from the Ministry of Education in Toronto, who patiently described their system of schooling and recent reforms to curriculum and the surveillance and improvement of the workforce, is not sufficient preparation for someone working in education in Quebec. For many, this is obvious; others may not appreciate the extent to which a discussion about Canadian politics, culture and education requires territorial caveats, qualifications and distinctions to render the story credible for an informed Canadian or Quebecois.

Many years ago, a colleague at a sociology of education conference in Sheffield properly pulled me up short for talking confidently, and as it happened superficially, about education in the UK. Once again, what do we mean when we speak of the UK? Even if we were to narrow the gaze to England, there are profound differences between the character and operation of schools in the leafy suburbs of Surrey compared with those that fight for space and opportunity in Islington, Southwark and Deptford; or between and within Hertfordshire and Newcastle.

So, too, for Australia. Schooling is not the same experience in the Aboriginal community school of Cherbourg in Queensland as it is for children in Wesley College in the Melbourne suburb of Prahran. And here I traverse the geopolitics of location and isolation, cultural identity, privilege and disadvantage, and public versus private schooling. However, while I will provide a thumbnail sketch of some of the broad features of the organization of schooling across Australia, I will not aim at the definitive primer – the *Lonely Planet Guide to Schooling in Australia*.

This is not to suggest that we jettison the project of international comparison in education. Following Delamont (1992), Ainscow (1999) reminds us of the value in making the strange familiar and the familiar strange to throw new light, new possibilities for interpretation and intervention, on our own turf. This remains the case, but there is recognition that how we pursue this has differential cultural impacts. Presenting and re-presenting the world as a laboratory for social scientific observation and analysis is not a benign project. Soto (2004) forcefully reminds us of the deep structure of power and powerlessness in researching and professing about inclusion and exclusion:

> Leela Ghandi's (2000) description is apt for how the 'othering' of the third world (in our case women of colour and our allies) can ultimately signify that 'we become someone's private zoo' (p. 85). The conception of a private zoo is powerful in helping to explicate the realities of voice and power within the complexities of cross-cultural research. How can we chart a liberating path leading toward a decolonizing space for research in cross-cultural contexts?
>
> (p. ix)

It is important to follow her argument further. The warning for authors in this volume is manifest, and manifold:

> For most scholars of colour and their allies we are the 'colonized', feeling the consequences of the Eurocentric, scientifically driven epistemologies in which issues of power and voice are drowned by the powerful 'majority' players reflecting the 'master's' ideology. For us, *there is no postcolonial*, as we live our daily realities in suffocating spaces forbidding our perspectives, our creativity, and our wisdom.
>
> (p. ix, original emphasis)

So, as Soto proclaims, the challenge is that we not collapse into essentialized accounts of 'disability' and 'inclusive education' and fail to acknowledge and interrogate the complexities that struggle within, across and against nation states (Appadurai, 1996). Here I take counsel from David Harvey who, while accepting the fluidity of identity (1996, p. 7) and rejecting the rigid Cartesian proclivities of 'cognitive maps' and traditional binaries, also rejects a collapse into post-structural relativism that defies intervention. He moves 'gently in contra-flow', suggesting that the reduction of everything to fluxes and flows limits the repertoire of response. To militate against the dismissal of narrative and political activism as the imposition of a supra-will, he advocates a *new metaphysics* that makes possible both values and political action. Might this foreshadow a return to critical pragmatism (Cherryholmes, 1988), where the boundaries of the *realpolitik* are heeded in shaping a theory for subversive impacts? And thenceforth forging an alignment between pragmatism and multidisciplinary analyses? In this respect, he is perhaps sympathetic with the spirit of, though not as strident as, Terry Eagleton (2003, pp. 221–222) who, in *After Theory*, asserts the demise of the small narratives of postmodernism and challenges us to *chance our arm* and break away from recounting narratives of class, race and gender to explore a new global narrative of capitalism, along with the war on terrorism.

Confronting the question of 'the just production of just geographical differences', David Harvey (1996, p. 5) contends that 'we need critical ways to think about how differences in ecological, cultural, economic, political and social conditions get produced ... and we also need ways to evaluate the justice/injustice of the differences so produced'. This is the essence of what inclusive education as a political and educational manifesto is morphing into. For 'meaningful political action (and, for that matter, even meaningful analysis) cannot proceed without some embedded notions of value, if only a determination as to what is or is not important to analyze intellectually let alone to struggle for politically' (Harvey, 1996, p. 10).

For some time now I have asserted a distinction between inclusive education as a technical fix, through elaborate policy ensembles, to assimilate disabled children into the unchanging field of regular schooling by adjoining special educational base camps and strategic intervention (swat) teams to the school and classroom (Slee, 1996a). In contradistinction, I have argued for the recognition of inclusive education as *cultural work* (hooks, 1994) in conjunction with the disability rights movement to envision new social and institutional relations. The former demands the latter. Peter McLaren puts it thus:

> Diversity that somehow constitutes itself as a harmonious ensemble of benign cultural spheres is a conservative and liberal model of multiculturalism that, in my mind, deserves to be jettisoned because, when we try to make culture an undisturbed space of harmony and agreement where social relations exist with cultural forms of uninterrupted accords we subscribe to a form of social amnesia in which we forget that all knowledge is forged in histories that are played out in the field of social antagonisms.
>
> (McLaren, quoted in hooks, 1994, p. 31)

Commencing as a rejection of traditional special education discursive practices and a struggle to insert the social model of disability (Tomlinson, 1982; Barton, 1987; Oliver, 1990) into new accounts of educational failure and disablement, inclusive education provided a bridge to the growing critical sociology of schooling. Consistent with Harvey's *new metaphysics*, inclusive education attempted to form a statement of value as a platform both for research and political action. This was lost on many traditional special educators such as Kauffman and Hallahan (1995), as Ellen Brantlinger reminds us (1997), who – in an astonishing act of occupational blindness (Connell, 1987) – argued that by declaring its ideological position, inclusive education forfeited research validity. That research can be *partisan*, and as reliable and verifiable as the so-called social scientific empiricists is not a new and untested proposition (Troyna, 1994). Zizek's (1994, p. 17) maxim that ideology is 'at work in everything we experience as reality' is apposite.

Inclusive education is a broad church to which a disparate, sometimes desperate, congregation is now attracted. Moreover, it has gained political legitimacy, as the discourse of inclusion and exclusion figures prominently in the policy scripts of 'third way' type governments (see also Chapter 4 in this volume). Labor government ministers of education across the Australian states and territories now speak with ease about their inclusive education initiatives. Critical scrutiny soon reveals divergence in the practices and understandings they describe. This chapter will consider whether the growing political respectability and frequent usage of the term represents either theoretical coherence or authentic progress towards more inclusive schools.

Comprising two sections, this chapter will first examine the development and atrophy of the field of inclusive education as a prelude to looking at the limits of government and education reform, in *my representation* of some trends in Australian education.

Inclusive education – substantive or functional rationale, vibrant new metaphysics, or flaccid liberal eduspeak?

Death sentence: the contraction of educational discourse

Former Australian prime ministerial speechwriter Don Watson (2003), commences his book *Death Sentence: The Decay of Public Language*, with a quote from Winston Smith, the erstwhile campaigner for truth in George Orwell's (1949) novel *Nineteen Eighty-Four*: 'Don't you see that the whole aim of Newspeak is to narrow the range of thought?'.

Having set the scene with the spectre of the Orwellian state, Watson assesses the constriction of public discussion and debate in Australian political and managerial discourse. Government and bureaucracy attempt to eliminate complexity by reducing issues to a digestible form for the electorate – to media grabs and one-page 'ministerials'. Buzzwords and clichés form sentences from which all meaning is wrung. They are then mobilized to dull the civic imagination. Public discussion is reduced to invented words, memorable couplets and staccato phrases that assume an agreed meaning and make for easy recitation. This default vocabulary (Slee, 1996a) is deployed to saturation level. Indeed, as Watson (2003, p. 15) declares: 'This kind of writing is now endemic: it is learned, practised, expected, demanded'.

'Value-added', 'benchmarking with world's best practice', 'flexible implementation', 'community partnerships', 'empowerment', 'performance management on core accountabilities', 'collaborative decision-making processes', 'management by results' and 'stakeholder society' is a random selection from management and government lexicons that have invaded and colonized education discourse. (As an aside, I recently met with a publisher who told me that management of his organization referred to academic journals as 'content platforms'.)

Focussing upon the rise of the discursive practices of the burgeoning education management industry, Thrupp and Willmott (2003) explore the 'limits to post-welfarist education reform'. Theirs is a study of the workings of the 'death sentence' in the field of education. The discourse of performativity (Ball, 2001) – competition, choice and standards – as mobilized through the neo-liberal education policy of New Labour – takes up the conservative mantle and is characterized by a number of key themes and features:

- The intensification of competition between schools around parent choice based on student results amplifies and reinforces social division (Ball, 1998; Gewirtz *et al.*, 1995). Oversubscribed high socio-economic status (SES) schools are given permission through a quasi-market to become selective of their student cohort. Undersubscribed low SES schools may exercise no such choice and often 'enter a spiral of decline' (Thrupp and Willmott, 2003, p. 39). There is, as Thrupp and Willmott (2003) observe, a social intensification of school intakes. Brantlinger (2003) traces this process of middle-class choice-making and its destructive impact upon schooling for working-class children in a North American neighbourhood to demonstrate this global convergence of schooling as an artefact of the marketplace. The implication of this for 'risky students' (Slee, 1998), those who are likely to jeopardize school results on academic performance league tables, and therefore for notions of inclusive education, are stark.
- Paradoxically, diversity policies frequently reveal themselves in the creation of niche or charter schools (Fuller, 2000). Unable to compete in the high-stakes academic main game of schooling, some low SES schools reconstruct themselves to cater for 'special populations' (Slee, 1998). As these fragile accommodations continue to be tested, the state invests heavily in a holding exercise where difficult students are kept away from schools in the rapidly growing panoply of alternative sites and referral units (Parsons and Castle, 1998).
- The mandating of national curriculum according to narrowly defined notions of academic outcomes, enforced through high-stakes standardized testing which employs limited understandings of the forms of and potential for educational assessment (Black, 1998; Gipps, 1994; Goldstein and Lewis, 1996), is not the friend of educational inclusion. Typically, there is a retreat to the disciplinary canons within defined cultural parameters that sponsor students from privileged backgrounds, jettison diversity and marginalize working-class and minority-culture

students (Brantlinger, 2003). Moreover, the claims about driving standards up rings hollow. Longitudinal research conducted by Ladwig, Lingard, Luke, Hayes and Mills to test the relationship between school-based management and improved student outcomes, reported a distraction of school management by administration and management to comply with centrally driven imperatives, as opposed to providing leadership in curriculum development and the improvement of pedagogy (Education Queensland, 2002). As a result, the performance across the state-wide cohort of schools revealed that schools were moderately successful in providing caring environments, but less than successful in establishing 'intellectual demandingness', student engagement in learning, and in teaching for diversity. Similarly, Thrupp and Willmott (2003) apply a critical analysis to the claims of government, suggesting tendencies towards overstatement and methodological problems behind the interpretations given when reporting student academic outcomes.

It is against this policy, and discursive backdrop, that I want to discuss inclusive education as a field of education theory and practices. While there exists a call for 'joined-up thinking', there remains a tendency towards reductionism when talking about inclusive education policy. Here, we need to unravel and reveal the complexities that are concealed within 'inclusive education'. Let me separate a number of interrelated issues as I attempt to establish some of the difficulties that education jurisdictions, and indeed education researchers and minority group activists, must contend with in the pursuit of inclusive education. I will concentrate on major tensions in inclusive education as a field of social theory and as an education reform agenda. These tensions arise from the trends towards reductionism and disconnection.

Scope, focus and multiple modernisms

Although there is an indivisibility of theory and action, there is a need to consider the way in which inclusive education presents as bodies of thought, and the problems therein, as a prelude to a consideration of inclusive education's contribution to education reform agendas. In order to do this I will draw from a recent essay by Edward Said (2000), 'Travelling theory reconsidered', from his collection of essays published under the title of *Reflections on Exile and Other Literary and Cultural Essays*. Said (2000, p. 426) discusses the way in which 'theories sometimes "travel" to other times and situations, in the process of which they lose some of their original power and rebelliousness'. He demonstrates his point by drawing upon Georg Lukács's theory of reification. In its original offering, reification was a powerful critique of hegemonic discursive instruments of oppression. At the time of writing, Lukács delivered an incisive set of conceptual tools for better understanding historically specific sets of social relations as a lever for political agency. Said's argument, not surprisingly, is clearest in his own words:

> the first time a human experience is recorded and then given a theoretical formulation, its force comes from being directly connected to and organically provoked by real historical circumstances. Later versions of the theory cannot replicate its original power; because the situation has quieted down and changed, the theory is degraded and subdued, made into a relatively tame academic substitute for the real thing, whose purpose in the work I analyzed was political change.
>
> (Said, 2000, p. 436)

Said follows the trajectory of reification:

> The point I made about all this was that when they were picked up by late European students and readers of Lukács (Lucien Goldmann in Paris, Raymond Williams in Cambridge), the ideas of this theory had shed their insurrectionary force, had been tamed and domesticated.
>
> (Said, 2000, p. 437)

Stretched to adhere to changed political circumstances, the newfound elasticity subverted the original intent. Add to this the fact that, as theories such as reification are 'picked up' and popularized, inside and outside the academy, they attract respectability and prestige. Subsequently, there arises the clamour for orthodoxy and dogma. In a recent Canadian television interview, jazz saxophonist Branford Marsalis recalled having to learn the 186 rules of harmony at the conservatorium. These rules were established from Bach's work. The question for a boundary-crosser like Marsalis was 'Whose rules did Bach break to establish the canon?'

As has been acknowledged earlier in this chapter, inclusive education grew out of a struggle against the dominance of defectiveness-based discourses to privilege the calibration and categorizing of students into segregated special education and the regulation of the lives of disabled children and their families. There are numerous accounts from disabled people of their experience of segregation (Humphries and Gordon, 1992; Potts and Fido, 1991) and of special schooling (French, 1996; Walsh, 1993) which provide compelling rationales for the profound struggles that they, their families and advocates entered into by testing the law for their place in the community and neighbourhood schools (Minow, 1990; Cook and Slee, 1999). Moreover, disabled researchers have established the importance of voice and narrative in building an insider knowledge of disability (Moore, 2000).

The epistemological incubus for inclusive education was not simply a question of location, of the right of disabled children to join their siblings and non-disabled peers in the neighbourhood school. The early work of inclusive education formed from the work of sociologists and disability studies scholars and activists, including: Finkelstein (1980), Tomlinson (1982), Ford *et al.* (1982), Oliver (1986), Abberley (1987), Barton (1987), Fulcher (1989), Morris (1989), Barnes (1990) and Shakespeare (1993). Collectively, they challenged the conceptual foundations of a defectiveness-based medical model upon which special education was built and practised. This was a model that reduced people to an essentialized set of characteristics that then forge teachers' expectations, 'appropriate and least restrictive' (Slee, 1996a) institutional arrangements for them and, ultimately, their life chances. At play, theoretically, are the very conceptions of ability, disability and disablement, and the patterning of power and social relations attendant with these varying conceptions (Oliver, 1996).

Disabled activist and author Jenny Morris (1989; 1992), while registering her disappointment in the silence of women's studies on disability, pathed an early articulation between feminist theory and disability studies. At a conference in the UK to celebrate the achievement of the journal *Disability and Society* (Barton and Oliver, 1997), theoretical tensions flared. Addresses by Marian Corker and Jenny Corbett applied poststructural and feminist lenses to interrogate the male and structural dominance of the social model of disability. Their intervention signified a growing interest in other genres such as cultural studies, queer research and poststructuralism to broaden the field of disability studies. Disability studies is an evolving research field offering an increasingly more sophisticated methodological toolbox, together with liberationist values, as a platform for action. It retains an insurrectionary edge in a world of disablement.

Following Foucault's genealogies of power as played out through the modernist knowledge projects of the 'psy' sciences, writers such as Rose (1989) examined the way in which the drive for governmentality fuelled the need to produce ways of knowing that would establish an authority to which the polity would defer, and in turn submit to the categorization and calibration of populations. Official knowledges proscribed the normative boundaries of ability/disability, morality and deviance, and sanity and madness. The ultimate achievement of the modernist project was to have people situate themselves within the regimes of truth and self-submit to liturgies of treatment.

Not so 'docile bodies' (Foucault, 1979) in schools, when assigned as attention disorders, become respectable, treatable and governable. That parents form themselves into policing self-help organizations enables institutions such as schools to move away from the spectacle of punishment, to assist in the administration of chemical interventions and thereby retain institutional equilibrium. The question may then be reframed: in whose interest does diagnosis, categorization and treatment work? If the goal is absorption and assimilation, then it may well be in the interest of the recipient of this intense scrutiny. If the goal is the recognition of difference as legitimate and valuable, then the answer forms a critique of the catechism and ceremonies of special education.

Power and voice are particularly important links in the theoretical chain. Relationships between disabled people and those who assert professional authority and seek to define their social geography (Gleeson, 1999; Harvey, 1996) are central to disability studies. How people are known, described and situated – whose story dominates the script and the consequent social and educational trajectories – are central to the development of inclusive education thinking, writing and practice. Put simply, inclusive education, according to this conception, becomes a field of cultural studies and politics, with the objective of social reconstruction. Traditional special education knowledge and practices are functional rationales (Mannheim, 1936) for the sustenance of a given social order. To be sure, the edges are polished and there are growing degrees of tolerance, but impacts are not respectful of the requirement for recognition and agency in the lives of disabled people. This is confronting for many special education researchers, teachers and administrators. It challenges them to reconsider the professional/client relationship and to consider the voice of disabled people in new ways. There exists a potential for non-oppressive research and professional practice (Oliver, 1996).

Lately, inclusive education has undergone a publishing and policy boom. Government discourse talks of the depletion of social capital through exclusion and the requirement, therefore, for inclusive schooling. Publishers' lists have become extensive where formerly powers of persuasion were stretched to have a proposal heard. 'How does it fix the problem of having a disabled child in a normal classroom?' drove researchers into their boutique publishing ghettos. Special educators, even those most resistant to the inclusive educational bandwagon, mindful of trends, practise linguistic alchemy to acquire the look of inclusion (Brantlinger, 2004). Special education conferences on inclusive education become trance-fixed on acceptable definitions for inclusion so that all theories are accommodated, all ideologies legitimized under the rubric of inclusion.

My short representation of antinomy between an authentic official brand of inclusive education and an unrepentant tradition of special education is itself problematic. Time has rendered the fields of which I speak more complex and they warrant a more forensic exploration and faithful representation. Reading the work of Julie Allan (1999; 2003) and Felicity Armstrong (2003) is good preparation for that research. Their respectful and insightful study into the work of teachers in 'special' classes and consideration of student identities and representations of their voices opens new possibilities for research and advocacy.

My task here, however, is provocation, as I suspect a dulling of the inclusive educational edge. I return to Edward Said for counsel. Has inclusive education travelled too far? Are we looking at recuperative jetlag? Or has inclusive education become a casualty to economy-class theory syndrome?

This is not glib. My concern about the potential to soften the insurrectionary edge of inclusive education by allowing special educators to describe old practices with a new liberal vocabulary is based on readings from other struggles. Barry Troyna (1993) proposed an education in anti-racism as multi-culturalism collapsed into polite 'samosas, saris and steel-band' events that issued no challenge to the pervasive presence of racism.

Paul Gilroy's (2000) *Against Race: Imagining Political Culture Beyond the Colour Line* is instructive. He describes the profound transformation in the way the idea of *race* is understood and acted upon. Raciology is a social construction of a fabricated scientific calibration and explanation to legitimate oppression. Though the impact of DNA has been to assign raciology to the dustbin of history, there remains a residual legacy:

> Raciology has saturated the discourses in which it circulates. It cannot be readily re-signified or de-signified, and to imagine that its dangerous meanings can be easily re-articulated into benign, democratic forms would be to exaggerate the power of critical and oppositional interests.
>
> (Gilroy, 2000, p. 12)

Let me compound the problem for theory-makers. Writing about inclusive education as identity politics magnifies the scale of our enterprise. At a colloquium in Newcastle in 1994, Tony Booth (Clark *et al.*, 1995) suggested that understandings of inclusive education are achieved through more rigorous attention to the processes and experiences of marginalization and exclusion. Such a proposition reinforced the need to examine the experiences, conceptualization and struggles of other marginal identities. In this way, the field became simultaneously complex and rich as the literature connected with research into those whose access to, and participation and success in, education is obstructed by factors such as socio-economic disadvantage, gender, racism, sexuality, mono-lingualism, and geographic isolation – and so on.

Typically, the discussion of inclusive education is simultaneously mounted as a general examination of exclusion and inclusion for all students and a claim on behalf of a particular constituency – disabled students, Aboriginal students, gay and lesbian students, and economically disadvantaged students – and so the list grows. The problem of inclusion into the modernist edifice of schooling, based as it is on the production of human capital for an industrial age (Apple, 2001; Hargreaves, 2003), becomes part of a general log of claims in the project of social reconstruction. Schooling was never meant for everyone. Only recently has compulsory schooling been extended to those who were prematurely ejected to the factory, shop, farm or street. Though the crisis in the unskilled labour market and anti-discriminatory legislation opens the door for increasing numbers of marginalized students, caveats govern their terms of engagement with schooling.

Echoing Basil Bernstein, Luke and Slee (forthcoming) argue that education 'in and of itself cannot right all wrongs ... the dilemma facing education in the West has been an overestimation, or more precisely, misestimation of the autonomous power of schooling and educational research'. Education systems can make a difference, but this is only achieved when there is alignment across government and other agencies to work at the 'multiple modernities' (ideas and institutions) (Taylor, 2004, p. 195).

Burdened by these theoretical concerns, let us consider inclusive education in Australia.

Inclusive education in Australia?

I previously posed this as a rhetorical question (Slee, 1996b) and promptly answered: Not yet! That answer does violence to a great deal of activity in schools and classrooms across Australia that is genuinely inclusive. This is corroborated by recent reports on research into individual schools in Queensland, Western Australia and Victoria (Carrington and Robinson, 2004; Deppeler and Harvey, 2004; Forlin, 2004). The picture for Australia *per se* is far more complex and beyond the scope of this discussion. What I will provide are some contextualizing remarks about exclusion from education in Australia as a backdrop to discussion of recent work in the state of Queensland.

The history of Australian education from its colonial origins is a story of systematic exclusion according to class, culture, language, gender, geography and ability (Connell *et al.*, 1982; Henry *et al.*, 1988; Bessant and Hyams, 1972). In this respect, schooling in Australia is a variation upon the Western tradition (Bourdieu and Passeron, 1977; Tomlinson, 2001; Tyack and Cuban, 1995). Streaming practices regulated the flow of working-class students into the unskilled labour market, while those of privilege pressed forward through to higher education. Exceptions implanted an impression that individual gifts and efforts translated into a triumph of agency over structure (Brantlinger, 2003; Connell, 1994). In the face of data revealing systematic and palpable inequalities, the *common sense* was that the provision of compulsory education was the liberal social guarantee of equality of opportunity (Apple, 1979; Connell, 1983).

Aboriginal attendance, retention and achievement rates remain a source of shame to governments rhetorically committed to inclusive schooling across Australia. Only recently has there been an official recognition of Aboriginal languages and a concession to students in Aboriginal and Creole languages. Queensland has recognized structural, curricular and pedagogic impediments to inclusive schooling for indigenous students. Accordingly, it has altered the structure of the school year in some communities in the Gulf region to reflect climatic conditions and familial obligations to travel. In the Cape region, it has supported the adaptation of the New Basics curriculum approach and given dispensation to schools not to teach the Eight Key

Learning Areas in order that a culturally relevant and engaging curriculum that makes sense to students, and teachers, is implemented. More fundamental has been the recognition in the *Partners for Success* (Education Queensland, 2001) compacts of the necessity of enlisting and listening to community voices in the project of educational reform. Whole-of-life issues are recognized as elements for the new curriculum. Simple examples of this revolve around health education to counter the disproportionate level of hearing impairment and chroming amongst Aboriginal students. These initiatives are central to the project of inclusive schooling. They embody a rejection of the impacts of racism and a determination not to do business as usual. Even so, much remains to be done when examining the disproportionate suspension and exclusion of Aboriginal students from school.

Segregated special education flourished for the provision of education to disabled students apart from their siblings and neighbours (Lewis, 1989; 1993). The provision of special education to disabled children was a reform representing an ambiguous détente between parental and professional advocacy, benevolent humanitarianism and a desire to permanently separate disabled children from the so-called normal child (Lewis, 1993). In this way, special education became a vehicle for social progressivism, charity and eugenicists. The concentration and building of resources in a separated special school sector remains an issue worthy of further investigation, as a recent report from University of Queensland economists, John Mangan and his colleagues, into the funding of education for students with special educational needs in Queensland revealed (Education Queensland, 2003). In this respect, Queensland is representative of funding of special education Australia-wide.

The overall funding of education in Australia is complex (Marginson, 1997a; 1997b). Some of the key features that are useful to set out for international readers are briefly outlined. Government funding for education comes both from the Department of Education, Science and Training (DEST) – the Federal Department of Education – and from each of the six states' and two territories' departments of education. The federal government is the principal funding agency for higher education (the university sector); however, the proportion of a university grant that comes from DEST has been shrinking over time so that it may range between 40 per cent for the Group of Eight universities (tier 1) to around 70 per cent for others. State governments also provide specific initiative funding for universities within their jurisdiction. As I write, Australian universities and their constituencies are locked into struggles over the deregulation of student fees (most universities opting for a 25 per cent 'top up' payment from students in addition to their HECS payment which is the government's student deferred interest-bearing repayment scheme). Together with international student fees, offshore programmes, patents, contracts, research grants, benefaction and various other sources, this makes up the total operating fund.

States and territories are responsible for the public (government or state) school system in their jurisdiction as a part of the total state government budget. State schools also receive funding for specific programmes, for example Asian language studies, boys' education, science education, Aboriginal education and students with special needs. DEST (federal government) funds a share of the cost of the provision of a large independent and Catholic schools sector across the states and territories. In fact, the allocation to this form of 'private' schooling exceeds their allocation to higher education. States and territories also contribute further to private schooling through a complicated arrangement known as the 'basket nexus' payment and through provision of shared services. This is especially so for the delivery of specialist services for disabled students in non-government schools.

The discussion of the funding of education is central to questions of inclusion and exclusion. In higher education, the rollback of public funding and an increasing reliance on student payment will translate to a return to traditional patterns of exclusion from higher education, and threatens a redirection of education research into more instrumental domains. This has already been seen in the setting of the research programmes that establish the fields of inquiry and what does not constitute worthwhile research in education. Lingard (1998) has traced the way in which federal funding has shifted from a broad range of participation and equity programmes, such as the disadvantaged schools initiatives, to conflate equity and social justice with the clamour for a return to basic literacy training. As such, we see greater expenditure on expensive short-term interventions such as 'reading recovery', which fail to contribute to school development or encourage government to think more boldly about underlying questions about redistributions in order to respond to the clearest predictor of academic failure and exclusion – poverty. As Luke (2003) intimates, it seems unlikely that there will be a phonics programme capable of ameliorating economic disadvantage, racism, sexism or disablement.

Educational privilege and disadvantage in Australia are structural (Ball, 2003; Brantlinger, 2003). Setting aside the clearest manifestation of privilege in the diversion of public funds to the so-called private schools sector and the diminution of public education funding, there exist vast disparities between public schools. Some are able to draw on affluent communities to support the extension of the school programme; others are not. Because postcode remains an index of failure and exclusion, inclusive education theory and practice must assert itself as a platform for an interrogation of the economics of education.

As stated, Aboriginal students, students from Non-English Speaking Backgrounds (NESB), students who are geographically isolated or who are from the emergent patterns of extreme rural poverty 'blockies', disabled students, and refugee children are also vulnerable and marginalized in the present arrangement of schooling. Recent debates about the failure and retention of boys in schools (House of Representatives, 2002) are worth unpacking to move closer to a growing realization that schooling curriculum and pedagogy are in need of reconstruction to meet the requirements of all comers. Inclusive education is a vehicle both for focussing on the impact of schooling upon particular identity groups and for mounting a general call for the reinvention of schooling.

From tourist farm to smart state – down to a new basics of educational reform

Traditionally, the state of Queensland in the sub-tropical northern climes has always promoted itself as Australia's Florida, 'Beautiful one day, perfect the next'. The Beattie Labor government repositioned Queensland as a centre for the development of the information economy and the intensification of biotechnology and medical research. The naming of government ministerial portfolios, and even of vehicle registration plates as 'The Smart State', reflected this makeover.

Education, through a policy blueprint: *Queensland State Education (QSE) 2010* (Education Queensland, 1999) was a centrepiece of the smart-state agenda. This document posed the question: What kind of schooling is necessary to equip commencing students with the requirements to successfully deal with the world upon their graduation in the year 2010? The document stimulated a policy environment where curriculum and pedagogy, workforce recruitment and development, school organization and inter-agency relationships were interrogated to improve the nature and quality of schooling and strike 'a new deal on equity'.

For the first time, an education jurisdiction mounted a comprehensive interrogation of social context to place what it called 'New Times' as a backdrop for a comprehensive reform of curriculum and pedagogy. The key features of its contextual analysis included, but were not restricted to, globalization, which refers to the contraction of time and space through new global economies and information flows (Castells, 1996; Giddens, 1999), resulting in the construction of complex and hybrid student identities. Also described is the profound transformation in knowledge and information production, recording and dissemination, and the construction of multi-literacies navigated by young people through communication and popular culture. The intensification of individualism (Fukuyama, 1999), the atomization of cultural groupings and the breakdown of extended familial and kinship patterns (Giddens, 1999) challenges educators to interrogate social futures and educate for a new communitarianism (Giddens, 1998). The tension between skilling and educating so that students are prepared for careers that do not yet exist, rather than being trained for disappearing jobs, is a feature of the new context of schooling (Education Queensland, 1999).

QSE 2010 targeted the poor retention rate of students in that state and aimed to raise student retention from 68 per cent to 88 per cent by the year 2010. Within this incubus of reform, Luke and his colleagues (1999) embarked on a comprehensive project of school reform that looked at school structure and professional work practices in schools, as well as repositioning pedagogy, curriculum and assessment. A *New Basics* (Education Queensland, 2000) was presented which asked what knowledge, skills and dispositions young people would require for negotiating the future. New knowledge organizers were established and content was thematically produced under a series of key questions. The first of the curriculum organizers was 'life pathways and social futures: who am I and where am I going?'

> The New Basics category, Life pathways and social futures, refers to that cluster of practices students need to master in order to flourish in a changing world. It involves both understanding the self and relationships with others, mental and physical health, and designing a place for the self in the changing contexts of work and community.
>
> (Education Queensland, 2000, p. 8)

Topics include: Living in and preparing for diverse family relationships; Collaborating with peers and others; Maintaining health and care of the self; Learning about and preparing for new worlds of work; and Developing initiative and enterprise.

The second category is Multiliteracies and communication media – how do I make sense of and communicate with the world? This category enables students to engage with technologies that use a range of codes, including traditional print literacies, visual literacies, aural and musical literacies, mathematical understandings of number, chance and data.

The third category is Active citizenship. The organizing question is: What are my rights and responsibilities in communities, cultures and economies? This category covers the following themes: interacting within local and global communities; operating within shifting cultural identities; understanding local and global economic forces; and understanding the historical foundation of social movements and civic institutions.

The final category, Environment and technologies, organizes work around the question: How do I describe, analyze and shape the world around me? The key themes for work in this category are: Developing a scientific understanding of the world; Working with design and engineering technologies; and Building and sustaining environments.

A total of fifty-nine schools enlisted in a trial of this integrated approach to knowledge, where rich tasks were the basis for teacher judgements about student engagement with, and mastery of, knowledge and skills that reflect both the worlds in which students are presently located and that to which they are heading. This is a far cry from the 'the curriculum as museum' as

Ball (1994) described the National Curriculum in England and Wales. The New Basics project is more than an attempt to redesign curriculum content. Incorporating lessons from the Queensland School Reform Longitudinal Study (Education Queensland, 2001), in which observations of over 975 classroom lessons in twenty-four schools across four dimensions, (intellectual quality, relevance, supportive classroom environment, and recognition of difference), New Basics represents an elaborated action research into school reform that engages with curriculum, pedagogy, assessment and school organization.

Inclusive education, I argued as a Deputy Director General of Education in Queensland (Slee, 2002), is about *all* students. It ought to provide a general framework for the reform of schooling through the reconceptualization of curriculum, the examination of teacher practices, and the creation of teacher professional learning communities to enhance pedagogic repertoires and to establish a focus on rich assessment schedules that eschews global pressure for high-stakes testing.

At the same time, under the umbrella of inclusive schooling for all, attention needed to be applied to specific marginalized identity groups, including the battleground of schooling for disabled students.

Queensland reforms, disabled students and the travellers

As mentioned, I want to identify some themes that emerged from working closely with one jurisdiction. I will characterize these themes as problems of travelling theory, on the one hand, and the limits of education reform, on the other.

The education of disabled students in Queensland was managed by the Low Incidence Unit. An immediate task was to change this extremely offensive nomenclature and call for the adoption and usage of a more inclusive lexicon. Language matters: it simultaneously reveals and conceals meanings – it sets the discursive field within which policy is framed. Some scrambled to level pejoratives such as there being 'a new order imposing political correctness'. Rather than be lured by such distractions, the Staff College for Inclusive Education was established as a vehicle for highlighting local inclusive activity and introducing the jurisdiction to divergent ways of thinking about inclusive education. An academic working with the Index for Inclusion (Booth *et al.*, 2000), Suzanne Carrington, was recruited as the Staff College Principal and a programme of activity that invited researchers such as Tony Booth, Mel Ainscow, Julie Allan, Keith Ballard, Tom Shakespeare, Mara Sapon-Shevin and Mark Vaughan, as opposed to traditional special education gurus, commenced.

To manage the Inclusive Schooling Branch of Education Queensland, I recruited a senior officer (devoid of a special education pedigree) from Disability Services Queensland, Michael Walsh. This was a deliberate attempt to loosen the grip of the traditional special education fraternity and implant new ways of thinking about disability, disablement and human services delivery. Shortly after his recruitment, the Minister, Anna Bligh, announced a Seven Point Plan for Students with Disabilities. Rather than list and describe the elements of the plan, there is greater value in high-lighting departures from precedent.

The first was the establishment of a Taskforce on Students with Disabilities to advise the Minister on key issues. The taskforce was a way of bringing a range of constituents to the table in order to host a discussion that had previously been conducted from behind barricades. Relations between government, teacher unions, parents and disability advocacy groups were dysfunctional. This taskforce enabled a range of views to be put and received in a climate of growing understanding and respect. Moreover, the voice of those who hitherto were not invited to the table, particularly parents and disabled people, was legitimized. This said, frustration grew around the table as progress slowed on central issues such as resources and policies surrounding the placement of disabled students. (In Queensland, most students enrol in neighbourhood schools; disabled students are placed.)

The second of the initiatives, already mentioned, was the establishment of the Staff College for Inclusive Education. This was a successful initiative in that it provides a range of incentives for the development and expansion of inclusive schooling initiatives at the local level by supporting and celebrating effective classroom practices and building communities of practice (Wenger, 1998). Inclusive education represented schooling for all students so that it worked to ensure that the consideration of disabled students' education was a part of the larger project of reconstructing schools as accessible and productive places for all.

A third area of work under the plan concerned the funding of education for students with disabilities. Like other jurisdictions, Queensland distributed support for students with disabilities according to a highly categorical six-tiered schema. Funding is only allocated for students considered to be at levels 4, 5 and 6. Not surprisingly, the increasing preponderance of students ascertained with disabilities was at level 6. Discriminations were not made for the kind of disability, nor was there a logic that suggested a building of school capacity as they acquired further funding for more disabled students. The most significant growth areas were behavioural, attention and emotional disabilities and speech language disorders. This, I have argued elsewhere, may reflect to varying extents schools' attempts to deal with students previously ejected to the unskilled labour market (Slee, 1995).

That there were significant disparities between regions in the rate and levels of ascertainment pointed to the lack of system and consistency, relying as it did on the voluntary services of guidance officers and special education bureaucrats in district offices. This marks a contrast with other jurisdictions such as New Zealand, where there is a central eligibility gate-keeping process that is tightly monitored by a senior officer and her team. There is little need to rehearse at length the problems attached to this approach to supporting the education of children with disabilities, as it has been the subject of numerous analyses (Galloway *et al.*, 1994; Pijl *et al.*, 1997; Rouse and Florian, 1997). From parents' points of view, it presses them to highlight the deficits of their children in order to garnish support; it quickly becomes adversarial; and they typically are reduced to an unequal negotiating position in the face of professional adjudicators (Armstrong, 1995; Marks, 1993). The gaze narrows to individual anatomical aetiology, seldom sufficiently interrogating curriculum, pedagogy, school organization, or education policy (Slee, 2001). From a government perspective, the exponential demand on the public purse as more students are gathered into the special educational net in order to render classrooms more functional as they struggle with diversity becomes extremely problematic. In Queensland, the budget allocation for students with disabilities through the ascertainment process exceeded that of Disability Services Queensland for whole of life support programmes.

The demand from Cabinet was to cap the level of funding and tighten the ascertainment schedules. We had attempted to consider the task in other ways. First, there was a political need to debunk ascertainment methodology and mythology and uncouple it from direct funding to individual students. Although it was widely regarded as flawed, ascertainment extended resources to schools and teachers and was thus supported by the Queensland Teachers' Union. Economic modellers, with experience in human services resource modelling, were contracted to evaluate the methodology and recommend alternative approaches. Their report to government highlighted deficiencies within the algorithms and consequent programme distortions. Simultaneously, there was an investigation to attempt to produce an alternative approach that moved away from categories of disability to focus upon teaching and learning and build capacity within and across schools. Resolution of these tensions is not easy.

As Ball (1994) suggested, education policy is messy and not as coherent as many academic accounts would have us believe (Dye, 1992). Electoral cycles, industrial struggles and internecine conflicts within and across bureaucracies disrupt some rationalities and privilege others. So, too, for Queensland where these struggles ensue, disrupting policy in deference to politics. Herein lie some of the limits to neo-liberal government reform agendas.

While there has been a determination for changes in the education of disabled students as an element of a more general programme of educational reform, there exists a large and resilient special school sector with a highly effective lobbying capacity organized by the Association of Queensland Special Education Administrators. To their credit, a number of the principals in this organization have effectively lobbied the qualifications authority in that state to generate options for disabled students locked out by extant qualification and certification requirements. There is a genuine desire from this quarter to advocate for disabled students from the platform of special education in Queensland. A number of special schools have entered into a consortium to apply New Basics curriculum and pedagogy to their programmes. The rhetorical reformist zeal is high, with principals and their teachers travelling to other states to disseminate these 'inclusive education' improvements in materials and instruction in special schools. This is described as inclusive education. Their argument pivots on the fact that many of their students would experience marginal engagement, neglect with respect to their diverse needs, and even hostility in regular schools. In this respect they are far too frequently correct. Many of our neighbourhood schools are not good places even for those children whose right to a desk therein is never questioned. Choice is framed around this unacceptable state of affairs – given the incapacity of neighbourhood schools, special schools fulfil an important need and represent a viable alternative, it is argued. This is travelling theory writ large – a new conservatism.

That parents have to accept segregated provisions because of the inability of present institutional arrangements does not represent choice. It represents the absence of options and presents a major obstruction to it ever being otherwise. The more diversity becomes commonplace in classrooms, the more it presents a valuable resource for an education for an inclusive future. I am mindful of a statement by Pierre Bourdieu (1998), where he declared that, 'between two evils, I refuse to choose the lesser'.

Inclusive education in Queensland occupies an extremely fragile position. Like other jurisdictions, it is rendered fragile by the tension it strikes with other policy aspirations. Disabled activists have not secured a reconstruction of the social relations of disablement, despite the renaming of policy, programmes and adjustments to the websites. The improvement of special schools and special educators is not inclusive education. Issues of professional power and parental choice are not adequately responded to. The relocation of special education to operate in neighbourhood schools does not challenge disablement. Inclusive education in this respect is a travel-weary theory. Just as soft multi-culturalism distracted from the pervasiveness of racism and did not lead to an interrogation of attendance rates and the exclusion and failure of Aboriginal children, this form of inclusive education subverts the project of equity for disabled students.

Inclusive education, a new metaphysics and democratic schooling

To be sure, there are many examples where schools and their communities have transformed the way they conduct themselves in order to engage with and build the success of all of their students. Many schools, despite the pressure of the education market place, remain committed to their neighbourhoods and aren't so choosy about their students with an eye to league tables. There exist schools where the practice of inclusion is more important than the rhetoric. These are genuinely reflexive institutions where the elements of community building are examined, where curriculum, pedagogy and assessment are subjected to critical scrutiny to build student engagement and teacher professional learning. This is inclusive schooling in action. For this reason I refuse to conclude that we jettison inclusive education as another failed modernist project.

Nevertheless, as a theoretical construct and blueprint for social action and education planning, inclusive education is gathering symptoms of Said's description of a travelling theory. We have explored a number of reasons for this. In this final phase of the chapter I want to further explore the epistemic foundations of inclusive education's potential implosion as a prelude to suggesting some ways forward.

I have described a struggle between inclusive education as a reform ethos and institutional stasis. Caveats are thus placed around the level of inclusion, if such a qualification is possible, so that the most difficult and different students don't disrupt the physical and educational capacity of current forms of schooling. Here lies a fundamental theoretical tension between traditional special education and those demanding the institutional changes required for educational inclusion. For, so long as special education uses the discourse of inclusion to protect their professional interest through cascading models of circumscribed engagement with the regular classroom, the integrity of inclusion is compromised. For, so long as 'regular educators' hold fast to notions of regular students and special needs students, inclusion is reduced to chimera.

This level of struggle signifies deeper antinomies. The bifurcation between special needs students and regular students represents but one epistemic possibility for disability. Disability studies present a range of divergent ways of thinking about disability, impairment, disablement and social division that challenge those whose understandings are built from medical and psychological bases. Called to account are traditional research relations and professional interactions with disabled people (Moore, 2000). This clash of the foundations of knowledge holds profound significance for the future of schooling for disabled people. A key to progress on this front is the presence or absence of disabled people in debates and the willingness of all to engage in building knowledge consistent with new times.

It is in this area that I feel most uncomfortable about inclusive education. Unless inclusive education builds on the timbre and pitch of disabled voices, it threatens to provide a vehicle for maintaining oppressive social relations of disablement. There needs to be a greater sense of outrage and urgency built around patterns of exclusion, and a determination for amelioration. This is where inclusive education becomes the credo of the cultural vigilante.

The general umbrella of inclusive education as a rallying point for a range of minority and disadvantaged identities is appropriate. It is when we delve into the individual struggles over theories, policy and practice that the tensions arise. I have referred to this in relation to multiculturalism and anti-racism, special education and disablement. Inclusive education remains softly spoken on the political economy of school funding and charterism. Education Queensland developed a definition of inclusion consistent with many others that I have read. Inclusive education refers to students having access to schools, being present and participating in the programme of learning and achieving success. Noteworthy is the fact that though we know that poverty is a clear indicator for academic failure and restricted patterns of educational participation, inclusive education is yet to provide a platform for governments to reform educational funding models.

Perhaps inclusion can be embraced within a broader educational theory to help us through present sticking points? Knight (2000) suggested that inclusion be incorporated within a general theory of education where ends and means are inseparable. For Knight (2000), inclusive education is a precondition of a democratic education:

> The principle of 'inclusion' becomes a mean contributing to defined ends; 'inclusion' is not treated as an end in itself. Proposed here is a cognitive democratic theory of education that merges 'inclusive educa-tion' and social inclusion, within broader epistemological principles.
>
> (p. 17)

Previously, Bernstein (1996) had announced a set of conditions and peda-gogic rights for an effective democracy. He distinguished between inclusion and absorption, and argues for enhancement whereby 'tension points condense the past and open possible futures' through critical literacy and civic practice (1996, pp. 6–7). Four years later, the English translation of Alain Touraine's (2000) work posed the question, *Can We Live Together?* He examines the politics of difference and distances himself from 'soft ideology' (p. 3) melting pots. He advocates for the power of schooling to 'recomposi-tion' the world. The relationship struck between different cultural identities is central to his argument:

> In a world of intense cultural exchanges, there can be no democracy unless we recognize the diversity of cultures and the relations of domi-nation that exist between them. The two elements are equally important: we must recognize the diversity of cultures, but also the existence of cultural domination. ... The struggle for the liberation of cultural minorities can lead to their communitarianization, or in other words their subordination to an authoritarian cultural power.
>
> (Touraine, 2000, p. 195)

For Touraine (2000), schools for social recomposition subvert the classical educational fare:

> A form of education centred on the culture and values of the society that provides the education in question is replaced by a form of education that gives a central importance to diversity (both historical and cultural) and to recognition of Other.
>
> (p. 270)

Setting out his principles for a new form of schooling, Touraine is emphatic about the redistributive (Rawls, 1971) function for schools:

> The third principle is the will to compensate for unequal situations and inequality of opportunity. … It gives the school an active role in the process of democratization by taking into account the particular conditions under which different children have to deal with both the same instruments and the same problems.
>
> (p. 270)

This preliminary foray into education and democracy yields a strong foundation of value – perhaps a new metaphysical claim on educational purpose that reasserts values into the political struggle for inclusion? It speaks to the politics of inclusion, difference, identity and representation. Issues of inequality are confronted as elements for intervention fundamental to a platform of inclusiveness. Moreover, in the reconstruction of schooling it presses us towards an interrogation of the differential privileges and impacts of curriculum, pedagogy and culture. I delineated principles of New Basics as a representation of Bernstein's call for a curriculum for enhancement. As I think about Said's description of the taming of Lukács' reification theory, I also think about the struggle around asserting the 'personal as political' (Oliver, 1996). Perhaps this present struggle that I have with inclusive education concerns a distancing within and by inclusive education of the educational as political?

References

Abberley, P. (1987). 'The concept of oppression and the development of a social theory of disability'. *Disability Handicap and Society*, 2(1), 5–21.

Ainscow, M. (1999). *Understanding the development of inclusive schools*. London: Falmer Press.

Allan, J. (1999). *Actively seeking inclusion: Pupils with special needs in mainstream schools*. London: Falmer Press.

Allan, J. (ed.) (2003). *Inclusion, participation and democracy: What is the purpose?* Dordrecht: Kluwer Academic Publishers.

Appadurai, A. (1996). *Modernity at large: Cultural dimensions of globalization*. Minneapolis: University of Minnesota Press.

Apple, M. (1979). *Ideology and curriculum*. London: Routledge and Kegan Paul.

——(2001). *Educating the 'right' way. Markets, standards, God and inequality*. New York: RoutledgeFalmer.

Armstrong, D. (1995). *Power and partnership in education*. London: Routledge.

Armstrong, F. (2003). *Spaced out: Policy, difference and the challenge of inclusive education*. Dordrecht: Kluwer Academic Press.

Ball, S.J. (1994). *Education reform. A critical and post-structural approach*. Buckingham: Open University Press.

——(1998). 'Educational studies, policy entrepreneurship and social theory'. In R. Slee, G. Weiner and S. Tomlinson (eds) *School effectiveness for whom?* (pp. 70–83). London: Falmer Press.

——(2001). 'Performativities and fabrications in the education economy: Towards a performative society'. In D. Gleeson and C. Husbands (eds) *The performing school*. London: RoutledgeFalmer.

——(2003). *Class strategies and the education market. The middle classes and social advantage*. London: RoutledgeFalmer.

Barnes, C. (1990). *Cabbage syndrome: The social construction of dependence*. Lewes: Falmer Press.

Barton, L. (ed.) (1987). *The politics of special educational needs*. Lewes: Falmer Press.

Barton, L. and Oliver, M. (eds) (1997). *Disability studies: Past, present and future*. Leeds: The Disability Press.

Bernstein, B. (1996). *Pedagogy, symbolic control and identity. Theory, research, critique*. London: Taylor and Francis.

Bessant, B. and Hyams, B.K. (1972). *An introduction to the history of state education in Australia*. Camberwell: Longman.

Black, P. (1998). *Testing: Friend or foe? Theory and practice of assessment and testing*. London: Falmer Press.

Booth, T., Ainscow, M., Black-Hawkins, K., Vaughan, M. and Shaw, L. (2000). *Index for Inclusion*. Bristol: Centre for Studies in Inclusive Education.

Bourdieu, P. (1998). *Acts of resistance: Against the new myths of our time*. Cambridge: Polity Press.

Bourdieu, P. and Passeron, J.C. (1977). *Reproduction: In education, society and culture*. London: Sage.

Brantlinger, E. (1997). 'Using ideology: Cases of nonrecognition of the politics of research and practice in special education'. *Review of Educational Research*, 67(4), 425–459.

——(2003). *Dividing classes. How the middle class negotiates and rationalizes school advantage*. New York: RoutledgeFalmer.

——(2004). 'The big glossies: How textbooks structure (special) education'. Unpublished paper presented at *Common Solutions: Inclusion and Diversity at the Center*. Syracuse, 20 March.

Carrington, S. and Robinson, R. (2004). 'A case study of inclusive school development: A journey of learning'. *International Journal of Inclusive Education*, 8(2), 141–153.

Castells, M. (1996). *The rise of the network society (The Information Age). Vol. 1*. Oxford: Blackwell.

Cherryholmes, C. (1988). *Power and criticism: Poststructural investigations in education*. New York: Teachers College Press.

Clark, C., Dyson, A. and Milward, A. (eds) (1995). *Towards Inclusive Schools?* London: David Fulton.

Connell, R.W. (1983). *Which way is up? Essays on sex, class and culture*. Sydney: Allen and Unwin.

——(1987). *Gender and power. Society, the person and sexual politics*. Cambridge: Polity Press.

——(1994). *Schools and social justice*. Leichhardt NSW: Pluto Press.

Connell, R.W., Ashenden, D., Kessler, S. and Dowsett, G. (1982). *Making the difference: schools, families and social division*. Sydney: Allen and Unwin.

Cook, S. and Slee, R. (1999). 'Struggling with the fabric of disablement: Picking up the threads of the law and education'. In M. Jones and L. Basser Marks (eds) *Disability, divers-ability and legal change* (pp. 327–341). The Hague: Martinus Nijhoff.

Dye, T.R. (1992). *Understanding public policy*. Englewood Cliffs NJ: Prentice-Hall.

Delamont, S. (1992). *Fieldwork in educational settings*. Lewes: Falmer Press.

Deppeler, J. and Harvey, D. (2004). 'Validating the British Index for Inclusion for the Australian Context: stage one'. *International Journal of Inclusive Education*, 8(2), 155–184.

Eagleton, T. (2003). *After theory*. London: Allen Lane.

Education Queensland (1999). *Queensland state education – 2010*. Brisbane: Queensland Government Printer.

——(2000). *New Basics project: New Basics – Curriculum organisers*. Brisbane: New Basics Branch.

——(2001). *Partners for success*. Brisbane: Education Queensland.

——(2002). *The Queensland school reform longitudinal study*. Brisbane: Education Queensland.

——(2003). *Report on resources methodology for students with disabilities*. Brisbane: unpublished consultants' report. Brisbane: Education Queensland.

Finkelstein, V. (1980). *Attitudes and disabled people: Issues for discussion*. New York: World Rehabilitation Fund.

Ford, J., Mongon, D. and Whelan, J. (1982). *Special education and social control: Invisible disasters*. London: Routledge and Kegan Paul.

Forlin, C. (2004). 'Promoting inclusivity in Western Australian schools'. *International Journal of Inclusive Education*, 8(2), 185–202.

Foucault, M. (1979). *Discipline and punish: The birth of the prison*. Harmondsworth: Penguin Books.

French, S. (1996). 'Out of sight, out of mind: the experience and effects of a 'special' residential school'. In J. Morris (ed.) *Encounters with strangers: Feminism and disability*. London: Women's Press.

Fukuyama, F. (1999). *The great disruption. Human nature and the reconstruction of social order*. London: Profile Books.

Fulcher. G. (1989). *Disabling policies? A comparative approach to education policy and disability*. Lewes: Falmer Press.

Fuller, B. (ed.) (2000). *Inside Charter Schools. The paradox of radical decentralization*. Cambridge MA: Harvard University Press.

Galloway, D., Armstrong, D. and Tomlinson, S. (1994). *The assessment of special educational needs. Whose problem?* London: Longman.

Gewirtz, S., Ball, S.J. and Bowe, R. (1995). *Markets, choice and equity in education.* Buckingham: Open University Press.

Giddens, A. (1998). *The Third Way. The renewal of social democracy.* Cambridge: Polity Press.

——(1999). *Runaway world. How globalisation is reshaping our lives.* Cambridge: Polity Press.

Gilroy, P. (2000). *Against race. Imagining political culture beyond the color line.* Cambridge MA: The Belknap Press of Harvard University Press.

Gipps, C.V. (1994). *Beyond testing: Towards a theory of educational testing.* London: Falmer Press.

Gleeson, B. (1999). *Geographies of disability.* London: Routledge.

Goldstein, H. and Lewis, T. (eds) (1996). *Assessment problems: Developments and statistical issues.* Chichester: John Wiley.

Hargreaves, A. (2003). *Teaching in the knowledge society. Education in the age of insecurity.* New York: Teachers College Press.

Harvey, D. (1996). *Justice, nature and the geography of difference.* Oxford: Blackwell.

Henry, M., Knight, J., Lingard, R. and Taylor, S. (1988). *Understanding schooling.* Sydney: Routledge.

Hooks, B. (1994). *Teaching to transgress.* New York: Routledge.

House of Representatives (2002). *Boys: Getting it right: Report of the Inquiry into the Education of Boys.* Canberra: Government Printer.

Humphries, S. and Gordon, P. (1992). *Out of sight: The experience of disability.* Plymouth: Northcote House Publishers.

Kauffman, J.M. and Hallahan, D.P. (eds) (1995). *The illusion of full inclusion: A comprehensive critique of a current special education bandwagon.* Austin TX: Pro-Ed.

Knight, T. (2000). Inclusive education and educational theory: inclusive for what? *Melbourne Studies in Education*, 41, 17–43.

Lewis, J. (1989). 'Removing the grit: The development of special education in Victoria 1887–1947'. Unpublished PhD thesis, Bundoora: LaTrobe University.

——(1993). 'Integration in Victorian schools: Radical social policy or old wine?' In R. Slee (ed.) *Is there a desk with my name on it?* (pp. 9–26). London: Falmer Press.

Lingard, R. (1998). 'The disadvantaged schools programme: caught between literacy and local management'. *International Journal of Inclusive Education*, 2(1), 1–14.

Luke, A. (2003). 'After the marketplace: Evidence, social science and educational research'. *Australian Educational Researcher*, 30(2), 87–107.

Luke, A., Matters, G., Herschell, P., Grace, N., Barrett, R. and Land, R. (1999). *New Basics: Technical paper.* Brisbane: Education Queensland.

Luke, A. and Slee, R. (forthcoming). *The future of education research: Pragmatism, alignment, multidisciplinarity.*

Mannheim, K. (1936). *Ideology and Utopia: An introduction to the sociology of knowledge.* London: Kegan Paul, Trench, Trubner and Co.

Marginson, S. (1997a). *Educating Australia: Government, economy and citizen since 1960.* Melbourne: Cambridge University Press.

——(1997b). *Markets in education.* Sydney: Allen and Unwin.

Marks, G. (1993). 'Contests in decision making at the school level'. In R. Slee (ed.) *Is there A desk with my name on it?* (pp. 159–184). London: Falmer Press.

Minow, M. (1990). *Making all the difference. Inclusion, exclusion and American law.* Ithaca NY: Cornell University Press.

Moore, M. (ed.) (2000). *Insider perspectives on inclusion: Raising voices, raising issues.* Sheffield: Philip Armstrong.

Morris, J. (1989). *Able lives.* London: Women's Press.

——(1992). 'Personal and political: A feminist perspective on researching physical disability'. *Disability, Handicap and Society*, 7(2), 157–166.

Oliver, M. (1986). 'Social policy and disability: Some theoretical issues'. *Disability, Handicap and Society*, 1(1), 5–18.

——(1990). *The politics of disablement.* Basingstoke: Macmillan.

——(1996). *Understanding disability: From theory to practice.* Basingstoke: Macmillan.

Parsons, C. and Castle, F. (1998). 'The cost of school exclusion in England'. *International Journal of Inclusive Education*, 2(4), 277–294.

Pijl, S.J., Meijer, C.J.W. and Hegarty, S. (eds) (1997). *Inclusive education: A global agenda.* London: Routledge.

Potts, M. and Fido, R. (1991). *A fit person to be removed.* Plymouth: Northcote House Publishers.

Rawls, J. (1971). *A theory of justice.* Oxford: Oxford University Press.

Rose, N. (1989). *Governing the soul: The shaping of the private self.* London: Routledge.

Rouse, M. and Florian, L. (1997). 'Inclusive education in the marketplace'. *International Journal of Inclusive Education*, 1(4), 323–336.

Said, E.W. (2000). *Reflections on exile and other literary and cultural essays.* London: Granta Books.

Shakespeare, T. (1993) 'Disabled people's self-organisation: A new social movement?' *Disability, Handicap and Society*, 8(3), 249–264.

Slee, R. (1995). *Changing theories and practices of discipline.* London: Falmer Press.

——(1996a). Clauses of conditionality. In L. Barton (ed.) *Disability and society: Emerging issues and insights.* London: Longman.

——(1996b). 'Inclusive education in Australia? Not yet!' *Cambridge Journal of Education*, 26(1), 9–32.

——(1998). 'High reliability organisations and liability students: The politics of recognition'. In R. Slee, G. Weiner and S. Tomlinson (eds) *School effectiveness for whom?* (pp. 101–114). London: Falmer Press.

——(2001). 'Social justice and the changing directions in educational research: The case of inclusive education'. *International Journal of Inclusive Education*, 5 (2/3), 167–177.

——(2002). 'Inclusive education: The heart of the reform agenda'. *Education Views*, 11(21), 16.

Soto, L.D. (2004). 'Foreword: Decolonizing research in cross-cultural contexts: Issues of voice and power'. In K. Mutua and B.B. Swadener (eds) *Decolonizing research in cross-cultural contexts. Critical personal narratives* (pp. ix-xi). New York: SUNY Press.

Taylor, C. (2004). *Modern social imaginaries.* Durham NC: Duke University Press.

Thrupp, M. and Willmott, R. (2003). *Education management in managerialist times. Beyond the textual apologies.* Philadelphia: Open University Press.

Tomlinson, S. (1982). *A sociology of special education.* London: Routledge and Kegan Paul.

——(2001). *Education in a post-welfare society*. Buckingham: Open University Press.

Touraine, A. (2000). *Can we live together? Equality and difference*. Cambridge: Polity Press.

Troyna, B. (1993). *Racism and education*. Buckingham: Open University Press.

——(1994). Critical social research and education policy. *British Journal of Educational Studies*, 42(1), 70–84.

Tyack, D. and Cuban, L. (1995). *Tinkering toward utopia. A century of public school reform*. Cambridge MA: Harvard University Press.

Walsh, B. (1993). 'How disabling any handicap is depends on the attitudes and actions of others: A student's perspective'. In R. Slee (ed.) *Is there a desk with my name on it?* (pp. 243–251). London: Falmer Press.

Watson, D. (2003). *Death sentence. The decay of public language*. Sydney: Knopf.

Wenger, E. (1998). *Communities of practice: Learning, meaning and identity*. New York: Cambridge University Press.

Zizek, S. (1994). 'Introduction: The spectre of ideology'. In S. Zizek (ed.) *Mapping ideology* (pp. 1–33). New York: Verso.

Chapter 8

Diverse socio-cultural contexts for inclusive education in Asia

David Mitchell and Ishwar Desai

Asia contains 60 per cent of the world's population and covers a vast area, extending from Iran in the west to Japan in the east, and stretching from Kazakhstan in the north to Indonesia in the south. With some of the richest countries (e.g. Japan, Singapore) and some of the poorest countries on earth (e.g. Bangladesh, Cambodia), levels of economic development vary widely within the continent; overall, some 45 per cent of Asians live below the poverty line.

As Maclean (2001) points out, Asia contains 70 per cent of the world's illiterates, a figure that conceals considerable variation within Asia, with nearly universal literacy in the developed countries such as Japan and Singapore, compared with only 42 per cent literacy in South Asia. Also, as noted by Maclean, although both gross and net enrolment rates have increased over the past decade, there are currently 74 million out-of-school children in the school age population (6–11 years old) in Asia's developing countries, mostly in South Asia. Of those who do enrol in school, at least one third drop out before completing the primary grades.

Asia has been marked by social and economic upheavals of great magnitude. As noted by Inaytullah (2003), these include: (a) the break-up of the former Soviet Union in 1991, which particularly affected countries in Central Asia, such as Kazakhstan and Uzbekistan; (b) the extraordinary growth of the East Asian 'tiger economies' in the early to middle years of the 1990s followed by the financial crisis that hit the sub-region in mid-1997; (c) the rapid growth of the economies of India and China; (d) the continuation of the border and territorial conflicts in parts of South Asia; and (e) the migration and settlement of economic and political refugees.

Given the differences present in the histories, resources, cultures, economic and political systems and the demographics of Asian countries, it is not surprising to find that the pattern of provisions for students with special educational needs is extremely diverse, ranging from negligible to comprehensive, from highly segregative to various mixes of segregated and inclusive programmes, from coordinated to uncoordinated services, from untrained to well trained personnel and from poorly resourced to well resourced provisions (Mitchell and Desai, 2003). Some countries have a long history of providing special education; others are only now taking responsibility for providing education for students with special educational needs.

Before attempting an overview of inclusive education in Asia, three points deserve to be highlighted. First, according to Kholi (1993), in Asia's developing countries only one per cent of children with special educational needs have access to any education at all, let alone quality inclusive education. Second, for most countries in Asia, special education has been, and still is, synonymous with the provision of special schools or special classes. Third, it must be recognized that any review of special education in Asia is fraught with difficulties, such as variations in the range and quality of information and the clear gaps between laws, policies and practices to be found in many of the countries.

During the past decade or so, almost every country in Asia has addressed special education through legislation and/or major policy initiatives, with many showing a growing commitment to inclusive education. Sometimes this commitment is limited in its expression to legislation and policies, but sometimes – and increasingly – it is shown through a range of practices, albeit on a small scale. Factors that have influenced the adoption of inclusive education policies include the Salamanca Framework (UNESCO 1994), the work of UNESCO in promoting Education for All initiatives, the impact of non-government organizations such as the Soros Foundation's Step by Step programme (in Central Asia), and the influence of foreign advisers and study abroad schemes (see Mitchell, 1999b, for a detailed analysis of the transfer of knowledge and experiences between countries). The following summary shows that countries are spread along a continuum of commitment to inclusive education or, as it is sometimes referred to, 'integrated education' (see Mitchell, 1999a, for a detailed analysis).

At one end of the continuum is Vietnam, which, of all the countries in Asia, seems to have made the most significant progress in implementing inclusive education policies (Villa et al., 2003). In a 1995 report from the Centre for Special Education of the Ministry of Education and Training, for example, it was noted that 'the model of education, integrating the disabled into the community, is not only humane, and part of the responsibility of society and the community, it is based on scientific principles and has proved to be effective and suitable to modern times'. As at 1995, programmes of integrated education for disabled children existed in 33 provinces and cities, with 66 districts, 926 communes, and 1,041 elementary schools catering for 26,102 children in 11,086 integrated classes. Some 11,031 teachers had received training at courses on integrated education. In three provinces, 80 per cent of the districts were implementing integrated education. Even so, it is significant that recent data show that of the estimated 1 million Vietnamese children with disabilities (3 per cent of the school age population, who have moderate to severe disabilities by Western standards), only 35,000 are enrolled in public schools, another 6,000 are placed in special schools, and the remaining 95 per cent are at home and do not receive any formal education (Villa *et al.*, 2003). In promoting inclusive education as the preferred service delivery model, the Ministry of Education aims, by 2005, to place 60–70 per cent of children with disabilities in urban and 'advantaged' areas, and 40–50 per cent in rural or 'disadvantaged' areas, in regular, age-appropriate classrooms. What is it, then, about Vietnamese culture and society that supports this drive towards inclusive education? Villa *et al.* (2003), identify five features:

> First, in the rural areas of Vietnam, people have lived together for generations; therefore there is a strong emphasis on collaboration. Second, communist ideology focuses on the building of equality and equity in society for everyone, including children with disabilities. Third, non-discriminatory behavior is a core curriculum competency expected from all children in schools. Fourth, Buddhism, the largest religion in Vietnam, teaches that if one member of a group is hurt, all are hurt. Fifth, inclusive education is in alignment with the Vietnamese communist party's policy of socialized education to make use of available resources in the communities where children live.
>
> (p. 30)

At the other end of the continuum are countries such as Mongolia and Indonesia. The former has made no commitment to inclusive education, its special education provisions being largely confined to special schools, even for mildly retarded students. Similarly, Indonesia has not expressed any significant commitment to inclusive education, special schools comprising the major form of special education – a pattern that seems likely to continue as its future strategic plan includes building a public special school in every district/municipality.

Occupying the mid range of the continuum are several countries that espouse a conditional approach to inclusive education. Nepal, for example, introduced a Special Education Programme in 1993 'to provide education for children with mild and moderate disability through an inclusive school approach under which children with disabilities participate in regular classrooms and school'. Nevertheless, like many other Asian countries, Nepal took a pragmatic approach by maintaining residential facilities, even while recognizing that such facilities are costly and that parents lose their feeling of responsibility for their children. South Korea's Special Education Promotion Law stipulated that 'without due reasons, school principals at regular schools should follow the request from the special education target population or their parents for integrated education'. Although Korea recognized that special education in regular classes was the ultimate goal, it, too, took a cautious approach, arguing that factors such as the following should be considered first: people with disabilities should be accepted and understood, regular teachers should have knowledge about special education, classes of 30–40 students need to be reduced, team teaching has to be accepted, educational administrators need to have more understanding of special education, and 'normal' children and their parents should not feel deprived. Pakistan's ninth 5-Year Plan (1998–2003) included two goals bearing on inclusive/integrated education: (a) programmes for integrated/inclusive education in normal schools should be initiated in each province; and (b) a special quota for disabled children should be reserved in all educational institutions. To enable this policy to be implemented, however, it was noted that ordinary schools should have the necessary infrastructure in the form of special education teachers, equipment, books, doctors, diagnosis and treatment procedures and an administrative mechanism for implementing integrated education programmes. Notwithstanding Pakistan's apparent commitment to introduce integrated education, the principal means of educating the relatively small number of children with special educational needs to be provided for in the Plan was to be special education centres, nearly half of which are operated by non-government organizations. In the Philippines, legislation and various policy documents provide a mandate for inclusive/integrated education. For example, the 1992 'Magna Carta for Disabled Persons' declared that 'Disabled persons are part of Philippine society, thus the State shall give full support to the improvement of the total well-being of disabled persons and their integration into the mainstream of society'. Again, there were significant caveats: although it was recognized that the ultimate goal was integration, there was also a recognition of the reality that not all children with special needs could be integrated in regular classes and thus various options and plans for educational placement remained open.

In this chapter, we have selected four countries for more detailed analysis: China, India, Japan and Singapore. They were selected because of their differing approaches to inclusive education and because of the authors' first-hand experience of them. As will be seen, China's movement towards educating students with special educational needs in regular schools reflects a blend of influences: Confucian values, Western ideas, and sheer pragmatism, the latter reflecting a recognition of the impossibility of providing sufficient special schools to serve such students. India, like China, would find it impossible to educate all students with special educational needs in special schools, so it, too, is turning to provisions in regular education. In both countries, this position raises the issue of addressing deeply held attitudes towards disability and how to accommodate students with special educational needs in over-crowded classrooms with inadequately prepared teachers. Singapore has a dual system of education: a special education system for students with moderate, severe or profound disabilities and a regular system for those without disabilities or those with mild disabilities, the latter receiving only limited accommodations. Japan has a similar dual system, but has placed considerable emphasis on resource class provisions for students with mild disabilities. This chapter will attempt to explain the underlying cultural and other influences that are giving rise to the various approaches to inclusive education in the four case study countries.

China: inclusive education in the context of Confucianism, socialism, Westernization and pragmatism

In general, according to Potts (2000), a long-time observer of special education in the People's Republic of China, recent years have witnessed a significant movement of children and young people from long-stay welfare institutions and family homes into special schools and from special into mainstream schools. China's educational policies and provisions for students with special educational needs reflect a blend of influences: traditional Confucian values, socialism (including Soviet influences), Western ideas, and pragmatism. In this section of the chapter, the impact of these influences on mainland China's emerging approach to inclusive education will be explored.

Provisions for students with special educational needs

In considering the educational provisions for students with special educational needs in China, perhaps the first thing to be taken into account is the sheer size of the country and its population (1.3 billion). Correspondingly, there are huge numbers of students with disabilities. On the basis of a 1987 survey, for example, it was estimated that there were 8.17 million disabled children and adolescents, aged from 0–14, 6.25 million of whom were of school age. This latter figure represented 2.66 per cent of the school age population, a figure that most Western observers would consider to be very conservative.

There have been several landmark events in China's recent history of making educational provisions for students with special educational needs. The first was the passage, in 1986, of the Compulsory Education Act. As suggested in its title, this Act marked the establishment of compulsory education in China. Significantly, for the present analysis, the Act's coverage included children with special needs, thus making their education a new focus of attention (Cheng, 1990). This is reflected, for example, in official district educational inspections including school entrance rates of students with disabilities as one of their criteria (Liang, 1990, cited by Deng and Manset, 2000). It is also shown in the dramatic increases in special education enrolments. In the ten years from 1988 to 1998, for example, the number of special schools expanded from 577 to 1,437, special classes from 599 to 6,148, and the number of students so catered for from 57,600 to 358,372 (Deng *et al.*, 2001). Impressive as these growth rates may be, they still represent provisions for only a tiny fraction of students with disabilities. As recently as 1991, according to Deng and Manset (2000), 90 per cent of students with disabilities, many of whom live in isolated rural areas, did not attend school.

This shortfall of provision led to the second landmark event, the decision that, while special schools would continue to be established, it would be logistically and economically impossible for them to provide comprehensive coverage for all students with special educational needs. Forceful measures would therefore have to be developed to help most such students to attend regular schools. Thus, following on from a National Conference on Special Education, held in 1988, the State Education Commission stated that, although separate schools would still be a part of the special education system, they would only constitute the 'backbone' of the system, while a large number of special classes and learning in regular classrooms will serve as 'the body'. This pattern of provisions was reinforced by the third important event – the 1990 Law on the Protection of Disabled Persons (Deng and Manset, 2000).

The learning in regular classrooms movement

In 1994, the above landmarks were followed by a fourth significant event, the implementation of a programme entitled 'Trial Measures of Implementing Learning in Regular Classrooms'. This had its origins in the Gold-Key Education Project, in which 1,000 children with visual impairments were integrated into regular classes within one year (Deng *et al.*, 2001). According to Deng and Manset (2000), the Learning in Regular Classrooms (LRC) movement has contributed greatly to the progress made in educating students with disabilities, even if it is difficult to get a true estimate of the numbers. They also point out that, despite the compulsory education law, LRC programmes are usually made available only to students with sensory impairments and mild mental retardation; those with severe and multiple disabilities, and some with moderate disabilities, are still excluded and do not attend school. Although LRC was directly influenced by the idea of mainstreaming in the United States, it retains characteristics of the Soviet Union's system, in that it emphasizes a remedial more than an educational-needs model. In contrast to the traditional whole-class lecture model for instruction, LRC teachers typically give instructions to the whole class, arrange tutoring schedules for students with special educational needs, organize peer tutors from among other students, and encourage cooperative activities so that students with differing abilities interact and study together (Deng and Manset, 2000). Also, students with special educational needs are set the same examinations as others, but are set lower pass marks and, rather than receiving a mark, they are given a set of comments. They are asked easier questions in class, sit with the 'best' students, who can help them, have easier homework, which the teachers go through with them individually, and are given extra help by their teachers after school (Potts, 2000).

Statistics on the expansion of special education in China from 1992 to 1996 provide some evidence of the LRC policy in practice. During this period, total enrolments of students with special educational needs grew by 148 per cent, enrolments in special schools for blind or deaf students grew by 1 per cent, 15 per cent, 36 per cent and 58 per cent (depending on type of facility), and enrolments in special schools for retarded children grew by 134 per cent. In contrast, enrolments of blind or deaf children in regular schools grew by 403 per cent and of retarded children in regular schools by 289 per cent.

This LRC initiative is not without its problems, however, and it is questionable as to whether it constitutes 'true' inclusion from a Western perspective. Several impediments are pointed out by writers such as Deng and Manset (2000), Deng *et al.* (2001), and Potts (2000; 2003):

1   While the main goal of the LRC programme is to give children with disabilities who have been excluded from any education the opportunity to attend school, 'there is no guaranteed right to an appropriate education, parent involvement, nor individualized educational program (IEP) once students are enrolled in general classrooms' (Deng and Manset, 2000, p. 125). This is exacerbated by inadequacies in teachers' skills and their lack of authority and experience to change curricula, assessment, or styles of pedagogy (Potts, 2000). However, there are signs of increasing flexibility in China's education system, which hold out promise for students with special needs. For example, according to Zhang (2003), the curriculum framework for the nine-year compulsory programme has been modified to allow variations, although still rather limited, including local contents and school-based extra-curricular learning activities. Furthermore, the previously unified textbook system that provided one set of books for all children throughout the country has been replaced with eight sets of textbooks to cater for the needs of children in different regions. While these modifications are not directed at students with special educational needs as defined in this book, they are perhaps signs of things to come.

2   In general, class sizes of 40–60 students make for difficulties in accommodating students with special educational needs. This is particularly a problem in rural areas where often only a few teachers are in charge of a whole grade level, which may contain up to six classes of sixty students each (Deng *et al.*, 2001). However, as reported by Blatchford and Catchpole (2003), research carried out on teachers' attitudes towards class size indicated that even though teachers from both urban and rural areas preferred teaching small classes to large classes (50+ students),

they did not believe they were necessary for academic achievement. While they believed that small classes facilitated classroom management and student-teacher interactions, it was more important for teachers to present knowledge in a manner suitable for learning.

3   Since the achievements of students with disabilities have not been required to be included in official programme evaluations, specific evaluation procedures have not been developed for them. A related point is that teachers feel encouraged to refer an increasing number of students as candidates for the LRC programme (Deng and Manset, 2000); in turn, this draws attention to the lack of systematic means for identifying students with special educational needs.

4   Within China's competitive educational environment, teachers usually do not have enough time, energy, or professional knowledge to help students with special educational needs in their classrooms (Deng and Manset, 2000). They worry, too, that that accepting students with special educational needs would interfere with the study habits and achievements of the other pupils.

5   As noted by Cheng (1990), it is students with IQs of 70 and above who are most likely to be placed in regular classes; these students are thought to be normal and are expected to achieve the normal graduation standard – an impossible expectation in most cases.

6   Since children with disabilities in the past were typically kept isolated from community life, even their parents question the expense and energy directed at educating such children. Generally they have mixed feelings. On one hand, they believe that it is desirable for their children to have social interactions with 'normal' children in regular learning environments and to be well prepared to be members of society; on the other hand, they are afraid that their children can't be treated well in the regular school. Some parents, particularly in rural areas, are reluctant to send their children with disabilities to school if, after graduation, they will have to stay at home as before. This accentuates the need for vocational education to be incorporated in their school experiences (Deng *et al.*, 2001).

7   As a consequence of the foregoing, in some LRC classrooms, students with disabilities have been observed sitting alone, isolated from classroom activities, or have even remained at home, despite the fact that their names are on the registration list.

The Chinese socio-political context

In seeking an explanation of China's evolving policies and practices in the education of students with special educational needs, consideration must be given to a complex amalgam of influences. These include traditional Confucian values, socialist ideologies, and, more recently, foreign (especially

Western) influences, all overlaid by pragmatic economic considerations. For example, according to Deng *et al.* (2001), LRC evolved out of a combination of adherence to the Western concept of mainstreaming and pragmatic considerations of Chinese social and educational conditions. They note that under Deng Xiaoping's reforms, 'socialism became more flexible, realistic, and marketable; extreme egalitarianism was replaced by an atmosphere of allowing or even encouraging differences' (p. 291).

Confucianism

Underpinning the Chinese culture (and some other Asian cultures) are the traditional values of Confucianism and Taoism (Deng *et al.*, 2001; Nanzhao, 1996; Potts, 2000). These centre on properly ordered social relationships in a hierarchically ordered society that is characterized by benevolence, harmony among people, respect for authority, obedience to rules, collective identities, and acceptance of one's status within society.

Collective societal interests are emphasized and individualism is abjured. Rather than the Western notion of society catering for individual needs, the Chinese tradition of collectivism believes that it is the individual who should adapt as far as possible to the system (Cheng, 1990). As Nanzhao (1996) expresses it, 'Confucianism emphasized the development of the individual as a social being, as an element of the family and of the society at large' (p. 241). He considers that this neglect of individuality results in the rights of individuals not being made compatible with their duties.

The Western concept of 'innate ability' is virtually non-existent in traditional Chinese culture. Instead, ability is something that can be improved through teaching. Teachers tend to believe that, with due effort, a child should be able to achieve the expected standard. As expressed by Cheng (1990), 'they believe that genetic factors are always secondary, so long as the pupils are trying hard. The motto, "diligence compensates for stupidity" is seldom challenged' (p. 164). To Confucius, according to Nanzhao (1996), 'man is perfectible and can be led in the right path through education, especially through his own effort at self-cultivation, within himself, but also through the emulation of models outside himself' (p. 240).

Within this traditional society, persons with disabilities occupy the lowest rungs, although they are deserving of sympathy. In this context, Cheng (1990) argues, it is not surprising that, until recently, the Western notion of 'special needs' was a foreign one.

Socialism

There are many parallels between traditional Chinese cultural values and the socialist ideology that took root in China in 1949 and that still holds sway in the present, although ameliorated somewhat by the drive to the market economy. Cheng (1994) reflects on these continuities, noting especially the similar views on the notions of individual needs and individual choice. In both ideologies, any emphasis of individual needs might be seen as reactionary and is never to be taken in its neutral sense. With regard to socialism, individualism is constantly a word for criticism; therefore, 'Education in the Chinese socialist ideology was to eliminate individualism rather than to cater for individual needs' (p. 66).

In a similar vein, Deng *et al.* (2001) point out that individual freedom has never been assumed to hold primary importance in China: 'In traditional China, the social ethics of duty and loyalty suppressed a sense of individuality; in socialist China, collectivism and loyalty to the Communist party have resulted in the neglect of individualism' (p. 297). As a result, 'individual differences have not been taken into account in curricula, teaching, and learning activities for children with disabilities, as in the West' (*ibid.*).

Foreign influences

As pointed out by Deng *et al.* (2001), special education in China has been considerably influenced by foreign countries at various stages of its history. For example, the first special schools were started in the nineteenth century by American and European charitable organizations, mainly churches, while the Soviet model of special education dominated from the 1950s to the 1970s. Since the 1980s, Western values, especially the concepts of mainstreaming and inclusion from the United States, have greatly influenced China's approaches to special education. While recognizing the important influence of foreign, mainly Western, ideas, Deng *et al.* (2001) emphasize that no theories from abroad are effective without considering the actual Chinese cultural and educational context. Even when innovative ideas such as student-centred approaches are introduced in the name of modernization, they are re-traditionalized, according to Dooley (2001) and Potts (2003). In other words, instead of the new replacing the old, the new becomes blended with the traditional, even to the point of it being negated. (This notion of new paradigms being co-opted into older paradigms, and leading to 'tensions and contradictions' (Potts, 2003, p. 241), is by no means restricted to China. Similar observations are made by Emanuelsson *et al.* in Chapter 6, Slee in Chapter 7, and Naicker in Chapter 10.)

Pragmatic considerations

Ideologies have a habit of coming up against realities. In the case of China (and most other countries for that matter), the reality is dominated by economics. Thus, the growing emphasis on inclusion not only reflects arguments in favour of its social benefits, but also recognizes the financial impossibility of funding special schools throughout the country. Thus, Deng and Manset (2000) quote a 1992 estimate that the nearly 5 million children with mental retardation alone would require establishing at least

210,000 new special schools. In addition, they cite a 1994 estimate that even if the existing teacher-training institutes could double their graduation rate, it would take more than a thousand years to educate enough teachers to meet the needs of just the students with mental retardation. A related point is that, since 80 per cent or more of students with special educational needs live in rural areas, it would be financially and logistically impossible for their families to send them to residential schools far from their homes (Yang and Wang, 1994).

Conclusion

Although China has a firm commitment to educating students with mild special educational needs in regular classrooms, there are many obstacles to overcome if these students are to be provided with an appropriate education. Some of these are logistical and economic; others reflect deep-rooted cultural values.

India: inclusive education in the context of a diverse socio-cultural and economic setting

In considering the educational provisions made for students with special educational needs in India, Jha (2002), whose assignment as Joint Secretary in the Ministry of Human Resource Development included responsibility for integrated and secondary education, states that while the agenda for inclusion in the West is concentrated mainly on the inclusion of students with physical and intellectual disabilities and those whose learning difficulties are due largely to emotional and behavioural factors, in India the focus extends beyond such groups. They include, also, children who are educationally deprived due to social and economic reasons: for example, street children, girls in rural areas, children belonging to scheduled castes and scheduled tribes, as well as various minorities and groups from diverse social, cultural and linguistic backgrounds. According to Jha, all these children are considered to have special needs. He argues that

> what is called "special needs" in Britain would be considered the "normal needs" of a large majority of children in India. Hence, the terminology, which has its origins in the medical world of diagnosing the disabled in the West, cannot explain the educational deprivation of large numbers of children in developing countries. The deprivation of these children is more on account of social, economic and historical factors; so the concept and context of SEN, introduced in Britain by Warnock, cannot meet inclusion expectations in India and other developing countries.

(p. 177)

The Indian socio-political and cultural context

In seeking an explanation for the diversity and extent of programmes and services available for students with special educational needs in India, a number of contextual issues and influences need to be considered. An examination of these will help shed some light on the present dilemma facing Indian educators regarding what is ideal and what is possible regarding the development of a fully inclusive system of education (Mani, 2002).

The country and its population

India is one of the oldest civilizations, with a rich mosaic of ethnic, religious, racial and tribal groups. Although it accounts for barely 2.42 per cent of the world's total landmass, it is home to more than a billion people – 16 per cent of the world's total population. There are eighteen official languages, with more than 1,500 dialects. The predominant religious groups are Hindus (81.3 per cent), followed by Muslims (12 per cent), Christians (2.3 per cent) and Sikhs (1.9 per cent). In addition, there are various smaller groups, for example, Buddhists, Jains, Parsis, and Jews.

There are also wide differences in the socio-economic status and educational attainment of its population. Enormous pockets of poverty and income disparities exist. Although there is a continuous flow of the population from rural to urban areas, about 70 per cent of the population still lives in rural areas. One consequence of this migration from the rural areas to the major cities has been that large numbers of people (estimated anywhere from 40 to 50 per cent) live in shacks and squatter settlements under slum conditions (Timmons and Alur, 2004). At the time of Independence in 1947, only 14 per cent of the population was literate and only one child out of three had been enrolled in primary school. Although there have been substantial improvements in school enrolments and literacy rates since then, Sachdeva (2003) asserts that 'the country has the dubious distinction of having the largest number of illiterates and out-of-school children in the world – 30 per cent of the world's adult illiterates (300 million) and 21.87 per cent of out-of-school children' (p. 3). Sachdeva further notes that at least 24 million children in the age group 6–14 are out of school, and of these about 60 per cent are girls.

The political system

India is a sovereign, socialist, secular, democratic republic with a parliamentary system of government. It comprises twenty-nine states and six centrally administered union territories. The Republic is governed by a Constitution, which came into force on 26 January 1950 following independence from colonial rule. The Constitution distributes legislative power between the Parliament and state legislatures but residual powers are vested in Parliament. The Constitution provides for a single, uniform citizenship for the whole country, guaranteeing its citizens such fundamental rights as equality before the law; protection from discrimination on the grounds of religion, race, caste, sex and place of birth; and freedom of speech and expression. In addition, the Constitution refers to free and compulsory education for all children up to the age of fourteen.

Responsibility for education

The provision of education is a joint responsibility of the central and state governments. Whilst decisions regarding such aspects as the organization and structure of education are largely the responsibility of the states, the central government has primary responsibility for the quality and character of education. At the national level, both the Ministry of Welfare and the Department of Education have significant roles in the delivery of services for students with special needs. According to Dasgupta (2002), the special school sector is dealt with by the Ministry of Welfare, whereas integrated education comes under the purview of the Department of Education. He states further that since the provision of education falls under the administrative control of the state governments, primary responsibility for the education of the disabled has to be taken by the state governments. Notwithstanding the involvement of both layers of government in the delivery of services for students with special needs, Alur (2001) points out that India still relies a great deal on voluntary organizations to provide educational services for children with disabilities.

Provisions for students with special educational needs

According to figures quoted in the Report on Manpower Development (Ministry of Welfare, 1996), the number of persons with disabilities in India was estimated to be approximately 45 million (5 per cent of the total population). This included only persons with physical, sensory and intellectual disabilities. If individuals with learning disabilities, leprosy and emotional disturbance were included, the figures would increase to approximately 90 million (10 per cent of total population). Estimates of the number of school-aged children with disabilities have ranged from 26 million (Ministry of Welfare, 1997) to 30–35 million (Singh, 2001).

Historically, the education of students with disabilities in India, as in many other countries, was provided primarily in segregated special schools. This trend continued unabated following India's independence from Great Britain in 1947, with various non-government organizations (NGOs) taking increasing responsibility for the education of children with different types of disabilities. For example, there were 25 schools for the visually impaired with 1,156 children in 1944, which increased to 115 schools catering for 5,000 children in 1966, and to 200 schools with an enrolment of 15,000 children in

1998. Likewise, the number of schools for hearing impaired children increased from 25 with an enrolment of 1,313 children in 1944 to 70 with an enrolment of 4,000 in 1966, and to 280 in 1988 providing special education to 28,000 children (Jha, 2002). The latest available figures on the education of the disabled, published by Dasgupta (2002), indicate that there are 1,400 special schools providing special education to 60,000 students.

In spite of this growth, many students with disabilities are still not provided with an appropriate education. The majority of the special schools are located in urban areas, whereas the majority of children with disabilities (approximately 70 per cent) live in rural areas. According to Rao (2000), special schools are able to meet the needs of only one per cent of students with disabilities. Therefore, integrated education (the term preferred in India) remains the only viable option (Chadha, 2000; Swaroop, 2001).

During the last three decades, the Government of India has taken a number of initiatives to promote integrated education: for example, Integrated Education of Disabled Children (IEDC), 1974; Project Integrated Education of the Disabled (PIED), 1987; and, more recently, the passage of the Persons with Disabilities (Equal Opportunities, Protection of Rights, and Full Participation) Act, 1995 (Ministry of Law, Justice and Company Affairs, 1996). Mani (2002) states that integrated education was conceptualized as the best 'alternative approach to bring all those unreached children under the umbrella of education. It was projected by governments and voluntary agencies as the economically viable, psychologically superior, and socially acceptable model for the education of disabled children' (p. 97).

The enactment of the Persons with Disabilities Act has been a major historical milestone in the education and welfare of persons with disabilities in India. It provides a legal and educational framework to enhance the status of persons with disabilities. The Act requires all states and union territories to ensure that persons with disabilities have access to the same educational opportunities and basic human rights as their non-disabled peers. The Act further emphasizes that, whenever possible, students with disabilities should be educated in regular school settings.

Two further legislative measures to enhance the full participation of persons with disabilities have also been taken. The first, the Rehabilitation Council of India Act, was enacted in 1992 for standardizing professional courses in rehabilitation and registering qualified professionals. The second, passed in 1992, was the National Trust for the Welfare of Persons with Autism, Cerebral Palsy, Mental Retardation and Multiple Disabilities Act, which, among other things, enables organizations representing these four disabilities to strengthen families in crisis and provides for the legal guardianship of persons with disabilities. The Act also encourages and supports the formation of parents' associations where persons with intellectual, severe and multiple disabilities are themselves unable or unwilling to engage in self-advocacy.

If fully implemented, such legislative measures have the potential to change the educational status of more than 30 million children with disabilities who currently do not have access to any form of education (Vaughan, 1997). The central government is working at present with over 1,500 NGOs in the disability field. According to Gopinathan (2003), there are over 750,000 students with disabilities in the mainstream of the education system where 1 million teachers in regular schools have had training in inclusive education. However, as noted by a number of researchers (Alur, 2002; Mani, 2002), when such statistics are viewed against the backdrop of the total number of children with special needs in India, it is clear that much remains to be done.

Mitchell and Desai (2003) point out that providing education to such a vast number of children with disabilities in regular school settings will require a number of challenges and issues to be addressed.

The challenge of modifying deeply held attitudes

School personnel, parents, students and the community generally hold deeply rooted negative attitudes towards people with a disability in India. A large majority of people who follow Hinduism, the predominant religion in India, believe in the doctrine of Karma. According to a number of writers (Baquer and Sharma, 1997; Bhatt, 1963; Davis, 2000; Desai and Desai, 1975; Karna, 1999) the doctrine of Karma has often militated against disabled persons because it is believed that their disabilities represent retribution for sins committed in a previous incarnation and, therefore, any efforts to improve their lot would interfere with the workings of divine justice. Thus, depending on the socio-economic and educational level of the Hindu family and the way it perceives its religion, reactions to the birth of a disabled child in the family can range from total acceptance to total neglect and the assumption of a fatalistic attitude towards the child. Dr Mithu Alur, who is a mother of a child with cerebral palsy and has undertaken extensive research in this area, found that disability was not seen as something normal or natural; rather, it was seen as an 'evil eye'. Families have become engulfed in guilt, stigma and fear, reinforced by negative attitudes from the community. Such deep-seated prejudice about disability, Alur adds, has affected the status in which disabled children are regarded and has led to much of the social exclusion of the disabled from their non-disabled peers in India (Alur, 2001; 2002). The modification of such attitudes, therefore, poses a continuing challenge to those involved in the process of implementing integration in schools.

Dissemination and public education

The community is largely unaware of the full intent and implications of the recently enacted legislation, the Persons with Disabilities Act (Sharma, 2001). Unless the wider community, especially parents of children with disabilities and school personnel, are made knowledgeable about the various provisions enshrined in the Act, the central and state governments' commitment to providing integrated education will be in vain.

The challenge of providing adequate levels of training to key stakeholders

The majority of school personnel in India are not trained to design and implement educational programmes for students with disabilities in regular schools (Das, 2001; Dev and Belfiore, 1996; Jangira, 1995; Jangira *et al.*, 1995; Sharma, 2001). In 1974, the central government initiated the IEDC scheme to promote the integration of students with mild to moderate disabilities into regular schools. Children were to be provided with financial support for books, stationery, school uniforms, transport, special equipment and aids. Each state government was provided financial assistance to implement this programme in regular schools. However, the programme met with little success. Rane (1983), in his evaluation of this programme in the state of Maharashtra, reported that the non-availability of trained and experienced teachers and the lack of understanding among regular school staff about the problems of disabled children and their educational needs were major contributory factors to the failure of the programme. Mani (1988) reported that by 1979–1980, only 1,881 children from eighty-one schools all over the country had benefited from this programme. Jangira (1990) attributed the lack of progress in implementing this scheme largely to the shortage of teachers specifically trained to work with disabled children. Appropriate levels of training targeted at preparing school personnel to implement effective integration programmes would, therefore, need to become a national priority.

Lack of coordination among various government departments

Alur (2000) points out that because of the lack of direction from the government and from NGOs, as well as factors such as ideological and conceptual issues, services for persons with disabilities are extremely fragmented. Her research suggests that the government has tended to rely too heavily on NGOs to educate children with disabilities. The NGOs, on the other hand, have contributed to this fragmentation by setting up centres of excellence that have removed the education of children with disabilities out of the public domain. As far as the education of children with disabilities is concerned, Alur states that there exists no cohesive policy.

Inadequate resources

The majority of schools in India are poorly designed and equipped to meet the unique needs of students with disabilities (Alur, 2000; Das, 2001; Sharma, 2001). Studies on integrated education in India continue to point to the lack of adequate equipment and appropriate instructional materials as a major impediment to the inclusion of children with disabilities in regular education classrooms (Dev and Belfiore, 1996; Rane, 1983; Sharma, 2001). If integration is to occur in schools, both the central and state governments will have to provide increased resources to address these issues.

Large class sizes

Most schools in India have large class sizes, with student-teacher ratios between 1:40 and 1:60. A number of researchers have reported that over-crowded classrooms are a major challenge to the implementation of inclusive education (Sharma, 2001; Swaroop, 2001). They warn that it may not be possible for teachers to accommodate students with disabilities in their classes unless this issue is given serious attention.

Educators' attitudes towards integrated education

Much of the research into integrated education during the past decade has been directed at exploring factors related to educators' attitudes towards the inclusion of disabled students into their schools. The following provides a brief synthesis of selected research on these aspects.

In 1991, Jangira and Srinivasan surveyed 59 educational administrators, 48 principals, 37 special education teachers and 96 regular classroom teachers from 47 randomly selected schools that were involved in the implementation of the IEDC scheme to determine their attitudes to the education of disabled children in regular schools. They found that the special education teachers expressed the most positive attitudes, followed by educational administrators and school principals. Regular classroom teachers exhibited the least positive attitudes. Panda (1991) examined the attitudes of 100 regular classroom teachers towards various types of disabilities in the state of Orissa. She found that teachers were generally negatively disposed towards children with epileptic disorders, emotional disturbance, and moderate and severe mental retardation. On the other hand, Dev and Belfiore (1996), who examined the attitudes of ninety-five teachers involved in the implementation of integrated education in Delhi, found them to be favourably disposed toward the inclusion of students with a disability. In a recent study, Sharma (2001) explored the attitudes and concerns of 310 primary school principals and 484 teachers working in government schools in Delhi regarding the integration of students with disabilities into regular school programmes. He found that the best predictors of teachers' attitudes towards integrated education were their length of teaching experience, contact with a student with a disability and perceived parental support for integrated education; while for the principals, perceived parental support for integrated education was the only significant predictor of their attitudes. He also found that both principals and teachers were concerned about the lack of resources (such as special education teachers and para-professional staff), the non-availability of instructional materials, the lack of funding, and their lack of training to implement integrated education.

Teacher competencies and perceived training needs

Mukhopadhyay (1990) surveyed teachers from four special schools located in Dehradun and Delhi and two higher secondary schools in Delhi and Coimbatore where integrated education was being implemented, in order to identify teaching competencies required to work with disabled children. The teachers ranked social goal setting, planning teaching activities, and ability to evaluate disabled students' learning outcomes as being the three most important competencies required to work with such students. The identification and placement of students with disabilities was ranked as the least important competency. Jangira *et al.* (1995) conducted a large-scale investigation involving 1,907 teachers (both primary and secondary) drawn from seven states in India to identify their training needs relative to integration. The teachers expressed a high level of training needs in the following areas: content of school subjects, methods of teaching, multi-grade teaching, play-way techniques for teaching and the preparation and use of improvised teaching aids. The most recent study on this aspect was conducted by Das (2001). Using a needs assessment strategy, Das surveyed 223 primary and 130 secondary school teachers to identify their perceived training needs to implement inclusive education programmes in Delhi. Several major findings emerged: both primary and secondary school teachers indicated a need for training in such aspects as professional knowledge, classroom climate, collaboration, assessment, classroom management, goal setting, resource management, instructional techniques, individualized instruction and evaluation. They particularly emphasized their need for intensive training in professional knowledge and assessment. Both primary and secondary school teachers identified conferences/conventions related to special education and workshops conducted by experts from outside India as their preferred mode for in-service training.

Conclusion

India appears to have established the necessary policy framework and legislation to implement integrated education. What is required, as noted by Mani (2002), is the acceleration of the services. Also, a number of challenges need to be addressed if students with disabilities are to be provided with an appropriate education in regular schools.

Japan: a cautious approach to inclusive education

While the vast majority of students with special educational needs in Japan receive their education in regular classes, for the most part these students are not identified, few adjustments are made to the curriculum or teaching strategies and little specialized support is provided. In outlining the ways in which regular schools accommodate such students, and the cultural values that contribute to the approaches adopted, this section will draw heavily upon the earlier work of one of the authors (Mitchell, 2002).[1]

Prevalence of students with special educational needs

According to the Ministry of Education, Science and Culture (Monbusho) figures for 1999, only 1.02 per cent of the school population received their education in special schools or special classes. There is good evidence, however, that the number of students needing special education support is considerably higher than this figure. Takuma *et al.* (2000), for example, present three sets of data that support this view. First, a 1967 survey revealed a prevalence rate of 3.69 per cent of students with disabilities in Japanese schools (Monbusho, 1967). Second, the National Institute of Special Education (1995) published the results of a national survey in which teachers reported on the proportion of students who were two or more years behind the expected level of achievement in the national curriculum in Japanese language and/or mathematics. By grades 5 and 6, nearly one in ten students were rated as being significantly behind their peers. The third study, which was carried out by Monbusho in 1998, reported that by junior high school and high school more than 20 per cent of students could not understand most or almost all of the content of lesson. While it is not possible to provide a firm estimate, the 'real' figure of students requiring special educational assistance would appear to fall within the range of 5–10 per cent, and possibly higher as students move through the school system.

Regular schools' provisions for students with special educational needs

Since the focus of this book is on inclusive education, special school provisions (which provide for just over 0.4 per cent of the school population and constitute a separate track within the Japanese system) will not be considered further.

Regular schools currently have three different types of arrangements for integrating students with officially recognized disabilities: special classes, resource rooms and limited integration for individual students.

Students in special classes

In 1998, there were 23,902 special classes attached to regular schools, accommodating a total of 67,974 students (Monbusho, 2000). The ratio of the total student population enrolled in these classes has been declining in recent years, dropping from 0.85 per cent in 1972 to 0.55 per cent in 1997. Most students in special classes spend an average of 7.5 hours per week in regular classes, mainly for 'non-academic' subjects (National Institute of Special Education, 2000). Students in special classes normally transfer to special schools on completion of junior high school, since high schools do not have special classes.

Students in resource rooms

In 1998, resource rooms attached to regular elementary and junior high schools accommodated a total of 24,342 students with mild disabilities (Monbusho, 2000). Since the inception of resource rooms in 1993, the ratio of students enrolled in them has been steadily increasing, rising from 0.13 per cent of the total student population in 1993 to 0.30 per cent in 1997. Students enrolled in resource classes are also enrolled in regular classes, where they spend most of their time. According to Mitchell (2002), three problems seem to be inherent in the resource room concept: (a) the travel time (approximately two-thirds of students enrolled in resource rooms have to travel to schools where these are located); (b) the lack of coordination of the programmes followed in the resource room and the students' home classes; and (c) the difficulties imposed on students in keeping up with the work in their home classes.

As well as the students with mild to moderate disabilities who are enrolled in special classes or resource rooms, a small number of students with severe disabilities attend regular classes as a result of parental insistence. These students may also receive support from special class or resource room teachers. No statistics are available on these students.

Schools' views on including students with disabilities in regular classes

In 2001, a Monbusho panel made a series of wide-ranging recommendations of direct relevance to the issue of inclusive education. The underlying principle was that education authorities should adopt policies to enable students with disabilities to become more self-reliant and integrated into society. Of most significance was the statement that, from 2002, 'students with disabilities that automatically qualify them for schools for the disabled, based on current standards, should be able to go to regular primary and middle schools *as exceptional cases if rational reasons are found for them to do so*' (emphasis added) (*Yomiuri Shinbun*, 15 January 2001). It must be noted that this highly qualified extension of access by students with disabilities was to regular schools, not necessarily to regular classes.

What, then, do schools think about the notion of classroom inclusion? In his study of eleven schools, Mitchell (2002) found that the broad concept was agreed to by the principals of eight of the eleven schools, with another two stating that it depended on the type of disability or the individual case and only one disagreeing with the concept. There was general agreement that if students with disabilities were included in regular classes, other students would learn to accept them (all eleven schools), they would learn more from other students (nine schools), their parents would feel happier (nine schools), and they would feel they belonged to normal society (seven schools). The schools gave mixed responses to the issue of such students having the right to be included, with only six agreeing with this proposition. General agreement was expressed about the following difficulties in including students with disabilities in regular classes: they would not be able to understand the lessons (ten schools), teachers are not trained to teach them (ten schools), the textbooks would be too difficult (nine schools), they need special equipment (nine schools), they would not be able to do the exams (eight schools), and they need special teachers and therapists (eight schools).

Mitchell (2002) also investigated how schools accommodated to students with special educational needs. He presented schools with a total of twenty-one categories of strategies based on initial observations in Japanese schools. Categories receiving a high number of mentions included teachers cooperating with parents of students with special educational needs (nine schools), the school nurse giving assistance (eight), teachers giving instruction outside of class time (seven), doctors giving assistance (seven), and teachers encouraging groups to assist (six). Some schools used a high proportion of the twenty-one strategies, with three schools using fourteen or fifteen, while some reported using as few as three.

As is the case in most countries, in Japan there are quite significant differences between elementary schools on the one hand, and junior high and high schools on the other, in their approaches to inclusion. As LeTendre (1999) has pointed out, the former are characterized by hands-on activities, problem solving, higher-order questioning, and creative manipulation of materials, whereas the latter are more drill-oriented and place less emphasis on creative problem-solving.

Critiques of special education

While it is clear that the majority of students with disabilities may be enrolled in regular classes, as Mogi (1994) notes, this does not mean that Japan has made great progress with mainstreaming. In fact, he claims, 'the majority of students with disabilities in regular classes cannot expect their disabilities to be taken into account' (p. 7). Similarly, according to Abe (1998), the rights of many students with mild handicaps or learning difficulties are being violated in regular classes, the most pressing problem confronting special education in Japan being that such students are placed in regular classes without adequate support.

Mitchell concluded that for inclusive education to be instituted more widely, many changes would have to be instituted. These include

(a) developing systematic screening and assessment procedures to identify students with special needs,
(b) adapting the curriculum and instituting individual education programmes,
(c) training teachers (especially at the junior high and high school levels) to use a greater range of teaching strategies,
(d) providing more professional advice to teachers on approaches to educating students with special needs,
(e) employing assistant teachers,
(f) expanding the number of school counsellors with educational psychology training, and
(g) involving parents more in decisions.

The cultural context

In coming to an understanding of Japanese schools' approach to inclusive education, it is vital to consider the prevailing cultural context. As LeTendre and Shimizu (1999) argue, 'Simply to label the system of special education in Japan as 'segregation' sheds no light on the psychological motives and ambivalence underlying the system' (p. 124). And further, 'Cultural values make certain choices available, and others difficult to obtain' (p. 128).

Several interlocking core values directly or indirectly impinge on attitudes towards inclusive education in Japan. (It should be noted, however, that these values are not necessarily universally subscribed to and, as LeTendre (1999) points out, many of them are undergoing change as Japan makes the transition to a post-industrial economy.)

Closed society

According to LeTendre and Shimizu (1999), the education of students with special education needs 'reflects on the concept of a "closed society" – a society that has closed off certain members of itself from participation in the full range of life of the community' (p. 116). Similar restrictions apply to cultural minorities who, as Motani (2002) claims, have been 'subjected to the assimilationist policies of the central government … [and] deprived of the opportunity to develop a positive identity as members of a minority group' (p. 227).

The notion of individual differences

Several writers have observed that Japanese schools are not much concerned with individual differences. Shimizu (1998), for example, cites a vice-principal who asserted that 'Japanese education, as a whole, is not set up to accommodate individual differences. What we do here is provide education according to collectively established frames of reference' (p. 79). According to Cave (2001), however, recent years have seen the emergence of the notions of individuality (*kosei*) and diversification (*tayoka*). While the ambiguity of these notions allows them to be used to justify a wide range of agendas, from neo-liberalism to progressivism, Cave argues that the latter tends to be favoured in practice.

With rare exceptions, people are born with equal capacities to achieve

In Shimizu's (1998) study, a principal explained that since a basic premise of Japanese education is that students are born with equal abilities, it does not make much sense to talk about 'ability differences' (*noryokusa*). Instead, it would be better to refer to 'difference in mastery levels' (*shujukudo*). The latter term 'would imply that individual differences are created as a result of schoolwork and individual effort, rather than naturally given ability' (p. 80).

Individual differences are created through cumulative effort, not innate ability

In general, Japanese believe that eventual success depends not so much on one's innate capacities, but on one's efforts over a long period to accumulate knowledge (*tsumikasane*) (Lee *et al.*, 1998; LeTendre, 1999; Shimizu, 1998; Stevenson and Stigler, 1992). Hence, 'potential is regarded in Japan as egalitarian – everyone has it, but some work harder than others to develop it' (White, 1987, p. 19). Except for students with clearly recognizable disabilities (who are mainly placed in special schools or special classes), teachers see all students as being capable of succeeding in school.

Since all students are equal, any special attention is seen as discriminatory

As Walsh (2000) has observed, a core cultural belief is that 'all students are equal and should be treated as such' (p. 127). Japanese teachers thus feel ability grouping is discriminatory and impinges on students' right to equal educational opportunity (Shimizu, 1998). Apart from violating the principle of fairness, Japanese teachers believe that ability-based grouping would have potentially detrimental effects on slow learners (Sato, 1998) and 'would hurt students emotionally so much that they would lose their motivation to study' (Shimizu, 1998, p. 100).

Self-discipline is important and is moulded through experiencing hardship

Japanese culture values self-discipline, a personality characteristic that is moulded through experiences involving 'hardship (*kuro*), endurance (*gaman, nintai, shimbo, gambaru*), effort (*doryoku*); and the utmost self-exertion (*isshokemmei*)' (Befu, 1986, quoted by Sato, 1998, p. 123). Japanese believe that hardship builds character, and that anyone can acquire the habit and virtue of self-discipline. As noted by White (1987), *kuro* (suffering or hardship) is believed to have a beneficial effect on the self, deepening and maturing it, removing self-centredness: 'Without *kuro*, one cannot be said to have grown up' (p. 29).

Effort and motivation to do well are as important as success

According to Shimizu (1998), the Japanese give higher regard to people who are motivated than to those with only ability or talent. In short, the motive to do well is considered to be a virtue in its own right. Furthermore, motivation is viewed as a characteristic that teachers can actively cultivate. Japanese teachers and parents often use the expression, 'If you tried your hardest, it wouldn't matter if you succeeded or not' (Shimizu, 1998, p. 92).

Much education is relations-oriented and emphasizes the importance of group life

According to several writers, Japanese culture prizes the relational aspect of self in interaction with others, the surrounding environment, aspects of oneself, and experiences (Rohlen and LeTendre, 1998; Sato, 1998). Further, 'the boundaries between self and other are not clearly distinguishable and are constantly negotiated as contexts change' (Sato, 1998, p. 122). Thus, in Japan, the educational enterprise is not just individual; instead, it is a series of carefully nurtured relationships, beginning with the family, extending to the school, and including identification with successively larger communities. In this life-long process, 'the starting point, means, and ends of education become caring relationships established between all members of a learning community' (Sato, 1998, p. 126). For the Japanese, according to White (1987), the most highly valued qualities are those that make a person 'human-like' (*ningen-rashii*) and the most valued quality is an ability to maintain harmony as members of a group or society. This ideal of group living (*shudan seikatsu*) means that while school achievements are important, they should be judged as a demonstration of a capacity to be a good social person (White, 1987).

This does not mean, however, that the individual is entirely subordinated. Cooperating with others does not necessarily mean giving up the self, but in fact results from inner self-control and self-discipline and is the appropriate means by which one expresses and enhances oneself (White, 1987). Thus, education centres on how individual rights and group responsibility go hand-in-hand, a process that requires negotiated trade-offs and degrees of sacrifice at every turn. As Sato (1998) noted, 'Constant attention to others is both restrictive of individual freedom and yet expansive in terms of the gains made possible through group connectedness and support' (p. 127). In a similar vein, Cave (2001) notes that while Japan is correctly seen as a group-oriented society, such a view should not obscure the genuine individuality that exists, even if the form that individuality takes in Japan is rather different from in most Western countries. The contrast is that the former perceive individuality in the context of interdependent relationships, whereas the latter perceive it as being an expression of independence.

Education should be concerned with the whole person

It follows from the preceding core values that schools would have as their goal the creation of well-rounded human beings, 'the trademark of [the Japanese] compulsory education system', according to Shimizu (1998, p. 98). Several writers have observed that this is indeed the case and that Japanese teachers consider students' emotional, social, physical and mental development to be as important as their cognitive development (Okano and Tsuchiya, 1999; Sato, 1993). Knowledge transmission is secondary to a more comprehensive emphasis on developing human beings (*ningen*), and at the core of *ningen* is *kokoro*, the centre of the physical, cognitive, spiritual, aesthetic, and emotional self (Sato, 1993).

Conclusion

Taken together, the cultural values that permeate Japan, to a greater or lesser extent, provide some understanding for the reluctance of Japanese schools to fully embrace a Western model of inclusive education. Such a model would, for example, challenge such notions as the relationship between individuals and the broader society, the rejection of innate differences, the importance of effort to achieve success, even if it means hardship, the importance of group identity, and concern for the whole person.

Singapore: a meritocratic market economy

In Singapore, there is a dual system of education: a special education system for students with moderate, severe or profound disabilities, whereas those without disabilities or those with milder learning, emotional, behavioural, sensory and physical disorders are in the general education system (Lim and Tan, 1999). Thus, efforts at inclusion have been limited to those students who have higher intellectual functioning. In general, students with special needs have low status in Singapore, a situation that, at least in part, reflects the country's adherence to the principles of marketization.

Provisions for students with special educational needs

In June 2001, 4,010 students (approximately 1 per cent of the school popula-tion) were placed in nineteen segregated special schools under the control of voluntary welfare organizations (VWOs) with substantial, but not full, government funding administered largely through the National Council of Social Services (NCSS) (Lim and Nam, 2000; Rose, 2000). In 2001, these schools were staffed by twenty-seven Ministry of Education (MOE) trained teachers and by another 628 teachers. There is no legislation or coherent set of policies governing standards for educating students with special educa-tional needs, the nine VWOs enjoying a high degree of administrative and professional autonomy. For example, special schools are under no obligation to follow Singapore's national curriculum, which means that once children enter a special school it would be very difficult to integrate or re-integrate them into the regular school system. The arguments for VWOs controlling education for students with disabilities, according to Lim and Tan (1999), centre on the assumptions that such organizations have a strong sense of mission and possess an autonomy that allows them to respond quickly to changing needs and demands.

Two services provided by VWOs support students with disabilities in regular school settings: First, 'TEACH ME' seeks to include children with physical disabilities within mainstream education. Second, a programme called 'WeCan', under the auspices of the Autism Resource Centre, facili-tates the inclusion of children with autism. This programme (earlier referred to as 'REACH ME') has three components: one aims to place autistic chil-dren into the mainstream by school entry, another to help such students to access the mainstream curriculum (but remain excluded), while a third works within an exclusive setting and separate curriculum. Also, since 1992, learning support coordinators work in most primary schools to assist them in catering for students with learning difficulties (Quah and Jones, 1997). Their task is made difficult by the widespread practice of whole class teaching, which is a response to large classes and a tight curriculum (Ng *et al.*, 1997). Furthermore, as Rao (1999) has pointed out, there is a growing trend among teachers in regular schools to refer students with mild disabili-ties to special schools because of their concerns about behaviour problems, short attention spans and their failure as teachers to cope with such students. Once referred to the special education system, such students rarely, if ever, return to the regular education system (Rao, 1999).

Low status of students with special educational needs

In that the education of students with special educational needs does not fully fall under the auspices of the MOE, but is the responsibility of VWOs, it may be seen as a form of charity, rather than as a right to be enjoyed by all students. This would seem to suggest that such students have a low status in Singapore. There are other indicators: First, even though the MOE funds special schools at around 2.5 times the recurrent costs of educating students in national schools, and NCSS funds at another 1.5 times, VWOs are required to seek donations to meet the full costs. Also, parents of students with special educational needs are expected to pay school fees and transport costs, although these can be reduced in exceptional circumstances. This situation is unlikely to change in the immediate future, as is clear from a 2001 speech by Dr Aline Wong, then Senior Minister of State for Education: 'In the provision of education for children in [special education] schools, an effective partnership involving concerned and caring individuals, voluntary welfare organizations, private companies and the public sector must always exist'. Further, in its August 2000 report, the Committee on Compulsory Education noted that it had been assured that the MOE

> will continue its funding and support for special education on a cost-sharing basis with NCSS and the VWOs. Such partnerships among MOE, NCSS and the VWOs are in line with the 'many helping hands' approach to looking after the needs of the less fortunate in society.

Second, students with special educational needs have less well-qualified teachers than other students. Students training to be special educators must complete their studies while at the same time carrying out their teaching responsibilities in their sponsoring special schools. This double load of teaching and studying means that students have little time to read widely in the field and are often tired and stressed. Because of the restricted time students can devote to their studies in the two years' part-time programme, the content of the programme is necessarily focused on 'survival skills' and cannot proceed much beyond introductory concepts. Given this lower level of training, it is not surprising that teachers working in special schools have significantly lower salaries than those working in regular schools. Further, they are not eligible to join the Teachers' Union, which exclusively oversees the welfare of those under the MOE.

Third, as recommended by the Committee on Compulsory Education (2000), and later expressed in the Compulsory Education Act of 2001, 'special needs children who are not able to attend national schools because of physical/ intellectual disabilities [should] be automatically exempted from [compulsory education] in national schools' (p. 19). Instead, the Committee recognized that 'children with learning disabilities are much more able to develop their full potential if they attend special education schools where they are taught by specially trained teachers, supported by para-medical personnel, and can learn at their own pace'. Instead of recommending compulsory attendance in such special schools, the Committee thought this would be 'unduly harsh on the parents of such children … particularly since the VWOs are not yet able to complete the building programme for special education schools, nor able to provide all the teaching resources for educating such children' (p. 19). A related point is that because of waiting lists in some special schools (229 in June 2001), some students with special educational needs do not have ready access to education.

Notwithstanding the above, it must be noted that Singapore is a signatory to two important UN documents relating to the education of students with disabilities. The first of these, the 1993 UN Standard Rules on the Equalization of Opportunities for Persons with Disabilities, includes the following statement: 'States should recognize the principle of equal primary, secondary and tertiary educational opportunities for children, youth and adults with disabilities, in integrated settings. They should ensure that the education of persons with disabilities is an integral part of the educational system'. The second document is the Asian and Pacific Decade of Disabled Persons 1993–2002. Among the Agenda for Action adopted by the signatory countries are the principles of 'specific inclusion of children and adults with disabilities in national formal and non-formal programmes to meet the goal of education for all', 'support for the participation of children and adults with different types of disabilities in the mainstream of the educational system', and the 'gradual integration of special education into mainstream education.'

Earlier, in 1988, the Advisory Council for the Disabled looked into the problems and needs of people with disabilities in Singapore, with a view to helping them integrate into society. Among the recommendations were that 'the MOE should take over the administration of special schools', and that

> where appropriate and feasible, special education should be provided within the regular education system. A child should be placed in a special school if [he/she] cannot be well educated in a regular school … integration should fit the disabled child to the most suitable educational environment.
>
> (pp. 37–38)

These recommendations did not lead to any significant move towards inclusive education.

Underlying philosophies

What, then underpins Singapore's segregationist policies? The answer perhaps lies in the elitist, meritocratic and market economics philosophy that has characterized Singapore since its inception as a country. At a broad, societal level, there seems to be a general perception that persons with disabilities are economic liabilities. As Parker (2001), points out, Singapore is not a 'welfare state' as might be understood by a Western audience. He goes on to cite the example that, initially, because the cost of elevators was deemed to be too high for the few potential beneficiaries, the Mass Rail Transit system was not made wheelchair-accessible (he also notes that this policy was changing and access features were being retrofitted).

According to Lim and Tan (2001), 'because inclusion demands fundamental school restructuring, the basic notions of schooling and education are called into serious discourse, debate and re-examination' (p. 178). They note a number of tensions in the Singapore education system that affect opportunities for inclusion: tensions between conservatism and innovation, competition and collaboration, diversity and uniformity, and elitism and equity. Earlier, they had pointed out that the principles of marketization that drive Singapore's education system 'produces forces and rewards that tear the very fabric of building school communities which teach students to embrace and value diversity' (Lim and Tan, 1999, p. 340). They argue that the marketization of education has two distinct features: increased autonomy for schools and increased competition among schools. First, several secondary schools have been granted various degrees of autonomy (although they are still subject to the national curriculum and examination system). Of relevance to the issue of inclusion is the fact that all independent schools are academically selective – a reflection of the well entrenched elitist philosophy of the Singapore government, according to Milne and Mauzy (1990). Second, there is increased stress on competition among schools, with schools being ranked annually since 1992. As noted by Lim and Tan (1999), the capacity to be selective provides schools with incentive for attracting students who are likely to be assets and, conversely, deters them from accepting students who might depress their scores. Lim and Tan argue that until performance indicators reflect a greater recognition of the diverse abilities of students, those with special educational needs will continue to be marginalized within the regular education system. Somewhat optimistically, they point to the recent emphasis on values such as graciousness and compassion for others as educational outcomes as encouraging portents of changing attitudes towards students with disabilities. Whether they become translated into a shift towards greater inclusion, however, remains to be seen.

Conclusion

Students with moderate to profound disabilities are well outside the mainstream of education in Singapore, while those with milder disabilities, although included in the mainstream, are often marginalized. This situation reflects the dominant role played by cost-benefit analyses of the economic worth of students with special educational needs.

Conclusion: contrasting countries

From this brief review, it is clear that inclusive education in Asia is filtered through a variety of contextual factors – cultural, political, economic and demographic; further, these factors change over time. For these reasons, only limited generalizations can be made across such a vast and diverse continent.

Although there is no common pattern of provisions for students with special educational needs, the countries of Asia (as elsewhere in the world) are facing a common set of dilemmas, and their associated (and inter-related) tensions:

The tension between the global and the local. While the philosophy of inclusive education has been promulgated globally, particularly through the UN and its agencies, each individual country must reach its own under-standing of how it can be incorporated into its own culture. In this chapter, we have seen several examples of this localization of the philosophy of inclusion: Japan with its reliance on resource rooms, China with its learning in regular classrooms initiative, India with its Persons with Disabilities Act of 1995 to promote integrated education, and Singapore with its minimal accommodations.

The tension between catering for students with mild disabilities and those with severe disabilities. Almost without exception, the notion of inclusive education in Asia has been limited to students with mild disabilities, those with severe or profound disabilities either being catered for in special schools, or, as is the case in most of the developing countries in Asia, not at all. The result in every country has been the emergence of a dual system of education.

The tension between Western and Asian philosophical assumptions. Since inclusive education had its origins largely in Western education systems, it is important to consider some of the conflicts that can arise when it comes to it being adopted in Asian contexts. In particular, as we have seen in this chapter, there is a tension between the value placed on individualism in the Western notion of inclusion, and the Asian values of collectivism. Thus, in both China and Japan, collective societal interests take precedence over individualism, reflecting the influence of Confucian thought and, in the case of China, socialist ideology.

The tension between pursuing equity on the one hand, and excellence on the other. This tension is one that occurs in most countries as they seek to obtain economic advantage through developing the skills of their populations, whilst at the same time paying regard to the needs of their disadvantaged citizens. This takes a related form in the tension between catering for the needs of the majority and the needs of minorities (including disabled persons). Thus, Singapore clearly has opted for the pursuit of excellence, with much less regard to equity imperatives; Japan seeks both equity and excellence; China and India have given priority to providing education for the majority of their populations.

The tension between the state assuming full responsibility for educating students with special educational needs and following a charity framework. Partly on economic grounds and partly in recognition of the low status of persons with disabilities, some countries (e.g. Singapore and India) rely heavily on voluntary agencies, expecting or allowing NGOs to make provisions for students with special educational needs. In others (e.g. China and Japan), the state assumes principal responsibility, even if, in the former case, this has not extended to making provisions for all such students.

The tension between pursuing the ideology of inclusive education and adopting pragmatic solutions in practice. While many of the countries in Asia have adopted international covenants on inclusion, practice often falls short of what has been advocated. This gap between theory and practice reflects a host of factors: economic, logistical, teacher attitudes and capability, parental attitudes, and cultural. The result often is that inclusion along Western lines is a rare occurrence, the most common pattern being something more equivalent to integration. When full inclusion appears to occur, it frequently takes the form of placement with little or minimal support.

These discrepancies between Western and Asian interpretations of inclusive education should not be surprising for, as Kyung-Chul (2001), writes: 'No social products, including educational change, can be transferred directly from one area to another. They are products of the social context and cannot be separated from their unique place and time' (p. 260).

Note

1 In preparing this section on Japan, permission to use parts of an article included in *The Journal of School Education*, volume 14, published by Hyogo University of Teacher Education, Japan, is gratefully acknowledged. David Mitchell would also like to acknowledge the support and guidance provided by Professor Shigeru Narita and his colleagues in his study of Japanese schools.

References

Abe, Y. (1998). 'Special education reform in Japan'. *European Journal of Special Needs Education*, 13(1), 86–97.

Alur, M. (2000). *Invisible children: A study of policy exclusion.* Paper presented at the International Special Education Congress, Manchester, UK.

——(2001). 'Some cultural and moral implications of inclusive education in India'. *Journal of Moral Education*, 30(3), 287–292.

——(2002). 'Introduction: The social construct of disability'. In S. Hegarty and M. Alur (eds) *Education and children with special needs* (pp. 21–22). New Delhi: Sage.

Baquer, A. and Sharma, A. (1997). *Disability: Challenges vs. response*. New Delhi: Concerted Action Now.

Bhatt, U. (1963). *The physically handicapped in India*. Bombay: Popular Book Depot.

Blatchford, P. and Catchpole, G. (2003). 'Class size and classroom processes'. In J.P. Keeves and R. Watanabe (eds) *International handbook of educational research in the Asia-Pacific Region* (pp. 741–754). Dordrecht: Kluwer Academic Publishers.

Cave, P. (2001). 'Educational reform in Japan in the 1990s: 'individuality' and other uncertainties'. *Comparative Education Review*, 37(2), 173–191.

Chadha, A. (2000). 'Special education: Empowerment through education'. *Journal of The International Association of Special Education*, 3(1), 17–22.

Cheng, K.M. (1990). 'The culture of schooling in East Asia'. In N. Entwistle (ed.) *Handbook of educational ideas and practices* (pp. 163–173). London: Routledge.

——(1994). 'Young adults in a changing socialist society: Post-compulsory education in China'. *Comparative Education*, 30, 63–72.

Committee on Compulsory Education in Singapore (2000). *Report*. Singapore: Ministry of Education.

Das, A. (2001). *Perceived training needs of regular primary and secondary school teachers to implement inclusive education programs in Delhi, India*. Unpublished doctoral dissertation, University of Melbourne.

Dasgupta, P.R. (2002). 'Education for the disabled'. In S. Hegarty and M. Alur (eds) *Education and children with special needs* (pp. 41–50). New Delhi: Sage Publications.

Davis, P. (2000). 'A drop in the Indian Ocean'. *Educare News, School profile series*, April.

Deng, M., Fong Poon-McBrayer, K. and Farnsworth, E.B. (2001). 'The development of special education in China: A sociocultural review'. *Remedial and Special Education*, 22(5), 288–298.

Deng, M. and Manset, G. (2000). 'Analysis of the Learning in Regular Classrooms movement in China'. *Mental Retardation*, 38, 124–130.

Desai, U. and Desai, I.P. (1975). 'Counselling the parents of handicapped children'. *Journal of the Faculty of Education, University of Durban-Westville, South Africa*, 1(2), 63–74.

Dev, P.C. and Belfiore, P.J. (1996). *Mainstreaming students with disabilities: Teacher perspectives in India*. Paper presented at the Annual International Convention of the Council of Exceptional Children, Orlando FL.

Dooley, K. (2001). 'Re-envisioning teacher preparation: Lessons from China'. *Journal of Education for Teaching*, 27(3), 241–251.

Gopinathan, A. (2003). Statement presented at the 2nd session of the ad hoc committee on a comprehensive and integral international convention on the protection and promotion of the rights and dignity of persons with disability.

Inayatullah (2003). 'Adult literacy in the Asia-Pacific Region'. In J. Keeves R. Watanabe (eds) *International handbook of educational research in the Asia-Pacific region* (pp. 293–304). Dordrecht: Kluwer Academic Publishers.

Jangira, N.K. (1990). 'Education for all: What about these forgotten children?' *Education and Society*, 1(4), 2–4.

——(1995). 'Rethinking teacher education'. *Prospects: Quarterly Review of Comparative Education*, 25(2), 261–272.

Jangira, N.K., Singh, A. and Yadav, S.K. (1995). 'Teacher policy, training needs and perceived status of teachers'. *Indian Educational Review*, 30(1), 113–122.

Jangira, N.K. and Srinivasan, A. (1991). 'Attitudes of educational administrators and teachers toward education of disabled children'. *Indian Journal of Disability and Rehabilitation*, July-December, 25–35.

Jha, M.M. (2002). *School without walls: Inclusive education for all*. Oxford: Heinemann.

Karna, G.N. (1999). *United Nations and rights of disabled persons: a study in Indian perspective*. New Delhi: A.P.H. Publishing Corporation.

Kholi, T. (1993). 'Special education in Asia'. In P. Mittler, R. Brouilette and D. Harris (eds) *Special needs education* (pp. 118–129). London: Kogan Page.

Kyung-Chul, H. (2001). 'Big change questions: Is finding the right balance with regard to educational change possible, given the tensions that occur between global influences and local traditions, in countries in Asia-Pacific?' *Journal of Educational Change*, 2, 257–260.

Lee, S.Y., Graham, T. and Stevenson, H. (1998). 'Teachers and teaching: Elementary schools in Japan and the United States'. In T. Rohlen and G. LeTendre (eds) *Teaching and learning in Japan* (pp. 157–189). New York: Cambridge University Press.

LeTendre, G.K. (1998). 'The role of school in Japanese adolescents' lives'. In *The education system in Japan: Case study findings* (pp. 137–182). Washington DC: National Institute on Student Achievement, Curriculum, and Assessment, Office of Educational Research and Improvement, US Department of Education.

——(1999). 'The problem of Japan: Qualitative studies and international educational comparisons'. *Educational Researcher*, 28(2), 38–45.

LeTendre, G.K. and Shimizu, H. (1999). 'Towards a healing society: Perspectives from Japanese special education'. In P. Garner and H. Daniels (eds) *World yearbook of education: Inclusive education* (pp. 115–129). London: Kogan Page.

Lim, L. and Nam, S.S. (2000). 'Special education in Singapore'. *The Journal of Special Education*, 34(2), 104–109.

Lim, L. and Tan, J. (1999). 'Marketization of education in Singapore: Prospects for inclusive education'. *International Journal of Inclusive Education*, 3(4), 339–351.

——(2001). 'Addressing disability in educational reforms: A force for renewing the vision of Singapore 21'. In J. Tan, S. Gopinathan and H.W. Kam (eds) *Challenges facing the Singapore education system today* (pp. 175–188). Singapore: Prentice-Hall.

Maclean, R. (2001). 'Educational change in Asia: An overview'. *Journal of Educational Change*, 2, 189–192.

Mani, M.N.G. (2002). 'Integrated education for disabled children: Cost effective approaches'. In S. Hegarty and M. Alur (eds) *Education and children with special needs* (pp. 97–103). New Delhi: Sage Publications.

Mani, R. (1988). *Physically handicapped in India*. Delhi: Ashish Publishing House.

Milne, R.S. and Mauzy, D.K. (1990). *Singapore: The legacy of Lee Kuan Yew*. Boulder CO: Westview Press.

Ministry of Law, Justice and Company Affairs, Government of India (1996). *The Persons with Disabilities (Equal Opportunities, Protection of Rights and Full Participation) Act, 1995*, New Delhi: Government of India.

Ministry of Welfare (1997). *Mid-term review meeting on the progress of implementation of the agenda for action for the Asian and the Pacific Decade of Disabled Persons.* New Delhi: Government of India.

Ministry of Welfare, Government of India (1996). *Report on manpower development.* New Delhi: Government of India.

Mitchell, D. (1999a). *Bridging the gap between expectations and realities: Special education in Asia and the Pacific.* Paper Presented at 15th Annual Pacific Rim Conference on Disabilities, Honolulu, 1–2 February 1999.

——(1999b). 'Transfer of beliefs, knowledge and experiences between countries'. In P. Retish and S. Reiter (eds) *Adults with disabilities: International perspectives in the community* (pp. 259–285). Mahwah NJ: Lawrence Erlbaum Associates.

——(2002). 'Japanese schools' accommodation to student diversity' *The Journal of School Education*, 14, 159–178. (Published by Hyogo University of Teacher Education).

Mitchell, D. and Desai, I. (2003). 'Inclusive education for students with special needs'. In J.P. Keeves and R. Watanabe (eds) *International handbook of educational research in the Asia-Pacific Region* (pp. 203–215). Dordrecht: Kluwer Academic Publishers.

Mogi, T. (1994). 'Current issues on human rights of persons with disabilities in Japan'. *Japanese Journal of Studies on Disability and Handicap*, 22(2), 5–10.

Monbusho (1967). *Situation of disabled pupils/students – Nation-wide survey of disabled students.* Tokyo: Monbusho. (Cited by Takuma *et al.*, 2000).

——(2000). *Statistical abstract of education, science, sports and culture: 2000 edition.* Tokyo: Monbusho.

Motani, Y. (2002). 'Toward a more just educational policy for minorities in Japan: The case of Korean ethnic schools'. *Comparative Education*, 38 (2), 225–237.

Mukhopadhyay, S. (1990). Identifying teaching competencies specifically for integrated education of the disabled children. Unpublished manuscript. New Delhi, India: NCERT.

Nanzhao, Z. (1996). 'Interactions of education and culture for economic and human development: An Asian perspective'. In J. Delors (ed.) *Learning: The treasure within. Report to UNESCO of the International Commission on Education for the Twenty-first Century* (pp. 238–246). Paris: UNESCO.

National Institute of Special Education (1995). *Report of special research project: Subtype and intervention research on pupils and students with learning difficulties in specific academic skills.* Yokusuka: The National Institute of Special Education. (Cited by Takuma, Ochiai and Munekata, 2000).

——(2000). *Nation-wide survey of curriculum and educational methods in special classes for students with intellectual disabilities.* Yokusuka: The National Institute of Special Education.

Ng, M., Chew, J., Lee, C.K-E. and D'Rozario, V. (1997). 'A survey of classroom practices in Singapore: Preliminary findings'. BERA Annual Conference, York, UK. Cited by Blatchford, P. and Catchpole, G. (2003). Class size and classroom processes. In J.P. Keeves and R. Watanabe (eds) *International handbook of educational research in the Asia-Pacific Region* (pp. 741–754). Dordrecht: Kluwer Academic Publishers.

Okano, K., and Tsuchiya, M. (1999). *Education in contemporary Japan: Inequality and diversity.* Cambridge: Cambridge University Press.

Panda, B.K. (1991). *Attitudes of parents and community members toward disabled children*. Unpublished doctoral dissertation, Utkal University.

Parker, K.J. (2001). 'Changing attitudes towards persons with disabilities in Asia'. *Disability Studies Quarterly*, 21(4). 105–113.

Potts, P. (2000). 'A Western perspective on inclusion in Chinese urban educational settings'. *International Journal of Inclusive Education*, 4(4), 301–312.

——(2003). *Modernising education in Britain and China: Comparative perspectives on excellence and social inclusion*. London: RoutledgeFalmer.

Quah, M.L. and Jones, K. (1997). 'Reshaping learning support in a rapidly developing society'. *Support for Learning*, 12(1), 38–42.

Rane, A. (1983). *An evaluation of the scheme of integrated education for handicapped children based on a study of the working of the scheme in Maharashtra*. Bombay: Unit for Child and Youth Research, Tata Institute of Social Sciences.

Rao, I. (2000). *A comparative study of UN rules and Indian Disability Act 1995*. E-mail obtained from cbrnet@vsnl.com on 17 March 2000.

Rao, M.S. (1999). *Beliefs and attitudes towards children with disabilities*. Unpublished M.A. dissertation, Nanyang Technological University, Singapore.

Rohlen, T.P. and LeTendre, G.K. (1998). 'Conclusion: themes in the Japanese culture of learning'. In T.P. Rohlen and G.K. LeTendre (eds) *Teaching and learning in Japan* (pp. 369–376). Cambridge: Cambridge University Press.

Rose, D. (2000). 'Special education in Singapore'. *Saudi Journal of Disability and Rehabilitation*, 6(4), 261–265.

Sachdeva, S. (2003). *Education scenario and needs in India: Building a perspective for 2025*. New Delhi: Centre for Policy Research.

Sato, N. (1993). 'Teaching and learning in Japanese elementary classrooms: A context for understanding'. *Peabody Journal of Education*, 68(4), 111–147.

——(1998). 'Honoring the individual'. In T. Rohlen and G. LeTendre (eds) *Teaching and learning in Japan* (pp. 119–153). Cambridge: Cambridge University Press.

Sharma, U. (2001). *The attitudes and concerns of school principals and teachers regarding the integration of students with disabilities into regular schools in Delhi, India*. Unpublished doctoral dissertation, University of Melbourne.

Shimizu, H. (1998). 'Individual differences and the Japanese education system'. In R.W. Riley, T. Takai, and J.C. Conaty (eds) *The educational system in Japan: Case study findings* (pp. 79–134). Washington DC: National Institute on Student Achievement, Curriculum, and Assessment, Office of Educational Research and Improvement, US Department Of Education.

Singh, R. (2001). *Needs of the hour: A paradigm shift in education*. Paper presented at the North-South Dialogue on Inclusive Education, Mumbai, India, February 2001.

Stevenson, H. and Stigler, J. (1992). *The learning gap*. New York: Simon and Schuster.

Swaroop, S. (2001). 'Inclusion and beyond'. Paper presented at the North-South Dialogue on Inclusive Education, Mumbai, India, February 2001.

Takuma, S., Ochiai, T. and Munekata, T. (2000). 'Contemporary issues and trends in special needs education in Japan'. In C. Brock and R. Griffin (eds) *International perspectives on special needs education* (pp. 251–275). Saxmundham, Suffolk, UK: John Catt Educational.

Timmons, V. and Alur, M. (2004). 'Transformational learning: A description of how inclusionary practice was accepted in India'. *International Journal of Special Education*, 19(1), 38–48.

UNESCO (1994). *World Conference on Special Needs Education: Access and quality. Salamanca Declaration and Framework for Action.* Paris: UNESCO.

United Nations (1993). *Standard Rules on the Equalization of Opportunities for Persons with Disabilities.* New York: United Nations.

——(1997/98). *Asian and Pacific Decade of Disabled Persons 1993–2002: Agenda for action of the decade.* Bangkok: ESCAP, UN.

Vaughan, M. (1997). Report on India conferences. URL: http://www.mailbase.ac.uk/lists-f-j/inclusive-education/files/india.txt

Villa, R.A., Tac, L.V., Muc, P.M, Ryan, S., Thuy, N.T.M., Weill, C. and Thousand, J.S. (2003). 'Inclusion in Vietnam: More than a decade of implementation'. *Research and Practice for Persons with Severe Disabilities*, 28(1), 23–32.

Walsh, D.J. (2000). 'Space and early schooling: From culture to pedagogy'. *The Journal of School Education*, 12, 123–137.

White, M. (1987). *The Japanese educational challenge: A commitment to students.* New York: The Free Press.

Yang, H. and Wang, H.B. (1994). 'Special education in China'. *The Journal of Special Education*, 28(1), 93–105.

Zhang, T. (2003). 'Education of children in remote areas'. In J.P. Keeves and R. Watanabe (eds) *International handbook of educational research in the Asia-Pacific Region* (pp. 171–188). Dordrecht: Kluwer Academic Publishers.

Chapter 9

Inclusive education and equity in Latin America

Todd Fletcher and Alfredo J. Artiles[1]

In this chapter, we discuss inclusive education in Latin America in the context of global educational reform initiatives, specifically, the growing commitment to provide an inclusive education for all individuals. We high-light the socio-historical contexts of inclusive education in Latin America as embodied in tensions stemming from the dialectics of the global and the local, the pressures to achieve economic development while strengthening democratic traditions and institutions, and the expectations to invest in and sustain inclusive educational systems that serve the needs of *all* culturally diverse populations. We use a case example to illustrate the development of inclusive education in one Latin American country, namely Mexico. The case example sheds light on the mediating role of the aforementioned tensions that emerge in the midst of the changing socio-cultural, economic, and political realities of a country.

The global context

Scholars characterize globalization as the dominant international system today that has major implications for the development and transformation of educational systems (Arnove and Torres, 1999). Globalization is defined as 'processes of change, generating at once centrifugal (qua the borders of the nation state) and centripetal (qua the post-national) forces that result in the de-territorialization of important economic, social, and cultural practices from their traditional moorings in the nation state' (Suárez-Orozco, 2001, p. 347). Friedman (2000) states that globalization may be best described as forces thrusting the world towards internationalization, inclusiveness, and integration. Globalization has three constitutive elements, namely '1) new information and communication technologies; 2) the emergence of global markets and post-national knowledge-intensive economies; and 3) unprecedented levels of immigration and displacement' (Suárez-Orozco, 2001, p. 345). The manifestations of these forces are apparent in educational reform initiatives that are occurring worldwide. They have a direct impact on current educational processes that are essentially changing the international educational and cultural landscape of the planet. Interestingly, the emergence of globalization is creating tensions between nations' economic development and their commitment to democratization processes and equity agendas (Arnove, 1999). Despite these tensions, however, we are witnessing a growing commitment to education for all – at least as reflected in official rhetoric. Specifically, there is evidence that globalization might be pressing nations to privilege competition and economic restructuring for the sake of competitiveness, and productivity at the expense of equity-minded development blueprints. This is certainly the case in the Latin American region (Arnove *et al.*, 1999).

The goal of this chapter is to provide an overview of inclusive education in Latin America in larger globalization processes and persistent social inequalities. Several important premises inform our work. First, we assume the study of reform and restructuring in special education must be examined in the larger context of global transformations taking place that are also affecting general education systems throughout the world. Second, education processes and outcomes need to be examined and interpreted as embedded in complex political and cultural dimensions. This means questions of historical trajectory, power, and the social locations of participants must be taken into account (Artiles, 2003). Third, the notion of inclusive education must be defined explicitly, as there is a variety of definitions and models used under this umbrella concept. Thus, it is critical that analyses of inclusion explicitly identify the varieties of inclusion under scrutiny. Fourth, even if two nations use the same definition of inclusion, it is critical to understand the precursors that shaped the development of inclusive education movements in each nation, as well as the functions that inclusion has served in those societies (Artiles and Larsen, 1998).

The Latin American demographic and socioeconomic contexts

According to the *Encyclopedia Britannica*, the definition of Latin America includes the countries of North and South America (including Mexico, Central America, and the islands of the Caribbean) whose inhabitants speak a romance language. Most frequently, the term 'Latin America' is restricted to countries whose inhabitants speak either Spanish or Portuguese, but the French-speaking areas of Haiti and French Guyana may also be included (*Encyclopedia Britannica*, 2003). Latin America is a rich and culturally complex region with approximately 50 million indigenous people, almost 400 different indigenous groups, and a multitude of languages, dialects and cultures that are of both aboriginal origin and the product of European and African migration (Comboni Salinas and Juarez Nuñez, 2000).

Latin America is a young subcontinent; UNICEF has estimated that 40 per cent of the world's population of children lives in the region (Albarrán de

Alba, 1996). Unfortunately, Latin America has greater income inequality than any other region in the world: 'at least one in three households and two in five persons live below the poverty line' (Reimers, 2000a, p. 57). Poverty and inequality persist and, in fact, characterize the region – this defining aspect, in turn, contributes to shape another distinctive attribute of the subcontinent, namely the sizeable gulf in educational achievement between the haves and the have-nots (Reimers, 2000b). Although the level of poverty was reduced between 1950 and 1980, by the end of the 1990s it was reversed to the 1980 level (Reimers, 2000b). In this region, the richest decile of the population received 40 per cent of the national income compared to less than 30 per cent in the United States. CEPAL (1999) reported that about 40 per cent of the population lived in poverty in 1997 (about 204 million people).

Latin American countries are fraught with inequality and poverty, as reflected in profound discrepancies in the distribution of resources and wealth, as well as access to educational opportunities and social mobility. The Inter-American Development Bank (1999) concluded that income inequality in Latin America is determined in part by educational inequality. According to Reimers (2000a), there is a positive link between equality of income and equality of educational distribution in Latin America, although there is evidence of a greater equality of educational opportunity than of income distribution.

Like other regions in the world with culturally diverse populations, there is a legacy in Latin America of 'national-popular' projects in which different groups coalesce to engage in politics with other groups and the state (Hale, 1997). In recent years, however, these socio-cultural projects experienced a shift to what Hale (1997) refers to as 'identity politics', which refers to

> collective sensibilities and actions that come from a particular location within society, in direct defiance of universal categories that tend to subsume, erase, or suppress this particularity. 'Location', in this sense, implies a distinctive social memory, consciousness, and practice, as well as place within the social structure.
>
> (p. 568)

The contents of emerging identity politics in the subcontinent can be characterized along two dimensions. First, Hale argues that Latin American identity politics challenges the assumption that a cohesive subject can 'represent' (i.e. both 'depict' and 'speak for') (p. 577) the inherent diversity of identities and social processes. Second, this identity politics subverts essentialism, foregrounding instead 'the hybridity of cultures and the multiplicity of identities' (p. 577). Interestingly, important tensions exist between these two dimensions that have yet to be examined – e.g. regarding essentialism and voice. The identity politics phenomenon can also be examined according to how political projects came into existence. In this vein, a distinction can be made between identities that were traditionally included – sometimes only in official rhetoric (e.g. women and racial/ethnic minorities) and those that have until recently confronted longstanding invisibility or neglect (e.g. gay and lesbian movements, human rights activism) (Hale, 1997). Another category in identity politics includes groups that once were in the spotlight of national-popular movements but have lost their appeal (e.g. peasants, workers).

What could be gained if we were to examine the experiences and struggles of people with disabilities in Latin America through an identity politics lens? Note that although some subgroups of people with disabilities might have engaged in national-popular projects in the nineteenth and twentieth century, particularly those with sensory (deaf, blind) and physical impairments, many such efforts were narrow in scope and were fraught with representation problems (e.g. a rhetoric of charity was prevalent and mainly articulated by non-disabled philanthropists) and essentialist bias. People with high-incidence disabilities (mild mental retardation, learning disabilities, and emotional/behavioural disturbances) have had limited engagement with national-popular or identity politics projects.

There is an emergent legacy of efforts that avoid the frontal confrontation-assimilation dichotomy that minority groups have historically been trapped into. In such efforts, groups manage to carve out a space in the national political landscape, while they also avoid engaging in belligerent, militant opposition to the establishment (see Hale, 1997). We must ask whether this movement can become a fruitful alternative for populations with disabilities in Latin America. Would this strategy allow people with disabilities to transcend the pity and paternalistic state-sponsored discourse that has characterized many past efforts? Could they coalesce with other groups with which they overlap, such as class-, race-, ethnicity-, gender-, and language-based communities? Considering the dramatic inequalities found in the Latin American subcontinent, an identity politics perspective might offer one productive tool for people with disabilities. We review next some general socioeconomic indicators, in order to gain a better understanding of the enduring inequalities that characterize this region.

The educational context in Latin America

The quest for modernization in Latin American education has been perceived as the exclusive privilege of elite groups whose intention had been to impose a form of modernity that aspires to imitate European and North American models. Until recently, the models of education proposed and initiated by international agencies and organizations in many cases have reflected the results of a policy grounded in a homogenizing paradigm.

By not recognizing and taking into account the context and reality of Latin America as represented by the diversity of its inhabitants, a homogenizing tendency characteristic of the processes of modernization involved in building nations has left no room for the multicultural dimension typical of Latin America (Comboni Salinas and Juarez Nuñez, 2000); in the words of the authors, 'The refusal to recognize the specific roots, identities and potential of Latin American communities has kept a considerable portion of the population, namely the indigenous populations who are still well represented on our continent, in poverty, ignorance, isolation and despair' (p. 106).

Reimers (2000a) recently concluded that schools in the region continue to be highly segregated by socioeconomic background. Social inequalities in Latin America mirror educational exclusion worldwide, and place those at a social disadvantage based on gender, disability, poverty, language and ethnicity as the most vulnerable and the most susceptible to continue on the margins of society. This pattern of educational disparity limits access to education and, subsequently, to social mobility and productive contributions to society.

It is important to note that equity issues in Latin American education are increasingly facing an interesting paradox. On the one hand, a policy of invisibility in place for centuries for socially disadvantaged groups is now being reversed on many fronts. Those placed at a social disadvantage because of poverty, disability, language, ethnicity and gender are now being included and considered in official pronouncements on educational opportunities (Porter, 2001). The primary impulse from international agencies, organizations and governments in the region now appears committed to the principles of inclusion and equal educational opportunities for all its citizens, as reflected in the numerous accords mentioned above. On the other hand, structural adjustment policies have had nefarious consequences for educational opportunities in the hemisphere (Arnove *et al.*, 1999).

For instance, the average Latin American citizen completes six years of education (compared to 9.5 years in OECD nations). Access to primary school has been improved substantially as 92 per cent of the eligible population is enrolled in school (OECD nations enroll 98 per cent of the eligible age group). In contrast, access to upper secondary grades is severely limited in Latin America, as reflected in the 32 per cent enrolment of the eligible population – the figure for OECD nations is 91 per cent. The illiteracy rate is 13 per cent of the region's population (Reimers, 2000a). However, as Latin American countries have made progress to provide universal access to primary school, inequalities have been displaced to the pre- and post-primary levels (Reimers, 2000b). Coupled with this trend, we observe an interesting paradox between the level of economic growth and the reduction of poverty. Although the region's economies experienced growth, in the last decade, poverty levels remained virtually unaffected. Reimers (2000a) explains that the economic growth trend is largely shaped by the region's participation in global markets, which disproportionately benefits individuals in high-productivity occupations who hold higher education degrees.

He further explains that as the number of graduates from lower levels of education increases, the economic advantages of attaining that level diminish. In this sense, education as a gateway to social opportunity is a moving bar. This is critical to understanding the paradox that even as access to education has expanded, deep inequalities remain in those levels that matter the most for social mobility. For those who have lower levels of education, there are few prospects of entering high-productivity employment and therefore to benefit significantly from knowledge-based economic growth (pp. 59–60).

In 1996, a task force on Education, Equity and Economic Competitiveness in Latin America and the Caribbean, a non-governmental commission, was established with distinguished citizens throughout the region. This task force was founded by the Inter-American Dialogue and the Corporation for Development Research (CINDE) as a part of the Partnership for Educational Revitalization in the Americas (PREAL) to examine school quality. In their initial report in 1998, the task force issued its first evaluation of the state of education in Latin America, entitled *The Future at Stake*, and outlined in report-card form grave deficiencies in the education being offered to children throughout Latin America. The commission stated that the most significant achievement during the past three decades had been the expansion of school enrolments, primarily at the elementary level. But, overall, only limited progress has been made and the quality of education remains low, inequality remains high, and few schools are accountable to the parents and communities they serve.

The initial report card in 1998 was followed by a second 'periodic' report (2001), three years later, and the results mirrored many of the initial report findings, with only limited progress towards these goals, even though many countries expressed a strong commitment to improve education and to undertake reforms to improve schools. Indicators from the report card reflect larger developmental trends that undermine educational advancements and impact on the greater society. On the positive side, most governments in Latin America have recognized the need for reform and subsequently have begun to address the quality, quantity, and equity gaps in education. The news of greater concern was published in the summary of their first report, *Lagging Behind: A Report Card on Education in Latin America*, where the authors concluded that 'Latin America is falling behind at a time when human resources increasingly constitute the comparative advantage of nations' (p. 6). This publication revealed major indicators of what the authors perceived to be the core problems in Latin America that have led to quantity, quality and equity gaps in the region. Scores reported on national achievement tests were disappointing, with few Latin American countries participating regularly in global achievement testing and only a few countries administering UNESCO's Latin America test of achievement.

In the *Report Card* document, findings stated that education levels remain low in spite of increasing enrolments, few students stay in school to complete their primary schooling, and even fewer finish secondary school. These patterns are also reflected in data reported by Arnove *et al.* (1999). Some of the inequities in the *Report Card* report also highlighted the fact that the wealthiest 10 per cent of twenty-five year-olds have had 5–8 more years of schooling than the poorest 30 per cent and, in almost every country, living in rural areas compounds education inequalities, as reflected in lower scores achieved by poor and rural students. Arnove *et al.* (1999) report that Latin American citizens living in rural locations are typically politically weak and poorly organized, have higher illiteracy rates, and have lower-quality educational opportunities, as reflected in fewer primary schools, overpopulated and ruined schools, lower teacher quality, and limited and inadequate curriculum materials. Thus it is not surprising, for example, that student dropout in rural Bolivia reaches 90 per cent, and that only 19 per cent of rural students in El Salvador complete the primary cycle (Arnove *et al.*, 1999).

The *Report Card* found that poor performance was more predominant among certain ethnic and racial groups, particularly in Peru, Bolivia, Brazil and Guatemala, with significant achievement differences being recognized as early as the first two years of schooling in Bolivia and Guatemala. Unfortunately, there is a dearth of research on educational opportunity across racial and indigenous groups in the region (Reimers, 2000a). Overall, however, the evidence suggests that racial minority and indigenous groups have far fewer educational opportunities and higher poverty rates than their non-indigenous counterparts; similar trends are observed in health status (Psacharopoulos and Patrinos, 1994). For instance, based on census data from 1989, Steele (1994) summarizes the dismal situation of indigenous groups in Guatemala, which, alas, reflects regional patterns:

> Overall, indigenous wages average only 55 per cent of non-indigenous wages ... 87 per cent of all indigenous households are below the poverty line ... 65 per cent ... do not have a safe water supply, 46 per cent have no sanitary services and 75 per cent have no electricity. ... On average, indigenous people have only 1.3 years of schooling and 60 per cent indicate that they are illiterate.
>
> (p. 126)

Another key indicator of the significant disadvantages of indigenous groups in the region is the return rate of education. Psacharopoulos and Patrinos (1994) report on the educational attainment and increase in earnings associated with an extra year of schooling in the four Latin American countries with some of the highest densities of indigenous populations. These data suggest that, although there is an increase in earnings for indigenous groups, these still lag behind the benefits received by their non-indigenous fellow citizens.

Finally, general spending for education reinforces the discrepancies and inequalities by concentrating disproportionately more funds on higher education, in spite of the fact that in some countries only 1 per cent of the population make it to the university level. Ironically, the 'growth rate of higher education in Latin America is the highest for any region of the world, approximately 3 per cent annually between 1975 and 1990' (Arnove *et al.*, 1999, p. 312); most of this growth has been propelled by the private sector. Overall, education spending has been deeply affected by the debt crisis that has flooded the region; the figures reported by Arnove *et al.* (1999) support this conclusion, both in terms of education investment as a percentage of gross national product (GNP) and total governmental expenditure (TGE). These writers argue that the neo-liberal economic policies imposed by the international donor agencies (e.g. the World Bank and the International Monetary Fund) that privilege market-driven measures have led governments in the region to cut back drastically on social spending (including education), deregulate the economy, and relax import policies. As part of this trend, governments embraced decentralization and privatization as key educational reforms. Unfortunately, these recent measures have reversed advances made in education in the 1960s and 1970s and have only exacerbated socioeconomic inequalities (Arnove *et al.*, 1999; Reimers, 1991). Among the negative consequences of these reforms, Arnove and his colleagues include lower teacher salaries, declining quality of public schools driven by decreasing public investment, and the vanishing of political pressure needed to maintain quality programmes (i.e. middle-class parents).

In conclusion, the lack of human resources development due to lack of educational investment will have little success in reducing poverty, combating inequality, and impeding economic development throughout Latin America. These results reflect a crisis situation in education in Latin America. Five processes mediate how social inequality converts into educational inequality for the poor, compared to the non-poor (Reimers, 2000a):

(a) limited access to various education levels (pre-school, secondary and higher education);
(b) differential access to a quality education (e.g. lower teacher quality, fewer resources, lower quality curricula);
(c) social segregation of students (which limits access to social capital and is associated with fewer resources);
(d) limited parents' resources and contributions to the education of their children; and
(e) failure to infuse a social justice agenda in schools' work, which contributes to the role of reproducing inequality currently played by schools.

Thus, one of the most important challenges for policy-makers and education professionals is to understand the intricate intersections of education, poverty and inequality. This is no easy task, as Reimers (2000b) explains:

> Poverty and inequality are not the same thing. It is possible to reduce inequality without influencing poverty, and it is possible to reduce poverty without influencing inequality. It is important to advance our understanding of these concepts and of their dynamic relationship. How does poverty relate to educational poverty; how do both of them relate to education and social inequality? How is this relationship influenced by the degree of educational expansion, by the rate of growth of the education system, and by other social and economic forces at work in different societies? How does the relationship between education inequality and poverty and between social class of origin and educational attainment change over time?
>
> (p. 12)

Towards the development of inclusive education systems

In most Latin American countries, laws and policies are in place which affirm individual rights and provide service delivery guidelines for individuals with disabilities. At the same time, however, the disability-related movements still suffer from a very low priority in most countries, particularly as people with disabilities are just one of a list of deeply disadvantaged groups that include 'rural dwellers, females, the poor, or minorities' (Lockheed and Verspoor, 1991, p. 168). Moreover, Latin American nations face grave issues such as exponential population growth, massive external debts, rampant poverty, and fragile democratic traditions and institutions. In such contexts, some leaders defend a hierarchical approach to addressing their societies' needs. 'How can we afford to invest in social services for the small population of people with disabilities', they argue, 'when sizeable segments of our non-disabled populations still have such deep basic needs?'. Although we disagree strongly with this biased logic, the lesson to be learned in order to understand the status of inclusive education in Latin America is that analytic efforts must be situated in the larger context of the social, economic and political factors that have an impact on general education.

Meanwhile, the concept of inclusion as a generic term is sweeping Latin America (Porter, 2001). This orientation, made manifest in the final meeting for the nations of the Americas in Santo Domingo prior to the World Forum on Education For All (EFA) in Dakar, Senegal in 2000, reflects a vision that 'represents a clear affirmation of the inclusion principle and a vision statement that will challenge the current status quo of segregation and neglect' (Porter, 2001, p. 24).

Despite the growing official endorsement of inclusive education policies, the scant statistics portray a dismal situation (Artiles and Hallahan, 1995). It is estimated that about 85 million individuals with disabilities live in the region and the vast majority have limited access to education, which eventually translates into limited participation in the workforce, low productivity, and, thus, greater dependence (Porter 2001). Between 11 and 18 per cent of children in the Central American isthmus have some form of disability (CACL, 1997; Porter, 2001), but less than 10 per cent of children with special needs are receiving educational services, and the modal service delivery option is the segregated special education school (Porter, 2001). These regional figures sometimes obscure deeper local problems that are consistent with the situation observed in most developing nations, where only 5 per cent of children have access to services, with less than 2 per cent attending schools (CIDA, 2000). In Nicaragua, for example, only 2.4 per cent (3,600) of the 150,000 children with special needs receive services (Porter, 2001). In El Salvador, less than 1 per cent of the 222,000 children estimated to have disabilities are served (Porter, 2001). In Jamaica, only one third of students with disabilities are receiving services (Porter, 2001). Milicic and Pius (1995) also report that Chile's prevalent service delivery option is the segregated special education school and that only about one third of the eligible population has access to such services.

The same factors that shape inequality in general education seem also to affect people with disabilities in the region (e.g. poverty, rural residence, minority status). This means the original spirit of Education for All (EFA) must rely on a multi-sector approach carried out within the context not only of education, but also within a responsible economic and social policy concerned with the welfare of the majority of the population. This assumes a holistic approach to problem solving. This statement also outlines the challenges and requirements facing Latin America to address the goals of EFA.

A system-wide view and restructuring is necessary, rather than the narrow conception implemented during the 1990s that focused only on basic education. This type of effort has resulted in a neglect of secondary and higher education and practically the abandonment of the education of pre-schoolers and adults during the past ten years. This requires a long-term vision of educational policy not to be limited by the dynamics of politics or that of international funding. In the EFA statement, a clear signal was issued regarding the globalizing process that is homogenizing and hegemonic in nature, and the authors call for the preservation and promotion of cultural and educational diversity. They suggest this can be accomplished through a review and re-conceptualization of the traditional model of international cooperation. They suggest that the role of international agencies should be to serve as catalysts oriented towards facilitating, promoting and communicating development and change.

An additional challenge to the consolidation of inclusive education models in the region is conceptual clarity, particularly with regard to disability definitions and the very notion of inclusion. The developed world has debated between categorical approaches, in which disability definitions continue to be contested to this day (e.g. the definition of learning disabilities in the United States) (Bradley *et al.*, 2002) and models based on the more fluid (though equally ambiguous) notion of special needs education (Evans, 2003). For instance, Corbett and Slee (2000) identified a three-tiered development model of inclusion that includes (a) surface inclusion, determined by policy and notions of school effectiveness, (b) structural modifications to the school environment and curriculum, and (c) 'deep culture, the hidden curriculum of fundamental value systems, ritual and routines, initiations and acceptance which forms the fabric of

Table 9.1   Varieties of inclusion

Variety of inclusion	Target group	What it means to 'be included'	Vision of inclusive society	Implications for schools
Inclusion as placement	Disabled children /those with special educational needs	To have the right of 'membership' in regular schools and classrooms	Rights-based	Schools must acknowledge rights and provide supports and adaptations to ensure access.
Inclusion as education for all	Groups with little, no, or poor quality education	To have access to school education	Welcoming, non-discriminatory	Schools must be capable of educating all learners.
Inclusion as participation	All learners, especially those who are marginalized in schools	To face minimal barriers to learning and participation	Rights-based, pluralistic and cohesive	Schools must critically examine current practices to identify and remove barriers.
Social inclusion	Groups at risk of social exclusion	To attain at high levels in school in order to thrive in the labour market and help shape society	Combination of rights and obligations, with active citizens and a competitive economy	Schools must have strategies for raising the attainments of low-achieving groups.

Source: Dyson, 2001. This table is published with the permission of Professor Alan Dyson, Manchester University, Manchester, UK.

daily life' (p. 140). Dyson (2001) also identified four approaches to inclusion, namely inclusion as placement, education for all, participation, and social inclusion. Each model identifies a different target group, defines inclusion in disparate ways, holds dissimilar visions of an inclusive society, and prescribes various implications for schools. Table 9.1 describes these types. It is not clear yet what models of inclusion dominate in the Latin American region. Based on this brief survey of the region, we could speculate that inclusion is being approached from the perspectives of inclusion as placement and education for all. Future analyses ought to examine more carefully the variations in understandings of this notion and the implications for educational reform.

In conclusion, despite the progress observed in Latin America's commitment to serve people with disabilities, many challenges lie ahead. Among the most significant challenges and needs we find the need to (Artiles *et al.*, 1995; Porter, 2001):

1   Improve the gathering of accurate disability prevalence data. This task is complicated by the intricate interactions between student socio-demographic factors (e.g. considerable ethnic and linguistic diversity, rampant poverty) and systemic inequalities (low teacher quality, scarce curriculum materials, high grade-repetition and dropout rates). Longitudinal data for research purposes are not available either (Evans, 2003).

2   Implement pilot inclusion models in local public schools or districts to test their effectiveness with different groups of students.

3   Strengthen personnel preparation so that general and special education teachers can work efficiently in inclusive contexts. This includes upgrading the current teaching force and moving teacher education to higher education.

4   Identify local leadership at the school, district, and state/regional levels to prepare them for the administration and evaluation of inclusive education models.

5   Fund special education research and development to improve this sector's infrastructure and to assist professionals, researchers, families and policy-makers in making informed decisions.

6   Create an internet-based information system to disseminate information about effective practices and to create systems of support for practitioners. This recommendation also requires investment in basic technology at the district and school levels so that access to technology is not an issue.

7   Strengthen partnerships between public, private and non-governmental sectors, as well as national and international agencies concerned with special needs education. This strategy will reinforce the creation of advocacy movements and intensify lobbying for disability-related movements and policies.

8   Maintain a focus on equity issues in all reform and development efforts, particularly as they affect traditionally marginalized groups (e.g. poor, ethnic and linguistic minorities, women).
9   Promote the creation of interdisciplinary perspectives in the policy, practice and research worlds, so that alternative paradigms about disability and special needs education are used in policies and knowledge bases.
10 Raise awareness about the fact that the process of knowledge transfer must be conducted with a concern for adaptation to local historical and cultural realities. This means a systematic approach to include multiple constituencies in knowledge transfer processes must be in place, particularly in ministries of education and in universities. Participatory approaches and respect for indigenous epistemologies must be relied upon heavily.

In the next section, we present a case example of Mexico's response to questions of social equity and the provision of a quality education to students with special educational needs. This case example will be couched in the context of international and national declarations trumpeting inclusive education as an effective response to educating students with special educational needs. We briefly trace recent educational declarations and legislation in Mexico that have framed educational reform efforts in special education, and present the current realities and challenges which appear as mirror images in the reform process currently sweeping Latin America.

Inclusive education and equity: the case of Mexico

Mexico is a multiethnic, multicultural and multilingual nation in the throes of educational reform designed to provide a quality education to all students within its borders. Within the educational reform process, the goals of the new General Education Law (SEP, 1993) call for the decentralization and restructuring of public education and the integration of regular and special education to enable it to respond to the basic learning needs of diverse learners, including those with cultural, economic, physical and cognitive variations. During the past decade, significant and systemic changes have occurred and made explicit the inclusion of students with disabilities into the mainstream. This shift, in accordance with international trends and outlined in national legislation and in the recent National Educational Program 2001–2006, contemplates the integration of special education and basic education, makes explicit the inclusion of all students into one integrated system, and focuses on the provision of quality educational services for all students.

Special education reform and educational integration

In the arena of special education, as noted by Guajardo Ramos and Fletcher (1998), Mexico has adapted and systematized measures recommended by UNESCO (1994) to provide a framework for the provision of quality educational services to all students. These measures were derived directly from international agreements and accords discussed, outlined and agreed upon by many countries at the World Conference on Education for All in 1990 and subsequently at the Salamanca World Conference on Special Educational Needs held in 1994. These have led to significant educational restructuring and reform within Mexico, designed to meet the challenges of educating all students from diverse backgrounds, including those with special educational needs. It is in the context of these international reforms and declarations that the impetus for education reform generally, and in special education specifically, was born. But even before the holding of international conferences and the issuing of joint declarations, political and educational forces within Mexico were underway and resulted in significant legislative and programmatic changes in special education.

The reform process began in earnest in 1992, with the National Agreement for the Modernization of Basic Education agreed upon by the federal government, the thirty-one states of the Republic, and the Education Workers' National Union (Gordillo, 1992). This was the beginning of a new federalism and, in particular, in matters related to the public budget, with the transferring of new responsibilities to individual states. Concurrent with this restructuring process, administrative decentralization at the federal level occurred and placed the major responsibility for supervision and coordination of special education under each state's jurisdiction, which has led to greater state autonomy in all matters related to education, not just special education. The result of the decentralization in essence provided more authority to and greater participation by each of the thirty-one states in terms of providing specific basic educational services required by their respective student populations, thus making them more responsive to the basic learning needs and diversity of all students with cultural, economic, physical and cognitive differences. As Guajardo Ramos and Fletcher (1998) state:

> The conceptual framework that serves as the basis for the restructuring process is attention to diversity supported by a new conception of basic education. Attention to diversity in this context is more broadly defined than just educational integration, although educational integration is assuredly an important aspect of it.
>
> (p. 40)

The result of the restructuring essentially decentralized the National Education System, providing sovereignty to individual states, which allowed them to provide basic educational services according to their unique and diversified populations, with the end goal of greater availability and completion of schooling (Pescador Osuna, 1992).

Although Article 3 of the Mexican Constitution provides for every Mexican to receive an education, and it was traditionally interpreted to provide for the education of children with disabilities, there was no designated federal mandate for special education in place. In 1993, Article 3 of the Mexican Constitution was amended with the passage of the General Education Law (GEL), which for the first time in the history of Mexico, enacted legislation at the national level that specifically addressed the education of students with disabilities. Article 41 of the new law states:

> Special education is earmarked for individuals with temporary or permanent disabilities, as well as those that are talented or gifted. It will strive to educate students in accordance with their physical differences, with social equity. With regard to children with disabilities, this education will promote inclusion into general education classrooms. For those who are unable to be integrated, this education will strive to satisfy their basic educational needs so they may achieve an autonomous, social and productive co-existence. This education includes guidance for parents and guardians, as well as for teachers, and elementary, general school personnel where students with special educational needs are integrated.

The GEL, now a legal mandate, makes explicit that no one with a disability can be excluded from receiving basic education services, from pre-school through to 8th grade. Prior to the passage of this law, children with disabilities were not permitted to attend public schools and were sent to special schools or remained at home. The law also refers to the total or partial inclusion of students in the general education classroom without restrictions, while still retaining the option of placement in a special school. All students, whatever their placements, are now taught through the same core curriculum and, as per Article 41 of the new law, special education students have the right to be provided with specific alternative methods, techniques and materials to meet their unique learning needs.

The emergence of special educational needs

The fundamental purpose of reorienting special education services was to combat the discrimination, segregation and labelling of students which in the past had dictated that education would be provided in a separate and segregated setting with a separate curriculum. Philosophical alignment with inclusive education and incorporation of the concept of special educational needs broadened the spectrum of students to be served in special education, and translated into the delivery of special education services to include children from socially disadvantaged backgrounds caused by poverty, gender or ethnicity, and, in some countries, gifted children. These policies and practices correspond with the definition of inclusive education as advanced by UNESCO (2003). Its definition states that it

> is concerned with providing appropriate responses to the broad spectrum of learning needs in formal and non-formal education settings. Rather than being a marginal theme on how some learners can be integrated in the mainstream education, inclusive education is an approach that looks into how to transform education systems in order to feel comfortable with diversity and to see it as a challenge and enrichment in the learning environment, rather than a problem.
>
> (p. 2)

Many countries in Latin America, including Mexico, have adopted the term 'special educational needs', which significantly broadens the concept of 'special education' and extends beyond those individuals traditionally included only in the disability categories. The term special educational needs was generated and became widespread as a result of the Salamanca Declaration (UNESCO, 1994). Since that Declaration, Mexico and most countries in Latin America have adopted the much broader definition of a student with special educational needs as that person who, in comparison to his or her peer group, has difficulties learning the established curriculum content, and as a result requires additional resources or different resources to achieve the educational goals and objectives of the curriculum. A primary feature of inclusive education programmes is that local neighbourhood schools are to be more site-based and self-contained in the way in which they provide additional support to students identified with special educational needs. This additional support might include greater flexibility in the establishment of class sizes and their composition, support provided to regular classroom teachers by specialists and their assistants, the reduction of teacher/student ratios, increased skills in ability to differentiate curriculum, more flexible pedagogies, and the development of curriculum materials to meet the needs of students (Evans, 2003).

In Mexico, the re-conceptualization of special education was followed by a restructuring in services designed to educate individuals with special educational needs with and without disabilities. This shift in policy and practice is based on changes promoted during the past decade in which special educational services made a transition from a clinical model with a therapeutic orientation towards a more inclusive educational response as a part of a total comprehensive package of educational reform. These changes have resulted in the establishment of support services to be provided to preschool and elementary education teachers in the regular classroom. These are provided by special educators through the Service Support Unit for Regular Education (USAER) team and through Multiple Attention Centres (CAMS) that educate children with more severe disabilities. These will be discussed later as an administrative and educational response to inclusive education with the goal of increasing educational efficiency for students with special educational needs.

The provision of special education services

In a relatively recent pronouncement, a new comprehensive initiative, entitled the National Programme for Strengthening Special Education and Inclusive Education (2002), was launched by the Fox administration. This programme reviews the current status of special education services and educational integration in Mexico. It outlines goals, objectives and action plans to be accomplished during the Fox presidency (2000–2006). To date, the responsibility to implement educational integration in Mexico has been perceived exclusively as a special education function. The responsibility for the nationwide implementation of the above programme falls under the jurisdiction of the Secretary of Basic Education. It will facilitate greater coordination among state educational agencies responsible for special education, and create the necessary linkages to guarantee the provision of a quality education to students with special educational needs, giving priority to those students with disabilities. The primary objectives and goals of the plan include:

1   Elaborate general guidelines to regulate the function and operation of special education services.
2   Establish the regulatory framework and the follow-up and evaluation mechanisms by which to evaluate the progress of educational integration.
3   Increase the coverage of special education services to all counties and school zones, with priority to students with special educational needs, with disabilities and with gifted abilities.
4   Guarantee professional development to educational personnel providing services to children at the pre-school and primary level, giving priority to those with disabilities.
5   Guarantee the outlay of material resources and technical support to insure the optimum level of service is provided to students with disabilities.
6   Inform and sensitize the greater community to related themes of disability and special educational needs.
7   Strengthen collaboration among the distinct sectors, institutions and civil associations to insure optimal attention to students with special educational needs, giving priority to students with disabilities.
8   Develop pilot research projects and innovative approaches that permit better provision of services to students with disabilities and special gifts and talents.

In addition to the eight goals outlined above, one facet of the new National Education Programme 2001–2006 of critical importance, and a foremost challenge facing other countries throughout Latin America, is the need to gather reliable data to document the incidence and needs of individuals with disabilities. Within the new programme, the push to promote greater inter-agency collaboration, design reliable instruments and establish mechanisms by which reliable descriptive and quantitative data can be gathered, is a key factor in determining the need for expanding services and programmes for individuals with disabilities and, subsequently, requests for additional financial resources. Fundamental in the development of a data collection system is the identification of the target population of students with special educational needs. But the relative ambiguity of the term 'special educational needs', and the lack of consensus among educational officials as to how to define, measure, and categorize it present a formidable challenge. Based on data gathered by the Centre for Educational Research and Innovation (CERI) at the OECD (2000, 2003), the term 'special educational needs' is widely used, but the definition varies considerably across countries. In some countries, it refers only to students with disabilities; in others it includes those with disabilities and learning difficulties, students from socially disadvantaged or ethnic minority backgrounds, and in some cases gifted children.

In the case of Mexico, discrepancies and disparities in data obtained from different federal agencies within the same government accentuate the problems in the gathering of comparable statistics, and the importance of the design and development of accurate instruments and systematic procedures to gather valid and reliable information about individuals with disabilities. The following information reported by the state and federal agencies within Mexico highlights the need for a unified system to obtain verifiable and reliable data. According to the 2001–2002 academic school year data reported by the state special education service providers in the thirty-one states of Mexico, approximately 525,232 pre-school, elementary, and secondary students were provided some type of educational service by special education personnel. Of the total number of these students served, only 112,000 were identified with a disability (SEP, 2002), indicating that approximately 413,000 students received some type of service in spite of the fact that they did not have an identified disability. Conversely, other data provided by the Secretaria de Educacion Publica (SEP, 2002) for the same school year, 2001–2002, indicated that of the 381,895 students with disabilities who were enrolled in public schools, only 112,000 students actually received services in special education, as noted above. In other words, 269,895 of identified children who required attention received no special education services. In Mexico, then, with a population of approximately 24 million children in the pre-school to middle school range, less than half of 1 per cent, or about 112,000, of these students currently receive some type of special education service.

According to education officials in Mexico, the number and percentage of students without disabilities, but who are 'lagging behind' academically and identified as students with special educational needs, suggests an ambiguity and vagueness in the definition and identification of students with special educational needs, thereby permitting the inclusion of students with learning problems or with low academic achievement into the special education domain. The magnitude of the student population lagging behind is reflected in a recent report by the National Institute for Adult Education (INEGI, 2003), which reports that 34.6 million Mexicans, or one in every two citizens over fifteen years of age, are considered to be *rezago educativo* (children who fall behind academically) for not being able to read or write or for not having completed primary or middle school.

In looking at the number of documented students with disabilities served by special education and those with special educational needs without a disability, one can see that special education in Mexico serves a broader agenda. These data also provide a picture of the function of special education personnel and services provided in Mexico, similar to many countries in Latin America, essentially indicating that these special education personnel primarily serve as a safety net for students without disabilities who are failing in school, falling behind academically, or at-risk of leaving school.

The Mexican government has touted the fact that in the past few years there has been a significant increase in the number of schoolrooms, teachers, and educational supplies, and it is estimated that, at the beginning of the twenty-first century, about 92 per cent of all children between the ages of 6 and 14 attended school (SEP, 2002). In spite of the fact that there has been a concerted effort to improve the educational opportunities and basic health care for its citizens, as in most Latin American countries, the social and educational infrastructure is still not available to all its citizens, particularly those in rural and remote areas. A detailed analysis of the INEGI report reveals that when the data are disaggregated and examined state-by-state, the reporting of national data in the aggregate masks ethnic differences, particularly in states with high indigenous populations. In states such as Guerrero and Chiapas, which have a high rural and indigenous population, the number of students entering school ranges between 19 per cent and 27 per cent, suggesting the persistence of factors maintaining educational inequalities in these regions. Indigenous groups in Mexico represent nearly 10 per cent of the population, but they constitute 25 per cent of the country's illiterate population. The enormous dispersion of the population leads to the isolation and exclusion of many communities, severely limiting educational services. Throughout Mexico, there are approximately 160,000 localities, of which more than 100,000 have populations of less than 100 inhabitants (Morales, 1999). Official reports from the Secretary of Public Education indicate that virtually no special education services are currently provided to indigenous populations in rural and remote areas of Mexico.

These findings are not surprising and corroborate research by Psacharopoulos and Patrinos (1994) and Steele (1994), who suggested that racial minorities and indigenous groups have far fewer educational opportunities than their non-indigenous counterparts, placing them at the margins of society. Additionally, the indigenous population of Mexico faces low retention rates, difficulties in staying in school, and social, economic and cultural inequalities that place them at a distinct disadvantage in comparison to students from urban areas. This reality is reinforced and is apparent in the lack of provision of special education services for indigenous populations throughout Mexico. For education in general, and special education in particular, this presents a challenging and complex scenario for the provision of schooling.

Special education coverage and service delivery models

The goal of providing greater coverage and quality education and services to special education students in the public schools throughout Mexico continues to be a formidable challenge. The goal remains largely a goal unachieved and unchanged since 1993. For example, statements made in 1993 by the former director of special education in Mexico City indicate that the same percentage of students was receiving services then as ten years previously:

> The potential demand for special education is ten per cent of the population, we cover about one per cent. We cover the explicit demand for our services, but when we encounter additional necessities, we have to campaign so that those children requiring special services receive them. …We are currently only providing for those who knock on the door, but we know that there are even greater needs among the population that we are not meeting.
>
> (cited in Garcia, 1993, p. 18)

According to statistics provided by the Secretary of Education (2002), the majority of the 4,097 locales offering special education services are in urban areas or more densely populated counties. Within Mexico, about 42 per cent of the counties provide some type of special education service. Special education currently provides services in about 16,000 schools throughout Mexico, which represents only 8 per cent of all schools, pre-school through middle school, in the country. As mentioned previously, the restructuring of special education and the adoption of an inclusive education posture to attend to diversity as a total educational response, is an attempt to engage the entire educational system in a quality education for all, based on social equity. During the past ten years, the number and type of services provided have grown consistently but have not kept pace with the student population requiring services. To increase educational efficiency and the number of students served by special education personnel, Mexico has framed its response to meeting the special educational needs of students through the development of two new service delivery models now adopted by all the federated states.

Multiple Attention Centres (CAM) are designed to provide education to individuals pre-school to high school who are unable to be successfully integrated into regular education classrooms and need additional accommodations based upon their special educational needs. These centres are organized by group and age to provide instruction to students with diverse disabilities in the same group. Each particular centre maintains autonomy and flexibility in the organization, planning, and instruction of the students they serve. The primary sources of referral to the CAMs are parents, social agencies, and the Service Support Unit of Regular Education (USAER). There are currently over 100,000 students being served in more than 1,300 centres within Mexico. Enrolments in the CAMs are made up of approximately 70 per cent students with disabilities and 30 per cent without disabilities.

The Service Support Units of Regular Education (USAER) are designed to integrate students with special educational needs into general education classrooms and schools. The role of special education teachers at a school site is no longer to teach special education classes or provide therapy, but rather to work collaboratively with the students' teachers and to facilitate the success of students with disabilities in the regular classroom. The primary goals of the USAER include: initial evaluations, intervention planning, intervention, ongoing assessment and monitoring. Curriculum-based assessments are used to determine the student's current level of functioning. Students identified are provided with curricular adaptations in the context of the regular education classroom based on their specific needs. USAERs currently operate in over 2,300 localities and serve approximately 320,000 students. Of the total number of students served, approximately 10 per cent, or 32,000 students, have an identified disability.

Teacher training and the changing roles of special educators

The availability of appropriately trained professionals is one of the key elements in the provision of quality special education services. Mexico recognizes this challenge of ensuring that teachers are equipped to teach pupils with special educational needs. To make inclusive education a success, teachers in training need a thorough pre-service and an on-going in-service training programme to develop new skills and approaches (Perner and Porter, 1998). Teaching is a profession of ever changing demands, and to make educational integration a success teachers require skills such as curriculum adaptation, using a variety of instructional strategies, collaborative and problem solving skills, designing individual education plans and monitoring student programmes (OECD, 1999).

Approximately 63 per cent of special education personnel have some type of special education preparation, while the other 37 per cent have preparation in related areas such as pre-school education, elementary education, educational psychology or pedagogy. The preparation of special education teachers has not kept pace with the transformation and restructuring of special education during the 1990s. The curriculum and programmes of study in undergraduate programmes imparted to students by the normal schools providing specialization in special education date back to 1985, and do not reflect current demands and changes in the orientation and provision of services to students. The current push for inclusive education and the provision of education to students with special educational needs requires that all teachers take responsibility for the learning of all students in their classrooms. Attention to diversity as a theme in the educational reform process requires all institutions providing in-service and pre-service teacher education programmes to include issues pertaining to inclusive practices, as in pedagogies for diversity, disability issues, and understanding processes to address barriers to learning and development.

An important question to ask as we survey the changing educational landscape of Mexico within the context of new legislative mandates, international and national decrees, and governmental initiatives aimed at retooling special education, is: To what degree have these reforms filtered down to the classroom and transformed the practices of teachers engaged in the education of students with special educational needs?

In a series of focus-group studies (Fletcher et al., 2003) carried out in urban and rural settings in Mexico, the authors examined the changing paradigm of special education since the passage of the General Education Law (SEP, 1993) and the resulting impact on the practices of regular classroom and special education teachers working within a new legal framework and newly designed models of service delivery. A number of important themes emerged from these studies. Among the most salient concerns expressed were the top-down manner in which the new system of educational integration was imposed on them, the general lack of preparation prior to the implementation of integration efforts, and the resulting confusion regarding the roles and responsibilities of practising regular and special education teachers. Other themes emphasized the absence of communication and dialogue among teachers working in integrated schools, the lack of administrative support in promoting and supporting inclusive education practices, and little parental involvement. Teachers found little time to collaborate and plan cooperatively, since the majority of teachers work two shifts at two different schools from 8 in the morning to 7 at night. Most of the teachers believed in the importance of integrating students with disabilities into the regular classroom, but expressed their unpreparedness to integrate students with disabilities into their classrooms and to make the curricular adaptations with class sizes ranging from 45 to 55 students in small, unequipped and crowded classrooms. In summary, the researchers concluded that regardless of the country, the problems faced by professionals who are working to change attitudes and policies are the same problems and require similar strategies to resolve them.

These findings are in concert with a report on inclusive education in Latin America by Willms (2000), who reported factors critical to improving the educational outcomes of children. The author cites class size, teachers working more than one job, lack of parental involvement, and ability grouping as salient elements to counteract if school quality and inclusive practices were to be improved.

Conclusion

Mexico, in step with the international community, has adopted, developed and implemented policies and practices that are designed to embrace a more inclusive educational approach providing for the education of all students. The changes implemented during the past ten years are unprecedented and suggest that Mexico 'is dismantling and streamlining its excessive bureaucracy and challenging the status quo at the economic, social, political, and educational levels of society with the goal of attaining educational equity for all' (Guajardo Ramos and Fletcher, 1998, pp. 39–40).

Despite the endorsement of educational integration, a lack of provision of basic education services, and a perpetuation of social and economic disparities and injustices among the most vulnerable populations, persists in Mexico. We see in inclusive education, in the case of Mexico, educational integration, the promise of an ideology that promotes and advances an equitable education agenda with outcomes designed to promote equity and justice for all students. But the passage of federal mandates and the issuing of directives must move beyond the rhetoric of governmental and educational officials, and prioritization must occur to ensure a quality education for all students. As recently as August 2002, Mexican President Vicente Fox, and Secretary of Education Reyes Tamiz, presided over a ceremony in which the 'National Commitment for the Quality of Education' was signed, announcing and outlining a new comprehensive and collaborative effort to improve the Mexican education system. During the ceremony, President Vicente Fox stated that 'We need an equitable education, giving everyone the opportunity to educational access at all levels, in spite of their economic condition'. The goals of the plan are praiseworthy and emphasize the importance of equal access and an equitable education for all of its citizens, but the achievement of these lofty goals remains elusive and continues to be a daunting challenge for the Mexican government. The rhetoric of government officials supporting even the most basic educational programme development has not resulted in the allocation of federal monies; in fact, education programmes are being downgraded. According to the recently released INEGI report (2003), the federal government implemented budget cuts over the past two years, severely curtailing programmes for literacy development and school completion.

In spite of the monumental reform initiatives and declarations during the past ten years in Mexico, pronouncements, declarations and mandates ring hollow if the resources are not allocated and provided. A Mexican saying, 'Entre dicho y hecho hay mucho trecho' (Between what is officially endorsed and what actually occurs there is a gap), characterizes the chasm separating discourse and reality in ensuring educational integration and equitable education in Mexico. As articulated by Artiles and Hallahan (1995), developing countries face monumental and difficult challenges in the provision of educational funding to support basic social and educational opportunities in the context of economies struggling under huge debt. This is affirmed by findings from the Partnership for Educational Revitalization in the Americas (PREAL) in their initial report in 1998 on the state of education in Latin America, in which they highlight insufficient investment in primary and secondary education as one of the root causes of the quantity, quality and equity gaps in education.

Ainscow and Ferreira (1999), in their discussion of programmes to support the development of inclusive education systems in Latin America, state that 'world-wide educational exclusion mirrors social inequalities, and the roots of these disparities are to be found in ideology, economy and politics' (p. 1). For the foreseeable future, educational opportunities for those populations socially disadvantaged by disability, ethnicity, poverty and gender will be few, and access will be limited, based on current budget outlays for basic education. As highlighted in the PREAL report (2001), governments and society are cognizant of the importance of education for development and social mobility, but, as documented, the allocation of financial resources is not viewed as a priority.

Conclusion

It is compelling, the challenge that lies before us as we survey Mexico and the Latin American region. The consideration of multiple factors, as outlined in this chapter, must be coupled with responsible economic and social policies concerned with the welfare of the countries' most vulnerable citizens. We firmly believe that the effort to give all children access to equal educational opportunities will advance the cause of social justice and equity, and will result in more productive citizens in whatever society individuals with disabilities live. Successful inclusive education programmes, in whatever locale, will require intersectorial, multidimensional, and interdisciplinary approaches that place the human rights of individuals with disabilities and disenfranchised populations front and centre in domestic aid and development programmes. Within the new context of educational modernization, the discourse of education justifies and ratifies education's function as a social and political strategy to include the excluded (Orozco Fuentes and Elizondo Carr, 1993).

Note

1 Dr Artiles acknowledges the support of the National Center for Culturally Responsive Educational Systems (NCCRESt) under grant no. H326E020003 awarded by the US Department of Education's Office of Special Education Programs.

References

Ainscow, M. and Ferreira, W. (1999). ALFA II – 2000–2005: *Supporting the development of inclusive education systems*. A draft proposal to set up a cooperative network involving universities in Europe and Latin America (pp. 1–3). University of Manchester, England.

Albarran de Alba, G. (1996). *En el Distrito Federal la infancia no es prioridad: Se multiplica la producción de niños que viven, crecen, y mueren en las calles* [In the federal district infancy is not a priority: The number of children that live, grow and die on the streets has multiplied]. *Process*, 1024, 16–23.

Arnove, R.F. (1999). 'Reframing comparative education: The dialectic of the global and the local'. In R.F. Arnove and C.A. Torres (eds) *Comparative education: The dialectic of the global and the local* (pp. 1–23). Lanham MD: Rowman and Littlefield.

Arnove, R.F., Franz, S., Mollis, M. and Torres, C.A. (1999). 'Education in Latin America at the end of the 1990s'. In R.F. Arnove and C.A. Torres (eds) *Comparative education: The dialectic of the global and the local* (pp. 305–328). Lanham MD: Rowman and Littlefield.

Arnove, R.F. and Torres, C.A. (eds) (1999). *Comparative education: The dialectic of the global and the local*. Lanham MD: Rowman and Littlefield.

Artiles, A.J. (2003). 'Special education's changing identity: Paradoxes and dilemmas in views of culture and space'. *Harvard Educational Review*, 73, 164–202.

Artiles, A.J. and Hallahan, D.P. (eds) (1995). *Special education in Latin America: Experiences and issues*. Westport CT: Praeger.

Artiles, A.J. and Larsen, L. (eds) (1998). 'Special issue: International perspectives on special education reform'. *European Journal of Special Needs Education*, 13, 5–13.

Artiles, A.J., Trent, S.C. and Hallahan, D.P. (1995). 'Special education for students with mild disabilities in Latin America: Issues and prospects'. In A.J. Artiles and D.P. Hallahan (eds) *Special education in Latin America: Experiences and issues* (pp. 251–283). Westport CT: Praeger.

Bradley, R., Danielson, L. and Hallahan D.P. (eds) (2002). *Identification of learning disabilities: Research to policy*. Hillsdale NJ: Lawrence Erlbaum.

CACL (1997). *Integration of persons with disabilities into the productive workforce.* Research study for the Inter-American Development Bank. Toronto: Canadian Association for Community Living.

CEPAL (1999). *Panorama social de American Latina* [Social panorama of Latin America]. Santiago, Chile: United Nations.

CIDA (2000 December). *CIDA's social development priorities: A framework for action.* Ottawa, Canada.

Comboni Salinas, S. and Juarez Nuñez, J.M. (2000). 'Education, culture and indigenous rights: The case of education reform in Bolivia'. *Prospects*, XXX(1), 105–124.

Corbett, C. and Slee, R. (2000). 'An international conversation on inclusive education'. In F. Armstrong, D. Armstrong and L. Barton (eds) *Inclusive education: Policy, contexts, and comparative perspectives* (pp. 133–146). London: David Fulton Publishers.

Dyson, A. (2001). *Varieties of inclusion.* Paper presented at the IV Jornadas Científicas de Investigación sobre Personas con Discapacidad, Salamanca, Spain, March 2001.

Encyclopaedia Britannica. Retrieved 11 November 2003, from *Encyclopaedia Brittanica* Online.

Evans, P. (2003). *Aspects of the integration of handicapped and disadvantaged students into education: Evidence from quantitative and qualitative data.* Paper presented at the Reunion de Lanzamiento del Proyecto OCDE sobre Estadisticas e Indicadores de las Necesidades Educativas Especiales, incluyendo Discapacidad, Dificultades para el Aprendizaje y Poblacion en Desventaja, 25–27 June, Mexico City.

Fletcher, T., Dejud, C., Klingler, C. and Lopez Mariscal, I. (2003). 'The changing paradigm of special education in Mexico: Voices from the field'. *Bilingual Research Journal*, 27(3), 409–430.

Friedman, T.L. (2000). *The lexus and the olive tree.* New York: Anchor Books.

Garcia, G. (1993). *Una demanda que toca la puerta* [Unmet needs in special education]. *Mira*, 16(7), 17–21.

Gordillo, E. (1992). *El SNTE ante la modernizacion de la educacion basica* [The education workers' national union and the modernization of basic education]. *El Cotidiano*, 51, 12–16.

Guajardo Ramos, E. and Fletcher, T. (1998). 'Special education and education reform in Mexico: Providing quality education to a diverse student population'. *European Journal of Special Needs Education*, 13(1), 29–42.

Hale, C. R. (1997). 'Cultural politics and identity in Latin America'. *Annual Review of Anthropology*, 26, 567–590. URL: http://search.eb.com/eb/article?eu=48395

INEGI (2003). *Tasa de asistencia escolar de la poblacion hablante de lengua indigena de 6 a 14 aos de edad por principales entidades federativas segun sexo, 2000* [Rate of school attendance reported by the principal federal entities for the population of indigenous language speakers between 6 and 14 years of age]. URL: http://www.inegi.gob.mx/est/contenidos/espanol/tematicos/mediano/ent.asp?t=ml en13&c=3340

Inter-American Development Bank (1999). *Economic and social progress in Latin America.* Washington DC: Inter-American Development Bank.

Lockheed, M.E. and Verspoor, A.M. (1991). *Improving primary education in developing countries.* Washington DC: Falmer Press.

Milicic, N. and Pius, M.P. (1995). 'Children with learning disabilities in Chile: Strategies to facilitate integration'. In A.J. Artiles and D.P. Hallahan (eds) *Special education in Latin America: Experiences and issues* (pp. 169–188). Westport CT: Praeger.

Morales, S. (1999). 'Bridge over troubled waters: Collaboration between the United States and Mexico on behalf of individuals with disabilities'. In T. Fletcher and C. Bos (eds) *Educating children with disabilities and their families: Blending US and Mexican perspectives* (pp. 109–120). Tempe AZ: Bilingual Review Press.

OECD (1999). *Inclusive education at work: Students with disabilities in mainstream schools*. Paris: OECD.

——(2000) *Besoins educatifs particuliers: Statistiques et indicateurs*. Paris: OECD.

——(2003). *Incapacites, troubles de l'apprentissage sociaux: Statistiques et indicateurs pour l'acces au cursus scolaire et pour l'equite*. Paris: OECD.

Orozco Fuentes, B. and Elizondo Carr, S. (1993). 'Educational reform in Mexico'. *International Journal of Educational Reform*, 2, 12–18.

Perner, D. and Porter, G.L. (1998). 'Creating inclusive schools: Changing roles and strategies'. In A. Hilton and R. Ringlaben (eds) *Best and promising practices in developmental disabilities*. Austin TX: Pro-Ed.

Pescador Osuna, J.A. (1992). *Acuerdo nacional para la modernizacion de la educacion basica: Una vision integral* [The national accord for the modernization of basic education: An integrated vision. *El Cotidiano*, 51, 3–11.

Porter, G.L. (2001). *Disability and inclusive education*. Paper presented at the seminar on inclusion and disability, Santiago, Chile, March 2001.

PREAL (2001). *Lagging behind: A report card on education in Latin America. The Task Force on Education, Equity, and Economic Competitiveness in Latin American and the Caribbean*. Washington DC: Inter-American Dialogue.

Psacharopoulos, G. and Patrinos, H.A. (eds) (1994). *Indigenous people and poverty in Latin America: An empirical analysis*. Washington DC: World Bank.

Reimers, F. (1991). 'The impact of economic stabilization and adjustment on education in Latin America'. *Comparative Education Review*, 35, 319–353.

——(2000a). 'Educational opportunity and policy in Latin America'. In F. Reimers (ed.) *Unequal schools, unequal chances: The challenges to equal opportunity in the Americas* (pp. 55–107). Cambridge MA: Harvard University Press.

——(2000b). 'What can we learn from studying educational opportunities in the Americas and why should we care?' In F. Reimers (ed.) *Unequal schools, unequal chances: The challenges to equal opportunity in the Americas* (pp. 3–23). Cambridge MA: Harvard University Press.

SEP (Secretaria de Educacion Publica) (1993). *Ley general de educacion [General Education Law]*. Mexico City: SEP.

——(2002). *Programa nacional de fortalecimiento de la educacion especial y de la integracion educativa. [National Programme for the Strengthening of Special Education and Educational Integration]*. Mexico City: SEP.

Steele, D. (1994). 'Guatemala'. In G. Psacharopoulos and H.A. Patrinos (eds) *Indigenous people and poverty in Latin America: An empirical analysis* (pp. 97–126). Washington DC: World Bank.

Suárez-Orozco, M.M. (2001). 'Globalization, immigration, and education: The research agenda'. *Harvard Educational Review*, 71, 345–364.

UNESCO (1994). *Final report of the world conference on special needs education. Access and equality*. Salamanca: UNESCO.

——(2003). Retrieved 8 October 2003, from UNESCO/Education – Inclusive Education. URL:http:/portal.unesco.org/education.ev.php?URL_ID=12078_DO_DO_TOPIC_ SECTION=201.html

Willms, J.D. (2000). *Standards of care: Investments to improve children's educational outcomes in Latin America.* Paper presented at Year 2000 Conference on Early Childhood Development (April 2000). Washington DC: World Bank.

Chapter 10

Inclusive education in South Africa

An emerging pedagogy of possibility[1]

Sigamoney Manicka Naicker

> Race and exclusion were the decadent and immoral factors that deter-
> mined the place of our innocent and vulnerable children. Through this
> White Paper, the Government is determined to create special needs educa-
> tion as a non-racial and integrated component of our education system.
> (Department of Education, 2001, p. 4)

In launching Education *White Paper Six on Special Needs Education:
Building an Inclusive Education and Training System*, the Minister of
Education, Professor Kader Asmal, in July 2001 committed the South
African nation to an inclusive education and training system. The period
from 1994, with the advent of democracy in South Africa, witnessed an
exciting and challenging process of policy development. One of the key aims
of the new policy was to address the inequalities of the apartheid past.
Education was no exception, with several new policy documents being developed. These included White Papers on education and policies on higher
education, adult basic education and training, early childhood education,
further education and training, and inclusive education.

The key transformation goals that underpinned the policy development
and policy implementation process included: (i) increased access to education;
(ii) deeper democracy in education structures and processes; (iii) greater equity
to redress the numerous inequalities of the past; and (iv) improved efficiency
(e.g. financial, management, learner flows) within the system (Centre for
Education Policy Development, 2001, p. 12). The period 1994–2004 has been
extraordinary for those in the new democratic government and civil society to
implement the above-mentioned goals. It was also a steep learning curve for
those responsible for implementation. The realization that transformation was
a complex and long-term task became clear as national and provincial governments in South Africa's nine provinces began to implement the new policy in
education. This chapter will make reference to some of the challenges and
complexities, specifically those that are central to the shift from special needs
education to inclusive education. More specifically, the chapter will discuss the
history of special education and the issue of paradigmatic shifts. It isolates the

history of special education and the paradigms followed in the past as being the most serious challenge and an obstacle to inclusive education. Concerns are also raised about the challenges of teacher training, central to the new curriculum, given the very conservative nature of teacher training in apartheid South Africa.

This chapter attempts to, first, provide a general account of policy development; second, discuss the history of special education; third, track the developments from a special needs education system to an inclusive system; and fourth, in the light of those developments, argue that a pedagogy of possibility is emerging within the South African education system despite the enormous challenges, mainly of an ideological nature, that need to be addressed for inclusive education to materialize.

Policy development in South Africa post-1994

In 1994, South Africa held its first democratic elections. One of the key tasks facing the new government was to address the inequities of the past. These inequities were deeply entrenched in society and in most institutions, mainly on the basis of race. In a country that lacked a human rights culture, one of the first achievements was writing a new constitution that attempted to entrench human rights. A new constitution was drafted and approved in 1996. With regard to the transformation of South African society, the Constitution was clear (Article 9[3]):

> The state may not unfairly discriminate directly or indirectly against anyone on one or more grounds, including race, gender, sex, pregnancy, marital status, ethnic or social origin, colour, sexual orientation, age, disability, religion, conscience, belief, culture, language and birth.

Education and transformation

Concerning future developments in education, the constitution also provided unambiguous leadership:

> The SA constitution (Republic of South Africa, 1996) required that education be transformed and democratised in accordance with the values of human dignity, equality, human rights and freedom, non-racism and non-sexism. It guarantees access to a basic education for all through the provision that everyone has the right to basic education, including adult basic education.
>
> (Department of Education, 2001, p. 4)

Quite clearly, the education system was viewed as an important transformation mechanism. The idea was to create the conditions within the classrooms of the country that lead to a more stable, democratic, non-racist, non-sexist and non-disablist society.

Of course, given the new human rights philosophy, the first target of transformation was at a systemic and structural level. Apartheid South Africa, based on ethnic and racial separation, had nineteen separate education departments. The challenge was to establish a single education system for all. This was achieved within the first year of democracy. Capacity had to be built within the unitary system, and there had to be recruitment of individuals who shared the goals of the new South Africa. Space was also created for personnel from the traditional establishment. However, many of the latter were part of the high attrition rate of the civil service since they could not identify with the new ethos. As mentioned earlier, several policy initiatives were undertaken with a view to transforming education. These are briefly described below.

In 1995, *Education and Training White Paper One* was approved (Department of Education, 1995). This outlined the main policy directions for the transformation of the educational system. An important foundation was that the education and training system was to be unified, and that it should provide equal access, non-discrimination and redress. This led to the National Education Policy Act (1996), which empowered the Minister to set norms and standards for educational planning, provision, governance, monitoring and evaluation through democratic decision-making. Provinces, regions, districts and institutions were obliged to work for equity, redress, quality and democracy.

The South African Schools Act (Ministry of Education, 1996) attempted to ensure that (a) all learners had the right of access to quality education without discrimination; (b) schooling be compulsory for all children aged 7–15; (c) schools were democratically governed; and (d) funding prioritized redress and targeted poverty. Further education and training (FET) was legislated in an empowering Act (1998), and elaborated in *Education White Paper Four* (1998) and the *National Strategy for Further Education and Training* (1999–2001). The FET sub-sector included mention of inclusion at the secondary level and in technical colleges. The Higher Education Act, passed in 1997, and *White Paper Three* (1999) provided for a unified national system of higher education, with the Council on Higher Education as a quality assurance mechanism. These developments were followed by the National Plan for Higher Education (2001).

Other key policies included the South African Qualifications Authority Act (1995), which legislated setting up a framework for an integrated education and training system; the Employment of Educators Act (1998), which unified the teaching profession, previously regulated by ethnic administrations, under the South African Council of Educators; and the Adult Basic Education and Training Act (2000). In addition, *White Paper*

Five focused on early childhood education and *White Paper Six* on inclusive education. The latter attempted to transform the mainstream schooling system, thus creating more space for vulnerable and disabled learners.

The history of special education

The history of South African special education provision and education support services, like all other aspects of South African life during the colonial and apartheid eras, was largely influenced by fiscal inequalities in terms of race.

In light of the different and complex developments in special education and education support services in South Africa, the history of special education and education support services has been divided into four phases, as outlined in Table 10.1 (Naicker, 1999).

Phase one was marked by the lack of provision. Phase two had three stages. Stage one dealt with special education provision by the church and private organizations, as well as the racist nature of the state. Stage two focused on the development of standardized tests. Stage three explained the development of the medical model.

Phase three was divided into four stages. Stage one focused on the beginning of institutional apartheid and the provision of disparate services. Stage two described the racially segregated education departments and the development of special education services within those departments. Stage three gave particular attention to the Homelands or Bantustans, which were created by the apartheid government to promote and politicize ethnic

Table 10.1   Different phases and stages in the development of special education

Phase	Stage	Characterization
1		Lack of provision
2	1	Provision by church and private organizations
	2	Development of standardized tests
	3	Development of medical model
3	1	Beginning of institutional apartheid
	2	Special education in racially segregated education departments
	3	Special education in Homelands and Bantustans
4		Developments in the new democracy

differences, a concept that was in keeping with the apartheid tradition of divide and rule. It also acted as a means to keep away from the cities large numbers of black South Africans. Stage four referred to the developments within the new democracy in South Africa.

There are difficulties in clearly demarcating phases and in portraying the complexities that existed within the fragmented African section of the population. These included:

(i)   the introduction of Homelands with their own separate policies (or rather, the lack thereof, which was manifested in very limited provision in, for example, the Transkei, Ciskei, and Bophutswana);
(ii) different policies of the Department of Education and Training (responsible for African education) and policies shaped by the Bantu Education Act (1953);
(iii) the fragmented nature of society based on racial distinction;
(iv) varying state policies, with differing intervention times for whites, Africans (divided into Homelands and locally), coloureds and Indians.

Nevertheless, in this chapter an attempt will be made to divide the history of special education and education support services, bearing the above difficulties in mind.

Phase one: absence of provision (1700s–1800s)

Here, as everywhere else in the world, the 1700s and early 1800s saw little provision for any type of special education need. Disability was mostly seen as a sign of 'divine displeasure', a superstitious attitude which led to the chaining, imprisonment and killing of people who later became recognized as mentally retarded, physically disabled, blind, deaf and so on. The 'divine displeasure' attitude influenced to a large extent the treatment of people who were construed as disabled within the South African context, since it was a colonized territory.

Phase two: white-dominated provision, and the important role of the church (from the late 1800s to 1963)

Stage one: provisioning by church, private organizations and society, and the racist nature of the state

The title of this phase is self-explanatory and intentionally used to reflect the oppressive nature of special education policy on the part of the state during the period 1863–1963. Whilst the effects of racial practices are still being felt today, long after 1963, this particular phase began to set the pattern for later years and was most striking in terms of racial disparities. These disparities become evident when one looks at the chronology of special education provisions.

No special education provision was made by the state for African children. It took a century for it to provide subsidies for African deaf, blind, and physically disabled children. This only occurred in 1963.

The church played an important role during this phase. It not only initiated the provision of special education for handicapped children in South Africa, for both white and 'non-white' children, through the Dominican Grimley School for the Deaf in 1863, but also continued to provide a service to 'non-white' children in the absence of state provision for these children for the next century. The state became involved in specialized education only in 1900 when it recognized the existence of white church-run schools and later promulgated Act 29 of 1928. In terms of this Act, the Union Education Department could now establish vocational schools and special schools for 'white' children. The Act provides the first signal of the model of special education that was to emerge in South Africa. Although it mainly concerned white learners, it revealed for the first time the model of special education in South Africa, which was later expressed in the Special Education Act of (1948). This latter Act worked on the assumption that learners were deficient and that their deficiencies were pathological, a viewpoint that was strongly influenced by then-current medical thinking. This pathological perspective associated disability with impairment and loss, and did not take systemic deficiencies into consideration. This is discussed in more detail later on in this phase, in stage three.

Whilst the church and other private associations and societies continued to provide support for 'non-white' children, the state increasingly favoured whites. The former groups were responsible for establishing (i) the Athlone School for the Blind for coloured children; (ii) a school for blind Indian children; and (iii) the Worcester School for coloured children with epilepsy.

The Special Schools Amendment Act, passed in 1937, created the first provision for hostels in special schools for whites.

Stage two: development of tests as a precursor to institutional special education and education support services

The 1920s saw the first development of intelligence tests in South Africa. Professor Eybers, of the then University College of Orange Free State, published the individual intelligence scale, which was called the Grey Revision of the Stanford-Binet Scale (Behr, 1980). The development of tests continued in white education, and was followed by their implementation in schools. In 1924, a committee appointed by the Research Grants Board of the Union Department of Mines and Industries, and under the chairmanship of Professor R.W. Wilcocks, designed a test, which came to be known as the South African Group Test of Intelligence. This marked the first connection between education and the labour market in South Africa and was the precursor to aptitude tests. Later, in 1926, Professor J. Coetzee of Potchefstroom University published the first standardized arithmetic test in South Africa for whites. In 1929, both the Wilcocks and Coetzee tests were used in the Carnegie Poor White Survey and later in the Bilingualism Survey (Behr, 1980).

As mentioned earlier, the Scale of General Intelligence for South African Schools was used until the mid-1960s. This was the precursor of categorization, labelling and the exclusive education system, since IQ tests were later used not only for whites, but also for all children to assess their intelligence and to place them in special education programmes.

These tests were a precursor to the later institution of special education and created a place at a later stage for psychological services in schools (currently associated with education support services). They also formed the basis for adaptation classes (in coloured education), adjustment classes (in Indian education) and remedial education.

Stage three: the genesis of the medical model

The 1948 Special Schools Act in white education introduced into special education a medical and mental diagnosis and treatment model. This model, which focused on the individual deficit theory and viewed the person as a helpless being, was firmly entrenched in the charity and lay discourses (Fulcher, 1989). The medical discourse shaped and largely influenced exclusive practices in the field of education, which continued for decades after their introduction. According to Fulcher (1989), the medical discourse

> suggests, through its correspondence theory of meaning, that disability is an observable or intrinsic, objective attribute or characteristic of a person, rather than a social construct. Through the notion that impairment means loss, and the assumption that impairment or loss underlies disability, medical discourse on disability has deficit individualistic connotations. Further, through its presumed scientific status and neutrality, it depoliticizes disability; disability is seen as a technical issue, [and is] thus beyond the exercise of power. Medical discourse individualizes disability, in the sense that it suggests individuals have diseases or problems or incapacities as attributes.
>
> (p. 28)

Thus, disability was associated with an impairment or loss. The entire focus was on the individual who was viewed as helpless and dependent. The individual deficit theory viewed the person as in need of treatment and assistance outside of regular education. No attempt was made to establish the deficiencies of the system; for example, a physically disabled person using a wheelchair required a ramp to gain access to a mainstream school, which was not provided for by the system. Access to education was prevented as a result of barriers, which reflected a deficient system and not a deficient person.

This was also the beginning of the professionalization, and consequently the mystification, of special education in South Africa for regular education teachers. Again, Fulcher (1989) is appropriate here in her comments about the medical discourse: it professionalizes disability: 'the notion of medical expertise allows the claims that this (technical) and personal trouble is a matter for professional judgement' (p. 28).

Thus, regular education teachers might have been led to believe that it was beyond their level of expertise to teach learners who were classed as disabled, that this had to be done by specialists, and that inclusive education was not a possibility. Fulcher's (1989) comments continue to be pertinent here and explain why the proliferation of educational psychology and related disciplines took place:

> A theme of professionalism pervades medical discourse and its associated discourses: psychology, social work, occupational therapy and educational discourse. ... Thus medical discourse, through its language of body, patient, help, need, cure, rehabilitation, and its politics that the doctor knows best, excludes a consumer discourse or language of rights, wants and integration in mainstream social practices.
>
> (p. 28)

Therefore, the depoliticizing, individualizing and professionalizing of disabilities led to the notion that learners who were viewed as disabled had to be taught in special schools and/or classes, while their rights and needs were ignored. Parents of learners were intimidated by the knowledge of professionals and therefore did not challenge the decisions concerning placement.

Phase three: 'separate development' and its impact on special education and education support services (1963–1994)

Stage one: institutional apartheid and disparate service provision for the four race groups

The year 1948 had ushered in the introduction of institutional apartheid into every facet of South African life. The National Party's policy of separate development ensured the division of Africans, coloureds, Indians and whites in all aspects of their lives. This had significant implications for special education and education support services. Whilst the concept of education support services (known traditionally as psychological services, or auxiliary services) evolved only at a much later stage in South African education (NEPI, 1992), it must be noted that the initial precursor was the introduction of the psychological services, initiated after the introduction of separate development. The School Psychological and Guidance Services of the Department of Education in the Transvaal, after the promulgation of Act no. 39 of 1967 for 'whites', saw clinics established and staffed by clinical psychologists, vocational guidance psychologists, orthodidacticians, speech therapists, sociopedagogic psychologists and occupational therapists (Behr, 1980). This proved to be a possible model for education support services several decades later (NEPI, 1992). Thus, the introduction of psychological services paved the way for the development of the education support services.

Stage two: segregated education departments take control of special education and education support services provision

Education, as one of the pillars of separate development, was used as an instrument to ensure that all four groups accepted the idea of that policy. The passing of the Coloured Persons Education Act, the Bantu Education Act, and the Indian Education Act, in 1963, 1964 and 1965 respectively, saw special education and education support services being taken over by the various departments.

The disparities in special education and education support provision were clearly racial and became very visible with the unfolding of separate development. Table 10.2 illustrates the disparities, as they existed in 1980.

At this time, 'whites' made up 17.5 per cent, 'Africans' 70.2 per cent, 'coloureds' 9.4 per cent and 'Indians' 2.9 per cent of the population. Table 10.2 thus shows that special education provision clearly favoured 'whites'. The problem regarding provision with regard to bias towards 'whites' was actually worse than it appeared, since the development of 'non-white' special schools had been initiated by churches and private organizations, while special education for whites had been provided mainly by the state.

In psychological services there were major discrepancies along racial lines. As mentioned in stage one, the four white Education Departments reorganized psychological services after Act no. 39 of 1967 in the different provinces. For example, in the Transvaal, under the wing of the School Psychological and Guidance Services, an elaborate system of child guidance clinics was established for each of the twenty-four inspection circuits. In this system, a clinic served a group of schools. A multi-disciplinary team conducted intellectual, scholastic and emotional assessments of pupils, and provided help in the form of psychotherapy, remedial teaching and speech

Table 10.2   Provision and schools for the different types of disability

Disability	White	African	Coloured	Indian
Aural	5 schools	7	2	1
Visual	2 schools	4	1	1
Cerebral palsy	4 schools	3	1	1
Physical	4 schools	None	1	1
Epilepsy	3 schools	None	1	None
Autism	2 schools	None	None	None
Mental retardation	41 centres	None	1	3
Industry / reform	3	None	5	1
Remedial	Provisions existed	None	None	Provisions existed
Educable mental retardation	Provisions existed	None	Provisions existed	Provisions existed

Source: Behr, 1980.

therapy. In addition, clinics were concerned with identifying and guiding children with learning deficits, cultural deprivation and behavioural problems. Other provinces had similar services, but not as elaborate as the Transvaal's (Behr, 1980).

The Department of Bantu Education did establish a section with psychological services, but it was restricted to assessing all pupils in Form I and Form III to help teachers and lecturers assess their teaching. Psychological services for coloureds were instituted. At least one teacher in each school was concerned with guidance. Training was provided for secondary teachers who had taken psychology as part of degree course responsible for guidance. School Psychological Services in Indian education focused mainly on assessing and placing pupils needing special education (Behr, 1980).

Except for Indian education, which had several psychologists, an inspector of psychological services and a school guidance office, there was little comparison between the resources of white education and other race groups. This disparity resulted in poor supervision of adaptation classes, remedial education and facilities at special schools, where they existed.

Stage three: the Bantustan or Homeland phase

The conferring in 1968 of Territorial Authorities to six 'Homeland' government departments, with separate education departments, did not result in any significant changes for African children with special education needs. There was little information on the actual development of special education and education support in these territories (NEPI, 1992). However, it followed the pattern and trends of the 'separate development' phase relating to the number of pupils in special schools as a ratio of total enrolment for the various races: Indians 1:42; whites 1:62; coloureds 1:128; and Africans 1:83 (NEPI, 1992).

From special needs to inclusive education

As mentioned earlier, the advent of the democratic government in 1994 saw wide-scale transformation taking hold throughout the country. The unification of nineteen education departments into a single Ministry of Education was tantamount to a revolution. The disparities and lack of provision for mainly black South Africans clearly reflected the need to conduct intensive research with a view to providing a service that could benefit all South Africans. It was against this background that the demo-cratic government appointed the National Commission on Special Education Needs and Training (NCSNET), as well as the National Committee on Education Support Services (NCESS), in 1996. Both NCSNET and NCESS, established as separate entities by the Ministry of Education, decided to work jointly as a single group in the light of over-lapping functions. This was clearly spelt out in the single report of NCSNET and NCESS. The first meeting of both bodies was held in mid-November 1996.

The work of NCSNET and NCESS lasted for a year (1996–1997), during which time these bodies consulted widely with key stakeholders in educa-tion. Workshops and public hearings were held in all provinces, since consultation with all interested parties formed part of the terms of reference of NCSNET and NCESS, and was regarded as crucial.

The terms of reference adopted by NCSNET and NCESS had to heed the major proclamations and other policy documents during the period of transformation. For example, the new Constitution of the Republic of South Africa had this to say: 'Every person shall have the right to basic education and equal access to educational institutions' (Department of Education, 1996, p. 16). The *White Paper on Education and Training* was also clear on the question of rights:

> It is essential to increase awareness of the importance of ESS [Education Support Services] in an education and training system which is committed to equal access, non-discrimination, and redress, and which needs to target those sections of the learning population which have been most neglected or are most vulnerable.
>
> (Department of Education, 1996, p. 16)

Further, the *White Paper on an Integrated National Disability Strategy*, produced by the Disability Desk of the Office of the Deputy State President in 1997, offered very clear direction to the NCSNET and NCESS:

> An understanding of disability as a human rights and development issue leads to a recognition and acknowledgement that people with disabilities are equal citizens and should therefore enjoy equal rights and responsibilities. A human rights and development approach to disability focuses on the removal of barriers to equal participation and the elimination of discrimination based on disability.
>
> (Office of the Deputy State President, 1997, p. 10)

In November 1997, in its report entitled *Quality Education for All: Overcoming Barriers to Learning*, the NCSNET and NCESS recognized the need for all learners to gain access to a single education system and thus be able to participate in everyday mainstream economic and social life. The recommendations of NCSNET and NCESS were largely phrased in the language of human rights, which differs radically from that of the medical perspective. It moved away from individualizing, professionalizing and depoliticizing disability by stating that

> barriers can be located within the learner, within the centre of learning, within the education system and within the broader social, economic and political context. These barriers manifest themselves in different ways and only become obvious when learning breakdown occurs, when learners 'drop out' of the system or when the excluded become visible. Sometimes it is possible to identify permanent barriers in the learner or system, which can be addressed through enabling mechanisms and processes.
>
> However, barriers may also arise during the learning process and are seen as transitory in nature. These may require different interventions or strategies to prevent them from causing learning breakdown or excluding learners from the system. The key to preventing barriers from occurring is the effective monitoring and meeting of the different needs among the learner population and within the system as a whole.
>
> (Department of Education, 1997, p. 14)

In identifying the system and individuals as reflecting or experiencing potential barriers to learning, NCSNET and NCESS had moved away from viewing disability as only an individual loss or impairment. They suggested that these barriers could be addressed in a regular school and that regular education teachers needed to be trained to identify and deal with barriers to learning and development. These barriers could include the following: socio-economic factors, attitudes, inflexible language and curriculum, inaccessible and unsafe built environments, inadequate support services, lack of enabling and protective legislation and policy, lack of parental recognition and involvement, and lack of human resource development strategies.

In their recommendations, and as part of the principles on which their work was based, NCSNET and NCESS called for 'equal access to a single, inclusive education system' in which

> appropriate and effective education must be organised in such a way that all learners have access to a single education system that is responsive to diversity. No learners should be prevented from participating in this system, regardless of their physical, intellectual, social, emotional, language, or other differences.
>
> (Department of Education, 1997, p. 66)

A development that preceded the work of NCSNET and NCESS had been the introduction of the new Outcomes-Based Education (OBE) curriculum. NCSNET and NCESS called for a single curriculum and urged that diverse needs be firmly located within this general curriculum development then underway in South Africa. This investigation argued that OBE had the capacity to deal with diversity as a result of its flexibility and its premise that 'all students can learn and succeed, but not on the same day in the same way' (Spady, 1994, p. 9).

Government's model to transform a dual system into an inclusive system of education

Education's *White Paper Six on Special Needs Education: Building an Inclusive Education and Training System* (Department of Education, 2001) suggested a twenty-year plan to transform the system from a dual to a single system of education. The twenty years were to include short-term, medium-term and long-term steps. In the short term, government intended to:

- Implement a national advocacy and education programme on inclusive education.
- Plan and implement a targeted outreach programme, beginning in government's rural and urban nodes, to mobilize disabled out-of-school children and youth.
- Complete the audit of special schools and implement a programme to improve efficiency and quality.
- Designate, plan and implement the conversion of thirty special schools into resource centres in thirty districts.
- Designate, plan and implement the conversion of thirty primary schools to full-service schools in the same thirty districts above.

- Within all other public education institutions, on a progressive basis, the general orientation and introduction of management, governing bodies and professional staff to the inclusion model.
- Within primary schooling, on a progressive basis, the establishment of systems and procedures for the early identification and addressing of barriers to learning in the Foundation Phase (Grades R-3).

(Department of Education, 2001, p. 42)

The intention here was to ensure that there was sufficient human resource development so that teachers would be well equipped to deal with diversity. Further, through physical resource/material resource development, schools would be made accessible. District Support Teams, which comprised curriculum specialists, psychologists, early childhood education specialists and related personnel, would also undergo training in the area of inclusive education. The purpose of identifying a relatively small number of schools was to ensure that there was rigorous development and research to establish the strengths and weaknesses of the plan. Ultimately, full-service schools (ordinary primary schools that would be converted into schools which cater for difference) would be established. Special schools within this plan should have more of an outreach role to assist and support, together with the District Support Team, the full-service school and the ordinary school. Advocacy focusing on inclusive education would be conducted within the thirty districts, as well as system-wide, to ensure that there were sufficient common understandings about government's plans. It was envisaged that this process would lead to the following outcomes:

- Costing of an ideal district support team.
- Cost of conversion of special schools to special schools/resource centres.
- Costing of an ideal full-service school.
- Costing of a full service technical college.
- Determining the minimum levels of provision for learners with special needs for all higher education institutions.
- Devising a personnel plan.
- Costing non-personnel expenditure requirements.

(Department of Education, 2001, p. 44)

According to *White Paper Six*, the completion of the short-term steps should take three years. Once the research has been completed and the findings known, the medium steps should involve more schools, further education and training and higher education institutions, depending on available resources.

The notion of inclusive education, as mentioned earlier in this chapter, is shaped directly by the recommendations of NCSNET and NCESS.

Therefore, the focus is not merely on disability, but rather on all vulnerable children, including over-age learners, children in prison, learners who experience language barriers, or barriers such as the attitudes of others, lack of parental recognition and poverty. The transformational goals mentioned at the beginning of this chapter become very relevant to inclusive education, where the emphasis is on creating access and skewing funding so that it is pro-poor.

Another concurrent activity launched by the Ministry of Education has been the training of teachers within the framework of a new curriculum that is outcomes-based. The emphasis on diversity is clearly expressed by the Director-General of Education, Thami Mseleku, in his foreword to the curriculum teachers' guide. In this, he states: 'These guidelines are geared to assist teachers in accommodating Learning Outcomes and Assessment Standards that are prescribed, yet create space and possibilities for the use of judgements and insights based on particular contexts and a diverse learning population' (Department of Education, 2003, p. iii). The guidelines document further states:

> The guidelines are intended to be implemented in conjunction with other policies, for example, the *White Paper Six: Special Needs Education: Building an Inclusive Education and Training System* needs to be read to provide background information on issues related to barriers to learning, as these have crucial impact on what happens in the classroom.
>
> (Department of Education, 2003, p. 1)

What emerges clearly from government's intention is that the system is being geared towards creating possibilities for the first time in the history of South Africa, a pedagogy of possibility, not only in terms of race but of ability, interest, intelligence and styles.

Whilst the intentions are very clear, several challenges face policy implementers within the South African context. The following discussion attempts to tease out the main challenges facing inclusive education, and later makes reference to specific curriculum challenges.

The challenges facing an emerging pedagogy of possibility

Given the history of special education and the new developments within a democratic South Africa, the challenge to South Africans was to make the shift from special education to an inclusive OBE. This constituted a paradigm shift.

Within the South African context, a shift towards an inclusive OBE model, where all learners experience success, will entail moving away from a dual system (special and ordinary) to a single system of education. The dual system of education of the past had its own theory, assumptions, models, practices and tools. Such a system with a 'special education separate sector', according to Barton and Oliver (1992), had its definitions, policies and practices shaped largely by medical and psychological perspectives. Tomlinson, cited by Barton and Oliver (1992), argued that this was a discriminatory system, since to be categorized out of 'normal' education represents the ultimate in non-achievement in terms of ordinary educational goals.

On the other hand, a single inclusive system of education based on a rights model, had its own theory, assumptions, models, practices and tools. Oliver (1996) was incisive in his critique of the inability of society to deal with disabling barriers and social restrictions when he said:

> At the ontological level this has led, not to a denial of the problem oriented nature of disability, but of its assumptions of pathology. At the epistemological level middle range theorizing has been turned on its head; disability is caused not by the functional, physical or psychological limitations of impaired individuals but by the failure of society to remove its disabling barriers and social restrictions. At the experiential level disabled people are increasingly seeing their problems as stemming from social oppression (Sutherland, 1981) and institutionalized discrimination (Barnes, 1991). In other words disability is something wrong with society.
>
> (p. 129)

Oliver argued that the rights model moved away from a pathological assumption, an individual deficit theory and institutional discrimination. Given the shift from apartheid and special education to an inclusive OBE system, different theories and practices must emerge. The Department of Education (1997), in a document titled *Outcomes-based Education in South Africa: Background Information for Educators*, suggested strongly that in order for OBE to materialize, there had to be a 'move from one paradigm to another; from one way of looking at something to a new way. A move to a new mind set, a new attitude, a new way of thinking' (p. 6).

This quote, however, does not capture the entirety of the concept of shifting paradigms. Paradigms include not only ways of thinking, ways of seeing and evaluative judgements, but also, crucially, practices. To make the shift from special education that existed outside the regular education system in the past towards OBE as a single inclusive system requires a paradigm shift. The OBE approach requires a change in philosophy, structure and consciousness concerning race, gender and disability.

Policy implementers have to take seriously the influence of psychological theory, since the majority of special education discourses are located within educational psychology frameworks and departments. According to Fulcher

(1989), 'the theme of professionalism pervades medical discourse and its associated discourses: psychology, social work, occupational therapy, rehabilitation, counselling, physiotherapy and educational discourse' (p. 28).

Many of the psychological theories underpinning much of the understanding around learning breakdown shapes the belief that problems are located within learners. For example, very little is said about system deficiencies. The manner in which learners are socialized, exposure to intellectual work, poverty and its concomitant social problems have not been taken seriously in understanding why there is a breakdown in learning.

Special education theory is located within a predominantly functionalist paradigm and is concerned with both learners who experience learning breakdown and those who are 'gifted'. The belief that the system worked and that any breakdown was caused by individual deficits resulted in invoking the pathological label. That there was something wrong with the individual is a common explanation for failure (Fulcher, 1989).

According to Naicker (1999), in order to shift paradigms, a rethinking is required around one's consciousness of disability, race, class and gender. The first step is to move from an understanding of disability that is shaped by the medical model to an understanding underpinned by a rights model. Second, barriers to learning in the system need to be identified and interventions need to be made. In other words, one needs to examine what impediments exist in the system that prevent access to learning. Arguably, there are some barriers that exist within children: for example, neurological impairment. But these barriers need to be addressed through pedagogical responses, not by carrying out psychometric tests that offer little in terms of programme planning.

In the case of the gifted, either enrichment or acceleration could be used to ensure that the gifted learner is not neglected. Enrichment will entail creating more stimulating opportunities for the learner. This could include linguistic, musical, logical-mathematical, spatial, bodily-kinaesthetic or personal areas of competence or expertise. Acceleration could also be utilized to ensure that the learner does not stay in a grade if he or she has mastered that component of work.

Table 10.3 attempts to highlight what shifts need to take place, both philosophically and structurally. It shows that a new service cannot be delivered within an old system.

The changes could or would mean the following:

- A shift from pathological medical/individual explanations to understanding system deficiencies; for example, interpreting a deaf learner's difficulty in engaging with the curriculum as a lack of responsiveness of the curriculum rather than the learner's problem.
- A shift from labelling and classification of learners to using the OBE notion of progression and inclusion.

- A shift in structural arrangements. A central feature of transformation will involve rupturing old structures that were meant to deliver a dual system of education. This means moving personnel from special education departments to regular education sections as dedicated personnel in curriculum services, early childhood education, adult and basic education, physical resources, finance and other sections of the single education department. Thus, system deficiencies will be identified and all learners will have equal access to a single curriculum.
- A shift from standardized tests to predominantly teacher-produced diagnostic tests that measure the learner's learning potential and identifies how it can be improved.
- A shift from the Special Education Act to the Amendment of the South African Schools Act to enable all children to go to neighbourhood schools, provided that support mechanisms are put into place.

For inclusion to be successful, a major reorientation is required, both with the shift from special needs education and also in teacher training, which is central to the new curriculum. The theoretical framework that informs how we teach and how we approach learning and teaching has been a critical barrier to learning and teaching. South Africans, historically, have been exposed to very conservative theories and practices. In most cases, an understanding of learning and teaching has bracketed out sociological considerations. Exclusionary practices resulting from such confined thinking have not benefited the learners who were placed out of the mainstream. The pedagogy that informs teaching and learning is the single most important factor that can create the conditions for responsible decision-making and protect the rights of all human beings.

Although some teacher training institutions used alternative theories, most of them persisted in teaching a narrow basket of psychopedagogics

Table 10.3   Shifting from special education to inclusive education

	Traditional paradigm	New paradigm
Theory	Special education theories	Outcomes-based education
Assumptions	Pathological, within-child deficits	System-orientated, takes into consideration diverse contexts
Practices	Segregation of learners into special facilities	Includes all learners
Tools	Standardized tests	Criterion-referenced tests: teacher-produced tests assessing the potential to learn
Model	Special Education Act	Amendment to South African Schools Act

and behavioural learning theory. Much of this had to do with the culture of control within apartheid-style institutions into which newly trained teachers graduated. It is also the case that many teachers and schools, through their own efforts and those of teacher organizations, had started to move away from these traditional methods of teaching in the later years of apartheid. However, this was not generally the case in all schools, and the problem remains. Much of this confined nature of thinking and practice has shaped exclusionary practices in South African classrooms. Many children were excluded as a result of systemic factors such as poverty and second language issues, or other barriers discussed earlier.

Teachers need to be reflective, critical thinkers if inclusive education is to be successful. The South African education system of the past was notorious for its deliberate policies to turn children into mere automata. Black children were to be schooled as workers, learning only basic language and manual skills at school; white children were to know very little beyond their 'group area', and so grew up ignorant of great leaders of resistance to racial segregation and apartheid, such as Nelson Mandela and Mahatma Gandhi. In this situation, the educator's role in the classroom was one of control. To be an educator, one was expected to be a controller of the minds of developing children.

Paulo Freire (1978) argues that any liberation project within a learning encounter must pay heed to two critical issues. First, dialogue is crucial. Taylor (1993), citing Freire, argues that, 'the thinking subject cannot think alone. There is no longer an I think, but a we think. This co-participation of the subjects in the act of thinking is communication' (p. 59). The five premises of a pedagogy of the oppressed are as follows:

1   The individual deprived of dialogue is oppressed.
2   Dialogue is the process and practice of liberation.
3   The individual engaged in dialogue is liberated.
4   Dialogue, by definition, requires more than one person.
5   More than one person can be called a society.

Thus, real change discourse that needs to be injected into the OBE curriculum design needs to take on board both the issues of dialogue and of conscientization. As Taylor suggests, being aware of a transforming context and who the oppressor is, is not good enough. There has to be a change in the conceptualization horizons of learners and educators. This cannot take place without dialogue. The act of liberating poses the question, 'What do we mean by challenging you to think correctly?'. There has to be a change of attitudes, a re-conversion and a re-Africanization for all people in South Africa.

Taylor, citing Freire, is again apt here:

This experience brings about a different kind of learning, or at least the potential for a different kind of learning, because it can become an act of knowing and a means of action for transforming the reality which is to be knowing and a means of action for transforming the reality which is to be known.

(p. 55)

The challenge for South Africa, according to the document, *A Lifelong Development Framework for General and Further Education and Training in South Africa* (Department of Education, 1996), is to achieve the following vision:

> The vision for South Africa encompasses a prosperous, truly united, democratic and internationally competitive country with literate, creative and critical citizens, leading productive, self-fulfilled lives in a country free of violence, discrimination and prejudice. The realization of this vision requires appropriate Lifelong Learning, training and development to empower people to participate effectively in all the processes of a democratic society and to excel in fields like human and natural resource development, human and natural sciences, the arts and technology.
>
> (p. 5)

How does one achieve this revolutionary project with learners and educators who have been marginalized from mainstream economic and political decision-making? How does one achieve this revolutionary project with learners who are regarded as the oppressed illiterate? How does one achieve this revolutionary project with those educators who have been victims of an oppressive apartheid ideology? These are the critical questions that need to be raised in advancing curricula within the new OBE curriculum. An inclusive OBE can only materialize where the spaces and possibilities are created to remove the ideological shackles of the past.

Space for a pedagogy of possibility

Three key factors create space for a pedagogy of possibility. First, there are the philosophical, structural and practical changes that have taken hold in South Africa since independence in 1994. At a philosophical level, the major proclamations and declarations referred to earlier in this chapter – for example, the White Papers and the Constitution – create space for transformation. By signalling an intention to create a human rights ethos in education, space is created for transformation at a legislative level.

Structural changes, which include the development of a unitary education system, attempt to ensure that there is a clear departure from a racist and segregated education system. At a practical level, the curriculum is being adapted to meet the needs of diversity.

Second, the major emphasis of the curriculum transformation is located within the framework of four major principles: human rights, inclusivity, healthy environment and social justice. The social goal, which is inextricably linked with the educational goal, provides a platform for creating inclusive spaces in South African educational institutions. Curriculum orientation and training is largely influenced by the social goal, and creates possibilities for viewing education differently. There is a clear link between education and society. South Africans are trying to create conditions in schools that will result in an inclusive society.

Third, the majority of South Africans, as indicated in the results of the last three elections, favour a democratic non-racist, non-sexist and non-disablist society, with major emphases on the principles of redress, equity and equality. The various proclamations and declarations mentioned earlier in this chapter, which were produced by the majority of South Africans, are underpinned by the principles of redress, equity and equality. Social movements and civil society, as reflected by the recent voting patterns, are firmly behind the democratic process. Thus, the transformation process enjoys substantial support from civil society and social movements that are in the majority.

Whilst this is the reality, the challenge is to produce new knowledge that is supported by solid implementation plans with realistic time-lines and resources. Educational transformation needs to be located within the framework of new theories, assumptions, models, practices and tools. There has to be a clear understanding that the deep change, which involves changes in consciousness, is an ambitious project. Much work needs to go into understanding the thinking and practices that underpinned apartheid and segregated education. Announcing principles relating to human rights and equity is only the beginning. Much work in the pedagogical terrain that debunks apartheid and segregated education at a philosophical and practical level has to be advanced in a sophisticated way. Further, a new philosophical and practical approach at a pedagogical level is required to replace conservative thinking and practices.

In general, South African educationists within mainstream education are perplexed by the notion of inclusive education simply because of a lack of exposure in the past and the current dominance of special education theory and practices. There is a lack of understanding and realization that common sense practices in special education are shaped by conservative theories and practices. Even progressive educationists within mainstream education who are in support of the principles of inclusion, are sceptical of including all learners in mainstream schools. Whilst substantial setup work is being done to deliver a new service, ideological constraints emerge as a major impediment among both policy developers and practitioners.

Philosophy shapes attitudes; attitudes shape practices. Unless South African educationists are able to engage critically with conservative philosophies and understand the implications of these philosophies for practice, change will be extremely difficult.

Conclusion

Transformation to an inclusive education system and society is not an easy task. The South African education system has put in place policy and is attempting to generate implementation plans that are consistent with that policy. With substantial support from civil society and government, there is hope that transformation will take place. South Africans have realized that the process of transformation is tedious, difficult and complex. Further, it is extremely difficult to assess progress with regard to change. Policy development shaped by the social goals of human rights, inclusivity, a healthy environment and social justice has been very successful. The success of policy implementation that generates new theories, structures and practices relating to inclusive education, however, is the challenge that South Africans will face over the next few decades. At this time, it is very clear that shifting assumptions and practices that are shaped by conservative thinking and theories is a major obstacle to real transformation. The main challenge that faces South African educationists and proponents of inclusive education is the theory and practice of special education. A radical departure and a bold approach are required to undermine the status quo. Transformation must not only exist in the minds of people; real transformation takes place when there is action.

Note

1 In preparing this chapter, permission to use sections of the book, Naicker, S.M. (1999). *Curriculum 2005: A space for all*, published by Renaissance, a section of Tafelberg Publishers Ltd, Cape Town, is gratefully acknowledged.

References

Barton, L. and Oliver, M. (1992). 'Special needs: Personal trouble or public issue'. In M. Arnot and L. Barton (eds) *Voicing concerns: Sociological perspectives on contemporary education reforms* (pp. 67–92). London: Triangle Books.

Behr, A.L. (1980). *New perspectives in South African education*. Durban: Butterworths.

Centre for Education Policy Development (2001). *Transformation of the South African schooling system*. Braamfontein: CEPD.

Department of Education (1995). *White Paper on Education and Training*. Pretoria: Government Printer.

——(1996). *A lifelong learning development framework for general and further education and training in South Africa*. Pretoria: Department of National Education.

——(2001). *White Paper Six on Special Needs Education: Building an inclusive education and training system*. Pretoria: Government Printer.

——(2003). *Teacher's guide for the development of learning programmes*. Pretoria: Government Printer.

Department of National Education (1997). *Quality education for all: Overcoming barriers to learning and development. Report of the National Commission on*

Special Needs Education and Training (NCSNET) and National Committee on Education Support Services (NCESS). Pretoria: Government Printer.

Freire, P. (1978). *Pedagogy of the oppressed*. New York: Continuum.

Fulcher, G. (1989). *Disabling policies? A comparative approach to education policy and disability*. London: Falmer Press.

Ministry of Education (1996). South African Schools Act. *Government Gazette*. Notice 503 of 1996, Vol. 370, No. 17136.

Naicker, S.M. (1999). *Curriculum 2005. A space for all. An introduction to inclusive education*. Cape Town: Renaissance, Tafelberg.

NEPI (National Education Policy Investigation) (1992). *National Policy Investigation: Education support services*. Cape Town: Oxford University Press.

Office of the Deputy State President (1997). *White Paper on an integrated national disability strategy*. Pretoria: Government Printer.

Oliver, M. (1996). *Understanding disability*. London: Macmillan.

Republic of South Africa (1996). The Constitution of South Africa, Act 108 of 1996. *Government Gazette*, Vol. 378, No. 17678. Pretoria: Government Printer.

Spady, W. (1994). *Outcomes based education: Critical issues and answers*. Virginia: American Association of School Administrators.

Taylor, P. (1993). *The texts of Paulo Freire*. Buckingham: Open University Press.

Chapter 11

Inclusive education in Middle Eastern cultures

The challenge of tradition

Ronald C. Brown

This chapter examines inclusive education as it is practiced in certain Middle East countries. Central to this exploration is the tension between rapid modernization and the requirements of tradition that characterize social change in this region. Countries that have clearly articulated their ambitions to address inclusive practices in the schools are now facing the challenges of forging action from their own public policy. Having few of the precursors associated with inclusive practices emerging from Western countries, the effort to translate rhetoric into action involves confrontation with the bedrock values and beliefs of the region. While many of the basic cultural values and sentiments toward the disabled provide a wellspring of potential support for inclusive thinking, deeply rooted cultural beliefs and traditions pose obstacles that are difficult to overcome. To illustrate this intrinsic conflict within some Middle Eastern societies, the independent countries of Qatar, Bahrain, and Kuwait have been selected. While they share many of their cultural attributes with other countries in the Middle East, they possess economic and practical advantages for implementing social and educational innovations such as educational inclusion.

With the growing recognition of significant numbers of educationally challenged students in the schools, the conflict between traditional education and modern educational practice is amplified. Special education practices associated with the identification, classification, placement and education of children in traditional categories of the disabled do not accommodate the needs of those with purely educational disabilities.

Modern educational and psychological strategies commonly recommended for poorly achieving students in regular government and private schools are in conflict with traditional beliefs about the nature of handicapping conditions and with normative educational practices. The invisibility of the disability experienced by children with mild degrees of cognitive impairment, ADHD, ADD, speech and language impairment and specific learning disabilities, has created confusion and contradictory responses among parents and educators. The absence of clear-cut, observable signs of the disability encourages denial and, frequently, neglect and misdiagnosis. The absence of a single set of specialized treatments for educational disabilities has resulted in confused, inconsistent, and fractured approaches to addressing these needs. At the same time that students in these newer categories may be more easily accommodated by inclusive educational practices, their identification in the schools is more likely to result in their exclusion. The extension of the psycho-medical disability treatment model, in common use with children with traditional disabilities (e.g. vision and hearing impairment, severe intellectual impairment or severe social and emotional disturbances), has encouraged the educational segregation of the new categories of exceptionality as a condition for receiving special education and related services.

Legislation and commitment

The region is rhetorically committed to the ideology of inclusion. All of the twenty-two countries represented by the Arab League are signatories to major international documents proclaiming the importance of integration of the disabled in all of its civic, social, vocational and educational institutions (UNESCO Regional Office for Education in the Arab States, 2000). Many have signed on to more specific regional agreements, and most have some form of legislation espousing the equality of disabled persons under the law. In practice, all of these countries face obstacles that are embedded in their cultures, as well as from external influences identified as economic, political, social, geographical (i.e. ruralism) and professional education. At this time, there are no coherent compliance procedures or governmental standards to serve as benchmarks to judge the existence or appropriateness of inclusive educational practices in any of the countries surveyed.

Because the concept of educational inclusion is new to the region, only time will reveal whether the legislative rhetoric of commitment to inclusion will be translated into practice. It is too early to judge with any confidence. Reliable official sources of information on the existence of inclusive practices are difficult to locate. Typically, they range from incomplete to simply erroneous. Definitions of inclusion vary widely, and reported incidence figures for the disabled do not account for the un-served or under-served. Verification of statistical and qualitative data by regional and international organizations that report it is rare. Terminology commonly understood among countries with the most experience of inclusion is frequently misapplied or reinterpreted. The study of cross-cultural patterns of inclusive practices in the Middle East remains a fertile area for new exploration.

Concept versus practice

Confusion and controversy over the semantics of 'inclusion' abound in many countries with long experience with its implementation, where the term is used to denote the integration of those with disabilities in the natural environments of home, school, neighborhood and larger community. When the term crosses over into use in other cultures, it is no surprise that it is interpreted and applied in even more different and, sometimes, contradictory ways. Where the concept has become associated with legislative, regulatory and legal processes, such as in the US and UK, specific practices or models have evolved to help define the meaning or at least provide examples of its application. As observed by Moghaddam *et al.* (1993), many research findings on common perceptions and practices in one culture do not cross over to other cultures. In this instance, terms such as 'inclusion', 'individualization', 'differentiation' and 'special education' are new to the region. They may relate to different practices and convey widely discrepant experiences when compared with the countries that have the most experience with their use. This discrepancy between espousing the values of full inclusion and the evidence of isolated and fragmented practices, reflects inconsistent and contradictory perceptions of the meaning of these terms. The underlying foundation for this inconsistency is discussed later in this chapter.

In the Gulf of Arabia, there is no historical or normative precedence for inclusion. Practices associated with the concept of educational inclusion are only beginning to emerge. Evidence of its occurrence is found, primarily, in the private international schools sector and only for categories of the disabled who are least likely to be perceived as 'handicapped.' While consumer and professional advocacy for the concept is evident in national legislation and in the brochure vision statements of government and private service providers, its impact is only beginning to be felt.

In all discussions of this complex topic, it is important to distinguish between inclusive thinking and inclusive practices. 'Inclusive thinking' refers to the internalized belief that society, and all of its institutions, will benefit from removing non-essential barriers to the participation of the disabled in natural environments within the community. In contrast, 'inclusive practices' refers to isolated examples of activities, events or special arrangements that allow for integration to occur, whether emerging from a segregated environment, such as a special education centre, or in the natural environment of the regular school. Inclusive thinking emerges from a philosophical posture, and encourages creativity, flexibility and resourcefulness in discovering or inventing opportunities for removing barriers and promoting integration. It also emphasizes conditions that promote the independence and self-reliance of the individual with a disability, while discouraging practices that promote dependence and helplessness.

When inclusive practices are the product of this belief system, they are usually sustainable, opportunistic, and have the effect of creating additional strategies for integration. When driven by a community of educators who share in this belief system, inclusive practices tend to reinvent themselves and expand to include more opportunities in the natural environments of the school and community. Frequently, inclusive practices are introduced in a school without such a driving philosophy. When dressed up as modern practices and imposed on a school, they are often viewed as separate from, or at odds with, the school's primary purpose. In these instances, inclusive practices may be sustainable only as long as the faculty or parents do not complain, the expected workload of the regular class teacher is not exceeded, the budget is not stressed, or the professionals and administrators who initiated it do not move on, leaving no support system behind. The probability is that they will not be sustained, as any of these factors can erode its support.

Inclusion in the Middle East

The concept of inclusion as a professional ideology is relatively new in the Middle East region, which is dominated by the values and beliefs of a traditional culture. Children and youth with traditional disabilities are educated, with few exceptions, in special schools or centres, characterized by isolation rather than inclusive practices. Traditional disability categories include students with severe physical, cognitive, emotional, or sensory disabilities, whose conditions are usually obvious to laypersons at an early age. A search for evidence of inclusive practices for these disabilities will reveal examples of specific events or opportunities for physical proximity or social contact between disability groups in regular school and community events. However, such isolated events do not contradict the observation that they are generally not integrated for educational, social, or proximity purposes.

This testimony underscores the point that 'inclusion' is now in the vocabulary of modernity used by service providers throughout the Middle East. It is increasingly seen as something to work toward, as the larger society is prodded toward acceptance. In the absence of traditions of assertive client and professional advocacy, it is perceived as part of the gradual, sometimes grudging, direction of change within Arab society, rather than as a separate set of practices to be employed by professional service providers.

In Qatar, Bahrain and Kuwait, inclusion is now accepted as an element in modern planning for the disabled. No practitioner wants to be thought of as being out of date or as resisting the opportunity to advance the welfare of his or her clients. At the same time, many obstacles within the traditional fabric of society are cited as the basis for the slow progress that has been made in that direction. The medical and social services for the traditional disability categories are extolled, while appropriate educational and social integration for both traditional and educational disabilities is restricted or non-existent. For this reason, the focus is on the opportunity for inclusive thinking to arise with students in the 'educationally disabled' categories, where the opportunity for breaking with the traditional patterns of exclusion is greatest.

Diversity in the Middle East

While there are marked similarities among the traditional cultures of the Middle East, generalizations across the region are not possible. The Middle East is characterized by pronounced diversity among countries in their specific cultural traditions, politics, languages, laws, religion, ethnic make up, social class structure and social institutions. When we strip away the stereotypes of the 'Middle East,' the assumption of continuity and homogeneity soon falls apart. Although the rich cultural diversity and effects of modernization that characterize the region (Lewis, 2000) has implications for differences in the progress made toward actualizing the rhetoric of inclusion, similarities do exist in the region's traditional response to disabilities. In many of the countries within this broad region, the forces of tradition have worked to both protect and care for the disabled while maintaining psycho-social borders preventing their integration into the larger society. This internal contradiction is at the centre of the cautious and hesitant emergence of inclusive thinking throughout the region.

The Gulf of Arabia

Because of the relatively high levels of affluence enjoyed by both the governments and most of their citizens, Qatar, Bahrain and Kuwait have the ability to fund innovative educational programmes and to introduce modern practices. In addition, each of these countries has enacted legislation supporting the integration of the disabled in society, achieved high rates of literacy, developed increasingly diversified economies, accommodated extensive exposure to forces of modernization, achieved relative political stability and democratic institutions, and established highly developed social welfare systems.

All are located along the Western shore of the Gulf of Arabia and primarily exist as city-states, in which most of the population lives in or close to the capital city, and where ruralism does not represent an obstacle to social and educational services. They all share a border with Saudi Arabia and have maintained much of the basic values of the region's traditional society. They are also well known for the speed with which they have adapted to the new technology and modern social forces that have rapidly affected their lives and, especially, the lives of their children. At the same time, they have maintained much of the bedrock conservative values and traditions of a predominantly conservative Muslim community.

They also experience considerable diversity within their populations, as the citizens of Qatar and Kuwait represent a minority of the inhabitants, while Bahrain citizens number two-thirds of its population. The demand for high-level expertise provided by expatriates from many different countries, from within and outside of the Arab world, coupled with the need for relatively low paid service personnel, has resulted in large expatriate populations (Cordesman, 1997).

Education in transition

The three countries in focus have placed a high value on education at every level, especially on post-secondary advanced education. As evidence of increasing exposure to Western educational practices, the number and size of private British and American elementary and secondary-level curriculum schools continue to grow as an integrated part of each country's domestic education system. In addition, each of these countries has, in recent years, approved the opening of American, British, or Australian universities, as an alternative to enrollment in government and private Arab universities. These developments reveal an increasing preference for Western-style education among an increasing number of their inhabitants. Diversification of the economies of these countries, and increasing demands for higher levels of general knowledge and technical skills, have combined to promote higher levels of education as an important value in defining the complete citizen.

This increasing demand for higher levels of education has received added impetus from the political and socio-economic urgency of reducing regional unemployment by preparing their citizens for skilled and professional jobs currently filled by expatriates. A significant, but more pervasive, incentive toward educational reform is related to the widespread perception across all Arab nations that both the pace and quality of educational development in the Arab world are increasingly falling behind their own projections (UNESCO, 2000).

With increased emphasis on higher levels of academic achievement and standards of education, recognition is growing of the large numbers of students whose educational disabilities will interfere with their meeting either the academic demands or, more significantly, the new cultural expectations related to advanced education. As secondary and higher education programmes are increasingly incorporated into societal norms for social adequacy and wholeness, the stigma of educational underachievement is magnified. The negative impact of the existence of a child with educational disabilities on the traditional family is exacerbated by this development, as discussed later in this chapter.

The implications of increased expectations for the levels and quality of education received by citizens are mixed. It does not follow that the reform of local education systems toward greater flexibility in methods, more demanding curriculum or higher academic standards will promote inclusive thinking. On the contrary, they may lead to greater exclusion of those who fall behind as standards are increased. When curriculum reform translates into meritocracy, the value in accommodating diversity in learning styles and achievement levels is lost (Kusuma-Powell, 2003; Teruhisa, 1994). In all school sectors of the countries under review, the modern reform concept of excellence is perceived as incongruous with accommodation of learning diversity. In this context, it may offer few incentives for the schools to adopt inclusive practices.

On the other hand, the existence of increasing numbers of Western curriculum schools and universities, with their greater emphasis on individualization and flexibility, provide the models in which inclusive thinking can develop within each country. For example, many of the new private universities are allied with universities in the West, which offer a variety of on-campus support services in their home countries. Also, their Gulf country affiliates undergo accreditation by international organizations, which also place value on providing for student diversity and individual learning needs. There is strong potential for these international schools, from kindergarten through university level, to model and promote inclusive thinking and the practices that emerge from it.

Even in international schools that do not provide specialized staff (e.g. learning disabilities specialists) to support inclusion, there is evidence that they have the potential to accommodate the goals of academic and social integration. For example, some schools will support educational inclusion for an individual student when the parents propose paying for a consultant and an extra teacher assistant. Where the family-funded assistant and consultant are in communication with the classroom teachers, the child can be successful in all spheres of regular school life. While individual parents initiate these arrangements, their success provides evidence that the school could achieve the same ends through its own initiative, when there is a commitment to inclusive thinking.

From charity to human rights

National legislation addressing public policy on social issues can only define the parameters for social change, by legitimizing and honouring the direction that change should take. All three countries discussed in this chapter have enacted national legislation that promotes the participation of individuals with disabilities in the schools, the workplace and in the larger community. Both the spirit and the intent of these laws support inclusive thinking in all spheres of life. However, unlike the laws of nations that have advanced inclusive practices, none of these Gulf countries provide regulations or a blueprint for accomplishing it. Specific rules may be given for such factors as special education class size, auxiliary services, and teaching credentials, but tests for compliance with inclusive practices are not included.

Kuwait is unique among the countries of the region, in its more permissive legislation, allowing government payment of school fees for children with disabilities in the private sector. This is affecting a growing number of students, not only among children with educational disabilities, but also those with more disabling conditions, including autism and moderate to severe degrees of intellectual impairment. The implications for inclusive education remain speculative, as most of the private school placements occur in segregated special schools or separate units within a school. However, as the government will also pay for part-time special education support services, the children may be permitted to remain in at least some of the regular international school classes in which they require little or no special assistance. This resource room model is currently applied with an increasing number of students in several of the American and British curriculum schools of Kuwait, and with a smaller number in Qatar and Bahrain.

One of the major contributions of these laws is their establishment of educational services for the disabled as a human and civil right (Hodgson, 1998; Mazurek and Winzer, 1994). This represents a major departure from the charity ethos, associated with compassion, recreation, cleanliness, custodial care, dependence and freedom from many of life's challenges. The shift from a charity obligation to a human rights ethic is highly significant as a support for the citizen and professional advocacy that has begun to make an impact. The concept of collective human rights for all individuals with a disability is a relatively new concept in a region that has taken pride in its traditions of charity. It entails a paradigm shift toward providing appropriate levels of education and training, beyond the traditional narrow focus on medical, recreational and social services. A reduction in barriers is emphasized, as evidenced by participation in the schools, the workplace, social and civic institutions, and society at large.

One example of the difficulty entailed in this shift is found in the manner in which those with physical disabilities are accommodated. While they may require no special supports in their academic program, the absence of inclusive thinking is apparent. Although there is widespread awareness among architects and engineers of the specifications for 'barrier free' construction and independent ambulation, the blueprints for new construction or renovations of regular schools would rarely qualify for the descriptor 'handicapped accessible'. Even when included in the original design, the finished product is often compromised by last-minute adjustments that prevent access to certain areas of a building. In addition, when buildings are retrofitted to accommodate wheelchair access, it is usually with the intention of allowing an assistant to navigate a steep incline and to hold the doors. The concept of independent mobility is not well understood or accepted in a culture that is motivated to do things for individuals with a disability rather than to burden them with activities directed toward achieving independence. This is a reflection of how traditional thinking contradicts the spirit and intent of human rights legislation in these countries.

Special centres

All three of the countries discussed in this chapter provide for the traditional categories of disabling conditions through specialized centres, offering medical, social, recreational and, to some extent, educational services. With some exceptions, children with traditional disabilities are not found in the regular schools of the Gulf of Arabia. They are generally identified early and enrolled in the special centre programmes or they remain at home, often with assistance from maids and nurses from countries where inexpensive labour is commonly recruited.

Inclusive practices in these centres include bussing clients to various formal ceremonies, recreation events or celebrations outside of the centre. Much of the contact with the society outside of the centres occurs through volunteers who visit or take them on trips in small groups. There is little evidence of any plan for inclusion in the norms for treatment or education. In all three countries, the concept of modernization and practical improvements in treatment and education are contained within the special centre system and are not associated with inclusive thinking. Although its absence may be attributed, in part, to the systemic obstacles confronted in all of the regular school sectors, much of it reflects the prevailing psycho-medical disability model that sustains the special centre concept. In this model, the clients are thought to benefit from the convergence of various specialized treatments, which can be administered more efficiently in a separate centre or hospital-like setting.

Emergence of educational disabilities

With the growing emphasis on achieving advanced levels of literacy and formal academic degrees, the phenomenon of 'educational disabilities' is becoming increasingly visible. In many schools in the West, these students would fall into the categories of specific learning disabilities (average or higher intelligence with specific weaknesses in learning), mild intellectual impairment (approximate tested levels of 50–55 to 75–80 IQ, depending on the intelligence test), speech and language disorders, attention deficit hyperactivity disorder (ADHD) or attention deficit disorder without hyperactivity (ADD). Parental expectations for appropriate and high-quality education, combined with the need to avoid family shame and social stigma, has resulted in some of these students going abroad to complete their education. More frequently, it has resulted in transfers from school to school in the hope that each new school placement would provide what was missing in the previous one.

The role of various school sectors in assisting students with educational disabilities is described below, with particular reference to opportunities for inclusive educational support. While inclusive education practices in any of these sectors are rare or non-existent, examples of those that do exist are serving as starting points for all of these small countries.

School sectors

In addressing this complex topic, it is helpful to distinguish among three general types of inclusion that have been practiced in many other countries:

(a) 'proximity integration', or location in or near other regular education programmes; (b) 'social integration', or arranging for participation in non-academic activities with students in mainstream classes or recreational settings; and (c) 'academic integration', or participation in normal academic studies in regular classes, with or without special education or reasonable accommodations.

The large majority of examples encountered in the Gulf region fall into the most basic category of inclusive practices, referred to as proximity integration. Opportunity for social interaction, during lunch, recess, and special events, is provided in fewer instances. Generally, academic integration occurs only with students who are described as mildly learning disabled, where their relatively higher levels of cognitive and social functioning are more easily accommodated. It also tends to be restricted to the early grade levels, where cumulative discrepancies in academic skill levels are not as pronounced.

The schools in Qatar, Bahrain and Kuwait support three distinct types of educational systems: (1) government-supported elementary, secondary and higher education schools; (2) private Arabic-speaking schools; and (3) foreign international schools catering to the dependents of host nationals and expatriate workers.

In the government and private Arabic-speaking schools, English is required from the early elementary through the secondary school years. Each country also provides for private foreign international bilingual schools, in which the school day is divided almost equally into course subjects taught in English and in Arabic. All schools, in each sector, teach a minimum number of periods of the Arabic language and Islamic studies. Host nationals represent many and, in some cases, the majority of students enrolled in the private British and American schools.

In the government school sector, infrequent opportunity for inclusion is found, apart from proximity and social integration. Here, we confront the theme of learning diversity versus conformity. While inclusive education incorporates the principle of learning diversity and individualization, prevailing government school practice adheres to conformity and standardization. These systems are frequently referred to as 'collective education', as they operate with the expectation of unswerving compliance with the approved curriculum regimens. They make no distinction among instructional objectives, learning resources, books, teaching techniques, and assessment methodology. These instructional components are welded into a single, unified package referred to as 'the government curriculum.'

The government schools have the opportunity to implement inclusive practices by fiat, through the authority of the ministries of education and social welfare. In Kuwait, this has occurred through the addition of special education classes for children officially categorized as slow learners and for certain other categories (e.g. Down's Syndrome). They are located in separate units of regular government schools, and are described as inclusive because they are not located in a special centre. Schools will differ in the extent to which they allow for social integration for non-academic subjects, but are consistent in their isolation of the full-time special classes within the regular school building. The Kuwait government schools provide an example of proximity integration with some provision for social integration. At this time, there is no system for academic integration.

For all three countries, significant barriers to academic integration are contained within the government curriculum, as it does not provide for differentiation or individualization of instruction at any level. Similarly, in the private Arabic school sector there are no established programmes specifically planned to address the needs of any category of disability. Because most of these schools closely follow the government-prescribed curriculum, it is unlikely that they would provide a forum for inclusive thinking or experimentation with inclusive practices. Similar in structure to schools in the private Arabic sector, are the national schools serving specific ethnic or national groups. They resemble the private Arabic schools, except that they offer their clients opportunity for instruction in their native language, in addition to courses in English and Arabic. These schools generally serve students whose families originated from India, Pakistan, Iran and the Philippines. Opportunity for inclusive practices in these schools would generally not occur.

It is in the private American and British international schools that the greatest potential for inclusive thinking occurs. Their administrators and many of their teachers practiced in home countries where inclusive thinking is normative and where models of inclusive practices were extant. With or without administrative endorsement or a commitment to inclusive thinking, they have the greatest potential to introduce and model appropriate practices. In Kuwait, where the government supports the school fees for Kuwaiti nationals with disabilities, a variety of experiments has arisen within schools offering British or American style curriculum formats. While some of these were judged to be unsustainable and were terminated, the government financial incentive for introducing inclusive practices remains strong. At this time, Kuwait offers a kindergarten to grade 12 private American curriculum school for college bound students with specific learning disabilities, a bilingual kindergarten to grade 10 American curriculum school providing special education classes and limited inclusion support services, and an Arabic medium special education school offering after-school tutoring and day school support for government school students identified as learning disabled. The stated purpose of the latter is to return students with learning disabilities to the regular government school programme after a period of intensive instruction in the Arabic medium, using the government school curriculum. A variety of other British and American schools in Kuwait also offer support for social and academic integration of children with mild learning and adjustment problems, on an individual basis.

In Qatar, a similar variety of special education services has developed, only without the impetus of direct payment of private school fees by the government. A private school for mixed disabilities has recently opened as a demonstration centre for instructional practices. The Qatar Foundation, a private initiative of the royal family, has supported a private international school offering limited inclusive education for those with mild learning disabilities, and a private special education school for those with moderate to severe learning disabilities. Although the Qatari government has encouraged the development of these private sector special education schools, it is currently reviewing proposals for conducting its own special education teacher training programmes with a focus on inclusive education. Other members of the British and American school sector in Qatar offer only limited support for inclusion of those with mild learning disabilities, in the form of resource teacher support or extra assistance from a reading teacher or ESL specialist.

Bahrain also offers a variety of British and American schools, operating at different fee levels and with different clienteles. One of the American international schools offers part-time, special education resource room services for its expatriate students (primarily dependents of the US military), based on written individual education plans (IEPs). Another American curriculum school, primarily serving Bahraini students, is offering IEP-driven support for children with mild to severe degrees of specific learning disabilities. In this new programme, the specific nature of educational inclusion is described in the IEP of each student, with regular class accommodations specified. Because it is the only inclusive education programme of its kind in Bahrain, it has the potential to absorb many of the students from the other schools in the region, including schools in Saudi Arabia, located just over the border. The programme opened in 2004 with government approval and encouragement but private funding.

Special education and reasonable accomodation

The common use of the term 'special education' in the Middle East might be loosely applied to any educational arrangement that departs from the highly structured and standardized educational regimens offered in the government schools. It is also used to describe the services of specialists, such as speech and language therapists, physical therapists, behaviour management specialists, or special education teachers. Most often, it refers to any of the various services that a student with an educational disability might receive. The existence of a written IEP implies that the student is receiving special education, whether or not any changes are made in the level or organization of the curriculum, assessment procedures, or methods of instruction.

The concept of 'reasonable accommodation' is an essential component of educational inclusion, but is rarely referred to in any of the school sectors. It is generally understood to refer to adjustments that might be made for any student with an educational or other type of disability, without the need for specially trained personnel, the addition of an assistant, or additional expenditures. In schools characterized by inclusive thinking, the application of reasonable accommodations is the first line of response and is often sufficient to support the success of a student with a mild educational disability. When used early, it often prevents the need for special education in later years (Lerner, 1989). In the absence of inclusive thinking at the administrative level, reasonable accommodations constitute the spontaneous adjustments that an individual teacher might make on behalf of a student without any expectation that they will carry over into other classes or that they will be carried on to the next school year. Without administrative support and encouragement for such accommodations, or a climate of support for making 'exceptions', continuity and predictability for inclusive practices are, at best, tenuous. This should not imply that inclusive schools are more successful without trained special education personnel. Many students experiencing educational disabilities require the assistance of the special education teacher and could not be maintained without it.

While the private English-speaking American and British schools offer the most promise for developing inclusive practices, in conjunction with special education services, there remains widespread resistance to taking this step. The perceived conflict between brochure descriptions of the pursuit of academic excellence and the presence of academically limited students represents a psychological barrier that few school boards, local sponsors, and school administrators choose to cross (Brown, 1995; Kusuma-Powell, 2003). Many are also reluctant to request additional fees from families to offset the increased cost of special services. The egalitarian ethos in the US and UK, that has supported learning diversity in the public sector in their home countries, does not readily translate into similar practices in the private British and American schools in foreign countries. Sensitivity toward the feelings of other parents, regarding the inclusion of children with special needs, will sometimes be the determining factor in not adopting inclusive practices.

The reputation of an international school for academic achievement is the major source of prestige and student recruitment and, in the perceptions of many, would be diminished by the existence of inclusive educational programmes. Some of these schools, in Qatar and Kuwait, have a history of attempting programmes for inclusive education, only to have them terminated when the expatriate education specialist moved on, when parental criticism or unrealistic expectations for a quick reversal of the disability mounted, or when the regular class teachers or administrators objected. In spite of these restraints, the private British and American schools have provided the best models, currently available, for what can be accomplished when there is commitment to inclusive education for individual students.

Individualization

The concept of individualization is not generally understood in the Middle East. Planning for effective academic integration of educationally disabled students is an individualization process. It normally involves changes in such variables as curriculum levels, methods, supplementary teaching materials, modifications in test-taking procedures, and homework assignments. Its absence in the organization of instruction represents a significant obstacle to the development of effective inclusive education practices.

While individualization of instruction is normally considered a prerequisite for effective inclusive practices, it is not always interpreted as necessary in the Gulf region. In the government school sector, it often refers to the process of removing students from a regular school programme and placing them in a separate special class. The very process of identifying an individual in the collective group as different, along with any separate treatment they might receive, is perceived as individualization. In this context, individualization is synonymous with exclusion, rather than a precondition for promoting inclusive practices.

The cultural norms for group identity, social cohesion, family unity and kinship are very strong in the Gulf region. In this collective paradigm, a child is often seen as errant if they demonstrate individual needs separate from the communal group. In the schools, the strong identification with membership in a subgroup is often demonstrated by the aggressive complaints of parents when a child does not continue in the same class from year to year. Remaining with the group, and with the same friends, is seen as more important than any particular benefits a child might receive from being moved to a smaller class or programme offering supportive services. In almost all cases, parents will advocate for services that occur in an inclusive context and resist those that require separation from the mainstream, particularly when it entails even temporary isolation from friends. It is ironic that when educational support services are offered, they almost always contradict these strong family preferences for inclusive education.

Diagnosis of educational disabilities

Familiarity with the Western concept of differential diagnosis and systems of diagnostic classification are relatively new in the Gulf region. While there is general agreement about classifications of those with traditional disabilities, there is a lack of consensus and considerable confusion among professionals in the region as to the categories that should be applied with educational disabilities (Brown, 1995).

One of the hallmarks of an effective system of classification is the specificity of criteria for describing a sub-population of the disabled (Hobbs, 1975). This is required for recommending the type and amount of appropriate medical, psychological and special education services that will need to be mobilized to support treatment programmes for those who fit a particular sub-classification. It is also essential for conducting needs assessment for administrative planning and allocation of budget to support the required human and material resources. Less obvious, is the need for clear and measurable criteria that will reduce the probability of misclassification leading to inappropriate educational placements. The absence of consensus on a system of classification for the disabled, and of trained diagnosticians to enforce one if it existed, affects all of these purposes.

Arguably, the existence of inclusive thinking should reduce the emphasis on classification systems as the focus is placed on the creative orchestration of regular and special education support services. The movement toward mixed-categorical, cross-categorical or non-categorical organization of special education services is clearly enhanced by the focus on matching student performance with appropriate arrangements for instruction. Countries with the most experience with educational inclusion have moved in this direction and away from classification of students for placement in segregated instructional environments. It remains, however, that instruction-ally relevant classification does contribute to organizing instructional options, selecting staff with appropriate training, and providing relevant professional development for teachers and support personnel. This applies whether the student is placed in an inclusive education programme or in a segregated special class. For the three countries under discussion, there is no officially accepted system for classification for any of the groups who fall within the broad description of those with educational disabilities presented in this chapter.

Differential diagnosis is generally an outcome of the training, country of origin, and particular specialization of the evaluators or of the organization responsible for serving specific sub-classifications of the disabled. The exam-iner may be a psychologist, counsellor, speech therapist, physician or other specialist. As there are no standards or licensing for evaluators, training varies widely and may have been completed at the B.A., M.A., M.Ed., Ph.D. or M.D. level. Training in the administration and interpretation of widely recognized psychological, psycho-educational, or academic achievement tests varies considerably.

In Qatar and Kuwait, where private foreign schools for those with specific learning disabilities have been established, American-licensed psychologists at the doctoral level have been responsible for the diagnosis of students referred for evaluation, using the American system of classification. In Bahrain, diagnosis is largely dependent on the availability of expatriate specialists working for a school or hospital with the skills to conduct the assessments. For the government school sector in all three countries, a psychologist or social worker, usually at the B.A. level of training, generally makes a diagnosis. An alternative source of diagnosis for many families is found in the government hospitals, where physicians make the judgement, especially where it involves attention deficit hyperactivity disorder or attention deficit disorder involving the possible prescription of psychoactive drugs. In the government school sector, there is little assurance of consensus among the diverse sources of diagnosis, owing to disparities in training, experience, and professional paradigms of the evaluators.

The recent introduction of the concept of educational disabilities poses a special problem for practitioners accustomed to addressing the needs of those within the traditional categories of disability. Most of these newly recognized disabilities have no clear aetiology, cannot be medically verified, are primarily demonstrated in school performance, depend on psycho-educational data for verification, and are thought to respond to a very wide range of non-medical treatment options (Lerner, 1989). The normal risk of misdiagnosis and inappropriate educational placements, faced by countries with long experience with standardized systems of diagnosis and classification, are exacerbated when there is no national or regional consensus.

The cultural context

Through the lens of culture, inclusive thinking and practices take on distinctive dimensions. Their presence or absence in the various education sectors has been reviewed in light of rapidly changing social forces within the Gulf region. In this section, we examine some of the cultural characteristics that influence the occurrence of inclusive education in the schools.

In the Gulf of Arabia, a family member's perception and response to a disability is expected to vary with exposure to modern practices in the West, their education levels and, to some extent, their socio-economic status in the community (Karola, 2002). While these factors influence the pervasiveness and intensity of family attitudes and behaviour, clinical observation over many years continues to reveal a commonality of response that cuts across all of these variables. For the three countries under discussion, the following cultural factors play a significant part in a family's response to evidence of a disability.

Image of wholeness

Every culture projects a certain image of the ideal person, representing the fulfillment of traditional cultural values and norms. This image is generally a composite of the individual characteristics that contribute to a sense of wholeness in the mature individual. In the Gulf region, the bedrock values of honour, courage, hospitality and generosity are to be displayed in an outward manner, so that others can judge them (Patai, 1983). In a similar fashion, the equally strong values and traditions associated with marriage, procreation, and active participation in the life of the family and community are major determinants of the individual's wholeness. Because the concepts of 'handicap' or 'disability' contradict the cultural image of wholeness, the impetus for rejecting information that confirms the existence of any imperfection is strong. Even in the case of the least debilitating conditions, the family is anxious that, once acknowledged, the potential for later marriage or future participation in the obligatory social and political life of the small community will be threatened. In some cases, this fear extends to the risk of limiting options for holding future political office, envisioned for a child from a prominent family.

Some of the logos of the special centres and societies dedicated to serving the disabled reveal this absence of wholeness in graphic form. Their logos and pictorial images of the disabled often reveal images of incompleteness or isolation, such as a puzzle with missing pieces, a motionless and isolated wheel chair, or a flower with a missing petal and partially missing leaf. In this paradigm, the concept of 'handicapped' is absolute, and not subject to consideration of the nature or severity of the condition or to a continuum of disabilities. Patai (1983, pp. 156–157) refers to this tendency in Arab cultures as 'polarization', or a tendency to observe opposites rather than gradations. These logos, and the literature that accompanies them, strive to portray a sympathetic image of their subjects by eliciting feelings of compassion and altruism. However, they have the effect of emphasizing the incompleteness of an entire class of individuals with disabilities and tend to represent their conditions as irremediable or fixed. These images also reflect the common perception of the disabled as members of a separate community, different and isolated from the mainstream of life. The absence of wholeness implies separation and segregation, conditions that are the polar opposites of the traditional values of communal unity (Moghaddam et al., 1993).

It is noteworthy that few practitioners or parents from the region would interpret these images in a negative manner. The prevailing culturally supported sentiments of compassion, kindness, and concern for the protection and happiness of children and youth with disabilities, mitigates any negative association with the incompleteness and isolation these visual symbols may convey.

In an earlier era, when wholeness depended less on educational achievement and participation in executive-level occupations and specialized professions, it was only those in the traditional disability categories that fell short of its requirements. As societal demands for increased levels of formal education accelerated to match the rapid social and economic advances in these affluent countries, however, the expectations of higher levels of education were incorporated into the norms for citizen wholeness. The evidence of educational disabilities places the individual in jeopardy of violating these newly enhanced norms for wholeness. Without understanding and acceptance within their own culture, and without supportive educational services to advance their learning to meet these new demands, a growing number of students will be at risk of failure in the judgement of their community. The changing norms of wholeness will be unkind to those it fails to understand and fails to provide for.

Shame and family honour

Most definitions of shame focus on the feelings of inadequacy or a state of remorse resulting from wrongdoing on the part of an individual or group. In Western countries, it is associated with the wrongful deeds of individuals and only rhetorically with the collective response of a whole group or subgroup. In the Gulf of Arabia, it more commonly refers to the loss of honour encountered by some misdeed or condition created by a family member. The misdeed has negative ramifications for the perceived status of not only the individual, but of the entire family (Patai, 1983). Intentionality is not always a factor, as it is sufficient that a condition violating cultural norms exists. In this context, the acknowledgment of a disabling condition in a child risks triggering the shame response for the entire family. It is difficult for professionals raised in the cultures of Western countries to comprehend the depths of the shame response when family honour is at stake.

Experiences of denial and grieving are not unanticipated responses from families in many other regions of the world. However, the response in the Gulf of Arabia is more protracted and complicated by the need to protect the family from the external judgement of inadequacy associated with the child's disabling condition. Although the anthropological concept of the disabled as a 'culture violator' is not new in other regions, its application to the shame response in Gulf societies is especially pertinent. In contrast to the feelings of guilt and self-blame associated with counselling families in North America or Europe, the shame response is all-pervasive and often elicits a constellation of protective measures by the family.

The cultural values of compassion, justice, equality, kindness, generosity and the acceptance of fate as God's will, prevalent in Islam and in local cultural belief systems, can represent supporting factors for the family. However, they do not sufficiently counteract the threat to family honour elicited by the diagnosis of a disability. The psychosocial response to the risk of shame is a complicating factor in providing opportunity for inclusive practices in the schools. Any suggestion of the need for individual assessment following academic failure, for example, may invite rejection of the school's intentions. The acceptance of special education support services may be tantamount to admitting the inadequacy of the child and, by implication, risks eliciting feelings of humiliation and shame among family members.

The immediate effect of the shame response is observed in the tendency to delay recommended evaluations or to reject professional diagnosis for as long as possible, in spite of mounting evidence of the disability. With a traditional disability, when its existence is obvious to most family members at a young age, the reaction may be to delay treatment until the child is older, keeping him or her in the home and in relative isolation from the extended family and the larger society. When the issue of educational disabilities arises, the evaluation and acceptance of a diagnosis may be delayed for a much longer period, as it is far easier to deny the existence of a condition that is not visible to others.

Denial

Denial operates as a psychological defense mechanism to protect individuals from painful confrontation with a reality they are not prepared to accept. It is a state of mind characterized by a refusal or inability to recognize and deal with a serious personal problem. While there are similarities in its occurrence across cultures, it operates in different ways in different societies. Western-educated mental health practitioners are trained to think of the stages of denial as grieving, anger, depression, and eventual acceptance of the new condition following psychic trauma or a profound sense of loss. The reaction of parents to the confirmation of their child's disabling condition is frequently described in these terms. It is expected that the parents will work through these stages toward acceptance of a new image of their child, one that is no less caring but defined by more limited expectations or altered ambitions.

For many parents in the Gulf of Arabia, this simplistic paradigm of the grieving process is never completed. The need to avoid family shame, associated with public and family recognition of the disability, will often prolong denial of its existence or leave it incomplete. This is especially true when it involves recognition of educational disabilities, where there are few or none of the stigmas associated with the traditional disabilities. While there is significant stigma and, often, parental blame associated with traditional categories of disability, they are at least recognized as being beyond the immediate control of the family. Denial may result in minimizing the obvious limitations the disability imposes for the present and future, but total denial of its existence does not readily occur.

The eliciting of denial in the families of children with educational disabilities may take a very different path. The invisibility of the learning disability or cognitive limitations may lead to repetitive cycles of acceptance alternating with denial. When extra support is provided, even small academic gains may be perceived as evidence of normalcy, sufficient to motivate the parent to deny the need for additional assistance or to blame the school for holding the child back. This may be followed by attempts to enroll the child in another school, where the cycle of failure, denial and blame will be repeated. Professionals in the region are accustomed to these contradictions, yet are often dismayed when their sympathetic attempts to educate the family to the seriousness of the educational disability are met with rejection.

Other family members frequently play a strong role in the denial process. The appearance of normality is often vigorously reinforced by extended family members who encourage the parents to reject any suggestion of a problem. The large number of private schools in the Gulf of Arabia countries offer ample opportunity to shift the problem from school to school before the accumulated academic discrepancies can no longer be tolerated by the school or hidden by the parents. Frequently, secondary problems of 'learned helplessness' and academic avoidance develop to the point where the student's disengagement from learning and emotional retreat represents the primary manifestation of the educational disability (Karola, 2000; Lerner, 1989).

While a pattern of gradual acceptance occurs for most parents, many never come to acknowledge any limitations throughout the child's school career. In other instances, one parent accepts the existence of the condition while the other parent does not. Because, in Arab society, the mother is traditionally considered responsible for the proper education of their children (Karola, 2000; Patai, 1983), much of the burden of protecting the family from the shame response falls on her. In this cultural context, the mother is primarily responsible for acting on the contradictory demands of advocating for the appropriate support services for her child, while simultaneously denying the existence of the problem to protect the family honour and the child's future status in the community.

The tension produced within the family matrix is usually enormous. Family members will often embark on a search for quick medical or magical cures while rejecting professional recommendations for special education and other long-term remedies holding the greatest promise for results. Suggestions by family members that the parents change schools and refuse to consent to psycho-educational assessments are common. There is a tacit fear that, once a diagnosis of an educational disability is confirmed, the child will be excluded from school and from full participation in the larger society. As noted earlier, this fear extends beyond the child's prospects for his school years into his ultimate status as a complete adult.

It is a poignant contradiction that many parents will accept segregated special education placement for a child with an educational disability, and follow through on school recommendations, while continuing to deny the existence of the problem. Denial may persist long after the child has been placed in a special education class. Parents will inform their relatives and friends that their child is attending a regular school programme, may rehearse the child to support this claim and sometimes dress them in a school uniform with their former school's logo. This often continues for as long as the child is enrolled in a special school. In other instances, after a child begins to demonstrate progress in a special education programme, the parents will demand that they be transferred to a regular school programme, in spite of evidence that the child is several years discrepant in his or her academic achievement and would receive no assistance in a regular class.

This residual form of denial cuts across all parental levels of education and economic status.

Denial can sometimes serve the objectives of inclusion by motivating the parent and school to support reasonable accommodations in the regular classroom as an alternative to the more threatening option of special class placement. Parents are much more accepting of special education services when they are provided in the regular classroom. For this reason, schools that offer even the possibility of academic or social integration in regular classes are preferred by almost all parents.

More frequently, it operates to frustrate efforts at early intervention as it delays initiation of appropriate special education services while allowing learning deficits to accumulate. Typically, the absence of early intervention leads to cumulative discrepancies in achievement, lowered self esteem, reduced achievement motivation, lowered expectations of success, and increasing disengagement from, and avoidance of, learning (Lerner, 1989). The consequences of family denial and its promotion of this failure cycle may result in ineligibility for programmes offering inclusive education. The possibility of academic integration is lessened, or lost all together, as the older child falls too far behind to be successful in an inclusive education programme designed for mild educational disabilities and, frequently, offered only at the early school levels.

Fatalism

Historically, traditional disabilities have been viewed as absolute and inalterable. The traditional belief in fate and the tendency toward thinking in absolute categories of experience is widespread in the region (Patai, 1983). When applied to the existence of a disability, it can contribute to parental resistance to any form of specialized professional intervention. In spite of exposure to modern views of treatment, these beliefs remain an obstacle to gaining early recognition and appropriate educational intervention. While there is willingness to seek out medical specialists, with the expectation of a rapid cure or reversal of a disabling condition, there is much less interest in pursuing a long path of rehabilitation and education. Special centres for children with traditional disabilities have reported on the arrival of parents with children, often aged twelve or older, who have never seen a specialist or attended school. Even when access to free medical and educational services is available, many parents will passively accept the condition, believing there is no hope of improvement. Unlike denial, which rejects reality, fatalism is based on the assumption that the condition exists but is unchangeable and intended to remain as it is. It emanates from the belief, common in pre-modern times, that without some form of divine intervention or, in some instances, non-religious magical remedies, there should be no hope of improvement.

Religion sometimes enters the picture, as many hold that the existence of a disabling condition is as God intended it to be. Various authors have reported on their findings in Islamic countries that parents frequently expressed the belief that it was a punishment from God (Dukmak, 1994; Riaz, 1994). Afrooz (1994), on the other hand, has emphasized the protected status enjoyed by the handicapped in the Holy Quran, noting that it was both a blessing and an honour to serve them. The beliefs and sentiments expressed in either of these observations (i.e. punishment or privilege) are not frequently expressed in clinical interviews with parents in the Islamic Gulf countries discussed in this chapter. In either context, it may be interpreted by family members that the condition should not be subject to improvement as it is fixed or unchanging.

Implications of fatalistic perceptions include parental apathy toward, or outright rejection of opportunities for special education support. While not readily acknowledged, there is substantial clinical evidence, from parent interviews, of the search for traditional folk remedies or magical interventions to cure the disability (Karola, 2000). This search may continue at the same time that they comply with recommendations for special education services and appropriate medical treatments. Parents may dramatically lower their expectations for achievement or refuse to cooperate with the school in ways that would contribute to their child's independent functioning and general welfare. Expectations for completed homework and for normalizing social behavior at home and in the school may be lowered. Excuse-making (e.g. 'He has a disability and he can't be expected to change'), shifting blame from the student to the school, and self-fulfilling prophecies of poor school performance or social behaviour are symptomatic of fatalistic beliefs.

Fatalism is an obstacle to inclusive education, as it promotes apathy and a wait-and-see posture at times when appropriate educational interventions could be most effective. It contributes to conflict between the home and the school, when shared expectations should be held for achievement in all areas of development. Fatalism, along with denial, represents a major obstacle to the development of early intervention programmes and the inclusive practices that could support it.

Early intervention

Early intervention by professionals knowledgeable about the developmental needs of young children has the greatest potential to enhance the achievement of the child's learning potential and to avoid more intensive intervention at a later date (Brown, 1995; Lerner 1989). Inclusive thinking, directed toward programmes at early ages, has a high probability of success in maintaining the educationally disabled child in a normalized learning environment. However, there are several factors that militate against parents accessing programmes established with this objective. These include the convergence of all of the cultural phenomena of denial, fatalism, absolutism and family shame.

Parents in the Gulf of Arabia often hold only a very general or vague perception of what constitutes developmental norms for their children. While there is intuitive knowledge of development for every age, the cultural tendency toward non-restrictive early child rearing practices (Karola, 2002), wherein children are not challenged to conform at an early age, often delays the recognition that a child is not meeting developmental expectations. The absence of books and mass media information on modern childrearing practices is another factor in delaying the recognition of problems that, in many other societies, would be identified by family members at an earlier age.

The accepted belief that it is better for the family not to know of the existence of an educational disability until it becomes obvious represents another obstacle. Among professionals from the region, there is often a reluctance to share suspicions of delayed development out of sensitivity toward the parents' feelings and the risks of eliciting the family shame response. In addition, many professionals responsible for the identification of these disabilities have limited training in the identification of young children, and act on the assumption that a child should fail in school for several years before being screened for these conditions. While the evidence supporting early identification and its association with successful inclusive practices is strong (Lerner, 1989), these cultural obstacles continue to deny such opportunity for most of those who will later be identified as educationally disabled.

Professional culture and teamwork

In the introduction to this chapter, the importance of 'inclusive thinking' was emphasized over the existence of isolated 'inclusive practices.' Optimizing opportunity for inclusive thinking involves a high level of communication, consultation, and collaboration among classroom teachers, educational specialists, administrators and other professional support personnel (Waugaman, 1994). In countries with long-established traditions of inclusive practice, we find a considerable emphasis on professional team planning and systems for problem solving.

An experiential background for team problem solving and collaboration among roles is rare among professionals trained in Middle East countries, where the emphasis is on specificity and rigidity of role descriptions, separation of professional functions, and on authority-based rather than shared expertise. The absence of a team ethos in the government and private Arabic school sectors conflicts with the requirements of team planning, creative problem solving and ongoing collaboration. With the possible exception of the classical psycho-medical disability model for multi-discipline team meetings in some special centres, there is little evidence of collegial collaboration or team meetings of any kind in the government or private Arabic schools.

In the private British and American international schools, collaborative team activity occurs with some regularity, although it is primarily focused on curriculum implementation and departmental organization activities. The emphasis on academic achievement and college preparation in most of these schools, combined with the normally high turnover of expatriate professional staff, does not encourage the institutionalization of standing teams focused on support for inclusive education. The professional culture in these schools may remain receptive to the team function, but requires administrative commitment and child-centred policies to activate it for this purpose.

Conclusion

The picture that evolves from surveying inclusive practices in the region is one of uncertainty, tentativeness, and confusion. The disparity between rhetoric and reality in implementing public policy on inclusion is great. However, supportive public policy has been established and the motivation to adopt modern educational practices for the disabled is strong. At the same time, traditional beliefs, norms and sentiments reinforce traditional practices that have emphasized segregation and isolation. To realistically introduce or extend inclusive practices in the schools, public policy developers, programme planners, practitioners and disability advocates will need to acknowledge and address the obstacles within the culture, rather than emphasize external restraints related to the absence of specialized professional training, local models, or a local research base.

The push and pull of tradition versus modernity is evident in many fields of development in the region. Because educational practices tend to conform to the side of tradition, the emergence of inclusive thinking will continue to stumble and lurch forward in inconsistent ways, following its own path, rather than emulating the direction taken in other countries. It is probable that local models of inclusive practice will need to be well established before the more flexible and creative patterns of inclusive thinking emerge from the requirements for sustaining them. In this instance, inclusive practice may precede the philosophical predisposition required for full-scale and long-term commitment of resources.

Governments may continue to look to the private international schools for examples of effective inclusive education practices, but will need to establish their own programmes to accommodate the large number of unserved students requiring them. As most of these have insufficient English to participate in the foreign international schools, and private school fees are a barrier to many families, it is inaccurate to say that adequate opportunity exists in any of these countries for gaining the necessary educational support services. The mainstream private sector will continue to serve only a very small number of selected students who would benefit from inclusive education, and these are likely to include only those of average or higher intelligence with specific learning disabilities or speech and language impairments.

In every country under discussion, the advocates for educational inclusion remain active. They are committed, patient and opportunistic. At each meeting with a public official, at regional conferences, and in the living rooms of private families they promote and persuade people of the region to think about the needs and rights of the disabled in a different way. They tirelessly maintain their focus on educational inclusion as a human right, and the education of all children as a moral and civic responsibility of their societies. On their side is the knowledge that the overwhelming preference of affected families in these countries is for inclusive education. This reality, more than anything else, will establish the direction for the future.

References

Afrooz, G.A. (1994). 'Islamic Republic of Iran'. In K. Mazurek and M.A. Winzer (eds) *Comparative studies in special education* (pp. 88–99). Washington DC: Gallaudet University Press.

Brown, R.C. (1995). *Specific learning disabilities in the Arabian Gulf: Issues and recommendations.* Paper presented at the 10th Asia and Pacific Regional Conference of Rehabilitation International, Jakarta, Indonesia.

Cordesman, A.H. (1997). *Bahrain, Oman, Qatar, and the UAE.* Oxford: Phoenix Press.

Dukmak, S.J. (1994). 'West Bank and Gaza Strip'. In K. Mazurek and M.A. Winzer (eds) *Comparative studies in special education* (pp. 44–69). Washington DC: Gallaudet University Press.

Hobbs, N. (ed.) (1975). *Issues in the classification of children*, Vol. 1. Washington DC: Jossey-Bass.

Hodgson, D. (1998). *The human right to education: Programme on international rights of the child.* Aldershot: Ashgate.

Karola, A.M. (2000). *Developing appropriate child-rearing practices within the Arab world to assist with integrating traditional culture with the need to accommodate the cultural shifts required for living within the twenty-first century.* Unpublished doctoral dissertation, Union Institute and University, Cincinatti OH.

——(2002). *Learned helplessness.* Paper presented at the First Annual Conference of the Professional Educators Association of Kuwait on International School Education, Kuwait City, Kuwait.

Kusuma-Powell, O. (2003). 'The changing face of learning disabilities'. *International Schools Journal*, 22(2), 34–45.

Lerner, J. (1989). *Learning disabilities: Theories, diagnosis, and teaching strategies.* Boston MA: Houghton Mifflin.

Lewis, B. (2000). *The Middle East.* London: Phoenix Press.

Mazurek, K. and Winzer, M.A. (eds) (1994). *Comparative studies in special education.* Washington DC: Gallaudet University Press.

Moghaddam, F.M., Taylor, D.M. and Wright, S.C. (1993). *Social psychology in cross-cultural perspective.* New York: W.H. Freeman and Company.

Patai, R. (1983). *The Arab mind*. New York: Charles Scribner and Sons.

Riaz, M.N. (1994). 'Pakistan'. In K. Mazurek and M.A. Winzer (eds) *Comparative studies in special education* (pp. 143–162). Washington DC: Gallaudet University Press.

Teruhisa, H. (1994). 'Education, legislation and economic performance: The case of Japan'. In W. Tulasiewicz and G. Strowbridge (eds) *Education and the law: International perspectives* (pp. 29–38). London: Routledge.

UNESCO Regional Office for Education in the Arab States (2000). *Arab regional conference on Education for All: The Arab framework for action*. Beirut: UNESCO.

Waugaman, W.R. (1994). 'Professionalization and socialization in interprofessional collaboration'. In R.M. Casto and M.C. Julia (eds) *Interprofessional care and collaborative practice* (pp. 23–31). Belmont CA: Wadsworth.

Chapter 12

Future directions

Todd Fletcher

This volume provides a general assessment of the reality of inclusive education throughout the world. While it documents significant advances, it also points to manifest problems as the world community struggles to provide basic quality education to all children by the year 2015, as pledged at Dakar in 2000 (World Education Forum, 2000).

Inclusive education is of crucial importance to all children with special educational needs, but particularly so to the estimated 400 million disabled children and adults living in developing countries who frequently occupy the lowest rungs on the socio-economic ladder and are rarely reached or included in development projects and global initiatives. The concept of inclusive education during the past twenty-five years has gained momentum and made significant inroads as education systems around the globe awaken to the reality that segregation and exclusion are no longer viable options. We are seeing the reversal of a policy of invisibility that for centuries was the dominant paradigm in education being replaced by one of equal access and education for all. This growing social consciousness is redefining the concept of access to education so that it is no longer seen as a privilege for a few, but as a fundamental human right for all children. It raises the need for effective global stewardship that embraces a policy of collective trusteeship and inclusion for all of the world's inhabitants.

One of the singular achievements of the last quarter-century regarding disability was the emergence of a new paradigmatic orientation in which key issues for disabled persons were approached within a human rights framework. This was accompanied by a shift towards a social model of disability, which is replacing the medical model orientation that has for so long dominated the field of disabilities. In essence, this latter shift places the locus of responsibility for disability on the society and not on the individual. The individual is no longer responsible for adjusting and adapting to society, but society, through the elimination of significant barriers such as prejudice, discrimination and inaccessibility, is responsible for change. Momentum for this shift in approach has the majority of governments worldwide assuming greater responsibility for enabling all citizens to participate fully and equitably in national and social economic development programmes.

A priority for the world community is to examine global trends and to seek solutions from a universalist perspective in order to minimize the discriminatory conditions, abuses, social injustice and marginalization suffered by individuals with and without disabilities. While disability is only one of multiple dimensions that must be considered, it must be recognized that, in many cases, persons with disabilities are the most dispossessed, marginalized and fragile.

Inequities must be addressed from multiple avenues. Nation states must go a step further and devise a more comprehensive multisectorial approach. This should involve consideration not only of education, but also of a responsible national economic and social policy with a priority placed on providing for the welfare of a nation's most disenfranchised and dispossessed populations. With reference to education, this will entail a system-wide view and restructuring of educational policy, including a re-examination of the policies that international agencies have promoted and advanced. The need for such a review is magnified in the age of globalization, with one of its most pernicious effects being the homogenization of culture and a consequent hegemonic impact that works against the preservation of cultural and educational diversity.

What is the intersection between globalization, development and disabilities? It is apparent that globalization presents significant challenges and risks to those on the fringes or margins of society. One of the most significant overarching and potentially positive features of globalization is integration (Friedman, 2000). But its worst quality, at least in the short term, is disruption, as noted in *The Millennium Forum Declaration and Agenda for Action* (United Nations, 2000) This forum, comprising over 100 countries and more than 1,000 non-governmental organizations, argued that steps must be taken to cushion the worst aspects of globalization from the most vulnerable:

> corporate-driven globalization increases inequities between and within countries, undermines local traditions and culture, and escalates disparities between rich and poor, thereby marginalizing large numbers of people in urban and rural areas. Women, indigenous peoples, youth, boys and girls, and people with disabilities suffer disproportionately from the effects of globalization.

(p. 1)

A global ethic and the principle of collective trusteeship

What is the vision of a future world community? How can we nurture and celebrate difference? Has the advent of globalization changed our concept of identity and promoted a greater sense of identification linked to the world community? The social evolution of humanity on the planet, with a trend towards recognizing one common homeland and its inhabitants as citizens of planet Earth, is, albeit at times, slow and imperceptible. The key elements for achieving increased educational opportunities and equity for all children will require a renewed commitment by all governments and their respective leaders to work together.

What are the universally recognized human values that can make inclusive education a reality? Cousins (1981) characterized the requirements of this stage in human development in the following way:

> A world consensus has never before been necessary. But we are living in a new and different world, a world that has suddenly become a single geographic unit. Such a world, in order to function safely and responsibly, needs all the thought and attention it can get. People of ideas have to operate on a world stage. They must find their way to each other across national barriers. They must not hesitate to proclaim their allegiance to the human family. They must make the human interest their prime concern, working with the sovereignties if possible and against them if necessary.
>
> (p. 66)

Human destiny is not merely the creation of a materially prosperous community, but also the construction of a global community responsive to the needs of the diversity of its citizens. Thus, the Commission on Global Governance (1995) asserted that the world faces a need for enlightened responses to the challenges in this new century, and voiced its concern at the lack of leadership over a wide spectrum of human affairs.

> At national, regional, and international levels, within communities and in international organizations, in governments and in non-governmental bodies, the world needs credible and sustained leadership. This cannot be leadership confined within domestic walls. It must reach beyond country, race, religion, language and life-style. It must embrace a wider human constituency, be infused with a sense of caring for others, a sense of responsibility to the global neighborhood.
>
> (p. 353)

How can this global ethic be fostered and nurtured, providing in essence the foundation for a sustainable world order? With regard to inclusive education, the magnitude and depth required for such a transformation was alluded to by Corbett and Slee (2000). They presented a three-tiered development model that is indicative of inclusive education development worldwide. The first, surface inclusion, refers to policies and notions of school effectiveness and efficiency; the second refers to structural modifications to the school environment and curriculum; and the third embraces 'deep culture, the hidden curriculum of fundamental value systems, ritual and routines, initiations and acceptance which forms the fabric of daily life' (p. 140). It is the third tier of the model that essentially embodies the achievement of the true recognition, appreciation and nurturing of diversity and difference. A fundamental shift in value orientation is the basis for the third tier to become a dominant global trend. The transition to that tier necessitates internalization of universal principles and core values into a systemic consciousness, a global culture, and an acceptance and recognition of the diversity of the 6 billion individuals who inhabit planet Earth.

Defining a role for the UN within the emerging world order

As noted above, one of the most critical and urgent requirements to ensure effective stewardship and coordination of efforts on a global scale is effective leadership. Thus, Mittler, in Chapter 2 of this volume, identifies the core problem in bringing inclusive education to a reality on the global level: the lack of authority currently ceded to an international agency of the stature of the United Nations by member states. There is a deep chasm between educational policies and reality as governments struggle to provide full and equal social, cultural, economic and educational participation in society. Education ministers have advanced an appeal to the governments of states throughout the world to ensure that first priority is given to education within their respective countries. But patterns of habit and attitudes adhered to for centuries will not be easily abandoned in response to legislative mandates.

Governments are not legally bound by UN mandates, and each nation interprets such international mandates in the light of their own histories, traditions, values and structures. In effect, the current machinery of the UN for monitoring, implementation and follow-up is woefully inadequate. Sufficient confidence or authority is not vested with the UN as it attempts to persuade governments to change their practices and policies. This lack of authority has resulted in an inability to bring the rhetoric of principles agreed upon and shared into reality at national and local levels. The stubborn clinging to antiquated paradigms and policies by member states undermines advancement. This reflects a general crisis in leadership and a lack of recognition of the principle of collective trusteeship. The UN must be re-tooled and given a more authoritative and meaningful executive function to serve the collective good, unmotivated by partisan or self-interest.

The role of an international executive agency could serve as a catalyst that facilitates, promotes and nurtures development and change within the local, state and national contexts. It is important to establish a long-term vision of a contextually relevant and meaningful educational policy, which is not to be altered by the dynamics of politics or by international funding. There is a growing consensus of the need for a systematic, planned and dynamic approach to coordinate and promote inclusive education in social and economic development projects. Past experiences reflect a disconnection between disability and mainstream development efforts. This accentuates the need for a mechanism, a global financial and institutional agency of sufficient magnitude and commitment with sufficient political will to secure the mobilization of financial resources of an unprecedented scale. 'This new collaborative mechanism would bring together bilateral and multilateral donors, international and national disability nongovernmental organizations, developing country governments and institutions, and practitioners' (Heumann, 2003).

Final thoughts

I would note one emerging trend that will begin to exert growing pressure on the world community, and that is how we can 'put our house in order' as we embark on this twenty-first century. There is an emergence of a sentiment for some form of world order that can facilitate global regulation and management, providing a sense of order to the current chaos and crises in human affairs. The response must fundamentally recognize the universal human family and the plight of individuals who are excluded socially and educationally from participation in society. The question of developing a global strategy to accelerate the recognition of the human rights of all individuals must be taken on by protagonists at all levels – members of governing institutions, international agencies and organizations, scientists and social thinkers, and non-governmental organizations. As noted by UNESCO (2003):

> While we are all committed to quality education, we acknowledge that we live in an unequal world – a world where enormous disparities make the possibility of equal opportunity to participate in a quality education a dream that is currently unattainable for many. To reduce, and eventually eliminate, these disparities is essential if we are to reach the goal of a quality education for all. The context in which we are striving for quality in education is one that is difficult to comprehend. The world of the twenty-first century is one of fast change and innovation. It is a world where access to technology, modern education, and resources play a major role in the ability to contribute to or adapt to change. Thus, the very means of gaining equity are particularly hard to obtain for those who are most disadvantaged.

(p. 3)

This trend and its emergence are observable as the world community makes steady efforts to forge a world political system that can provide for humanity the possibilities of justice, equality, and prosperity. The United Nations as an international organization has demonstrated humanity's capacity for united action in the past and 'has affirmed our collective moral will to build a better future, evinced in the widespread adoption of international human rights covenants' (Baha'i International Community, 1995, p. 2). The ultimate safeguard would be a model of world governance to accommodate the world's diversity within a united framework and provide comprehensive, practical and sustainable strategies for addressing social issues that perplex the planet.

This book, in providing a searching review of inclusive education in several regions of the world, has generated more questions than answers. In contemplating the current state of our global community, difference continues to be a dominant theme leading to dilemmas. How do we encourage new patterns of thinking and behaviour that duly serve as an agency for change? What is the community that we hope to build for future generations? The most optimistic scenario is a world of diversity where billions of people representing an infinitely diverse range of backgrounds, cultures, philosophies, religions and languages, work together to advance human civilization, to celebrate the successes and to provide opportunities for all communities to participate equally.

References

Baha'i International Community (1995). *Turning point for all nations*. New York: United Nations Office. URL: http://www.bahai.org/article-1–7–5–1.html

Commission of Global Governance (1995) 'Report of the Commission of Global Governance' *Our global neighborhood*. New York: Oxford University Press.

Corbett, C. and Slee R. (2000). 'An international conversation on inclusive education'. In F. Armstrong, D. Armstrong and L. Barton, L. (eds) *Inclusive education: Policy, contexts, and comparative perspectives* (pp. 133–146). London: David Fulton Publishers.

Cousins, N. (1981). *Human options*. New York: W.W. Norton.

Friedman, T.L. (2000). *Understanding globalization: The lexus and the olive tree*. New York: Anchor Books.

Heumann, J. (2003). 'World bank international dialogue on disability and development'. *Disability World*, 19, 1–9. URL:
http://www.disabilityworld.org/06–08/development/dialogue.shtml

UNESCO (2003). Communiqué, Ministerial Round Table on Quality Education, UNESCO Headquarters, 3 and 4 October 2003. Paris: UNESCO. URL:
http://portal.unesco.org/education/ev.php?URL_ID=23609_DO=DO_TOPIC&URL

United Nations (2000). *We the People's Millennium Forum Declaration and Agenda for Action: Strengthening the United Nations for the twenty-first century, adopted by the Millennium Forum on 26 May 2000*. New York: United Nations.

World Education Forum (2000). *The Dakar Framework for Action. Education for All: Meeting our Collective Commitments*. Text adopted by the World Education Forum, Dakar, Senegal, 26–28 April 2000. Paris: UNESCO.

Index